American Rhapsody

American Rhapsody

JOE ESZTERHAS

Alfred A. Knopf   New York   2000

THIS IS A BORZOI BOOK
PUBLISHED BY ALFRED A. KNOPF

Copyright © 2000 by Barbarian, Ltd.

www.aaknopf.com

Knopf, Borzoi Books, and the colophon are registered trademarks of
Random House, Inc.

ISBN 0-375-41144-5

Manufactured in the United States of America
Published July 25, 2000
Second Printing, July 2000

For Naomi, Sunlight

Love is like a cigar. Once it goes out,
you can't light it again. It's never the same.

—RICHARD M. NIXON

Contents

Act Three   SUSPICIOUS MINDS

Author's Note

Nearly three years ago, afraid that my public persona as a screenwriter was overwhelming my creative life, I went to the island of Maui with my wife and our three children, shut my phone down, stopped doing interviews, and pretended I wasn't a public man.

I played with my wife and played with my kids, let the sun beat me up, and thought about things. About values and success. About the sixties. About my past relationship with the women I'd used and my present relationship with the wife I adored. Somehow or other, those thoughts about my life inevitably led me to Bill Clinton.

I thought I recognized and knew Bill Clinton and what made him tick. I understood the ambition, the success, the political duplicity, the Hollywood charm. I understood the mad priapic obsession that had always fuel-driven his life . . . because it had driven mine until I met Naomi. I understood the fierce boom-box rhythms of his inner life the same way I understood and loved the demons shrieking in the darkness inside the Stones, the Doors, the artist now known again as Prince, and Dr. Dre.

I started reading everything ever written about Bill Clinton when we finally came back to Malibu, our phone still shut down, living a near-reclusive life now, not even calling agents, lawyers, and friends back, still refusing all interview requests. I was lost in a mirrored sea of my own creation, in snorkeling pursuit of myself and Clinton, swimming through his past in search of my own soul.

As the impeachment psychodrama began, I watched every minisecond of it, bleary-eyed, haggard, and grizzled, maniacally flicking channels, indulging gluttonously in the national bacchanal of information and bulimia of rumor. I read everything, I saw everything, digested whatever I could, and learned a lot . . . about myself and Bill Clinton and about America, the country I love as only an immigrant who grew up in the ethnic ghettos of Cleveland can love her.

I wasn't just thinking of Bill Clinton anymore, but about a generation, *my* generation, which, in some ways, even though it was entrenched in power, creeping up on sixty, was still struggling to find itself. I was thinking about the state of the union and the state of our hearts and privates as we tried not to stumble and slide on the treacherous Internet ice of the new millennium.

The book you are holding in your hand is filled with everything I thought about and learned. Ah, yes, except it's not that simple. If only it were . . . but it never is.

I am loath to confess that I have had a writing partner who has cursed my career from the time I was in the sixth grade at Saint Emeric's School and published a class newspaper, thanks to the toy printing set that I had received as a Christmas gift. I wrote some of the stories in the *Saint Emeric's Herald* and my writing partner wrote others. I wrote childish investigative reports about the river in the valley below the school, in the smoky part of the city known as the Flats, a river so polluted with industrial chemicals that it burned your eyes as you watched it from the bluffs above. (Many years later, the river literally burst afire!) My writing partner wrote sensational exposés about which girls in our class were kissing which boys. (Hot off the press! A *Herald* exclusive! Frances Madar and Robert Zak!)

By the time I got to Hollywood, I knew my partner well enough to acknowledge him condescendingly in interviews as "the twisted little man inside me." We wrote about different things, you see, but it all came out under my name. I wrote *Music Box, Telling Lies in America, F.I.S.T.,* and *Betrayed.* He wrote *Basic Instinct, Showgirls, Sliver,* and *Jade*—although sometimes he even intruded his back-alley homunculus self into *my* work: Why, after all, was there a need for lengthy, sexually graphic courtroom descriptives in a movie as aesthetically ambitious and as morally lofty as *Music Box?*

And as I wrote this book—about a cultural shadow war that resulted in the figurative assassination of a president (Bill Clinton)—I realized that the Twisted Little Man was writing feverishly, too. And hallucinating. Daydreaming. Wet-dreaming. Projecting. About Kenneth W. Starr's secret lust. About George W. Bush and Tricia Nixon. About Hillary and her forlorn, intimate relationship with Eleanor Roosevelt. About Al Gore's heartbreaking, cuckolded fears. About Bob Dole and his electable missing shoulder. About "John Wayne" McCain's painful broken promise and his love of identical Long Tall Sallies. About Monica and her spoiled-princess extortion of the president of the United States. About Bill Clinton and his eternal true love, his Willard.

Are the things the little lowlife wrote about true? Well, as a matter of fact, no. But that's also not so simple. Because in the little scuzzball's cockeyed, fun-house view, they are. He uses facts wickedly to shape his outrageous fictional perspective. He is a contortionist and a juggler of the historical record. No mere imposter, he is an abysmal, excrescent python who swallows his subjects, spits them back out, and spews *his* venom from *their* mouths. Is this little vermin a liar? Well, you know, in Bill Clinton's mind, oral sex isn't sex. Is the little slime, as Mark Twain defined himself, "a professional liar," making up fictions to reveal truths? Well, he is certainly supporting himself in Hollywood by professionally dressing up his tawdry, realistic lies.

I have decided, finally, after all these years of living with him as my writing partner, that it is time to distinguish what is his and what is mine.

If you are reading this typeface, the writing is mine, sometimes interpretive but based on well-researched facts.

If you are reading this typeface, the writing is fictional and his, starting with well-researched facts but blasted through and transformed by his hallucinatory dreams.

I'll put it another way, too. If you get angry while you're reading this brazen book, blame it on the crude, insulting little prick—Lord knows, he's gotten too many people terribly angry through the years. If you find things in this reflective book that frighten you, or if you find yourself laughing against your determined will, blame it on a little boy endlessly watching a sun-kissed river that makes him cry.

Writing my book about Bill Clinton, his political peers, and our national ethos has had a pronounced personal effect upon me. Now I want to play with my wife and children *all the time!* I want to pretend permanently that I am not a public man. Our phones, while not shut down, have gatekeepers with disembodied voices to safeguard our family's bliss. Me, my wife, our boys, the massive pinheaded bulldog we call Rep. "Mud" Nadler, the anti-impeachment Democrat from New York . . . and the Twisted Little Man.

The little devil and I had a nerve-racking, maddening, revolting, hilarious, and climactic time writing this book. We hope that your time reading it will be similar.

Joe Eszterhas
Point Dume, California

[Act One]

HEARTBREAK HOTEL

From my own voice resonant, singing the phallus . . .

The President with pale face asking secretly to himself,
What will the people say at last?

—WALT WHITMAN, *Leaves of Grass*

[1]

The Whole World
Is Watching

"We gotta get you laid," Monica said.
"Oh, God," Linda Tripp said, "wouldn't that be something different? New and different. I don't know. After seven years, do you really think that there's a possibility I'd remember how?"
"Of course you would."
"No," Linda Tripp said.

My friend Jann Wenner, the editor and publisher of *Rolling Stone*, the rock and roll bible, called me excitedly the day after Bill Clinton was nominated for the presidency. He had spent the previous night at a party, celebrating with Clinton. "He's one of us," Jann said. "He'll be the first rock and roll president in American history."

I had come to the same conclusion. He *was* one of us. Even if, on occasion, he tried to deny it. *Of course* he had dodged the draft, just another white Rhodes Scholar nigger who agreed with Muhammad Ali and had no quarrel with them Vietcong. *Of course* he had smoked dope, inhaling deeply, holding it in, bogarting that joint.

Bill Clinton, Jann told me, had always read *Rolling Stone*, so I smiled when, shortly after the election, he was photographed jogging in a *Rolling Stone* T-shirt, the same T-shirt I had worn to my son's Little League games. Well, this really was a cosmic giggle: *Good Lord, we had taken the White House!* After all the locust years—after Bebe Rebozo's boyfriend, after the hearing-impaired Marlboro Man, after that uppity preppy always looking at his watch—*America was ours!* In the sixties, we'd been worried about staying out of jail. Now the jails were ours to run as we saw fit.

Carter had given us false hope for a while, but Bill Clinton was the real deal: undiluted, uncut rock and roll. Carter, we had discovered, wasn't one of us. Oh, sure, Jimmah allowed his record-mogul pal Phil Walden and Willie Nelson to smoke dope on the White House roof, and he had told *Playboy* he had "committed adultery in my heart many times," but the unfortunate, terminally well-intentioned dip was such a cheesy rube, definitely *not* rock and roll, with his beer-gutted Libyan-agent brother, his schoolmarm wife, and the Bible-spouting sister who was secretly having sudsy, lederhosen romps with married German chancellor Willy Brandt. No, definitely not rock and roll, proven forever when he fell on his face jogging, claiming breathlessly that a bunny rabbit had jumped in front of him, falling on his face while wearing *black socks.*

His Secret Service agents nicknamed Bill Clinton "Elvis," but we knew better. Elvis had been Sgt. Barry Sadler's ideological sidekick, a slobby puppet on a carny barker's strings, in love with his nark badges, informing on the Beatles, toadying up to Nixon, The Night Creature. Those wet panties hurled onstage at his concerts were size 16 and skid-marked. Bill Clinton wasn't Elvis. With his shades on and his sax gleaming, Bill Clinton looked like a pouchier Bobby Keyes playing backup for the Stones. No, that wasn't quite right, either. Not Bobby Keyes, but a pop-gutted Jumpin' Jack Flash and graying Street Fightin' Man . . . Bill Clinton was Mick on cheeseburgers and milk shakes, Taco Bell, and Chef Boyardee spaghetti.

Rolling Stone called his inauguration "the coming of a new age in American politics." Fleetwood Mac was playing "Don't Stop." That *was* Fleetwood Mac up there, not Pearl Bailey or Sammy Davis, Jr., or Sinatra or Guy Lombardo or Fred Waring and the Pennsylvanians. That *was* rock and roll we were hearing, not the Sousa Muzak the big band–era pols in the smoky back rooms had forced on us for so long. Dylan, our messiah, was there. And that *was* Jack Nicholson at the Lincoln Memorial, Abe's words brought to life by our lawyerly Easy Rider. Bill Clinton's White House was rock and roll, too, full of young people, full of women, blacks, gays, Hispanics; a White House, as Newt Gingrich's guru, Alvin Toffler, said, "more familiar with Madonna than with Metternich." That was just fine with us. It looked like Bill Clinton was continuing what he had begun in Arkansas, where he'd been criticized for having a staff of "long-haired, bearded hippies" who came to the office in cutoffs and patched jeans. The boss himself had been seen in the governor's mansion barefoot, in jeans and a T-shirt.

He had a Yippie-like zaniness about him we could identify with. Out on the golf course in Arkansas, one of his partners noticed that he could see Bill Clinton's underwear through his pants. "They weren't bikinis he had on," the partner said, "but it was some kind of wild underwear." Bill Clinton's favorite joke was one he had told over and over on the Arkansas campaign trail, a joke closer in spirit to Monty Python than to the Vegas lounge meisters favored by so many other presidents: "There was a farmer who had a three-legged pig with a wooden leg. And he bragged on this pig to everybody who came to visit. The farmer would tell how this pig had saved him from a fire. People would be amazed! And he'd say, 'Well, that's not all; this pig saved my farm from going bankrupt.' And the folks would be amazed. And the farmer would say, 'That's not all; this pig saved the entire town once when the dam broke.' Then somebody said to the farmer, 'Well, gosh, it's pretty amazing that you have this pig, but you never did explain why it only has three legs.' And the farmer said, 'Well, hell, you wouldn't want to eat a pig this special all in one sitting!' "

He certainly was a rock and roller. The light blue eyes, the lazy, sexy smile. The lips that were called "pussy lips" in Arkansas. Girls loved him. At age twelve, a classmate said, "Little girls were screaming, 'Billy, Billy, Billy, throw me the football.' All the girls had crushes on him. He was the center of their attention." A reporter covering one of his Arkansas campaigns said, "You could see the effect that he had on people in the eyes of the teenage girls who came to see him. Their eyes would light up. You would think that a rock star had just come into the Wal-Mart." He had rock and roll habits, too. Gennifer Flowers remembered the time he told her, "I really got fucked up on cocaine last night." There was even a Jagger-like androgyny he allowed some of his women friends to see. He put on girlfriend Sally Perdue's dress one night, high on grass, and played Elvis on his sax. He asked Gennifer to meet him at a bar dressed as a man, and he liked her putting eyeliner, blush, and mascara on his face. Underneath it was a rock and roll restlessness, what Gennifer called his feeling that he was "bullet-proof," which allowed him at times to flaunt his relationship with her.

There was no doubt he loved the music. Janis's "Pearl" . . . the Seekers' "I'll Never Find Another You" . . . Peter and Gordon's "A World Without Love" . . . "Here You Come Again" (which reminded him of Gennifer) . . . Steely Dan . . . Kenny Loggins . . . the Commodores' "Easy" and "Three Times a Lady" . . . Joe Cocker . . . Jerry Lee Lewis . . . anything by Elvis. He had his own band when he was a kid, called The Three Kings, which the other kids called Three Blind Mice because they all wore shades. A high

school friend said, "I remember driving down this road and Bill singing
Elvis songs at the top of his voice. He loved to sing. He just liked music and
he was always playing music. I think that was one of the reasons he went to
church so much as a kid. To hear the music."

One of the things that attracted him to Gennifer was that she was a rock
singer with her own band—Gennifer Flowers and Easy Living—at about
the same time that his little brother, Roger, had his band—Roger Clinton
and Dealer's Choice. Roger was like Chris Jagger to Mick: He wanted to be
a rock star, but he wasn't very good. Roger's taste leaned to Grand Funk
Railroad, REO Speedwagon, and Alice Cooper. But Roger shared his love
of the music. Bill Clinton's memory of his first appearance on *The Tonight
Show* was that Joe Cocker was there. "He was telling me about the show,"
Arkansas Democrat columnist Phillip Martin said. "He was telling me about
Joe Cocker's band. He said 'Man, they were bad; they were just a kick-ass
band, man!' You know, he really wanted to play with Joe Cocker rather than
going out there and playing 'Summertime' on his sax. But he was afraid to
ask. He was really in awe." And when Stephen Stills asked Roger up onstage
once, he said, "I was so excited, I thought I would pee my pants."

He was one of us, it became apparent, in another special way, too, the
classic sixties child in love with, addicted to, the pleasures provided him by
his penis, which he called "Willard." There was even a cartoon flyer circu-
lated around Arkansas early in his political career that showed Bill Clinton
looking down and saying, "Dick, you kept me from being the President of
the United States."

He was a *southern* rock and roller, a hillbilly cat like Elvis and Jerry Lee,
growing up in Hot Springs, Arkansas, a neon-lit haven of gamblers and
whores, once patronized by Al Capone, Bugsy Siegel, and Lucky Luciano.
Bill Clinton may have been born in Hope, but he grew up in Sin City, with
a mama who painted her eyebrows, pasted on false eyelashes, loved the racetrack, and helled around in her convertible, drink in hand, from the Vapors
to the Pines to the Southern Club, with or without her husband. A ripe
peach of a woman, there to be tasted.

He developed a lifelong yen for those ripe peaches, for rock and roll, and
for convertibles. It all came together in August 1977, the perfectly realized,
transcendent Bill Clinton rock and roll moment, when he was already a
married man, the attorney general of Arkansas. Dolly Kyle, a ripe-peach girl-

friend he hadn't seen for a while, now also married, came to see him in his office. He introduced her around the office as an old and good friend and then walked her out to her car and he . . . just flipped out! It was a brand-spanking-new turquoise Cadillac El Dorado convertible, 500-horsepower, nineteen feet long, eight-track tape player, AM/FM radio. It was the ultimate hepcat thing, a chrome-plated, poke-your-eye-out, southern gothic Elvismobile, hotter even than the Caddy convertible Chance Wayne (and Paul Newman) drove in *Sweet Bird of Youth*.

He asked if he could drive it, and Dolly said sure, so Bill Clinton got behind the wheel and took her out on the freeway and juiced her up over a hundred, veering, skidding a little, laughing like a kid. He took his foot off the pedal then and let her drift, just gliding along, grinning. Elvis was singing on the eight-track and he sang along . . . "Treat me right, treat me good, treat me like you really should."

Bill Clinton pulled off into a field, with no houses nearby, and got out and popped the hood open and looked at her motor. Then he looked into her trunk and found some blankets and got back in the front seat and started kissing Dolly. He put the blanket over the front seat and pulled the convertible's top down and told Dolly to take her dress off. He took off every stitch of his clothing, including his cuff links, and put his clothes neatly into the backseat. The sun was shining . . . it was a radiant, warm day . . . the Cadillac was gleaming . . . and they got it on. He put his finger into the sweat inside her belly button and he licked his finger. He reached into the backseat, put his pants back on, and walked back to the trunk for some water. He drank, offered her some, and took his pants off again. He moved her hand to Willard and said, "Touch it." They got it on again. They got dressed and started driving back to his office. He put the Elvis eight-track back on and he started humming along to the song.

"Today's my wedding anniversary," she told him.

"Are you happy?" he asked.

"Are you?" she said.

He said nothing until they got to his office.

"Good-bye, pretty girl," he said, and walked away. She got behind the wheel and popped the tape out to put in another one and she heard the disc jockey on the radio say that Elvis Presley was dead in Memphis. She started to cry and drove away, the tears streaming down her face.

The transcendent rock and roll moment . . . and it ended with a crash and a burn. Roaring down the highway in a brand-new Cadillac, rock and roll blasting, the sun shining, a beautiful girl with her legs up on the dash, a little water to slake your thirst, getting it on again, and then . . . *death.*

A slice of life at Altamont, only four months after Woodstock, love and peace and beads splattered by blood, the beauty of naked bodies at Woodstock obliterated forever by an obscenely naked fat man with a knife plunged into his mottled, greasy flesh. Oyez, oyez, darkness once again at the heart of rock and roll. Darkness and danger and sex. Knives and guns and Cadillacs careening into the pitch-black night. Forget the Beatles and their "good day sunshine." Rock and roll was about sex, not about love. It was about excess, not about romance. Bill Clinton understood that. It was exactly why he loved it. Bill Clinton was a rock and roll hog.

So was I. I knew it, too, having seen it, even tasted it, firsthand. As a writer for *Rolling Stone,* I had helicoptered into a crowd of 100,000 drunken, naked kids in Darlington, North Carolina, with Alice Cooper and Three Dog Night and watched as Alice guillotined chickens onstage, spraying blood over these sunburned and sweaty, naked kids, who'd rub the blood into one another's privates. I'd sat, afterward, around the pool of a Holiday Inn with the bands and a hundred local groupies as everyone got naked and the night blazed into a chlorine-smelling human blur of contorted wet bodies.

As a screenwriter, I'd waited in the living room of a Denver hotel suite at eight one morning for Bob Dylan to emerge from his bedroom. A half-full quart of Jim Beam stood on the living room cocktail table, along with three or four broken lines of coke. A pair of black silver-toed cowboy boots was under the table. One girl came out of Bob's bedroom, then another, then another. They looked tired and sleepy and were scantily and hastily dressed. They said hi in a shy and embarrassed way and then they left. Five minutes later, Bob came out, bare-chested and barefoot, wearing jeans, his hair an airborne jungle, his complexion graveyard gray. He sat down at the cocktail table, took a long slug of the Jim Beam, did a line of coke, smiled, and said, "Howya doin?"

That's what rock and roll was about! Brakes screeching, knives flashing in the moonlight, bodies aswirl in a lighted pool, blood spraying naked flesh, Mick with a whip in his hand, Keith's skull ring gleaming, a bottle of Jim Beam, silver-toed cowboy boots, a girl in a Cadillac with her legs up, a finger being sucked clean of the juice in her navel.

Rock and roll was Elvis doing "One Night" and "Mystery Train" before Colonel Parker and Hollywood tried to turn him into the Singing

Eunuch . . . Jerry Lee Lewis spraying more lighter fluid on his already-burning piano . . . Otis Redding running down a fire escape as an irate husband shot at him from a window above . . . Chuck Berry videotaping himself as he urinated on a hooker . . . Little Richard getting a backstage blow job as the curtain went up from the groupie whom Buddy Holly was doing doggy-style at the same time . . . the Stones passing that catatonic naked blonde over their heads in *Cocksucker Blues.*

Rock and roll was a young Jerry Lee sneaking over to Haney's in Natchez and watching an old black man play boogie-woogie piano. It was a young mascaraed Elvis sneaking down to Beale Street in Memphis, watching an old black man with a tin cup singing a Robert Johnson song. It was a young Billy Clinton watching the curvy, ripe-peach painted women taking their tricks into the Plaza or the Parkway or the Ina Hotel in Hot Springs.

All three learned to play their instruments in proximity to that corrupt, exhilarating, and life-giving red neon glow. Jerry Lee had his piano, Elvis had his voice, and Billy Clinton had a silver tongue.

It was easy to forget now, in the nineties, when we were parents or grandparents so busily reshaping our pasts to become role models for our children or our junior executives, that behind the idealism and the social commitment and the herbal experiments related to self-awareness, the sixties were about sex.

Even the drugs were tied to it: grass made us ecstatically sensitive to the slightest flick of a dry-mouthed tongue. A little bit of coke on our willard or her labia was a marathon stuntlike sex act. Quaaludes tranced us into an endless stretch toward orgasm. The sixties were, in a world without the lethal dangers of AIDS, a sexual smorgasbord. No small talk, no courting, no foreplay, just "Do you wanna fuck?" Or, if you wanted to be a little Jane Austenish about it, "I'd really love to ball you."

I spent the years from 1971 to 1975 as a senior editor at *Rolling Stone* in San Francisco, recently arrived from the Midwest, and found myself dining at this pink smorgasbord quickly and heartily. Some of the women at *Rolling Stone* were going to Braless Day rallies, where they hurled girdles, bras, and panties into a "Freedom Trash Can." All the *Rolling Stone* editors, all of us male, expressed fervent solidarity with the gesture.

The women at *Rolling Stone* were young, nubile, attractive and liked the phrase "I really want to ball you." And they *did.* Goodness knows, I did,

too . . . with Deborah and Kathy and Shauna and Sunny and Robin and
Leyla and Janet and Deborah again, realizing quickly that they were balling
the other editors on alternate nights, that this was about nothing, really, but
a little bit of exercise and lots of pleasure. It was about having fun. It was a
combination of athletics and theatrics, intimate communal performance
art, best exemplified by the staffer who took his girlfriend into the parking
lot each noon while other staffers lazily watched from the windows upstairs
as she fellated him. (We named the show "Clarabel and the Zit Queen.")
When Jann went out of town, some of us borrowed his office for our couplings, but he came back from one trip, enraged to find "coke and come" all
over his desk, and started locking his door.

As I watched Bill Clinton with Hillary and heard Gennifer's account of
how Bill wanted to have sex with her in a rest room while Hillary stood outside, a few feet away, I remembered that during those years at *Rolling Stone,*
I was married . . . and so were many of the other editors. And after those
office or parking lot or backseat or Van Ness Avenue motel couplings, I'd go
home to my wife, still smelling of sex, with Acapulco Gold coursing through
my blood, and she and I would talk about Watergate or the price of not-yet-
taboo abalone at Petrini's.

My wife wasn't one of the hot and willing young sweetmeats at *Rolling
Stone.* She was, in fact, sort of like Hillary: smart, poised, responsible, a partner in most ways, except the sexual ones. I didn't marry my wife for sexual
reasons, and it became obvious to me that Bill Clinton didn't marry Hillary
for sexual reasons, either. You could call Hillary many things, but not sexy.
Drawn to Lucy in the Sky with Diamonds, Bill Clinton had married Judy in
Disguise with Glasses.

Was it possible to imagine Bill wanting to take Hillary into that rest room
while wife Gennifer was standing out there? But there was another deadly
flip to that question: Would Bill Clinton have felt the need to take anyone
into that rest room had he been married to Gennifer instead of Hillary? No
one was saying that Bill and Hillary didn't have a sex life, but the whole
world knew by now that it didn't amount to much.

So our rock and roll president started having what the press called
"affairs," although, except for Gennifer, the euphemism didn't bear scrutiny. These weren't affairs—they were backstage exercises, Mick cutting a
swath through groupies, the political rock star run amok at the sexual smorgasbord. All women were Connie Hamzy to him. Connie was a rock and
roll groupie whom he'd met in Little Rock. Not just any groupie, royalty
groupie, made famous as "Sweet Sweet Connie" in Grand Funk Railroad's

smash hit "We're an American Band": "Sweet sweet Connie was doin' her act . . ." Connie had done singers and drummers and managers and roadies and bus drivers by the time Bill Clinton spotted her by a hotel pool, and the first thing he said to her was, "I want to get with you."

He was using women's bodies still, the way he and we had callously and selfishly used one another's bodies in the sixties. The point was a pair of lips, a pair of tits, a nice ass. The point was skin, flesh, meat. The point was a hole. And was it any wonder that he hadn't matured? That, simply due to age and wisdom, he hadn't learned to treat his fellow human beings with more humanity? Well, look at Mick Jagger, who was pushing sixty. He was just a rock star, not even the most powerful man on earth, the president of the United States. Mick still wasn't interested in women. He was still interested in holes.

The trouble with holes, if you were a politician, was that you couldn't run on them. The public smirked when Mick knocked up a new honey, and they said, "Look at that Mick! And he's almost sixty!" But you couldn't run for president and say, "Listen, people, I'm married and I love my wife, but I've got this thing about vaginas and fellatio and if I don't get enough, I'll sit around the White House masturbating."

If you couldn't say that, and if you were a career politician whose only talent was to collect votes, you had to lie. You had to become a practiced and constant world-champion liar. And if you saw yourself getting away with this lie for many years, and continued collecting votes in the statehouse and in the White House, then why not lie about everything? If your whole inner dynamic was structured on a fundamental lie that you were getting away with, then why not adopt the same successful strategy—*lying*—about everything? You dodged the draft? Lie and say you didn't. You smoked dope? Lie and say you didn't inhale. You were humping Gennifer whenever you could? Lie and say it never happened. A White House intern? "I want to say one thing to the American people. I did not have sex with that woman, Miss Lewinsky."

A semen stain on a blue dress? DNA? *What? Hoo-boy! Jesus God!* We didn't need the National Center for Atmospheric Testing to tell us there was a skunky odor in the air. America felt like it needed a psychic disinfectant. We were Grossed Out, Pissed Off, and Ready to Throw Up—a nineties twist on "Tune in, turn on, drop out."

It was the stain that got him, of course. Technology. Who would have thunk it? Exposed as a liar forever, impeached, red-faced, jabbing his finger, lying. In the same boat as Nixon. "I am not a crook." The same boat as Nixon! Nixon the Night Creature! Devil incarnate to us in the sixties! Not Nixon at the end, sneaking into Burger Kings in New Jersey for a forbidden cheeseburger, but Nixon at full bore: lying about Pat's cloth coat and Checkers and Ellsberg and the break-in at the Watergate. Exposed, too, as gutless as Nixon, which was why Nixon lied too. Nixon could have admitted it, could have said the break-in was wrong and a mistake, but he didn't have the guts to do that or to burn the tapes. ("If he had destroyed the tapes," former House Speaker Tip O'Neill said, "he could have remained in office until the end of his second term. Not to destroy them was irrational.")

Clinton could have admitted it, could have said, Yes, I've always had a problem with sex. My marriage has never fulfilled me. I'm a horndog, dadgummit! But no, it was impossible for him. He had lied from the beginning about everything because he had lied about . . . the holes . . . and gotten away with it. ("It's not a lie," former Reagan secretary of state Al Haig said, "it's a terminological inexactitude.")

Oh boy, a sad, sad story. A sixties kid, waging the good fight against the forces of racism and intolerance, against Nixon and the Marlboro Man and the right-wing pentecostal nutbags possessed and held in thrall by the unborn fetus and the Confederate flag and the Protocols of the Elders of Zion . . . and then this happened! In the same leaky boat as the Night Creature, way up shit creek . . . revealed, disgraced, and all this after a landslide victory over Bob Dole, an old man who had ED—erectile dysfunction. (Everyone sensed something, but no one knew.) Bob Dole couldn't even get it up, at the same time Bill Clinton was frolicking with Willard on aide Nancy Hernreich's couch. Oh boy. Sad.

Only Hunter Thompson, our mad prophet, had had any reservations about Bill Clinton, claiming that Clinton made him uncomfortable, that he didn't have a sense of humor, that he hogged the french fries. When Bill Clinton said he hadn't inhaled, Hunter wrote, "Only a fool would say a thing like that. He's just a disgrace to an entire generation. . . . Bill Clinton doesn't inhale marijuana, right? You bet. Like I chew on LSD but don't swallow it." Hunter didn't like Bill Clinton from the first time he met him. "He treated me like a roach from the get-go. Like maybe he had such a pure, clear goddamn nose from never inhaling that he could actually smell what he thought was some kind of drugs in my pocket. Or maybe it was me that was actually responsible for what happened to his brother. Sure! Like it was me that told the cops to go ahead and put the poor despised little bas-tard in a federal prison. For his own good, of course. Nobody would have Roger locked up for their own political reasons, would they?" But Hunter endorsed Bill Clinton anyway, despite his reservations, just like he'd endorsed Jimmah, because he thought Bill Clinton would be the first rock and roll president in American history: one of us.

So he was one of us and now many of *us* couldn't wait to get him out of sight—what the hell, a lot of us had seen too much of Mick's tired circus act, too. Eighteen months before his final term ended, America had already turned to the next election. The news shows were covering it as if it were next week. Why so early? Why were we so caught up with an election eigh-teen months away? Because so many of us wanted it to be over already, because so many of us wanted Bill Clinton gone. He was the first rock and roll president of the United States and he had become the first elected pres-ident to ever be impeached. Impeached for lying about his ripe peaches. He should have been infibulated instead of impeached.

It sure wasn't supposed to end this way. Our first rock and roll president was supposed to rock the world . . . but not like this. He was supposed to put our kick-ass primal inner beat into the Oval Office. He was supposed to tell the truth—finally—after all the White House liars we'd grown up and grown older and grown more cynical with.

He made us feel queasy now. We saw a freeze-frame of a fifty-three-year-old man, tired, red-faced, overweight, a father, sitting alone in a plush office, his fly open, Willard in hand, staring, coming. Bill Clinton was the literal nineties realization of that mythical moment in the sixties: Jim Morri-son onstage in Miami, unzipping his fly, showing off his dick, and simulat-ing masturbation and oral sex in front of thousands of people. Bill Clinton was the wet spot on America's bed.

It had gotten so tawdry in Washington that even the reporters, as they were asking their questions, seemed shocked by their own actions—as shown in an exchange between White House correspondents and Clinton press secretary Mike McCurry.

A reporter: "Does Clinton have a sexually transmitted disease?"

Another reporter: "Jesus!"

McCurry: "Good God, do you really want to ask that question?"

Another reporter: "Mike, are you saying the President does not now have and has not since he entered the White House been treated for a sexually transmitted disease?"

McCurry: "Boy, I tell you, I'm astonished you're asking that question."

The reporter: "I don't want to."

McCurry: "Look, I'm trying to keep some level of dignity here."

Another reporter: "We really have reached a new low."

Walter Lippmann, James Reston, and Joe Alsop had been replaced in the press corps by Xaviera Hollander, Dr. Ruth, and Stuttering John Melendez.

I saw Bill Clinton wearing his shades in the summer of 1999 on his way to lunch with Barbra Streisand near my home in Malibu, just around the corner from Kenny G's and a few doors down from a convicted drug dealer's. Most people in Hollywood knew he and Barbra had a special friendship, though a lot of years had passed since the night she'd stunned the world by letting us see her derriere through her Scassi pajamas on the Oscars. Even Gennifer had said, "She went so overboard while Bill was campaigning, gushing over him and buddying up to his mother. She seemed like a woman hypnotized."

They held traffic up now as the big Secret Service Suburbans came barreling through. For a moment, Bill Clinton's limousine stopped and he glanced at the row of cars waiting there. He saw a group of us watching him. He looked quickly away in the other direction. Those of us watching said not a word. Nobody waved.

[2]

Monica, Andy, and Handsome

"Why don't you just fuck your father," Linda Tripp said to Monica, "and get it over with."

She told her second-grade teacher she would be the president of the United States. She made it into the Oval Office, but . . .

Monica grew up in Beverly Hills, 90210. Her father was a doctor, a cancer specialist. Her mother wrote for a newspaper, *The Hollywood Reporter*, which chronicled the lives of movie stars. Her father called her his "little noodle."

She got good grades, but she was physically clumsy. It took her a long weekend to begin to learn how to jump rope. She was fat. The other kids called her "Big Mac" and "Pig Mac." She called her father "Dr. No." He wouldn't let her get a Snoopy phone. He wouldn't buy her a Minnie Mouse dress at Disneyland. Dr. No wasn't all bad, though. He bought her a pink bike with a banana seat.

Her mother was her soul mate. She looked and talked like her mother. She reached puberty early. She hated being fat. The summer before she entered the eighth grade, her mother enrolled her in a fat camp in Santa Barbara. At fourteen, she met her first boyfriend, Adam Dave. She went to his baseball games; she spent hours on the phone with him; she let him touch her.

Her mother and father weren't getting along. She ate more and got fatter. She was hurt and upset that her parents were arguing most of the time; she'd grown up watching *The Brady Bunch*. Her mother filed for divorce.

Her father was telling a woman patient that she was dying of lung cancer when his secretary interrupted to tell him there was a process server outside. Monica's mother told her that the reason she'd filed for divorce was that her father was having an affair with a nurse at the office.

She was often in tears. She spent whole days alone at the movies. She gained more than fifty pounds in her freshman year at Beverly Hills High. Her nicknames had followed her. "Big Mac!" The kids laughed. "Pig Mac!" While she was skipping her classes at Beverly Hills High, she was spending a lot of time in the drama department. She sewed costumes for the school plays. She got a tiny part in *The Music Man*. The drama department was her sanctuary. Often she'd eat lunch by herself there.

Her mother transferred her from Beverly Hills High to Bel Air Prep, where there was less emphasis on physical perfection. She fell in love with poetry, especially that of Walt Whitman and T. S. Eliot. She wrote a poem that began:

> *I crouch in a corner all by myself fighting the war of emotions,*
> *Battling against FEAR, ENVY, DEPRESSION, and REJECTION,*
> *I struggle.*

Although no longer a student there, she still went back to the drama department at Beverly Hills High. She made a little money now sewing costumes. That's where she met Andy Bleiler, the school's new drama technician. He was twenty-five, eight years older, involved in a relationship with a divorcée eight years older than he. She knew he had a reputation as a lothario. He walked her back to her car one night after a play. He kissed her good night and he touched her breasts. Andy was good-looking and slim.

When she graduated from Bel Air Prep, she applied to Boston University. Dr. No said no. It was too expensive. She enrolled at Santa Monica College instead. She got a job at the Knot Shop, a place that sold neckties. She loved working with the ties, dazzled by the fabrics and colors. But she was putting weight on again.

Her mother sent her to a psychotherapist. Dr. Irene Kassorla was known as "the psychologist to the stars." In 1980, Dr. Kassorla had written a book called *Nice Girls Do*. The book advised women to get in touch with their "magical push muscles." Dr. Kassorla advised women to go to the bathroom, sit on the toilet, and begin to urinate. Then to stop in midstream. Then to hold it for a few seconds. Then to start urinating again. Stopping and starting this way, Dr. Kassorla said, would enable women to find their "magical push muscles." Her book talked about "plunging into a passionate ride," "turbulent, fleshy moments," "sensual storms," "romantic electricity." "Your body swells with expectation," Dr. Kassorla wrote, "your flesh is rosy with excitement and warmth . . . soon the hot juices will flow through you."

As she was seeing Dr. Kassorla, Andy Bleiler, the drama technician at Beverly Hills High, now married to the divorcée Kate Nason, started hitting on her again. He told her she was sexy. He told her she was beautiful. He asked her to give her panties to him. They started spending afternoons together at local motels. She wouldn't have intercourse with him at first. She felt guilty he was married. But she went down on him. She felt she was in love with him.

She told Dr. Kassorla she was sleeping with Andy. Dr. Kassorla warned her about having an affair with a married man, but the author of *Nice Girls Do* didn't tell her to break it off. On the other hand, Dr. No said no. Her father told her to stop seeing Andy immediately. Her mother was furious. She thought Bleiler "a piece of garbage" for hitting on a woman so much younger.

When Andy's wife was four months pregnant, Monica told Andy she felt bad about what she was doing, and she ended the affair. Two weeks later, when he made another pass at her, she started having sex with him again. She was *s-o-o-o* in love with him. She got him a birthday cake shaped like an iguana. She made love to him in the lighting booth of the school auditorium. She sang "Happy Birthday" to him the way Marilyn had sung it to JFK.

Just before Andy's baby was born, Andy told her he was breaking up with *her*. He wanted to be a good father to the baby, he said. But weeks later, he started seeing her again, and she thought she understood now that this was the way married men behaved. They felt guilty; they wanted to stop, but they couldn't.

When she finished Santa Monica College, she opted to attend Lewis and Clark College in Portland, Oregon, because it felt like Bel Air Prep to her. She knew there wasn't a chance she could end the relationship with Andy in L.A. She didn't have the strength to say no. He was hot, good-looking, sexy. She felt herself to be none of those things.

She shared a house with two guys near campus. She went to flea markets to decorate her room with floral patterns (she loved roses) and embroidered pillows. "She was a slob," a friend said, like most kids in college. She called her mother to ask how to clean the bathroom and always had her hair done and her legs waxed when her mother visited.

There was a Knot Shop in Portland, too, and she got a job there, working with the ties that she loved. She helped out at a meeting place for the mentally ill, the Phoenix Club, and tried to make matzo ball soup for the members, but the soup she made was inedible.

Her new friends noticed that she talked a lot about sex and a lot about her weight. Some described her as larger than life. Some said she was too loud. Most, though, liked her directness and sense of humor.

She went out with a few guys casually, but she badly missed Andy. So she called him in L.A., and, back home for Thanksgiving, she slept with him again. She slept with him again and again in L.A. during the winter and spring—when she discovered that he was cheating not only on his wife but on her, too.

In late spring, Andy called to tell her that he, his wife, Kate, and their baby boy were moving to . . . Portland. She was excited and distressed. She felt she still loved him, but she knew that if he came up to Portland, she wouldn't be able to break it off.

Andy came up in June, but he came up alone. He told her he'd have to find a place to work and a place for his family to live before they could join him. He told her he was in love with her. He said she was sexy and beautiful. He stayed in Portland without his family the entire summer. She and Andy were together all the time, intimate every day.

When Kate and the baby came to Portland in the fall, Andy told her, once again, that he felt so guilty, they had to stop being intimate with each other. She tried, but she couldn't do it. When she met Kate, she liked her. She and Kate became close friends. She felt that her feeling for Kate was partly the result of how much she loved Kate's husband. She started baby-sitting for Kate and buying clothes both for the baby and Kate's older daughter. And she slept with Andy at her apartment.

When Andy kept flying to L.A. on "business," she became suspicious. She made some calls to friends in L.A. and they told her Andy was sleeping with a teenager at Beverly Hills High. She got the teenager's number and called her. The teenager was angry that Andy wasn't seeing her enough. The girl felt abused and said she was thinking about calling Andy's wife and telling her everything.

Monica confronted Andy and told him the teenager was thinking about calling his wife. Andy cried like a baby and said he was going to kill himself. He begged for her forgiveness and begged her to help him. She called the teenager back and convinced her not to call Andy's wife. In return, Andy agreed that he wouldn't just sneak away from Kate for a few hours to have sex with her. He'd take her out for a drink or dinner and treat her like a woman he loved. She still kept baby-sitting for Kate. And, to get back at Andy, she slept with Andy's younger brother, Chris. Andy had said Chris would never like her because he "only liked tall and willowy women." Chris liked her. She made sure Chris liked her.

She schemed with Andy to provide excuses to Kate so he could get out of the house to see her. Whenever Kate left the house, Andy told her that David Bliss, shop foreman of the Lewis and Clark theater department, had called to offer him a few hours or a full day's work. Kate became suspicious of these calls coming exactly when she wasn't there. Andy was panicked about Kate's suspicions and came running to see Monica at her apartment. She knew what to do. She went down to the theater department and stole a piece of stationery. She wrote a letter to Andy, offering him work, and forged David Bliss's signature at the bottom.

While she was seeing Andy, she was also a teaching assistant in a course called Psychology of Sex. She was the group leader in a "sex lab." When the others were shy about discussing their intimate lives, she charged boldly ahead, talking honestly about her weight problem and its effect on her sexuality. At the same time, she and a girlfriend paid forty dollars to hear a lecture entitled "How to Find a Mate."

The day after she graduated, she accompanied two friends who were going to do a bungee jump. At the last moment, without even giving it a thought, she jumped as well.

Her father encouraged her to think about a career in the public defender's office in Portland. Her mother, who knew about her continuing relationship with Andy Bleiler, had a better idea, an idea that would get her out of town, away from Andy.

Her mother had a friend named Walter Kaye, a friend of Hillary Clinton's, a big Democratic contributor, whose grandson had been a White House intern. It would, her mother said, only be a six-week summer job, unpaid, and she'd be one of two hundred interns, but it sounded like fun, didn't it? What a thing to have on a résumé!

Her mother was already living in Washington, to be near her sister, Monica's aunt Debra. Monica could move in with her mother at the Watergate and have Bob and Elizabeth Dole for neighbors. Monica told her mother that it *really* did sound like fun. And her mother said she'd call her friend Walter Kaye, who perhaps would call his friend Hillary Clinton.

. . .

She made out an application and . . . she was accepted! She would be working at the White House! She spent one final night before she left Portland
with Andy Bleiler. She knew she still loved him.

She had a couple weeks before her job at the White House began, and
she and her mother spent it at her aunt Debra's big, sprawling house in Virginia. Her Aunt Debra also had a small in-town apartment at the Watergate,
so Monica was seeing a lot of her. But she couldn't get Andy out of her
mind. She called him and then decided, after only two weeks away from
Portland, to fly back to see him on the Fourth of July. He was only able to
sneak away from Kate and the baby for a few hours, but they enjoyed the little time they had together.

On July 10, 1995, in room 450 of the Old Executive Office Building, she
was given her White House assignment. She'd deliver sorted mail from the
Old Executive Office Building to the West Wing, where the Oval Office was
located. The first time she passed the Oval Office's mahogany door (a Secret
Service agent standing guard), her pulse raced. She called Andy and breathlessly told him about what she'd felt as she'd passed the mahogany door.

The women at the White House, she soon discovered, were in awe of the
forty-second president of the United States—not just as the president but as
Bill Clinton, the horndog. She knew his reputation with women, but here
she heard the gossip about specific women working at the White House:
Marsha Scott, an old Arkansas girlfriend, an administrative assistant, who
reportedly had spent the night with Bill Clinton when Vince Foster killed
himself; Cathy Cornelius, young and stunning, Cybill Shepherd–like, who
accompanied him on many of his trips abroad; Debbie Schiff, former stewardess on his campaign plane, now a White House secretary. She didn't get
it. From what she'd seen on TV, Bill Clinton had a big red nose. His hair
was gray and lusterless. He wore geeky sunglasses. He was old.

Sometime in mid-July, only a week or so after she'd started her internship, Walter Kaye invited her mother and her to watch an arrival ceremony
for the president of South Korea on the White House lawn. It was a hot day.
She was sweating. She wore a flimsy sundress and a straw sombrero-type hat.
It was so hot, she was worried about fainting. "Ladies and gentlemen," she
heard over a loudspeaker, "the President of the United States, accompanied
by the First Lady." She heard military music from the Marine Corps Band.
She saw him. Her heart skipped a beat. She felt short of breath. Butterflies
circled inside her. She only saw him from far away, but it was enough. He
was *s-o-o-o* handsome.

She saw him up close a week later when the interns received permission to watch a presidential departure. He came down a roped-off path, shaking hands, smiling. When he got to her, she felt like air. She felt like a tree or a plant. He barely glanced at her.

A little more than another week later, on August 9, she went to another departure. She wore a tightly fitting sage green dress her mother had recently bought for her at J. Crew. Here he came again, walking down the rope line. He was talking to another intern's father as she stood nearby, and he suddenly glanced at her . . . and held her gaze as he continued talking to the others. He was smiling at her . . . and then he came over to her and shook her hand. His smile was gone now. He looked deeply into her eyes. She felt she was alone with him. She felt he was undressing her. He moved down the line, and, dazed, she bumped into a friend. She caught his glance again as he moved farther down the line. He was looking at her.

At work the next day, still reeling from what had happened to her on the rope line, she learned that the interns had been invited at the last minute to attend a surprise birthday party for the president that day. He was forty-nine. She was twenty-two. She drove home quickly to put her tight-fitting sage green J. Crew dress on.

It was a Wild West party. Vice President Gore arrived in an old woody station wagon. Some of the president's aides came in on horseback. And, finally, here *he* came, down the line again, smiling at her as he approached. When he shook her hand, immersing himself into her eyes again, she said, "Happy Birthday, Mr. President," repeating the Marilyn Monroe imitation she had tried out on Andy Bleiler. Everything was in slow motion and freeze-frame again . . . and as he moved away, his arm casually brushed her breast. She watched as he walked down the line. He glanced at her at the end of the line and headed back inside the White House; then he stopped suddenly, turned, and looked at her. She blew him a kiss. He threw his head back and laughed.

When she got home, she told her mother and her aunt Debra what had happened. Her mother laughed and said she was getting a crush on the president of the United States. Aunt Debra said, "Maybe he's interested in you or attracted to you or something."

She went out to a bookstore that was still open and bought a copy of Gennifer Flowers's book and spent the night reading it. Gennifer said that Bill Clinton called her "Pookie." Monica read that he liked women who were "ripe peaches," and she thought of herself in her sage green dress. She read Gennifer's account of "overheated eye contact" and "psychological foreplay" and thought about how he had looked at her on the rope line.

She was excited to see Pookie describe him as "a natural born lover man . . . with more sexual libido" than Pookie had ever seen. Monica noted how much he liked sexy lingerie—lace and garters, tiny black teddies, little white nighties. She couldn't believe how kinky he was—dripping ice on Pookie's body, asking Pookie to drip candle wax on him, dripping honey on her body, asking her to tie him to the bed, to use a dildo on him.

Everything that Gennifer wrote about him turned Monica on. "His stamina amazed me," Monica read; "we made love over and over that night, and he never seemed to run out of energy. . . . He proved he could go on all night." Bill, according to Pookie, was a wild man who kept dope in his pockets and casually lighted up, who liked Pookie to meet him at a hotel wearing nothing but a fur coat, who loved phone sex—"Bill loved to talk dirty and to have me say things back to him"—who liked pouring catsup and milk all over her body and licking it off, who liked oral sex. "With Bill, oral sex seemed like the natural thing to do." Pookie also made Monica wonder about his relationship with Hillary, whose friendship with Walter Kaye had gotten Monica her job. "Bill said he had known for a long time that Hillary was attracted to women," Gennifer wrote, "and it didn't really bother him anymore. His first clue came from her lack of enjoyment of sex with him. He said Hillary was cold and not playful at all in bed. Hillary didn't like to experiment and insisted on the missionary position and nothing else. Because she wasn't enjoying herself, neither was he. Sex with Hillary became a duty, nothing more." Bill told Gennifer, "She's eaten more pussy than I have."

Monica laughed when she read that he called his penis "Willard." Willard? *Willard!* What an odd name for a penis. Wasn't there an old movie called *Willard?* About a boy and his rat? But she liked his explanation to Gennifer of why he called it Willard: "It's longer than Willie."

She was off from work the next day, but she never left the apartment. She was sure she was going to get a call from the Secret Service telling her the president wanted to see her. She had heard that that was what the Secret Service had done for JFK. The phone rang a lot that day—she felt her heartbeat race each time—but it was never him.

Her six-week internship was nearly over and she went to her supervisor and asked to re-up for a second six weeks. She was, her supervisor felt, conscientious and enthusiastic, and so her second internship was approved.

She started reading everything she could find about him. Her heart broke for him. To have had to grow up in that awful racist state, where black people had been lynched as recently as the 1920s! To have had to be brought up by his grandparents for two years because his mom could only find work in another city! She could just see his mom as he had: kneeling on the ground and sobbing after a visit with him. And her heart broke for herself, too. *He* was the fat *boy*. The only pair of jeans that fit him in the waist were so long that he had to roll them halfway to his knees. He had a cute little Hopalong Cassidy outfit and the other kids made him jump rope in his cowboy boots—*he couldn't jump rope, either!*—and they pulled the rope out from under him. He broke his leg and the other kids yelled at him as he lay on the ground: "Sissy! Sissy! You're a sissy!" And he, too, had cowered alone in his room as his parents yelled at each other.

She remembered how, in grade school, she had said she was going to be the president of the United States, and she smiled when she read that when he was in grade school, a teacher said that *he* was going to be the president of the United States . . . and now he was.

The moment of his life that touched her the most took place when he was a little boy and he was singing "Frog Went A-Courtin' " with his music teacher.

He sang, "Miss Mousy will you marry me, uh-huh! uh-huh! Miss Mousy will you marry me, uh-huh! uh-huh!"

His music teacher sang, "Without my Uncle Rat's consent, uh-uh! uh-uh! Without my Uncle Rat's consent, I wouldn't marry the President, uh-uh! uh-uh!"

She held the image in her mind: a clumsy little fat boy with a crew cut, his jeans rolled up, his tummy sticking out, singing, "Miss Mousy will you marry me, uh-huh! uh-huh!" It made her feel close to him. *S-o-o-o* close to him.

She went to another departure ceremony in August with a group of interns, and when he stopped and chatted with the group, she introduced herself and made sure to say that she was staying for a second internship term. He smiled and nodded. A week or so later, she was in the basement lobby of the West Wing, talking to a member of the Secret Service, when he came by with two women guests. He turned away from the two other women and turned to her.

"Hi, Mr. President. I'm Monica Lewinsky," she said.

"I know." He grinned, looking her up and down, undressing her with his eyes again. She sucked in her tummy. She was happy she was wearing black.

She went to her supervisor and applied for a paid White House job after her second internship was up. She didn't see him then for more than two months, but she thought about him all the time and told her girlfriends about him, too, describing the way the president of the United States had undressed her with his eyes. Her friends were wary. One of them, who worked at the White House, even warned her there were rumors he was leaving the White House late at night to meet someone at the Marriott downtown.

As she was telling her friends about the crush she had on the president, she flew across the country, back to Portland, to see Andy Bleiler again. He sneaked away from his wife to spend a few hours in bed with her, but then he told her once again that it was over, that he was feeling too guilty about cheating on his wife.

She was crushed and hysterical. She had flown all the way across America just to make love to him . . . and now he was giving her the same old awful, hurtful, duplicitous song and dance. She sobbed her way back to Washington.

She got good news the morning she got back. There was a job opening in Legislative Affairs at the White House. She interviewed with senior officials and she got the job!

There was, though, a temporary glitch. Newt Gingrich and his Republicans were causing a budgetary impasse and there was going to be a government shutdown. It meant that senior staff were forced to go home, that the 430-person White House staff would be cut down to 90 while the impasse lasted.

But it also meant that interns, who were unpaid, could work and would have additional responsibilities. Since she had not officially begun her Legislative Affairs job, she would work during the shutdown—technically, still as an intern.

On her first day of work during the shutdown, she wore a navy blue pantsuit. She was working in Chief of Staff Leon Panetta's office, answering the phones, which kept ringing off the hook because Rush Limbaugh had given Leon's phone number to the dittoheads who wanted to complain about the shutdown.

She saw "Handsome" as he walked past her office in the hallway. She mouthed *Hi* at him while she was on the phone. He said, "Hi," smiled, and kept going.

Later that day, there was an informal birthday party for another aide, and he unexpectedly showed up, smiling and looking at her as she kept dealing with the loony-tunes on the phone.

He went into Leon's inner office, and she got up from her desk and waited for him to come out. When he did, she turned her back to him and lifted the back of her jacket with her thumbs, letting him see the thong underwear showing above her waistline. From reading Gennifer's book, she knew how much he loved underwear and other lingerie. As he passed her, he looked at her and smiled.

Throughout the course of the evening, he kept coming back to Leon's office as she worked at her desk, looking at her every time, claiming he was trying to find aides who he knew weren't there. Going to get something to drink, she passed George Stephanopoulos's office and saw Handsome sitting there . . . all alone.

"Come on in here for a second," he said.

She went in.

"Where did you go to school?"

"You know," she replied, "I have a really big crush on you."

He laughed and looked at her for a long moment, staring at her breasts. "Come into the back office," he said.

In George's inner office, he put his arms around her and held her tightly. His eyes were "soul searching, tender, very needing, very wanting, very loving." She also thought there was a sadness about him she hadn't expected.

"You're so beautiful," he said. "Your energy just lights up a room." And he asked, "Can I kiss you?"

He kissed her—"softly, deeply, romantically." He stroked her hair and her face.

"I've done this before, you know," she said. "It's okay." She was talking about her affair with Andy Bleiler, a married man. She wanted to put Handsome at ease.

"I knew when I saw you on the line out there that I'd kiss you," he said. He looked at her a long moment, smiled, looked at his watch, then said he had to get back to work.

She was sitting alone in Leon's outer office three hours later, around ten o'clock at night, when he came in. She was expecting him. She had written her name and phone number on a piece of paper, and when he came in, she handed it to him.

He smiled and said, "If you'd like to meet me in George's office in five or ten minutes, you can."

"Yes." She smiled. "I would like to do that."

She waited ten minutes and then walked down to George's office. She went into the outer office, where the lights were on, and he wasn't there. Then the door to the inner office opened and he was standing there in the darkness, aiming that slow, sexy smile at her. He gestured for her to come in.

He kissed her as soon as she stepped into the inner office. She unbuttoned her jacket and he touched her breasts, her bra still on. He lifted her bra up and he felt her breasts and he kissed them. He explored her body with his hands and moved a hand under her panties. A telephone rang. He picked it up and started to talk to a congressman about Bosnia while he kept moving his hand between her legs. She had an orgasm as he talked, and she knelt down in front of him. She tried to unbutton his pants, but, used to zippers and not buttons, she was having trouble doing it. He unbuttoned his fly for her, still talking on the phone. Willard was suddenly there. She began nurturing Willard with kisses while he was still on the phone, still talking about Bosnia. When he finally hung up, he stopped her.

"Please," she said. "I want to make you come."

"I don't know you well enough," he said. "I don't trust you for that."

He pulled on the pink intern pass around her neck and said, "This could be a problem." She told him that she had just been hired as a legislative aide and would soon have the blue pass, which would give her access anywhere in the White House.

"That's great." He smiled.

He looked at her and then he said, "Well, I've got to go, kiddo."

She said, "Okay," and he was gone. She felt that she had found her "sexual soul mate." When she got home, she woke both her mother and her aunt Debra and told them the president had kissed her. She didn't say anything about Willard.

He ignored her the next day. The day after that, she waited all day for him, but he never came around Leon's office. She stayed late with some others, still waiting for him, among them the president's secretary, Betty Currie. They ordered a pizza. When the pizza arrived, she went down to Betty's office to tell her it was there.

She saw him then, finally, talking to some people. He didn't even glance at her. Betty came back to Leon's office, and so did the others who were working late. One of them bumped into Monica and smeared pizza all over her new red jacket. She went into the bathroom to clean it off, and when she came out, Handsome was standing in the doorway of Betty's office, as though he'd been waiting for her.

"You can come out this way, kiddo," Handsome said, smiling, and he led her into the Oval Office, toward his private study.

He stopped her in the hallway, where there were no windows, and kissed her. He felt her body with his hands.

"You've got such a beautiful smile," he said.

She asked him why he hadn't called her at home.

"What about your parents?"

"It's okay. I've got my own line. You don't have to worry. I told you—I've done this before."

He kissed her again, feeling her, pulling her closer to Willard.

"I bet you don't even remember my name," she said.

He grinned and said, "What kind of a name *is* Lewinsky, anyway?"

"Jewish."

He started to kiss her again, and she said, "I'd better go. They're going to wonder where I am." She wanted to show him that she was on his side, that she didn't want anyone to get suspicious.

He grinned. "Why don't you go get me a couple slices of pizza?"

She went back to Leon's outer office and grabbed two slices of vegetarian pizza. When she returned, Betty Currie was sitting at her desk outside the Oval Office. She told Betty that he'd asked her to bring him some pizza. Betty opened the door to the Oval Office and said, "Sir, the girl's here with the pizza."

She went inside, and he led her back to the hallway and started kissing her again. He unbuttoned her blouse and he kissed her breasts. She unbuttoned his shirt and she kissed his chest. She felt him suck his stomach in. She said, "Oh, you don't have to do that—I like your tummy."

Betty Currie was suddenly at the door leading to the hallway. They froze.

"Sir," Betty Currie said. "You've got that call you were expecting."

He said, "Thank you, Betty." His voice was hoarse.

He led her into the bathroom off the hallway—it was dark in there—and he picked up the telephone. He was speaking to another congressman about Bosnia. As he spoke, he unbuttoned his fly and Willard came out to see her. She knelt down and . . . He pushed her head away and made her stop again.

"Please, just let me finish."

"No. I told you. I don't know you well enough."

She didn't understand the distinction; he knew her well enough to let her nurture Willard, but he didn't know her well enough to let her bring Willard to closure.

He told her again that she had "a beautiful smile" and "great energy."

"I'm usually around on the weekends, when there's hardly anybody here," he said. "You can come see me, kiddo."

"Okay." She smiled. "Call me."

"I will."

He didn't call her. She saw him in the corridors sometimes and he smiled and said hi, but he always called her "kiddo."

Late in November, she went to see Betty Currie. She asked Betty whether she'd pass a necktie on to him if she got one. She explained about her jobs at the Knot Shops and told Betty how much she'd always loved ties. Betty said sure.

She bought a beautiful hand-painted, hand-stitched Zegna and gave it to Betty for him. A few days later, Betty told her he'd loved the tie so much that he'd had himself photographed wearing it and that he was going to give her a picture.

Early in December, she was walking through the West Wing, when she saw him with a group of people. He turned away from them when he noticed her and said, "Did you get the picture of me in that tie?" She told him no and walked away. Later that day, Betty called her at her desk and asked her to come over. Betty told her to go into the Oval Office so he could sign the picture for her.

As soon as she walked in, he said, "God, you look really skinny." She knew she wasn't skinny. She'd never been skinny. She'd never *be* skinny. But she was trying s-o-o-o hard to lose weight and he was s-o-o-o sweet to say it. He gave her the picture of him wearing the tie and signed it for her. Betty came in then.

Monica said, "Thank you, Mr. President."

He said, "Okay, kiddo," and then she left.

She told her mother and her aunt Debra and her friends that she was falling in love with him. They didn't take her seriously. If nothing else, she thought, Handsome was getting her over Andy Bleiler. Finally. She knew that women sometimes needed one man to get over another, but she'd never thought that it would take the president of the United States to get her over Andy.

[3]

The Uproar Is Deafening

"Every President," Monica said to Linda Tripp, "every President we have ever had has always had lovers because the pressure of the job is too much. Too much! Too much to always rely on your wife, with whom you have too much baggage—which you inevitably will if you get to that point."

The Comeback Kid knew this one was going to be tough. The uproar from this would hurt his ears. Turning down the new hearing aid he'd recently gotten at Bethesda wouldn't help. The uproar would be loud and painful, louder than the uproar over . . .

O.J.'s acquittal . . . Nixon's tapes . . . Gennifer's tapes . . . Carter's attempt to free the hostages . . . Chappaquiddick . . . Ford pardoning Nixon . . . Bob Packwood's diary . . . Tyson biting Holyfield . . . Vince and Hillary . . . Nixon and Bebe Rebozo . . . Ronald Reagan and Selena Walters . . . Bob Dole and Meredith Roberts . . . Nelson Rockefeller and Megan Marshack . . . Nancy Reagan's "three-hour lunches" with Frank Sinatra . . . Nixon and Bob Abplanalp . . .

Jimmy Carter's chief of staff, Hamilton Jordan, grabbing at the front of the dress of the wife of the Egyptian ambassador and saying, "I've always wanted to see the Pyramids" . . . Hamilton Jordan spilling a drink of amaretto and cream down a young woman's dress at a Georgetown bar . . . Elton John saying Keith was "a monkey with arthritis trying to go onstage and look young" . . . Tip O'Neill saying George McGovern was "nominated by the cast of *Hair*" . . . Donald Trump saying, "I have seen Darryl Hannah on many occasions and she is simply in need of a shower or bath" . . . Senator John McCain saying Newt Gingrich's poll numbers were "worse than mass murderer Jeffrey Dahmer's" . . . Prince and Kim Basinger . . .

Bush throwing up on the Japanese prime minister . . . LBJ saying, "Gentlemen, I've got a hard-on for the presidency" . . . Dukakis wearing that silly helmet in the tank . . . Hugh Grant and Divine Brown . . . Carter admitting "lust in his heart" . . . Nancy whispering into Reagan's ear . . . George Bush and Jennifer Fitzgerald . . . Ford falling down all the time . . . Bob Packwood singing Sinatra songs . . . George Bush commenting on his television debate with Geraldine Ferraro, saying, "We tried to kick a little ass last night" . . . Carl Bernstein and Elizabeth Taylor . . . Bob Dylan and Elizabeth Taylor . . .

Hustler's selection of Jerry Falwell as "Asshole of the Month" . . . J. Edgar Hoover and sixteen-year-old boys . . . LBJ picking women out of crowds, his aides pimping for him . . . Jimmy Carter's poems . . . LBJ stealing furniture from the White House and flying it to his ranch . . . Eddie Murphy and the transvestite . . . George Bush saying, "Read my lips—no new taxes" . . . Dick Morris and Sherry Rowlands . . . JFK using Judith Exner as his bagman to the mob . . . LBJ staggering drunk and cussing up a storm in the White House . . . Jack Kemp's time-shared Lake Tahoe apartment . . . Joan Kennedy's life . . . Eugene McCarthy's poems . . . Geraldo and Marion Javits . . . Ike and Kay Summersby . . . Vince Foster's suicide note . . . JFK and Marilyn in that loft above the attorney general's office . . . LBJ lifting his dogs up by the ears . . . George Bush examining a price scanner at a grocery store . . .

Barney Frank and Steve Gobie . . . Ruth Carter Stapleton and Larry Flynt . . . Paula Jones's nose . . . Bobby and Marilyn . . . Dustin Hoffman saying about Carl Bernstein, "I understand why Carl did so well on Watergate. Carl is essentially a fuckup and he has to fail, and Nixon is a fuckup and he has to fail, so Carl could always understand Nixon" . . . the videotape of Peter Jennings blowing his nose onto the ground . . . Jimmy Carter picking his nose in that photograph . . . Iowa senator Tom Harkin blowing his nose without a handkerchief on C-SPAN . . . Pat Buchanan saying, "Congress is Israeli-occupied territory" . . . Texas gubernatorial candidate Clayton Williams comparing bad weather and rape: "If it's inevitable, relax and enjoy it" . . . Bob Kerrey telling Bill Clinton that joke on C-SPAN: "Jerry Brown walks into a bar and sees two hot women. A guy in the bar says to him, 'Don't waste your time, Governor; they're dykes.' Brown says, 'How do you know?' The guy says, 'They like going down on each other.' Brown says, 'I like that, too. Does that make me a dyke?' " . . .

LBJ ordering Marine Corps helicopters to herd the peacocks on his ranch . . . JFK doing three hookers at a time in his hotel suites . . . LBJ say-ing, "I don't trust a man until I have his pecker in my pocket" . . . Spiro Agnew saying, "If you've seen one city slum, you've seen them all" . . . Ronald Reagan saying, "If you've seen one redwood, you've seen them all" . . . the picture of Gary Hart and Donna Rice . . . Barry Goldwater say-ing, "This country would be better off if we could saw off the Eastern Seaboard and let it float out to sea" . . . Dole falling off the stage . . . Ford drunk on *Air Force One* on the way back from Russia . . . Ford saying, "There is no Soviet domination of Eastern Europe," while Russian forces were stationed there . . .

Wayne Hayes and Elizabeth Ray . . . Houston mayoral candidate Louie Welch saying the way to control AIDS was to "shoot the queers" . . . LBJ explaining to reporters why we were in Vietnam by unzipping himself, tak-ing out his willard, and saying, "This is why" . . . Roseanne's crotch grab after singing the national anthem . . . George Bush, with a guitar embla-zoned THE PREZ, jamming on stage at his inaugural ball . . . Ted Danson in blackface at Whoopi's roast . . . Gerry Ford, after a long martini lunch, skip-ping several dozen pages of a speech . . . A Nancy Reagan aide, refusing to schedule a meeting between the First Lady and a child with muscular dys-trophy, saying, "Absolutely not. The First Lady doesn't want her picture taken with some drooly kid on a respirator." . . .

What Sally Field did to Burt Reynolds in *Playboy* . . . George Hamilton and Lynda Bird Johnson . . . Roger Mudd's interview with Ted Kennedy . . . Reagan saying, "Keeping up with my opponent's promises is like reading *Playboy* magazine while your wife turns the pages" . . . Dole on TV with his Exercycle, wearing shorts, a dress shirt, and French cuffs . . . Betty Ford, drunk, being carried off *Air Force One* . . . Nixon and Kissinger kneeling together, praying . . . Melissa Etheridge, Julie Cypher, and David Crosby's sperm . . . LBJ turning to the side and taking a whiz at an outdoor press con-ference . . . LBJ telling a tailor, "I need some more goddamn ball room in these pants" . . . Nixon walking on the beach with his wing-tip cordo-vans . . . Reagan falling asleep during cabinet meetings.

Gerry Ford's flatulence . . . Pat Buchanan saying, "Women are less equipped psychologically to stay the course in the brawling arenas of busi-ness, commerce, industry, and the professions" . . . Gary Hart telling the media, "Follow me—I don't care if anybody wants to put a tail on me. Go ahead. They'd be bored" . . . LBJ displaying his gallbladder and kidney-stone surgery scars for the cameras . . . Jimmy Carter holding Joan

Kennedy's hand as Rosalynn kept her eye on his . . . LBJ's three Texan secretaries, none of whom knew how to type . . . Quayle using the spelling "potatoe" and "beakon" . . . Carter using the White House stairs as his jogging track . . . LBJ smoking cigarettes with the presidential seal on them . . . Michael Jackson and his chimp . . . Roxanne Pulitzer and her trumpet . . . Alfred Bloomingdale and Vicki Morgan . . .

Wilbur Mills and Fanne Fox . . . Dan Rather saying, "Courage" . . . Haldeman and Ehrlichman . . . David Geffen and Keanu Reeves . . . Ford examining the change cup at McDonald's . . . LBJ's nickname, "Bull Nuts" . . . Pat Nixon's four martinis for lunch . . . Howard Stern's ass on prime-time television . . . LBJ buck naked on *Air Force One* with his wife, his daughters, and his secretaries . . . Jimmy Swaggart and the hooker . . . LBJ watching a crowd and saying, "You dumb sons of bitches, I piss on all of you" . . . Jimmy Swaggart's apology . . . Dan Rather and "What's the frequency, Kenneth?" . . . LBJ discussing the Civil Rights Act: "I'll have them niggers voting Democratic for two hundred years" . . . Tricia Nixon wearing a cape and broad-brim hat when she went into the water to go swimming . . .

LBJ talking about Vietnam: "We're going to liberate those poor little boogers and I'll be known as the Great Emancipator" . . . Woody Allen and Soon-Yi . . . Hubert Humphrey in a cowboy hat . . . Luci Baines Johnson looking for an assistant: "You go find my nigger! Right now! Find my nigger" . . . Jesse Jackson talking about New York City as "Hymietown" . . . Kitty Dukakis drinking her husband's aftershave . . . Ted Kennedy's testimony at the William Kennedy Smith trial . . . Reagan wearing a USC Trojan helmet . . . LBJ ordering *Air Force One* to land somewhere and buy some root beer . . . JFK doing that blonde who could have been a Communist secret agent . . . LBJ doing the same blonde who could have been a Communist secret agent . . . Kissinger shoving vegetables off his plate onto the floor of *Air Force One* . . . Bruce Lindsey saying to the press, "You all have been asses ever since we started" . . . LBJ stealing an electric bed from Walter Reed Army Hospital and flying it to his ranch . . . Richard Gere and the gerbil . . . *Showgirls.*

The Comeback Kid knew this would be more painful than . . .

Almost getting drafted . . . the *60 Minutes* interview . . . meeting Monica's parents at his radio address . . . being interviewed by Woodward . . .

golf without mulligans . . . a Sam Donaldson prediction . . . sitting on a dais with Don Imus . . . Hillary throwing things at him . . . the way Monica's father looked at him . . . watching Nixon on TV with his arms held high . . . being breathed on by Yeltsin . . .

The way Monica's mother smiled at him . . . Hillary yelling, "You stupid fuck" . . . Bob Dole's jokes . . . shaking hands with Nixon . . . watching Al Gore dance . . . watching Roger sing . . . Hillary yelling, "You dumb shit" . . . Harold Ickes bursting into the Oval Office . . . Hillary yelling, "You fucking bastard" . . . Monica going "Da-da-da-da-da" . . . Hillary saying, "Get that whore away from me" at the Little Rock airport . . . the way Hillary's mother looked at him . . . a Helen Thomas birthday party . . . making a speech at the Vietnam Memorial . . . hearing Monica making those Yoko Ono noises . . .

Hillary asking "How's Gennifer?" . . . Joe Klein writing a sequel . . . Monica wearing boots identical to Chelsea's . . . Chelsea's spaniel, Zeke, getting hit by a car . . . Hillary with her legs unshaven . . . that condescending look on Blumenthal's face . . . Hillary moving away from his kiss at the inauguration . . . Vince holding Hillary's butt in public . . . Monica having her period that day . . . the way Betty Currie didn't look at him . . .

Reading William Safire . . . watching Al Gore campaign . . . dinner with George and Mari Will . . . talking to Monica about Hillary . . . watching Tipper from the rear . . . the broiled chicken breasts Hillary wanted him to eat . . . Hillary saying, "Get your dick down! You can't fuck her here" . . . trying to find poor Web Hubbell some work . . . meeting William Safire . . . sitting on Nancy Hernreich's couch in a meeting . . . dinner with Hillary's brothers . . . reading about Chelsea in the tabloids . . . seeing Hillary naked.

[4]

America Gags,
Hollywood Swallows

"Hey, there's a Barbara Walters interview with Barbra Streisand and James Brolin tonight," Linda Tripp said.
"Oy," Monica said. "I hate her! She's so annoying!"
"She gets prettier as she gets older."
"Yeah. What do you think that's from?" Monica said. "Plastic surgery. She's probably had everything done but her nose."

The only place where I'd ever seen a cigar inserted in related fashion was in grandly decadent movie producer Robert Evans's mink-rugged bedroom. And even in Bob's inner chamber of horrifying pleasure, it wasn't in real life; it was in a photograph up on the wall: a voluptuous young woman, one of Bob's collectible queen bees, stark naked, on her hands and knees, an English bowler on her head and a lighted cigar sticking out of her magnificent upraised behind. I had no idea whether Evans, or the photographer, Helmut Newton, finished smoking the cigar after the picture was taken, or if the young woman finished smoking it in her own special way.

I did know that as far as the Clinton-inserted cigar was concerned—now the most famous cigar in world history, more famous than JFK's, more famous than all of Winston's—I'd heard no one raise the basic policy-wonk questions: Was it a Cuban cigar and therefore an Oval Office violation of the president's own Cuban embargo? Was it good battle judgment for the president to have a cigar in the Oval Office even as the big guns were blazing in America's war on big tobacco? No one wanted to know about the cigar, and the truth was, there were reasons to pretend it didn't exist, reasons that went deeper than parental need to avoid Pay-Per-View, Howard Stern dialogue at the dinner table.

We were the free-speech generation of the sixties, the generation of free love and communal sex, of one-night stands and no guilt, of bedroom experimentation and athletics, of laughing condescendingly at our poor parents, copulating away once a week, doing the old in-out, in-out, in the same boring missionary position. Dad grunted a few times and came too fast; mom lay there staring at the ceiling, doing her duty and thinking about tomorrow's discount on pork chops at the A&P; and foreplay consisted of a few sticky kisses and a dab of the K-Y jelly that was kept in the nightstand (mom applied it).

All that was true . . . many years ago. But now we were moms and dads ourselves and it scared the freaking bejesus out of us that our kids would act the same wild and crazy way we had acted in bed. We were shaping a better America, and our definition didn't include the things we had done in our youth: Wesson oil parties and body painting and stunt sex and drugs. We had gotten off in a thousand kinky ways, rubbing our privates red-raw, and we didn't want our kids acting like that in a better America. We loved our kids and wanted the best for them: We wanted them to be not like us, but like our parents, like grandpa and grandma sitting watching the sunset after fifty years of mostly monogamous marriage, talking about that long-ago, misty senior prom as they sipped their warming his and hers mugs of tea and honey.

We had read Bukowski and Kerouac and Henry Miller when we were our kids' age, but now we wanted them to read Tom Clancy and Tom Brokaw, or if they really wanted to go out there, then maybe Stephen King. Nothing too graphic, nothing too sexual, nothing that would jangle our kids' ganglia and innards so they'd wind up like some of us, on Prozac and hostage to shrinks.

We had seen movies like *A Clockwork Orange* and *El Topo* and *Mean Streets*, movies that had purposely diddled with our heads, and we sure didn't want our kids' heads diddled with like that. Some of our generation, who became our most important movie critics, like Janet Maslin of the *New York Times* and Kenneth Turan of the *Los Angeles Times*, crusaded against movies with foul language, movies that were "vulgar" and "dispiriting," campaigning for Jane Austen and Dickens and Shakespeare and Merchant and Ivory. (Some filmmakers were angry about what they called "the New Puritanism." "Sometimes I have an overwhelming temptation to grab one of those critics by the throat, head-butt them, and leave them bleeding in the corner," said English director Mike Figgis.) When we weren't creating our own personal, unfilmed porn movies in the sixties, we were watching the Mitchell brothers or Linda Lovelace or Marilyn Chambers or Ralph Bakshi, but we were terrified now about what our kids were watching as they surfed the Net.

And now, suddenly, to have all this hedonistic sixties stuff, the cigar, the blow jobs, the whacking, plopped down on the kitchen table at dinner—by the man we'd voted for, by the man who shared our vision of a better America—we didn't want any part of it. We didn't want to hear it; we didn't want to see it. Period! We were not nostalgic, at least not publicly, about those good old days of excess. Many of us, now Little League coaches and soccer moms, were downright ashamed. How could we possibly have acted like such little pigs and little sluts? Well, our kids—Dylan and Caitlin and Sky and Montana—weren't going to act that way. We'd make good and damn sure of that, even if it meant blocking out what our president was very publicly teaching our kids.

Perhaps the masturbation part wasn't that bad, if you had pubescents. We weren't like mom and dad, who told us that if we did it, hair would grow on our palms and we'd go blind. We told our kids that masturbation was just fine, dear, that everybody did it, even mom and dad. Now we could expand and strengthen the argument. Everybody did it, dear, even the president. See? He didn't have any hair on his palms. So there was something nearly positive there, something almost role model–like in what Bill Clinton did. His habit might ease our kids' guilts. Though, hopefully, none of our kids would ask, "Am I still going to be doing it, Mom, when I'm as old as the president?" Or "How old are you, Dad? Do you still do it?"

Another reason why America didn't want to deal with these black billows of toxic smoke from this historic cigar was because—of all the bizarre, cockamamy things you could ever imagine—Gloria Steinem and Jerry Falwell had climbed into bed together! The oddest mating, certainly, since Mick and David Bowie, since Portnoy and his piece of liver, since Marilyn Manson removed his rib to mate with himself. Gloria, always the hotchacha of the women's movement, classy and iconlike, and the Reverend Jerry Falwell, with his triple spare tires, his oleaginous smile, and his lechery for our Lord and Savior. But they were joined together on one issue: what they viewed as porn. As far as Steinem was concerned, it demeaned women. As far as Falwell was concerned, it was a sin and we'd burn in hell.

The Left and the Right had intertwined and the combined force of their moral fervor, their propagandists, and their media fellow travelers had already had a palpable, chilling effect on the motion picture and television industries. Those writers and directors who liked pushing the sexual envelope and who enjoyed being in battle with the Reverend Jerry Falwell and the Reverend Donald Wildmon and the army of Reverend Others found themselves coldcocked, not by the Right, but by the Left, by liberal editorialists of their own generation, who called them not free-speech warriors pitted against the armies of narrowness and night, but sleaze meisters and pornographers exploiting women for financial gain. In other words, sinners just like the Reverend Jerry Falwell said, but not sinners who would go to hell and burn.

Sinners whose movies would be picketed by angry women at the box office. The Reverend Donald Wildmon didn't even have to go out there with his placards. He could rest up at home, preparing next Sunday's fire-and-brimstone serving, while all those liberal, posthippie women did his job for him.

The climate for graphic and even not-so-graphic sex was so frosty—at the exact moment America caught its first suspicious sniffs of the Oval Office cigar—that Hollywood actors who'd become stars by playing sexpot parts—Sharon Stone in *Basic Instinct*, Julia Roberts in *Mystic Pizza*, Annette Bening in *The Grifters*—were now putting "no nudity" clauses in their contracts, cutting their hair, dressing like Russian apparatchiks, and making themselves look as sexually unappetizing as they possibly could on-screen, thereby flooding the market with an awful lot of box-office clinkers. Stone even took it a step further: She told the world she'd found Jesus at Cecil Williams's Glide Memorial Church in San Francisco. But it was possible Stone had good reason to take it further and find Jesus. Of the three, only Stone had showed the world her pubic hair.

Refusing to smell the smoke from Bill Clinton's cigar was symptomatic of something else, too. There seemed to be a tendency among many in our generation to want to sanitize, cosmeticize, and pasteurize life, to put a rosy spin on daily existence, to pretend some things didn't exist or happen. The attitude smacked of the kind of narrowness we were victims of in the sixties, when we were accused of un-Americanism. AMERICA, the bumper stickers said back then, LOVE IT OR LEAVE IT.

I thought I heard echoes of that from the former victims, who were now crucifying Kenneth W. Starr for his report, who were now objecting to vulgar language and sex and violence on the big and little screens. Never mind that tens of millions of Americans often used vulgar language or that violence was rampant or that folks were having sex—some people in our generation didn't want to hear about that any more than they wanted to hear Public Enemy or Snoop Doggy Dogg. They wanted to hear Yanni or music made by mating whales or the *Beatles Anthology*. They wanted to see movies that were touchy-feely and gauze-lit. They wanted to see Spielberg, not Spike Lee, and they absolutely did not want to hear that Hillary used the word *fuck* more times in one paragraph during meetings with the White House policy wonks than any president, including LBJ (who should have had the word, his favorite, on his tombstone).

And they absolutely *did not, did not, did not* want to hear about the cigar. Smoking was too sore a subject anyway—the only thing some of us liked about Kevin Costner's woefully awful *Waterworld* was that the scuzzball, low-life bad guys were called "the Smokers." Releasing the *Starr Report* in this climate was like reading parts of Henry Miller, Terry Southern, Iceberg Slim, and Luther Campbell to the residents of a nunnery.

While the rest of America didn't want to sniff the cigar, Hollywood, it seemed, wanted to sniff it, lick it, inhale it, ingest it, digest it, and take a stool sample. This was the biggest Hollywood news (although no one said anything publicly, of course, of course, of course) since Ovitz left CAA . . . since they almost killed Lew Wasserman at Cedars . . . since Hugh Grant and Eddie Murphy got in trouble with *their* blow jobs.

While it was the greatest dish, Hollywood wasn't *shocked* by any of it. Hollywood, as someone said, had always been a big beautiful blonde with soiled underwear. I had heard most of the stories during a quarter century of screenwriting, told with the kind of booster's pride you might find at a place like the City Club in Kansas City. But these stories weren't Kansas City stuff; they were the windswept legendary grime that had encrusted in the cracks of the gleaming marble stars along Hollywood Boulevard.

Hollywood was the kind of place that appreciated the honesty of Bugsy Siegel's mistress, Virginia Hill, who said, "Hey, I'm the best damn fuck in town and I've got the diamonds to prove it." Bill Clinton's excesses were *bupkes* compared with those of Marlon Brando, who decorated walls with his old girlfriends' Tampax and collected stool samples from his visitors while living on his private Fijian island . . . Robert Mitchum, who defecated on Harry Cohn's white rug during a contract dispute and bent over and passed gas into the face of a passenger who asked him not to smoke on an airplane . . . Errol Flynn, who unzipped his willard at parties and played the piano with it, who walked over to the house of his next-door neighbor, gossip columnist Hedda Hopper, and masturbated on it.

A blow job in the White House from a Beverly Hills airhead who looked and talked like a Valley Girl—oh, mama, the whole thing was s-o-o-o Hollywood! Hollywood was Blow Job City, an industry historically identified with this particular act. What did Marilyn Monroe tell the press when she signed her first studio contract? She said, "This means I'll never have to suck another cock in this town again."

Way back in the pioneer days, the old guys, Cohn and Goldwyn and Zanuck and Thalberg, the founding fathers—all those cigar smokers—they'd have a nice lunch at the Brown Derby or Musso's or, later, Scandia . . . and maybe they'd take a little steam after . . . and they'd go back to the office and light up a cigar while they got their . . . *manicure.* A nice little after-lunch, after-steam, during-cigar . . . manicure. The manicure girls knew what they were doing. They knew how to do it so it didn't have to take too long. Beautiful young girls from the Valley (the best manicure girls were always from the Valley and always in demand), down there under the desk, so if the secretary or the wife walked in, she didn't even see her.

It was the perfect activity, this manicure—not too much exertion after a rich meal and all that hot steam; the ticker wouldn't stress. It was the perfect position, too, for a man of power, a titan, a founding father to enjoy. Down on her knees, her skirt hiked up, panties pulled down, taking it happily in her mouth, the same kind of well-kept mouth with which their PMSing, high-maintenance wives had driven them nuts for years. There was something satisfying, too, to the titans in the gagging and the swallowing. The highest paid Valley Girls always swallowed. Then they left and the titans finished their cigars and closed some important, boffo deals.

There was even a phrase for the sleepy condition of the willards of these men at this time of day as they underwent their routine daily manicures, not completely focused, distracted, but getting the manicure anyway because it was a perk and a part of the schedule, like getting the Bentley detailed on Monday. The willards of these semierect men were called "Hollywood loaves."

And now here was this Beverly Hills Valley Girl of the nineties, this Lewinsky, a nice Jewish girl with big lips, her mother a little screwed up maybe — *what was that business about the mother pretending to sleep with Pavarotti?* — and the titans of *today* got it, instantly understood even what the rest of America didn't get: Yes, she blew him, but they didn't have sex.

Because a blow job in Hollywood wasn't sex. A blow job was a little break in a busy afternoon . . . the traditional way to aid the digestion after a long lunch . . . better than Mylanta, better than Tums . . . a blow job was almost like a different way of taking a pee, for God sake! . . . A blow job was . . . a *manicure*.

So what was the big deal? Bill Clinton was a good president building a better America, a dream that many of today's titans, sixties kids, shared. Other presidents had had manicures. Bill Clinton was Hollywood's president anyway, in a town with deep liberal Democratic roots.

People here still talked about Mark Rosenberg, the late former head of production at Warner Bros. and one of the heads of the Students for a Democratic Society in the sixties. People here still talked about Gary Hart and how his binding friendship with Warren destroyed him. Gary, the joke was, wanted to be Warren — the greatest Hollywood swordsman since Milton Berle, and Marilyn had once said Uncle Miltie had the biggest willard she'd ever seen — and Warren wanted to be Gary, the serious social thinker.

At least Bill Clinton didn't have any destructive friendships like that, except for the smarmy pollster, Morris, who liked sucking hookers' toes. Bill Clinton's pals in town were Steven Spielberg — sexually, Steven was Saint Steven; Jeffrey Katzenberg — devoted to money and his wife, Marilyn; and David Geffen, who was gay.

Oh, sure, there had been some Hollywood buzzings about Bill Clinton through the years. Bill and Sharon, who had dinner together while some people prattled about Stone engaged with the president in the same kind of yipping, leg-elevated positions we saw her faking with Joe Pesci on-screen. And Bill and Barbra — but Barbra was almost dowdy now, older than Hillary even, no longer what producer Jon Peters once called "the nicest ass in town."

Bill Clinton even had a family connection to Hollywood, although it was awfully low-rent. Barbara Boxer's daughter married one of Hillary's brothers . . . and Boxer's daughter used to work for the producer Rob Fried. The connection got Rob some golf with the president at Burning Tree, but little else.

. . .

While godless and immoral Hollywood had been amusing itself with manicures for nearly a century, the blow job, we felt, was our generation's gift to
American popular culture in the sixties. We didn't call it a "blow job" for
aesthetic reasons (way too uncool). We called it "head."

Head was ours the way the missionary position was our parents'. We'd
seen our moms flush crimson when dad picked the chicken neck out of the
pot and, grinning, held it up . . . and the idea that mom (or Mamie Eisenhower or Pat Nixon or Debbie Reynolds or Doris Day) was going to, you
know . . . not in a million years!

Even in the sixties, most midwestern or southern or rural girls went,
"Ooh! Yuk!" at the slightest suggestion that they lower their pretty heads.
But California girls knew all about it: They had the talent their mothers
would never have. They strengthened their jaw muscles with cucumbers
and bananas and did oral yoga exercises with their lips, mouths, and
tongues. They went to the dentist to file down teeth so they "wouldn't get in
the way." They learned to put condoms on with their mouths. They performed after licking ice or eating jalapeño peppers or chewing a Red Hot.

Head was the perfect sixties sex act. It was, literally, still outlawed in
many states between men and men, as well as between men and women.
You could go to jail for it. It was fast; you didn't even have to take your
clothes off. And the fact that we were certain our parents hadn't done it was
an important consideration at a time when fools like Abbie Hoffman and
Jerry Rubin were telling us to "kill your parents" (while not killing theirs).
Part of its outlaw appeal was that it was a black act more than a white one.
Old blues songs like "Hog Me Baby" and "Down on Me" and "Scratch-
Throat Blues" had celebrated it.

We had adopted black culture fervently and wholeheartedly in the sixties, to the point where if Black Panthers showed up at a party in the Haight
and admired one of our "chicks" or "old ladies," we longhaired white boys
got out of the way and went outside to smoke some dope while she moved
into the bathroom with the Panther. Both we and our chicks felt this was
ideological penance, a personal way to redeem ourselves for slavery and
untold generations of white racism. Some of our old ladies—not all—
objected only when Panthers like Huey Newton, a successful pimp, tried to
turn them out to perform for the dollars our generation pretended to
disdain.

Head also caused some men to open doors they had forced closed all their lives. Stoned enough or drunk enough, they discovered they didn't really care if the form kneeling there in the lava light with lips bared and mouth open was a man or a woman.

The porn industry quickly picked up on what we'd started. Massage parlors opened everywhere suddenly, fluorescent-lighted churches in an America that was overnight becoming the Diocese of Fellatio. The naked priestesses in these grubby temples would never have intercourse, but they could be convinced with a donation to do massage with their lips and mouths. Men all over America ducked into these churches for quickie noontime prayer; the bells they heard going off in their ears had nothing to do with salvation.

By then, our generation had found its own miracle-dispensing sex symbol. Our fathers may have had B.B. and M.M. Our kids would one day have S.S. We had L.L.—Linda Lovelace, the Empress of Head. Her movie was called *Deep Throat* and everyone of our generation—future president Bill Clinton, future Supreme Court justice Clarence Thomas—saw it. It featured Lovelace doing nothing but head, taking it *all in* without gagging, every sixties man's dream. She was somehow able to relax, perhaps paralyze, her throat muscles completely. She claimed that her clitoris was in her throat. Her manager, an ex-marine named Chuck Traynor, explained it: "Once your throat opens, your esophagus gets quite large, like a sword swallower's." We heard that Linda was doing a cross-country media tour where she was demonstrating to critics that what we saw on-screen wasn't movie magic. Head shampoo announced it was considering putting her in a television commercial.

When Richard Nixon was brought down by the source named Deep Throat, we thought it was poetry. Richard Nixon, doing a Linda Lovelace, taking it all in.

Hollywood had warm and fuzzy feelings about Bill Clinton, and there was the conviction that if he loosened up—like JFK when he came to town; producer Irwin Winkler's guest house is where JFK and Angie Dickinson used to tryst—Bill Clinton would fit right in. It was easy to visualize him hanging out in Evans's bedroom with Jack Nicholson, sharing a joint and watching as a magician twirled a girl around and around, C notes coming out of her every orifice. Listening to Evans talk about a girl he'd urinated upon, who got up and broke three of his ribs. Hanging out. Having fun. Just being human in Hollywood. The big house in Bel Air, the beach house at Carbon Beach, the two black Mercedes, the black Ducati, the black Dodge Ram, a daily manicure. You know . . . normal life. Listening to Sharon tell him how Bob Evans once kept one of her friends in a dog collar. Going over to the wall in Evans's bedroom and checking out the Helmut Newton photograph of the girl with the smoking cigar in her . . .

There was even some relatively serious talk that Bill Clinton would move to town after he left office. Didn't he say, "The best part of the White House isn't Camp David or *Air Force One;* it's all the movies people send me"? And he did like these three little guys—Steven and Jeffrey and David—very much, and they seemed to like being in the big guy's presence. He probably would have made a good CEO or CFO or whatever honorific the hard-nosed Geffen would have thrown the ex-president of the United States.

It wasn't even hard to see Bill Clinton at an important script meeting. He knew movies. He told Mel Brooks he watched *Blazing Saddles* every year, not once, but *six times!* He didn't say that publicly, of course; the six times may have raised some eyebrows. Publicly, he said his favorite movies were *High Noon, Casablanca,* and *The Ten Commandments.* (Really.) He claimed to love movies that were about "love, honor, and courage—stuff people care about." And movies "about people who managed to stay human under inhuman conditions." He loved Bogart—"He could get away with everything because he was so authentic"; De Niro—"He's got real range"; Meryl Streep—"one of the two or three greatest actresses ever"; and frequent Clinton contributor Tom Hanks—"tactile, compelling." And he was relatively literate. He liked *Leaves of Grass,* and Walt Whitman was certainly better than average for Hollywood. After all, Michael Eisner's sole point of creative reference seemed to be O. Henry. And if Bill Clinton was able to handle the Indiana Jones–jacketed Newt and glassy-eyed Dick Armey and that rat-catching creep Tom DeLay, he could certainly convince screenwriters to rewrite and directors to reshoot. There would be no shame in being finessed by the man who'd finessed Bibi and Arafat—even though, with full-blown Hollywood egos, few screenwriters saw themselves as the fallen Bibi. And no director would ever tell the truth and admit to acting like Arafat.

Some people at Spago or Crustacean or Le Dome even talked about Hillary coming out with Bill. But Hillary didn't seem the right fit for a

Hollywood wife. A little tummy tuck? A little liposuction? A little lip infla-tion? A little time in a tanning salon? A twice-a-week top-of-the-line facial at Veronica's on the PCH, where both Mel Gibson *and* his wife went? But it was all wrong. . . . *Wrong! Wrong! Wrong!*

People thought about it and realized they just couldn't see Hillary in the new patio dining room of the Bel Air Hotel, talking about whether Wolfgang was still a better caterer than Along Comes Mary, whether Merv would make it much past the millennium with his prostate, whether Mark Can-ton's affair with Luc Besson's secretary would last, whether Michael Eisner was justified saying about Jeff Katzenberg, "I hate that little midget." Every-one realized Hillary was too afire, too revved up, too alive to be doing that. How could you possibly have the patience to work with Wolfgang's wife, Barbara, organizing a charity tent event if you'd already co-run the whole world? How could you worry about the rhesus monkeys running amok in south central Florida, leftovers from a 1940s *Tarzan* movie shot there, if your normal frame of reference was global, perhaps even stratospheric? Besides, every Hollywood wife was 100 percent sure that, once out of office, she would dump him.

Some old-time William Morris agents who hung out in the bar of the Regent Beverly Wilshire, once Hernando Courtwright's glorious Beverly Wilshire Hotel, sucking on their unlit cigars, even started spitballing a whole new career for Bill Clinton, post-term, post-Hillary. They convinced themselves he could act, and the false rumor mill went into hyperactive overdrive for a few days.

Bill Clinton was still a young man, after all, and, with Sly's trainer and Michael Jackson's plastic surgeon, they could see it, these wise old showbiz hoot owls: Bill Clinton and Sharon in *Basic Instinct II*, Bill Clinton and Redford in *Butch and Sundance II*, Bill Clinton and Warren in *Shampoo II*. (He already had Hollywood's hottest hairdresser, Christophe.)

It made some sense. That ten-second eye-contact empathy turned on a camera *directly*, instead of on nearby cameras with human beings around — if Redford was so good as the Candidate, wasn't it possible the lifelong pro-fessional candidate would be as good as Redford? Some sashimi instead of cheeseburgers, Geffen's masseur, a little karate with Ovitz, some of Steven's mom's vegetables, who knew? . . . Jackie Chan's speech coach, sincerity tips from Sydney Pollack, a little Thai from Sharon's Chrome Hearts hash pipe . . . a star *could* be born.

He came out to Hollywood often during his darkest days, vamping fund-raisers, pressing friendly and selected flesh, and playing golf with a group of Hollywood players, one of them now primarily a grass dealer and gofer for movie stars. Bill Clinton, the gofer told me, never asked him for any dope (he knew the gofer had the best in town), but he really enjoyed lighting up a cigar after a few rounds of golf. Bill Clinton told the gofer it was the only place he could smoke a cigar anymore. The Secret Service agents always made sure nobody took any pictures while the cigar—it was a Davidoff, not a Cuban—was in the president's mouth.

Hollywood, the home of manicures, ultimately didn't care about the smoke from the Oval Office cigar, either, and the town's attention was soon diverted to another—this time, locally scandalous—blow job. It took place at a party in the Palisades, at the home of New Age former fur salesman turned agent Arnold Rifkin. The sister of another Morris agent was seen on a balcony giving New Line head of production Mike DeLuca a blow job. The balcony performance made the front page of the business section of the *Los Angeles Times*. "I have become what I beheld," DeLuca told friends. The newspaper account missed the party's other sensational event: Farrah Fawcett, finding the bathrooms full, went outside and pooped the front lawn while the partygoers watched from inside.

The two events, the balcony performance and Farrah's pooping, obliterated all talk in Hollywood of any of Bill Clinton's actions and habits for some time. America may have been in purposeful denial about what took place in the Oval Office, but Hollywood was in a gleeful dither about Arnold Rifkin's balcony and front lawn.

Bill Clinton was old news now. All this sound and fury . . . about another manicure done by a wanna-be Valley Girl . . . all this Sturm und Drang . . . all this kvetching . . . *Big deal!* It wasn't Farrah.

[5]

Hillary Lives, Tammy Wynette Dies

"I don't think he can be magnanimous," Linda Tripp said. "It's not him. He admitted as much to you."
"You mean monogamous?" Monica said.

One of the many cheesy ironies in the whole lurid, sleazy melodrama was that as the president transmogrified into the Big Creep, Hillary was reborn as Saint Hillary. Because while, if you were a man, you couldn't run on holes, you could, if you were a married woman, go a long way on scorned holes.

The woman who told us she was not Tammy Wynette stood by her red-faced, finger-jabbing man, and Americans, both men and women, loved her for it. Women loved her because many of them knew that their own husbands were cheating. Men loved her because she wasn't leaving her husband, thereby justifying what they were telling their own wives, if forced to: Honey, you know how much I love you and the kids. It didn't mean anything, honey. It was just sex.

We were asked to believe that Hillary was shocked and wounded by her husband's dalliance with the thong-snapping, Altoid-sucking Monica. We were asked to believe that Hillary's marriage was shattered by her priapic beast of a husband. We were asked to believe that the First Family needed time for healing. Saint Hillary and her husband appeared in church; he even had a Bible in hand—and Saint Hillary wore dark shades, beneath which, Americans just knew, there were hot, angry, and martyred tears. And most of us wanted to believe it. We wanted to because the alternative was worse.

The alternative was this: The only part of Lewinsky even surprising to Hillary was the cigar. She knew the man she stood by. She knew him when she married him; she asked her dad to go down to Arkansas when Bill was campaigning, to try to make sure he kept his pants zipped. She wasn't stupid. She knew that the Arkansas state troopers drove him to Gennifer's apartment (with its zebra-striped couches). She knew about the girl in the basement of the statehouse. She knew that his jogs detoured into the bushes. But she didn't care anymore. Maybe, in the beginning, when she sent her dad down there. But not anymore. Her husband was an animal. It didn't matter what he did . . . as long as it didn't explode on the front page and on the evening news . . . and embarrass her and Chelsea.

Hillary and Bill Clinton had a cynical deal, whose roots were found in the idealism they'd shared in the sixties. They thought they could make this country, the country they loved, a better place. He'd run for office and she'd be there hand in hand with him. They'd share the power, and as long as they shared it, as long as he listened to her about public affairs, he could have his own private ones. She'd stand by her man . . . and he'd stand tumescent, telling others to "kiss it."

He liked the deal. He had a smart wife with a passion for making this a better America, a savvy political theorist who wasn't afraid to take the gloves off against the forces of right-wing Republicanism, which were trying to undo the many legal and political victories achieved since the sixties. Hillary had real, heartfelt, and thought-out beliefs that weren't dependent on polls. She was a huge asset to have in the room when the subject was the state of the state or the state of the union. She was a real partner to him in a conference room, which is where she belonged, as surely as Gennifer belonged in a bedroom.

She liked the deal. She had a charismatic husband with a gift for eye contact and one-on-one, ten-second empathy. He was a relentless campaigner. He shook hands with fire hydrants and waved at telephone poles. He could work a room better than anyone she'd ever seen, a Method actor playing out a redemptive, lift-your-spirits drama on an endless rubber-chicken circuit.

No wonder all those bimbos got dewy-eyed just shaking his hand. There was something sexual about the way he touched people and seduced them into pulling the ballot lever. She knew she didn't have his ease — his *lubric-*

ity—she had been stiff, wallflowerlike, and dry all of her life. He was like a sleek and dazzlingly waxed Cadillac. Well, fine. Then she'd drive it. Drive that Cadillac all the way to the White House and make sure it didn't turn into an Edsel. She believed in public service. If the price of doing good, of making this a better America, was letting him be privately serviced by white-trash mechanics in zebra-striped service stations, so be it.

There was one part of the deal that was dicey. He couldn't ever leave her while he was in office. He could *talk* about leaving her (he did with Gennifer and with Monica), but he couldn't *do* it . . . not if he wanted to stay in office. All of his polls said that if he broke up with her, he'd be history. Nor could he allow her to leave him. Dick Morris was adamant that no president could survive White House divorce. So all he could do was talk about it, playing with the notion, teasing the possibility of a life without Hillary in his own mind, and then dismissing it with a self-deprecating joke. He'd have to pee twenty times a day at a certain age, he told Monica. True, but he also knew—hot damn!—that he'd still be getting it up.

He also knew he couldn't afford to piss Hillary off . . . *too* much. He needed her for his presidency and he needed her to shape his policies . . . and he knew that *she knew* how much he was screwing around. This was a woman who read everything, who had her own network of mostly women friends, street-smart and cynically idealistic political operatives who heard everything and told her everything. Yeah, she threw things sometimes and called him names, but she wasn't going anywhere. She was running the country with him. She was "Mrs. President Mary Todd Clinton." They were partners to better America. She couldn't get a gig like that anywhere else, with anybody else. There was no other gig like that in the whole world. So he was safe. He could piss her off . . . just not too much.

Then it almost hit the fan in 1992, in New Hampshire. Gennifer, the slut! She had tapes! He lied and denied and somehow got away with it. Partly thanks to Gennifer herself making money off of all this with the tabloids. (Thank God for women who needed money; their credibility was destroyed by the dollars men paid them.) Partly, he got away with it because 60 *Minutes* sent simpatico and mild-mannered Steve Kroft instead of that junkyard watchdog Mike Wallace. But mostly he got away with it because of Hillary. She sat there holding his hand. She put a dollop of hominy and a teaspoon of grits into her midwestern voice. She stood by her man. He lied with his words, but it was Hillary's lie—with her eyes, her body language, her hands—that got him off.

. . .

There were moments when Monica first hit Drudge's Web site that he thought it was the ball game. The details terrified him. Would the details get out? The death of his presidency—historical ignominy—lay in the details.

If this could be spun into an "affair" with a young woman—well, maybe there was some light at the end of the tunnel. But the details he remembered all too clearly and fearfully—the cigar, all the jacking off—would Monica give them the details? Would the details be in that smug, self-righteous, pompous dork's report? If the details wound up on the front page, how would Hillary handle it? Would his own daughter have to know that he put a cigar in there and then put it into his mouth and said, "Tastes good"? He had no choice but to lie. The details were Freddy Krueger hiding in the closet.

So Monica would have to be turned into trailer trash, too, just like Paula and Gennifer. She was a stalker. She was neurotic; she was sick; she needed psychiatric help; she couldn't be believed! Those twisted, perverse details that she fabricated out of whole cloth showed how sick she was! A cigar indeed! Right out of Krafft-Ebing! Beverly Hills trailer trash!

So he denied it to everyone—to Hillary, to Chelsea, to us—forcefully, emotionally, looking us in the eye, an outraged, innocent man, falsely accused. We said to ourselves, Maybe he really is innocent. Look how angry he is. Sure, politicians lie, but with this kind of vehemence? This kind of passion? This baldly? Right in our faces? Nixon's lame "I am not a crook" defense sounded like a lie when he said it—flat, dispassionate, masked words. But Clinton's words were fighting words: a guy sitting in a bar, ready to come across the table at you if you said it again.

Hillary was equally convincing. "A vast right-wing conspiracy." Sure! Groovy! Right on! Power to the people! We knew they were out there—the conspiracy nutbags and abortion clinic bombers and militiamen and the flag-bedraped bigots and racists and homophobes. It made sense they wanted to get Bill Clinton, who was one of us. They wanted to get him *because* he was one of us. Because he dodged the draft and loved blacks and talked about gay people being in the army. They wanted to get him because they were still pissed off about the shit storm we'd unleashed in the streets thirty years ago. They were still pissed off that we'd ended that stupid and bloody and senseless war in Vietnam they had so much fun with.

When the *Starr Report* came out, Bill Clinton's worst nightmare came true, and then went away . . . like he'd had a nightmare about having a nightmare. The details were there all right. The cigar, the tongue, the Altoids, the onanism into the sink, and onto Nancy Hernreich's couch. But they were buried in footnotes and addenda.

The mistake Starr made politically wasn't that his report was too salacious. The mistake he made politically was that he was *afraid* of making it too salacious. So he buried the details, the Freddy Krueger details Bill Clinton was most afraid of, in small print in thousands of pages. He never brought all those poisonous little pellets of sleaze together in the body of his report. He never asked if the man in the Oval Office needed to be removed to get some hasty therapy.

Even though the details were out, the sordid nature of the details themselves came to Bill Clinton's defense. They were the blow jobs that rocked the world—bad enough for parents sitting at the dinner table to ask, "What did you do in school today?" only to hear, "Mom, what's oral sex?" in reply. But a cigar? The president of the United States sitting there playing with himself? On the front page? On the evening news? Are you kidding me?

And it didn't happen, either. It was as though the squalid nature of Bill Clinton's own actions was getting him off the hook. It was much safer and sanitized for the media to spin it as an affair, to cosmeticize, almost romanticize it, to put a Hollywood gloss on it, instead of showing the harsh, shadowy black-and-white reality: a middle-aged man using a young woman as a piece of meat.

Hillary, we were told straight-faced by her aides, didn't even read the *Starr Report*. Right. Her partner, that sleek Cadillac that she drove to the White House, was in danger of being booted and towed, and we were asked to believe that she didn't even bother to read the citation. She was allegedly off wonking over policy, making Post-its for the millennium.

No recent First Lady had been humiliated this way. Pat Nixon had been humiliated and had turned to the bottle, but *his* humiliation never reflected directly on her. Lady Bird Johnson knew that LBJ was using Bobby Baker's whoors, but she didn't have to read about it in the papers. No one knew that JFK was bringing three hookers at a time into his hotel suites. And if George Bush had a special friend who'd been his secretary for a long time, well . . . but none of them had used the Oval Office itself, the tabernacle of America's government, as a four-dollar-an-hour motel room. None of them had been caught spilling themselves on the White House sinks and couches. Some of them had smoked cigars, but . . .

I wondered if Hillary feared in those darkest days that her husband would wind up like Spiro Agnew, bribed with a bagful of frozen steaks, living reclusively on international flights and in the desert until the day he died. Or as a new partner at Dreamworks, keeping a twinkly eye on that new development girl with the nipple ring.

But she stood by him, wearing her grieving woman's shades, playing out the whole touchy-feely opéra bouffe of healing and forgiveness, pretending that Lewinsky was a mortar to her heart, that she really hadn't known. Hillary was a smart woman playing dumb to keep herself looking like the victim she had never been, knowing that her Saint Hillary incarnation was playing just fine in Peoria and upstate New York.

She even got Chelsea, the daughter she loved, to play a crucial public part in this extraordinary family soap opera. When she and Bill went vacationing in Martha's Vineyard, when we were all microscopically watching their every little twitch (Was Hillary holding his hand? How close was she standing to him?), she somehow got Chelsea to go up and down the reception line that was waiting for them. There was Chelsea, truly the innocent victim, shaking hands with the folks, pressing the flesh near her dad, smiling like an old pol, a true Clinton. The message we were meant to receive was clear. If Chelsea forgave him for his inner squalor and his lies, shouldn't we? It was the *60 Minutes* Gennifer Flowers ploy, shamelessly reenacted all over again. Hillary had gotten her husband off the first time. Now she'd pimped her daughter to perform the same act.

During the year of Saint Hillary's incarnation, Tammy Wynette died. Her daughters promptly accused her husband of killing the woman who had sung "Stand By Your Man" and made it a household phrase. Was there grisly, dark meaning here? Was that the ultimate fate of women who stood by their men? Would it happen to Hillary, too, someday in a figurative, political sense?

But then police officials cleared Tammy Wynette's husband of any involvement in her death. He, it seemed, had stood by his woman, too. It gave false hope to those who thought Bill Clinton would stand by his.

[6]

Hillary, Barry, and Nixon

"Do you know what I have?" Monica said to Linda Tripp. "I hope I didn't throw it away. I have a picture of me from his birthday party but he's like bent over—just his butt—and it's me looking at his butt."

illary's first political romance, back in her prom-flower sweet-sixteen years, was with the right-wing conservative Barry Goldwater. He was the perfect bridge to her New Left and movement politics of the sixties, even though the cowpoke Arizona senator voted against the Civil Rights Act and would have bombed North Vietnam into a moonscape. I understood Hillary's crush. In 1964, at Ohio University, I wore a Goldwater pin and was a member, like Hillary, of the Young Conservatives. Two years later, I was out in the streets breaking windows at an ROTC office, reading Marcuse and Fanon, and smoking dope.

Hillary and I had a crush on Barry Goldwater not because we shared his sometimes wacko political ideas, but because he was finally what we'd been dreaming about for our America. A politician who was honest. A politician who dared to reveal his humanity in public. A politician who didn't talk magnolias like Lyndon Johnson, or out of all of his orifices like the loathsome Nixon, or put us to sleep with mush-mouthed by golly–isms like Ukulele Ike. I interviewed and covered Goldwater as a young student reporter during his doomed 1964 campaign for the presidency and remembered the moment in Cleveland's Public Hall that defined him for me. Here were thousands of true-believing, wild-eyed zealots chanting first "Viva!" and "Ole!" and then "We want Barry! We want Barry! We want Barry!" and the candidate stood there watching them as if they were badly behaved orangutans at the zoo . . . and he finally put his arms up and growled, "Well, if you'd just shut up, you'd have Barry!" Talk about taking the wind out of sails; the orangutans gaped at him as if they'd been struck by a tranquilizer bullet, and Barry proceeded to laugh at them for twenty seconds in his deep, phlegmy baritone.

If you want to define politics within a rock and roll context, Goldwater, who would inspire Newt Gingrich and Trent Lott and Dick Armey and Tom DeLay to consider public service, was Bill Haley without the curlicue and the belly fat, a cowpoke in suits and horn-rimmed glasses. Some of his fellow senators called him "Senator Branchwater," and before he began his campaign, he told a reporter, "You know, I don't really have a first-class brain." When he was nominated, he said, "Christ, we ought to be writing a speech telling them to go to hell and turn it down and let somebody else run." A thousand psychologists signed a petition saying he'd be "psychologically unfit for office." He appeared on his campaign plane sometimes wearing a white sombrero with a yellow-and-white-striped Mexican blanket slung over his shoulder.

His enemies, solid LBJ Great Society liberals, many of them formerly JFK aides, feigned horror and shock at some of the cowboy's antics. How could he have waded into a crowd and snarled, "Get that damn baby away from me!" when some mother lifted the thousandth baby of the day to be kissed? How could he have put a sign on his campaign plane that said BETTER BRINKSMANSHIP THAN CHICKENSHIP? They dug up what they considered damning actions in his personal life, actions that I loved, like taking a minicamera to a party and trying to catch his friends in compromising positions without their mates; putting a microphone and a loudspeaker into the bathroom of his house and booming, "Hi there, honey!" as women guests did their business; floating for hours at the bottom of his pool, a weight bag across his stomach, a snorkel sticking out of the water because, he said, "I get damn tired of answering the damn phone." There was also the matter of his behavior as a city councilman in Phoenix. He kept a toy set of windup teeth near him and when someone rambled on too long, Barry would set the teeth clattering (the perfect Christmas gift for future president Bill Clinton).

I was depressed when Barry Goldwater was decimated in the election, my mood brightened only by the comments made by his vice presidential running mate, the obscure and abysmally undistinguished New York congressman William Miller: "What we have said was apparently little noted by the electorate, and certainly will not be long remembered. But it is for us the living, and not the dead drunk, to here resolve: That this government, of the birds, by the birds, and for the birds, shall not continue on this earth." Barry's response to Miller was typically right on point: "No campaign crew in history drank more booze, lost more laundry, or bet more money on card games than his."

Yet, ultimately, through the years, I did remember, and so did many others, two things about landslide loser Barry Goldwater . . . even as I got involved in the movement politics of the sixties and seventies. He was right about Vietnam when in his nomination acceptance speech he said, "Yesterday it was Korea; tonight it's Vietnam. Make no bones of this. Don't try to sweep this under the rug. We are at war in Vietnam. And yet the President . . . refuses to say . . . whether or not the objective over there is victory. And his secretary of defense continues to misinform and mislead the American people." (It wasn't until 1997 that Robert McNamara would finally admit misleading and deceiving us. And he did it in a book—for which he was paid a lot of money.)

Barry was also right about Walter Jenkins, whose situation presented a relevant and somewhat analogous issue to ponder in the year of Bill Clinton's impeachment travail. In 1964, White House aide Walter Jenkins was Lyndon Johnson's closest adviser, his personal assistant. Married and the father of six children, Jenkins was arrested at the YMCA, a block from the White House, for committing a homosexual act—a month before the election. Reporters learned of the arrest and also of a previous arrest for the same act, in which the charge read "Pervert." Walter Jenkins was a scandalous front-page story in the most fevered days of a presidential election. Against the counsel of his advisers, Barry Goldwater issued orders that Walter Jenkins's arrest not be used in the campaign. (Johnson, on the other hand, ordered a poll before he issued "a statement of sympathy" for his old friend.)

As much as Hillary and I loved Barry Goldwater, we loathed Richard Nixon, his successor as the Republican standard-bearer, with an equal fervor. "Richard Nixon," Barry Goldwater had said, "is the most dishonest man I've ever met." Harry Truman agreed. "Richard Nixon," he said, "is a no-good lying bastard. He can lie out of both sides of his mouth at the same time, and if he ever caught himself telling the truth, he'd lie just to keep his hand in." Yes, that was exactly right, and it was the basic reason my generation had such a visceral and deep distrust of him. Nixon literally was, as Barry had said, "a four-square liar."

We had watched Tricky Dick as we grew up, a shadowy presence in a sharkskin suit on our evening news. His body language was stiff and stilted, like Ed Sullivan's or like Charlie Chaplin burlesquing Hitler in *The Great Dictator.* His Pinocchio nose seemed longer to us every day, the greasy mangrove of Brylcreem atop his head a nest of crawly things. His muscles moved independently of one another: the arms sweeping up as though jerked by puppet strings, stiffly held V-for-victory fingers thrust at us the way Nelson Rockefeller used to thrust his middle finger at reporters. His smile was the frozen, gleeful smile of the KGB or Gestapo torturer, about to turn up the current. His eyes were the black holes in a mossy Transylvanian graveyard where bats with furry wings cavorted among gorgons, Gothic crosses, and tombstones. His mouth was another, larger black hole, a mass grave tended by a serpentine tongue that spewed lies and (we later discovered) scabrous four-letter racist, sexist, homophobic, and anti-Semitic words.

That's how I felt and that's how my generation felt. We loathed the man. We had seen him on television using his wife's "Republican cloth coat" to get himself off a hook we were certain he deserved to hang on. This was a man who was even willing to use his dog, Checkers, to elicit our sympathy. (Visually, Bill Clinton would use Buddy the same way.) This was a man willing to persecute Alger Hiss to further his own career. We thought him an empty, ambitious careerist. He had no heart. He was the personification of the word *phony* to a generation that had grown up believing itself armed with Holden Caulfield's shit detector.

When JFK beat him, we were . . . in rapture. We were rid of him, free finally of what seemed to have been a childhood disease, a dark-shadowed presence who was a daily depression. And JFK was *ours,* even though we weren't of voting age yet, a president with a sense of humor and a real, unstaged laugh, who talked about compassion and the rights of our fellowman, of loving one another, regardless of skin color. As Hubert Humphrey said, JFK "brought form to our amorphous yearnings."

JFK offered us hope for an America without dark shadows and night creatures prowling the mossy graveyards. *The* Night Creature, meanwhile, was beaten in California even for governor, a loser in his own state. He said, "You won't have Nixon to kick around anymore." Yes, *rapture!* Nixon was in that hole in the graveyard himself now, politically dead and buried, and we busied ourselves trying to help build the golden place called Camelot.

And then, in one furious apocalyptic moment . . . *six gray horses, followed by the traditional riderless black horse.* The bats and demons and gorgons from the graveyard were back, and they took JFK from us. After a few years—LBJ and that surreal mink-trimmed ten-gallon Stetson—Nixon crawled out of his political grave. Two other bodies later (Martin and

Bobby), Richard Nixon, the Night Creature, was president of the United States. (He beat Humphrey in 1968 with one of the earliest uses of negative television advertising: a shot of Hubert laughing over images of cities burning, protesters being beaten, and stacks of dead GIs in Vietnam.) We were of voting age by then. We were old enough to hurl bricks that broke windows. We were cynical enough to answer his four-letter expletives with our own shrill ones.

Everything he stood for was symbolized to us by the goofy uniforms he designed for the White House police. Double-breasted tunics trimmed with gold braid and gold buttons, worn with helmets that looked like they belonged in the Ukrainian army. Some of us even stopped watching "Laugh-In" when they allowed him on the show. "Sock it to me!" he said, and the sound of exploding TV sets was figuratively heard across the land. Considering the rage we felt toward him, Nixon was lucky some acid-burned, mind-blown one of us didn't frag him—DICK NIXON BEFORE HE DICKS YOU our signs said. Dick Tuck, our merry political prankster, even hired two obviously pregnant women to march outside the Republican National Convention with a sign that said NIXON'S THE ONE!

We chortled knowingly when novelist Robert Coover revealed the real Nixon to us in *The Public Burning*. Coover's Richard Nixon said, "I'm a private man and always have been. Formal. When I have sex I like to do it between the sheets in a dark room. When I take a shit I lock the door. My chest is hairy but I don't show it off. I don't even like to *eat* in public. . . ." And we absolutely rejoiced when Coover revealed the scar that made Nixon tick: a brutal anal rape committed by Uncle Sam himself. Nixon: " 'No!' I cried. 'Stop!' but too late, he was already lodged deep in my rectum and ramming it in deeper—oh Christ! It felt like he was trying to shove the whole goddamn Washington Monument up my ass! . . . I lay there on the spare-room floor, gurgling, sweating, half-senseless, bruised and swollen and stuffed like sausage, thinking: 'Well, I've been through the fire. . . . I recalled Hoover's glazed stare, Roosevelt's anguished tics, Ike's silly smile. I should have guessed.' "

No dummy, Nixon knew how fervently we loathed him. He was our enemy and we were his. He described us as "bums" and "derelicts."

We defined ourselves to be everything that Richard Nixon wasn't. We *were* sex, drugs, and rock and roll. We believed in the buttons that adorned our scrawny bodies: TUNE IN, TURN ON, DROP OUT; DON'T TRUST ANYONE OVER THIRTY; BURN POT, NOT PEOPLE; MAKE LOVE, NOT WAR; STAMP OUT PAY TOILETS; IF IT MOVES, FONDLE IT.

We traded in our neckties for beads and ankhs. Peace symbols dangled around our necks. We got rid of our blue button-down shirts and wore embroidered denim or denim jackets with an upside-down American flag on our backs. We wore fringed Wild Bill Hickok coats and navy-surplus pea coats. (Bill Clinton had a long one when he came back from Oxford.) Those of us who worked in offices where beards and mustaches were banned bought fake ones for the weekend. We wore no underwear, and the funkier our bell-bottoms looked, the hipper they were, especially if there was a copy of Chairman Mao's *Little Red Book* in the back pocket. We never read the book—it was in sync with yelling, "Ho Ho Ho Chi Minh, the NLF is gonna win"—but we kept it in our pockets the way we kept a rubber in our wallets. We were too zonked to read much of anything, although the more scholarly were memorizing passages from Tolkien and *Siddhartha* and Kahlil Gibran.

We swore by our genitals the way Nixon swore by his "old Quaker mother." We were our own vast Bay of Pigs—roiled up and flooding the Berlin walls of Puritan resistance. The Stones' *Sticky Fingers* cover featured a real zipper with a bulge to the left of it. John and Yoko were naked on the cover of *Two Virgins.* Yoko made a movie called *Bottoms,* starring 365 naked ones. Andy Warhol painted with his willard, as did Tom of Finland, who said, "If my cock did not stand up when I was working on a drawing, I could not make the drawing work." The Plaster Casters turned willards into art objects. One member of the troupe would get a famous rock willard interested; then another caster would quickly dunk the interested willard into a malt shaker of caulk. The plaster willards (Hendrix's reputed to be the largest) were exhibited as holy relics at underground art shows.

We wore jeans so tight, they cut the circulation off, and we stuffed Kleenex or Kotex or a beanbag *down there.* Eldridge Cleaver, former minister of information for the Black Panthers, commercialized that idea by manufacturing "Cleavers"—pants with codpieces. (The Panthers, in love with guns, were always willard-focused.) We celebrated the Age of Aquarius by attending be-ins where, within minutes or hours, we usually *were* in, though we often didn't know each other's names. We put our sexual show on the road in comfy Volkswagen campers, which freed us from backseat immobility and leg cramps. We discovered water beds and Slip'N Slide, a twenty-five-foot plastic sheet that we'd wet down and use for intertwined skinny-dipping on summer nights in the backyard. We found more intimate uses for our new electric toothbrushes. We yelled "No!" in chorus when, on-screen, Dustin Hoffman said to Mrs. Robinson, "Do you think we could say a few words to each other first this time?" The Noxzema commercial was our ad—"Take it off! Take it all off!"—the way "Lay Lady Lay" was our song. We made Burt Reynolds a star after he showed a little pubic hair in *Cosmopolitan*.

The emblematic sixties moment may not have been Woodstock or the Summer of Love, but a scene at a Village club in New York. Hendrix was up onstage, playing his guitar. Morrison and his date, Janis, were in the audience. Jimi was stoned and Morrison and Janis were stoned and drunk. Morrison got up, went to the front of the stage, unzipped Jimi, and put his willard into his mouth. Jimi kept playing. Joplin ran to the stage, tackled Morrison, and the two of them swung at each other. Jimi zipped himself up and kept playing.

When we weren't flaunting our genitals, we were getting high. Marijuana was as important to us as catsup and cottage cheese were to Nixon. We fired up our doobies with Smile lighters. When we ran out of grass, we smoked dried banana-skin scrapings, oregano, corn husk, and pine needles. Marijuana scented America's air. Even some of the older folks got into the zeitgeist of it. The socialites Alfred and Betsy Bloomingdale hosted a party—their guests: the Jack Bennys, the George Burnses, and the governor of California, Ronald Reagan and his wife, Nancy. According to his former executive assistant, Alfred, always a live wire, lit up a joint and passed it around. The governor and Nancy and Jack and George all took a couple of hits, inhaled, and then said, not surprisingly, that they didn't feel a thing. (The same Ronald Reagan who at the same time was ordering his National Guardsmen to use the same skin-stinging powder against us in the streets that was being used against the Vietcong in the jungle.) It seemed like everybody was getting high somehow: Even the astronauts smuggled mini-bottles of brandy onto *Apollo*.

Sex, drugs, and rock and roll defined our politics, as well. John Lennon's words were a manifesto: "Christianity will go. It will vanish and shrink. I needn't argue about that. I'm right and I will be proved right. We're more popular than Jesus now. I don't know which will go first—rock and roll or Christianity." We burned bras, draft cards, and American flags, burning bridges, we naïvely thought, to the values our parents had taught us. We attended teach-ins, wearing our most serious faces and our tightest jeans, looking for someone to share a joint with and in-depth exploration of our bodies and the body count so gratifyingly far away in Vietnam. Moratorium Day was our callow response to Memorial Day and the Fourth of July. One hundred thousand of us, longhaired and unwashed, streaming past the White House, candles in our hands, as Nixon Peeping-Tommed us from behind his tacky gold-flecked White House drapes. In our juvenile, messianic arrogance, we didn't care that while we were having fun protesting, getting high, getting laid, our black and farm boy brothers in Vietnam were writing things on their helmets like WE ARE THE UNWILLING, LED BY THE UNQUALIFIED, DOING THE UNNECESSARY, FOR THE UNGRATEFUL.

We were feverishly proud of being part of a political movement—The Movement—but even our politics were intertwined with sex. "The sexual and the political are one," Bernardine Dohrn, one of the leaders of the Weatherpeople said, and her words came from the horse's mouth. Because while the media vamped Jane Fonda as the sex symbol of our revolution, we knew that was crap. Jane was a movie star, a movement public-relations commando. Our pinup girl, our real babe in bandoliers, was Bernardine, leading her troops in what she called "Wargasms." As another Weatherpeople guerrilla, Mark Rudd, said, "Power doesn't flow out of the barrel of a gun; power flows out of Bernardine's cunt."

She was twenty-six years old, tall, long-legged, tanned, brown-eyed, voluptuous. She was pouty, in-your-face sensuous. All the men I knew in the sixties and early seventies dreamed of "getting it on" with Bernardine. She appeared on protest stages in front of tie-dyed seas wearing a brown minijumpsuit with thigh-high Florentine leather boots; barefoot in a tight miniskirt, her shirt open to her navel; in a purple skirt with a tight orange sweater with buttons that said CUNNILINGUS IS COOL, FELLATIO IS FUN; in hip-hugging jeans and a sheer low-cut top, her hair dyed the color of Ho Chi Minh's flag; in a black motorcycle helmet and tear-gas gloves, playing with a steel pipe the way Mick played with his mike. She staged formal Weatherpeople orgies we were all *dying* to be invited to. She was our clenched-fist, red-hot Fidelista, who took a breast out one day as a man was looking at it and said, "You like this tit? Take it." Bernardine was our own sweet thing, our own pink shot, the sex bomb who called herself "a crazy motherfucker" and said she wanted to "scare the shit out of honky America."

We were a counterculture, an America within Amerika, arrogant, self-righteous, even jingoistic about our values, heroes, and music. "I Can't Get No Satisfaction" was our "Battle Hymn of the Republic"; "Sympathy for the

Devil" our "Star-Spangled Banner"; Woodstock our D day; Altamont our
Pearl Harbor; Dylan our Elvis; Tim Leary our Einstein; Che Guevara our
Patrick Henry.

We did not have "our" Richard Nixon. It was a shared faith among us
that our generation, committed to letting it all hang out, to the truth setting
us free, would never produce a Richard Nixon, a president who would look
us in the eye, jab his finger in our faces, and lie.

Yeah, there were a lot of us—*a whole lot of us*—and the Night Creature knew
we were a lot of trouble and turned his worm-encrusted ghouls loose on
us . . . Ulasciewicz and Segretti and Liddy and Hunt and Haldeman and
Ehrlichman . . . and the cross-dressing, sanctimonious pedophile, J. Edgar
Hoover. The Night Creature gave frenzied, polarizing speeches (written by
Pat Buchanan and William Safire), whetting the living dead's appetite for
blood—*our* blood—shed by police batons and billy clubs and National
Guardsmen, until they finally shot and killed four of us at Kent State. But it
was all starting to come apart by then; Nixon had lived and been resurrected,
thanks to his lies, and he was about to die (once again) as a result of them.

Hillary, God bless her, was in the front lines, working for the House
Impeachment Committee, working endless hours, helping put together the
case that would drive him from office. The Night Creature's own tapes
drove the stake through his heart. Not only did they confirm his role in the
Watergate cover-up but they showed America that the Oval Office had
become the Night Creature's rat's nest—a place of filth and dead fingernails
and foul-smelling wetness. It was Barry Goldwater, in poetic justice, who
pushed the stake the final inch into the Night Creature's black heart by
telling him he'd be impeached if he didn't resign and by saying he was going
to vote for impeachment himself. (By the nineties, Barry was firmly on *our*
side, saying, "Jesse Helms is off his rocker," referring to Ronald Reagan as
"just an actor," and warning, "The Religious Right scares the hell out of
me." In 1994, he was named "Civil Libertarian of the Year" by the Arizona
ACLU for his support of the constitutional rights of gays and lesbians and
his commitment to the reproductive rights of women.)

Driving a stake through the Night Creature's heart was such sweet
revenge! They had taken JFK from us and then Martin and Bobby . . . and
the Night Creature had come out of his darkness and now we'd cast him
back there where he belonged. Thanks to the efforts of Hillary and Barry
and millions of us who'd united to throw this "four-square liar" out of office.

At the moment of his resignation, I had sat in an office at *Rolling Stone*, with the entire staff there, undrugged for once, watching the Night Creature on TV flipping us his final V-for-victory fingers. Across from me sat a young intern who'd bought champagne for everyone. Bobby Shriver was JFK's nephew, and as he watched the set, he had tears streaming down his face. I started to cry, too, as I watched Bobby.

I saw Richard Nixon in 1993, months before he died, in the dining room of the Ritz-Carlton hotel in Laguna Niguel, California. He was dining with friends at a table not far from us and I watched him as he ate.

I had met him once before, as a young reporter covering a campaign stop he was making in the lily white Cleveland suburb of Fairview Park in 1968. He was on remote control that day at a press conference, his eyes dead, until I asked him if he knew that Denny McLain of the Detroit Tigers had just won his thirtieth game. Nixon came briefly alive, asking about the score and the number of McLain's strikeouts, the frozen smile replaced by something faintly human. "I'm a big Denny McLain fan," he said. Neither of us knew that day in 1968 that McLain would wind up in jail for pimping and gambling and that Nixon would escape jail only thanks to Gerry Ford's kamikaze pardon. The day his pardon was announced, I was waiting for Evel Knievel, yet another goon, to rocket across the Snake River in Idaho . . . and when word of the Night Creature's pardon worked its way through the unwashed, longhaired, outlaw crowd, a bit of the old ultraviolence infected the boys: Windows were broken, bonfires lit, teeth smashed out, and women stripped and held high at the edge of the abyss-fronting cliffs so they could watch Knievel fly. Evil was in the air the day Evel crashed.

As I watched Richard Nixon in the dining room of the Ritz-Carlton in 1993, so many years later, he looked feeble, beaten, and old. I was wearing a sport coat and a T-shirt and tight black women's leotards stuck into my cowboy boots. Jeans were outlawed in the dining room and I had no other pants to wear, so my wife had lent me one of her leotards. As Nixon passed us on the way out, I got up and shook his hand and wished him well. Maybe it was my way of making personal peace with the Night Creature as he approached his final and unnegotiable grave. But Nixon just kept staring at my wife's tight black leotards on my burly frame and made the kind of empty pleasantries he's probably still making in hell.

After Nixon left, I reflected that maybe that's why I'd *really* gotten up to shake his hand . . . a final act of protest for his weary eyes: *Yeah! Dig it, Dick! This is what happened to your America. . . . It's a place where men wear cowboy boots and leotards.*

[7]

The President
Shrieks and Shouts

"You know," Linda Tripp said, "I wouldn't mind seeing him have to admit in public that he has a problem."
"My God, I'd die," Monica said.

There was a chancre growing on the presidency, growing daily. Gone was—sure as hell!—any hope for an eternal flame. Gone were the William Jefferson Clinton postage stamp and his beet red mug on future ten-dollar bills. Gone were the USS *Clinton* and the Clinton F-54 bomber and Clinton freeways and boulevards, national airports, promenades and malls. Gone were the William Jefferson Clinton Pavilion in LA and the Clinton Memorial Tower in New York. Gone was the Nobel Peace Prize, although, thanks to Jann Wenner, he probably still had a shot at the Rock and Roll Hall of Fame in Cleveland.

His contributions to America would be overshadowed now by his contributions to the English language: "to Clinton"—to parse and lie skillfully; "to get a Clinton"—to receive fellatio. His finger-pointing television denial would be as famous as the Zapruder film. Hugging Monica in her beret would get as many laughs as the Tonya Harding and Jeff Gillooly honeymoon video.

It was an extraordinarily painful way for a man to step on his own willard. He'd been the Comeback Kid since the day in high school when, forgetting about a science project due that morning, he'd bought a hot dog and a piece of tin and put them out in the sun. Presto! A solar hot dog cooker. But what could the Comeback Kid do now to get out of this one? Could he . . .

Stonewall? Make a Checkers speech? Claim it was executive privilege?

Borrow Ted Kennedy's Chappaquiddick neck brace? Hide behind Betty Currie the way Nixon hid behind Rose Mary Woods? Crawl into a bottle like Joe McCarthy? Get electroshock like Thomas Eagleton? Decompose like Ed Muskie? Blame it on Addison's disease? Boo-hoo like Jimmy Swaggart? Impregnate Hillary? Go down on Patricia Ireland? Dahmer Linda Tripp? Kopechne Paula Jones? Ned Beatty Kenneth W. Starr? Defenestrate Helen Thomas? Horsewhip Maureen Dowd? Deep-six his copy of *Vox*? Move to Paraguay? Move to Malibu? Stop hanging out with Sharon, Barbra, and Eleanor? Put a sweater on and try a fireside chat? Flagellate himself in Times Square? *Cut it off?*

If all that wasn't bad enough, that dumb, miserable Paula Jones, turned out now by the right-wingers covering her legal costs, said she could describe "distinguishing characteristics" about Willard.

He'd be out there raising money to build a better America, gushing charisma, and he'd see people looking at him . . . *funny*. He knew they were thinking about Willard. Was Willard too small, like Hitler's? A pencil? A knockwurst? A thimble? A mushroom? A horseradish? An olive? It wasn't fair! He was giving his constituents words and policies they could rock on and they were looking at his willard! (It was as though his fly had been permanently unzipped by the headlines. Would he, for the rest of his life, be permanently looking down, checking it?) Lyndon Johnson had scrotal skin hanging halfway to his knees and no one knew about *that*! No one was looking at LBJ's willard.

His own lawyer, Bob Bennett, that self-righteous prig Bill's brother, started talking to his Hot Springs buddies, his oldest friends, guys he'd been in high school gyms with, asking them about Willard, saying if Jones really knew something known only to those who'd been healed, blessed, ministered to . . . Bennett almost went into a rest room with him once but chickened out at the last minute. Well, at least Bennett didn't go to Hillary to ask if she faintly remembered anything that was . . .

No, Bennett went to his doctors, former and present, and they swore out affidavits that Willard was just fine, thank you. Bennett told him he had to see the Obi-Wan Kenobi of willards, the urologist who'd studied Reagan's and Bush's privates, and he had to sit there as this "unbiased Republican expert" poked and pulled and squeezed. But even *that* wasn't enough! Jones's lawyers said what if . . . what if . . . whatever Jones saw appeared only when Willard was erect? There was talk he'd have to sit there in front of Obi-Wan Kenobi teasing Willard until he stood up to his full, proud, and hungry height. But at least Bennett, aware of what he called "the ugh factor" here, finally didn't allow that. Bill Clinton remembered Al Gore's words: "A moral compass should always point north," and knew that was a good part of his problem. Willard had always pointed north, north of the North Pole.

It was a sixties problem once again, a problem the men of my generation had struggled with now for thirty years. We were always so . . . into . . . our willards. For many years, before women saw through our self-obsessed, preening nonsense—it was more than thirty years before John Wayne Bobbitt's was sliced off by his wife—we acted like we were saving the world with our willards. But instead of saving the world, we got into a lot of trouble. Women got tired of hearing about how many women the Kielbasa Man— Wilt Chamberlain (twenty thousand)—or Warren Beatty or JFK or Mick had used . . . and they got justifiably pissed off.

Truth was, we just *had* to give our willard room, dangle it out there, and stick it into *something*. Maybe we were suffering from Clara Bow syndrome, the inability to say no in any sexual situation (Clara couldn't say no to the USC football team). Maybe it was erotomania or some form of priapism. It got hard. It made us uncomfortable. It had to be softened . . . by anybody and everybody. Some of us, even those of us with high public profiles, had had a difficult time with our . . . *condition*. Geraldo Rivera's description of himself fit many of us: "a grunting, voracious pig in heat."

I saw Michael Douglas, whom I'd previously met, in the bar of the Westwood Marquis, shit-faced, sitting next to, and all *over*, a sultry, nymphet-like sex bomb. I finally went up to Michael from across the bar and said, "Hey, Michael, man, get a room!" And he laughed and did. A few years later, Michael's wife walked in on him at the Regent Beverly Wilshire, while Michael was in frenzied flagrante delicto with his wife's best friend, and his wife left him. Michael checked himself into an addiction clinic in Arizona and got up in front of the group and said, "I am a sexaholic" and confessed everything—all the way back to admiring Kirk, one of the greatest swordsmen of all time. (One of his fellow addicts taped the confession and sold it to the tabloids.)

I saw Jeff Bridges, the compleat sixties guy, on the *Jagged Edge* set, begging to do the first scene of the movie himself, the scene where a naked woman is tied to the bed and murdered by a ski-masked figure. "Jeff," the director told him. "You're in a ski mask. You don't have to do this scene yourself; your stand-in can do it." But Jeff did it himself, six times, over and over, insisting on doing it "till we get it right."

And I saw the penultimate sixties marriage blow up, the countercultural royal couple in Splitsville, over that damn zipper. Jane Fonda was a ballsy and stunningly beautiful woman, and Tom Hayden was a ballsy, if geeky-looking, man, the former head of Students for a Democratic Society, author of the Port Huron Statement, our generation's call to arms, one of the Chicago Eight, *our* Magnificent Seven. And Hayden, the putz, the pimply-faced shanty Irish putz, with Jane Fonda in his bed, still couldn't keep it zipped. It was like cheating on the holy grail of female sexuality, grabbing for the brass ass when you were already king of the world. But he grabbed anyway, and Jane left him, forced by California's divorce laws to pay tens of millions of dollars to this idiot who'd wronged her.

As we headed toward the millennium, sixties men had been made to feel like the pigs we often were. The truth was that in the battle between the sexes, many of us were war criminals. *Cocksman* became a pejorative word, though a lot of men were still playing the same old self-centered, sexually abusive game. They weren't talking anymore, though, about banging their brains out and moving on to the next piece of tail. They were wiser now, and more one-on-one sensitivity-savvy. They were talking about "failure to communicate" . . . "lack of commitment" . . . "emotional fatigue" . . . before they moved on to the next piece of tail. They kept cutesy stuffed animals in their bedrooms to demonstrate their own nonmacho and cuddly natures . . . and to disarm suspicious, liberated soon-to-be victims.

Bill Clinton had learned that new language, too. Even while he was still using Monica as a sex toy—not her lips anymore, but her voice, in two-hour marathon phone sex—he bought her gifts: a stuffed animal, joke sunglasses, a small box of chocolates. He even let her play with his new puppy, Buddy, now that she wasn't playing directly with him, only indirectly over the phone. He wasn't one of those abusive sixties men anymore. He didn't just tell Monica to get down on her knees. She meant something to him—at least a small box of chocolates. And then, naturally, when he got bored with her, when he started entertaining thoughts of Eleanor Mondale maybe— the daughter of the former vice president was certainly safer and prettier than Monica, whom Vernon Jordan, a man with a keen eye for horse flesh, dismissed as "flaky and chubby"—the breakup with Monica would be in civilized nineties terms—in this case, using the world's oldest June/December dismissal: I'm too old for you, sweetheart, I'll be peeing twenty times a day and you'll still be beautiful. (What could he say—*flaky and chubby?*)

The end of another tragic romance in the nineties, weepy and touchy-feely, as the non-cocksman gives her one last "Christmas kiss" in the cramped porn-cubicle that was the hallway between the Oval Office and his private one. Goodbye, Monica, we had fun, I'll think about you forever, and one night maybe at two fifteen (with Willard) I'll call you, kiddo (wink wink, oink oink).

Everything, Bill Clinton was old enough to know, had a silver lining. Nineteen sixty-eight, for example, was the worst year—Martin and Bobby and Nixon's election, but still . . . it was the year McDonald's put the Big Mac on its menu. *But where was the damn silver lining here?*

What he felt like doing, he told his chief of staff, Leon Panetta, was punching Kenneth W. Starr in the gut. The preacher's son had turned on an evil, roving spotlight and it had gotten stuck right on his willard. If Reagan was Teflon, then Willard was Velcro.

Bill Clinton was over-the-top enraged about what he aptly called the "drip, drip, drip" from all of this. He wanted to take a swing at somebody the way he'd almost swung at Dick Morris after tackling and knocking him down during the governor's race in Arkansas. He found himself smashing the sides of his chairs while talking to aides, shouting, screaming, shrieking (an aide's description). *Goddamn these son of a bitch, right-wing motherfuckers, grouped around the windows of the Texas School Book Depository!*

What about Ronald Reagan? Why didn't anybody talk about *his* damn sexual habits? The father of family values? Reagan told his biographer, Edmund Morris, about all those groupies when he was an actor: "They tore at his clothes, beat on his hotel room door." He admitted to Morris that when he was an actor, he slept with so many women that one morning he woke up and didn't know who was lying next to him. He didn't tell Morris that even as a young man, he could sometimes have used some of Bob Dole's Viagra. Starlet Jacqueline Parks said, "He really couldn't perform sexually." Former girlfriend Doris Lilly said, "Intimately, he was nothing memorable." Ex-wife Jane Wyman put it bluntly: "He was lousy in bed." The problem seemingly was an old one. Army buddies remembered how Reagan liked to tell gross, embarrassing X-rated jokes in front of women, prompting one woman to tell him finally, "What's the problem, Ronnie? Don't you fuck too good?"

There was even a lot of talk about Nancy Reagan. Had she really gotten her movie parts by sleeping with the head of casting at MGM? Was it possible that in her youth the Ice Queen was a Hollywood bimbo? Did she really entertain the dirtiest old man, Frank Sinatra, who liked to eat eggs sunny-side up off of hookers' breasts, in the White House? During three-hour, do-not-disturb "lunches"? Spencer Tracy, who knew her as an actress, didn't think so. "She projected all the passion of a Good Humor ice cream," Tracy said. "Frozen, on a stick, and vanilla."

What about the Reagan *administration?* All those hypocritical, pharisee Republicans seemed to have forgotten their own dirty, juicy sex scandal! Never mind the blow jobs and the cigar and the whacking, this one involved genuinely Republican kinks. Beating women with belts, riding them bareback, and drooling. All done by Alfred Bloomingdale, Reagan's close friend and adviser and heir to the department store fortune. Vicki Morgan was seventeen years old when she first catered to Alfred's needs. Alfred was fifty-seven. "There were two women who were nude," she said, "and I was told to take my clothes off and Alfred was already taking his off. He asked one of the girls to get the equipment, which was Alfred's belt, the ties he wore around his neck and, excuse me, a dildo. He then proceeded to have everyone line up against the wall and beat them with his belt. . . . He'd have these girls crawl on the floor and he would sit on their backs . . . and drool, okay? I mean, he'd drool!" *These hypocritical, pharisee Republicans!* Even Dan Quayle was alleged to have had sex with a lobbyist. His wife, Marilyn, defended him by saying, "Dan would rather play golf than have sex any day."

Jesse Helms, that evil, poisonous troglodyte, was behind it all! The three-judge panel that had appointed Starr was headed by Judge David Sentelle, whose "rabbi" (a word Helms didn't prefer) was Helms. Bill Clinton felt like biting someone's lip off! His mood was even transmitted to the public by his press secretary, Mike McCurry, who, after columnist William Safire called Hillary a "congenital liar," said that if Bill Clinton weren't president, he'd make a comment "to the bridge of Safire's nose" . . . invoking badly needed positive images of good old nonphilandering, all-American Harry Truman, who'd once threatened to punch out a reporter for criticizing the quality of his daughter's piano playing.

Even as Bill Clinton raged and shrieked and smashed his chair arms, there were other new allegations: A White House makeup person didn't like the way she said he "flirted" with her. . . . One of the stews on the campaign plane said he'd folded his arms and wiggled his finger across her nipple while Hillary was only a few feet away, napping.

It seemed he'd continue to have, in his aide's phrase, more "personal exposure" on this issue, and in his frustration and rage, screaming and shrieking, Bill Clinton wished he could be more like one of his aides, Harold Ickes, who had said to the White House counsel, "You better get this fucking straight and listen up! You better keep your fucking nose out of this! And if you don't like it, you can just go fuck yourself!" God, Bill Clinton thought, how he'd love to say that to Kenneth W. Starr! God, the president of the United States thought, how he'd love to make that speech live, prime-time: "Good evening, my fellow Americans. Listen up! Keep your fucking nose out of this! If you don't like it, go fuck yourself!"

It was no fun being around the White House. Imagine: The preacher's son, that sanctimonious wimp, was talking about sending over a search war-rant . . . a search warrant! As if the White House were some kind of crystal meth lab! . . . Looking for Hillary's Rose Law Firm billing records. Then the FBI had come over to fingerprint first Hillary and then himself, the presi-dent of the United States . . . the whole deal you see on *NYPD Blue* . . . a full roll of every finger, then the palm and the side of the hand. White House staffers were wearing rubber gloves, looking at files they were afraid Starr might want. And all this time, that evil roving spotlight was fixed on the center of his private gravity, the place where he'd led so many hands. He scheduled another trip to L.A. . . . to raise some more cash to better Amer-ica . . . to play some more golf . . . to smoke his cigar in his golf cart.

Time flew fast in L.A., the place where real life was only a few reels long. Nobody in Hollywood cared anymore about Mike DeLuca's blow job, or Farrah Fawcett's defecation, either. Everybody was talking now about the size of Mötley Crüe drummer Tommy Lee's willard, exposed in a video with Pamela Anderson Lee that was being messengered all over the studios. I got mine by messenger from an executive at Disney in the same package with *The Lion King* and *Beauty and the Beast*.

The women in Fox's publicity office weren't impressed, though. They had something called the P-file—a collection of stills taken from the out-takes of movies. Plenty of big male stars. All full-frontal nude. Forget Tommy Lee, the women said. Check out Willem Dafoe. Hurray for Holly-wood! The president of the United States found solace in the only place in America, maybe on earth, where people were talking about other willards.

[8]

The War on Acid Reflux

"I didn't kiss a boy for four years," Monica said.
"Really?" Linda asked.
"When I was in high school," Monica said, "oh, this was like
the most depressing time of my life. How depressing is that?"
"Well," Linda Tripp said, "you sure made up for it, dear."

G*ood evening, Mr. and Mrs. America and all the ships at sea.* Let's go to press! It was a million-megaton story. Bill Clinton was hip-deep in the Big Muddy now, under the Tallahatchie Bridge, gasping for air like Brian Jones.

The Pentagon Papers hadn't been as publicized as the *Starr Report.* Nixon's incursion into Cambodia hadn't gotten as much bad press as *his* semi-incursion into Monica. If the failure of Nixon's Vietnamization policy hadn't resulted in calls for Nixon's resignation, then why was his masturbation prompting so many calls for *his* resignation? Nixon was guilty of aerial atrocities; all he'd done were oral sodomies. Nixon had had it easy. Well, yes, there was the war and there were all those demonstrations, but Nixon had all those orbitings and moon walks and *Apollos* and *Saturn Fives* and *Surveyors.* "I am not a crook" didn't sound *that* bad in the context of "Houston, Tranquility Base here; the eagle has landed."

Bill Clinton had dodged the draft and now found himself the target of a television air war, tap-dancing around land mines on the slippery slopes of a slimy Ho Chi Minh trail, strafed, bombed, barraged by editorialists howling, "Resign! Resign! Resign!" Even Bob Dole had been drawn into the scandal. Dole, the lobbyist now that he always should have been, Monica's next-door neighbor at the Watergate, was handing out doughnuts to the press camped outside, sharing the weekly supply he received for doing Dunkin' Donut ads.

"If you're in big trouble over something," Dick Morris had said to Bill Clinton before Dick's own disgrace, before Dick's preference for toes shared the same tabloid pages with Marv Albert's werewolf imitation, "the best strategy is to distract 'em." Or, as Harry Truman said, "If you can't convince 'em, confuse 'em."

But how could Bill Clinton *distract 'em* or *confuse 'em* when the media Beast was feeding on this in its own gluttonous way—"All news all the time! Continuous twenty-four-hour-a-day coverage!" What could he throw the Beast so it would feed on something or someone else? What could the Beast possibly enjoy more than this feast of food so rich that ratings were skyrocketing even on Fox News?

Searching for a distraction, his more pointy-headed aides argued for "a redefinition of the big picture, a reframing of historical context," to make a case that there was nothing that was really unseemly or un-American or unpresidential or *unique* about Bill Clinton's actions. Researchers turned into private eyes, snooping the history books and memoirs for anything that might be . . . *relevant* to this.

George Washington was probably bisexual (irrelevant). . . . Thomas Jefferson fathered a black child (bingo! jackpot! very relevant). . . . Benjamin Franklin liked threesomes (maybe relevant). . . . James Buchanan may have been gay (probably irrelevant). . . . Warren Harding made love to a young mistress in the White House closet (so relevant), but Harding was such a corrupt sleazeball—*Whitewater was not, was not Teapot Dome!*—that any attempt to craft a Harding shield would only hurt. . . . FDR and his mistress Lucy Mercer, one of several, had a lot of oral sex (full-scale relevance alert!), but FDR was bound to a wheelchair, so oral sex was a near necessity. . . . LBJ said, "I get more pussy in twenty-four hours than Jack Kennedy got his entire life" (probably relevant), but LBJ was such a barnyard hick that drawing parallels between LBJ and Bill Clinton could boomerang. . . . JFK was a sex fiend (directly relevant, but, unfortunately, old news, gorged and gobbled by the Beast way too often to distract it from what was on the table now).

Besides researchers turned into private eyes, veterans of more recent scandals were out there, too, tipping the White House to juicy morsels that might distract the Beast. They remembered the stripper Fanne Fox and octogenarian Arkansas congressman Wilbur Mills . . . nontyping secretary Elizabeth Ray and near-octogenarian Ohio congressman Wayne Hayes . . . Teddy Kennedy under the table at Sans Souci, plastered out of his mind, trying to force an unwilling waitress to . . . (Oh, not relevant! Sad-eyed old congressmen and fat old Teddy, the little brother who couldn't, disgraced forever anyway for fatal cowardice at Chappaquiddick.)

And Gerry Ford? Gerry Ford had had more problems with women than anyone, but no one understood why. Why did Squeaky Fromme want to kill him? Why did Sara Jane Moore want to kill him? And what about that seventy-seven-year-old woman who rammed the White House gates with her car, got arrested, got released, went home, got in her car, and rammed the gates again that same night? What was there about flatulent, pipe-smoking, mild-mannered Gerry Ford that made women want to kill him?

Unfortunately, there was no riskless way to reframe the historical context. The history of American politics was an unswept minefield and rusted shrapnel posed the danger of tearing Bill Clinton's head off. Besides that, the Beast was being savagely criticized by the soccer moms for feasting on all this garbage. To throw more maggoty food atop the table now would further enrage those moms . . . and then someone (Hillary?) had a brilliant idea. Feed the Beast a different taste to distract it—something sweet.

Sweet? But what? What was *sweet* in this story? A small box of chocolates as payoff for phone sex and blow jobs? A last "Christmas kiss"? *Sweet?* No, no, Monica was the wrong woman to focus on. The right woman was Chelsea. And her mom and dad. A family in crisis. A family healing. A family forgiving. Give the Beast a soap opera, feed it schmaltz, play it some violins. How could the Beast not like that?

It was beautiful! It was uplifting! The Beast gobbled it up . . . and so did we. It was sugar-coated breakfast cereal that snapped and popped in our mouths. Not for nothing had we become the sensitive, in-touch-with-real-feelings generation. The generation of communication, intervention, closure, and venting. We had designed ourselves, ever since the sixties, to buy this story. "Love is all you need," the Beatles had said.

And so, out of the detritus of cigar butts, we conjured for ourselves—at the Beast's urging—a sappy, universal love story. He cheats. He's sorry. He loves his wife. They love their daughter. Will mommy and their daughter forgive him? Stay tuned! "All news all the time! Continuous twenty-four-hour-a-day coverage!"

We were torn away now from the Oval Office and Bill Clinton's private office, the scene of the noncrime crime. We were watching a different show: *The First Family in Crisis!* We were away from XXX into PG country, away from *Boogie Nights* and safe with *The American President* or a nineties remake of *Kramer vs. Kramer*. Some of us got tears in our eyes. Oh, look at poor, brave Chelsea! Trying to carry on so heroically with her hellish schedule at Stanford after daddy's screwed the pooch! Poor, poor Chelsea, even her nice, clean-cut, white-bread swim-star boyfriend dumped her because he didn't want anything to do with someone whose father . . . Poor, poor Chelsea! *People in the streets were dressed up as human cigars! Signs on overpasses screeched* HONK IF HE SHOULD RESIGN! How could poor Chelsea possibly deal with this? Such a brave, noble, innocent, *sweet* young woman?

And look at poor Hillary, her fate the fate of most of America's women. Betrayed, humiliated, victimized! Oh, she thought she was so highfalutin for a while there, didn't she? Wearing her fancy black coat with the silver Deco design into the grand jury hearing, even autographing her book for a juror, acting in general like hers didn't stink . . . *not anymore!* Brought down off the throne now, just one of millions of cheated women now, one of us now. But how brave she was in the face of this smell. Noble. Crying behind her sunglasses. Because she . . . loved . . . him . . . and . . . he . . . loved . . . her! You could just tell . . . and they both loved their little girl and they'd love each other forever and live happily ever after and he'd never cheat again! The Beast was happy and so were we. We fell for it like Monica fell for him. Jesse Jackson and ministers everywhere waved their applause signs at us in case we had second thoughts: LOVE! HEALING! FORGIVENESS! NOT RESIGNATION! NO IMPEACHMENT! FINISH OUT THE TERM!

Yes, there were a few critics who said, Please! It's horse manure! Tripe for the masses! Dick Morris's distraction strategy at full throttle! . . . Morris had also said, "My job is to run the pump and the motors, not to fix the hole at the bottom of the boat" and "Polls are the ultimate master of the Western World" . . . but there was no doubt the strategy was working. Bill Clinton's approval rating was sky-high and, now that she was off of her throne and one of us, now that she'd been humiliated, Hillary's approval rating was sky-high, too. (Some of her aides worried about that a bit. If we liked Hillary only after she'd been humiliated, did that mean we liked humiliating her? Do you really like a person whom you want to humiliate?)

First we watched A *Time to Heal!* . . . Bill Clinton saying he was sorry, over and over again, sometimes choked up, though it was difficult to determine what exactly he was sorry for. In his words, "inappropriate actions"—which could have meant anything from using the N word, using the F word, or cutting a loud and rude one aimed at Arafat while at Camp David. In an increasingly appropriate America, it could have meant just about anything, but whatever it was, Bill Clinton was sorry. So sorry, so very, very sorry. During this period of healing, he hung out with ministers the way he'd hung out with Steven and Jeffrey and David, and clutched his Bible like a man with emphysema clutches an oxygen tank, or like a man robbing a bank clutches a gun.

Then, after this period of healing, choreographed for a monthlong period, like a ratings-sweep television miniseries, we watched *A Time to Forgive!* Hillary, back at his side, the sunglasses gone, Chelsea between them, even Buddy, the puppy, wagging his tail once again (and no longer squatting on the Rose Garden lawn).

Even the most successful show, however, comes to an eventual end: Those insane Republicans kept yammering about impeachment—"The elephant has a thick skin, a head full of ivory, and, as everyone who has seen a circus parade knows, proceeds best by grasping the tail of his predecessor," Adlai Stevenson had said—and the Beast, jittery and petulant, was showing signs of suffering sugar rush. So, to act out the screenplay written by Dick Morris, *another* distraction was needed. *Impeachment?* Had the Republicans completely lost their minds? *Impeachment?* With Bill Clinton's approval rating sky-high and the economy booming? *Impeachment?* With even Hillary, the big loser in the midterm election of 1994, triumphant again thanks to her abject humiliation, admired again in her disgrace. *Impeachment?* No way! Not a chance! Nada! Zip! But still, just to make sure . . . another distraction was imperative.

The policy wonks got together and wonked! An issue, maybe? Gay marriage? A new offensive in the war on big tobacco? How about a sequel to health care now that Hillary wasn't radioactive anymore? More empowerment zones? A war against a new disease? How about a war against one of those diseases people were always hearing about on TV? *That* would guarantee an already-receptive, preconditioned audience. A war against hemorrhoids? Incontinence? Diarrhea? Male-pattern baldness? The ever-elusive Epstein-Barr virus? Constipation? A war against acid reflux?

Some of the more hypochondriacal policy wonks waged a spirited campaign to expand the putative medical offensive from the *limited* target of acid reflux to the wider *killing zone* of heartburn. In arguing for the War on Burps—it admittedly didn't have the ring of the War on Poverty or the War on Illiteracy—they pointed out that antiburp medication was already a $1.4 billion industry. A lot of dyspeptic Americans would rally gassily, their gastric juices sloshing, behind this distracting New Age flag.

The War on Burps, some policy wonks explained, would also be seen as part of the administration's Holy War on Cancer. Overflowing gastric juices left the esophagus with scar tissue and altered the cells that line it, thereby making those altered cells more likely to develop the dreaded terror, so much scarier than Saddam and all those other war criminals in biblical robes, Public Enemy Numero Uno . . . *the Big C!* But no, the wonks were just being wonkish. Cancer had already been wonked and milked even by liberal Republican wonks, the Compassionate Conservatives (which, some Hollywood wags said, was as oxymoronic as saying "lady producers").

What Bill Clinton needed desperately was a wild boar national tragedy, some hard-shell and awfully cynical pols felt (the kind of pols who thought Lee Harvey Oswald's bullets passed the first Civil Rights Bill and James Earl Ray's the second; who thought Reagan would have been nailed for Iran-Contra without Hinckley). Bill Clinton needed a humongous hurricane with thousands of deaths, or anthrax in Central Park, or a Three Mile Island meltdown on a Chernobyl scale, or the Big One in California voiding a chunk of coastline into the sea, or a Texas tower–type sniper in a ballpark. *Something* . . . on that tragic level. (The shootings at Columbine High School in Colorado, much later, would have been perfect.)

Bill Clinton needed an event that would break America's heart for a month or two. We'd go through the horror itself first. Then videotaped replays of the horror for weeks. Then we'd go through the grieving. Then videotaped replays of the grieving for more weeks. Prayers. Sermons. Sobbing faces. Children holding on to their mommies. Parents screaming. *All mourning all the time!* Then the experts would pontificate on *Larry King Live*, night after night, analyzing the horror and the grieving and the closure from all the replays, still picking through ruins—a child's Raggedy Ann doll, a smashed photo of a smiling young couple found in the rubble, an old lady crying on an old man's shoulder—as the camera panned across fresh graves at a turn-of-the-century cemetery . . . at *sunset*.

Bill Clinton needed a Mike Tyson uppercut to our hearts. Something to soften us up. To put us into a more sensitive mood. To make us feel more forgiving. To make us feel better about him. (Reagan, his polls down during Iran-Contra, said, "Maybe I should go out and get myself shot again.") Bill Clinton needed a great and horrible and welcome and opportune tragedy to put everything in perspective.

·   ·   ·

He didn't get it. He didn't get the apocalypse he needed, but he got something. The explosions at the American embassies in Tanzania and Kenya, final proof that the Good Lord was on Bill Clinton's side. (Some would have their doubts later, when another act of God, a tornado, wiped out Bill Clinton's former Little Rock statehouse, including Chelsea's tree house.) *Yes, Virginia, there was a Santa Claus! Bill Clinton was as happy as the day grocery stores started selling frozen pizzas!* This act of God, these explosions, coming during the period when Bill Clinton was clutching his Bible, were truly heaven-sent. The explosions were planned and carried out by Arab terrorists.

Forget the War on Burps; this war would be against Arab terrorists, and it would be real. The Beast would be showing America at war. The explosive cacophony of all of those bombs, live on CNN, would surely drown out the jibbering, jabbering cries for impeachment. The Creep would be recast as the Commander in Chief, clothing himself in the flag some insisted he'd burned in the sixties, draping Old Glory over the most inglorious part of his body.

Just to firm up his support a bit, he dragged his Saddam scarecrow out of the Pentagon's closet and hurled some more bombs and Tomahawks Saddam's way, too. Oh, he flew through the air with the greatest of ease, the high-flying Creep on his political trapeze, dropping Tomahawks on Baghdad and Afghanistan and the Sudan! *Boom! Boom! Boom!* What a lovely, handy, perfect little boomer war this was! Even the old-style, dadgum, shit-kicker rednecks (who hated him) got booby-trapped by this one. Yessir, Amurrica was at war, by God! And by God, we had to support our boys, by God, and support the commander in chief, by God, by God (even if they hated him), because, by God, he *was* the commander in chief.

Well, sure, some people upchucked. Republicans Trent Lott of Mississippi and Gerald Solomon of New York, who'd seen that saddle burr *Wag the Dog* movie and thought they knew how to distinguish a reel show—first *A Time to Heal!* and then *A Time to Forgive!* and now *A Time for War!*—from real life. But when they criticized the cynicism and self-serving mendacity of the president of the United States, the nauseating and brazen timing of this, they were ambushed by their core constituencies. All those shit-kickers and By God Amurricans supporting our boys and the commander in chief. They had to stage a fast and undignified retreat.

Lott and Solomon knew they were on slippery, dangerous ground anyway. There were crazy people out there on the Internet claiming that Bill

Clinton had bombed our embassies to save his skin, with the help of the CIA. They were the same sort of ding-a-lings who in the past had claimed that LBJ and the CIA murdered 129 people (connected in some way with JFK's assassination), and that LBJ, on the flight from Dallas to Washington, had stuck his willard into JFK's wounds. *Yea, verily,* Trent Lott and Gerald Solomon did a big-assed retreat indeed . . . and our Tomahawks kept falling around the world.

Cross-dressed in Old Glory now, fighting a victorious multifront war, officially and publicly forgiven by Hillary and Chelsea, riding his polls and approval ratings, the commander in chief thought for the first time that he could win the battle of his life. Not against big tobacco or the burps, not against terrorism and Saddam Hussein, but against Kenneth W. Starr. The war against Kenneth W. Starr would be the final distraction, the rarest filet mignon, served up to the Beast. Bill Clinton and his aides and his friends in the media (mostly sixties kids) would take this preacher's son, whom Clinton considered "filthy and sleazy," and turn him into the ghost of drunken Joe McCarthy: Kenneth W. Starr portrayed as peepingly sticking his nose into the holy of holies—America's collective bedroom.

Bill Clinton would Saddamize the preacher's son the way Nixon had Saddamized McGovern. He would make Kenneth W. Starr the issue, not Bill Clinton. He would not allow himself to be ruined. He would ruin Starr. ("Here ruining reputations is considered sport," Vince Foster had written in his suicide note.) Clinton would exploit Starr the way he believed Starr was trying to exploit him. He would accept the wisdom of his first White House counsel, Bernie Nussbaum, who had advised him "to do harm to enemies if you can."

Kenneth W. Starr, Bill Clinton was convinced, was a Republican hatchet man, the demonic Helms's creature, the former chief of staff from 1981 to 1983 to Reagan's attorney general, William French Smith. He'd been appointed to the U.S. Court of Appeals by Reagan in 1983. Who really needed more proof than that? Starr was obviously a Helms man, a Reagan man—but there *was* more proof. Even as Starr was investigating Bill Clinton as special prosecutor, Starr was still getting a million dollars a year representing . . . big tobacco! Helms, Reagan, and big tobacco! And the pious twit was claiming that he was being fair? *Fair?* With friends and allies like that?

Bill Clinton wasn't discouraged. He contemplated the advice his mama had given him: "Nothing good comes easy. . . . We just have to be strong to pull ourselves together. . . . We've climbed mountains before and we've got one more to climb. . . . You can't saw sawdust."

It was back to the barricades for Bill Clinton, back to the sixties: The pigs were lined up in phalanx, holding billy clubs and tear-gas guns, and they were lofting the canisters in, and flashcubes were sparkling, and Bill Clinton was out there, the Stones and the Who blasting inside his head. Arkansas's own Street Fightin' Man with his Prince Valiant Beatles haircut wouldn't ever get fooled again. Throwing those canisters right back at Judge Pig Starr, Bull Connor Starr, Rusty Calley Starr, Paul Harvey Starr, Judge Julius Hoffman Starr, screaming "Fuck you!" into the acrid, choking, dark night of his travail. *Look, top of the world, Ma!* Abbie Hoffman (now dead), Jerry Rubin (also dead, after turning into a real estate salesman), Bobby Seale (now selling barbecue sauce), and our lollipop-dispensing baby doctor, Benjamin Spock (dead now, too) would have been proud.

It was all starting to swing the commander in chief's way: The shows—*A Time to Heal!* and *A Time to Forgive!* and *A Time for War!*—had all been successful. This new show—*A Time to Saddamize!*—would play, too . . . but Bill Clinton was still uneasy.

There was that moment in Vancouver, up on the balcony, when Boris Yeltsin, the doddering sot, had seen Bill Clinton waving to producer Bud Yorkin's beautiful wife, the actress Cynthia Sikes, down below, holding Bud and Cynthia's baby . . . and Yeltsin had turned to him with his vodka red cheeks and said, "Is dat *your* baby?" *That was wrong!* The president of a bust-out derelict country had no right to speak to the president of the United States that way!

And then there was the uncomfortable moment in Hollywood, at that cocktail party, when he'd walked into the room, floating on his own charisma, and Sharon Stone was sitting there with her back to him. She didn't even turn to look at him. She just sat there with her legs crossed, thighs showing, and didn't even turn. Aware of him behind her, she arched her neck back and said, "Hi, Bill." *Hi, Bill? Bill?* Like he was an ex-fiancé or something! He was the president of the United States! The commander in chief! She was an aging actress with *one* hit movie! Was that any way for a piece of fluff to greet her commander in chief?

Within hours, people in Hollywood told the story of how Sharon Stone had greeted Bill Clinton. In a place where a good title means dollars, their meeting already had a million-dollar title: *The Flasher and the Masher!*

(9)

Kenneth W. Starr Confesses

Forgive me, Lord, for I have sinned. Cast out the evil that has corrupted my flesh. Grace me with Your strength. Infuse me with Your spirit. Save me from the flames of perdition.

I have been Your servant. I sing Your hymns on my morning jog. I read Your Scripture when Alice and I go on our Sunday-afternoon drives. I have never cheated on my Alice. I am a straight arrow, a learned, affable man, courtly, thoughtful, and deliberate. I try to carry myself in a judicial and Christian manner. I have been a good husband to my Alice, who has been a good wife to me. Once a Mendell, once a Jew, she is now a Starr; she is Church of Christ. *I have never cheated on my wife!*

But I will never, to my dying day, forget the look on my poor Alice's face when she found me down here in the basement, abasing myself with the Internet, my eyes red and lusting, ravishing Pookie's body. Alice has gone back upstairs now. I hear her puttering in the kitchen, and I know she can hear the abject sobs of my ruin. For a man of my judiciousness, decorum, and equanimity to be discovered by his faithful wife sitting at his computer in striped pants and morning coat, looking at *his* strumpet's naked body—His! His! Not mine!—is, I will be first to admit, an abomination. *I have never cheated on my wife, Lord!*

I can't even bring myself to refer to *him* by his name. Nor can I force myself to violate myself further and call him the president of the United States. I will call him, then, POTUS, the inhuman acronym used by the Secret Service on their location maps. Please do not think, my God, that I am apportioning any of my blame to him by referring to him. I am on my knees as I hear Alice, sniffling upstairs now, begging to be forgiven for *my* sins, not POTUS's. I will use the worn-out and now meaningless phrase I have heard so often sitting high on my judge's bench: the truth, the whole truth, and nothing but the truth, so help me God.

You know I have done my best to serve You and America my entire life. I say that not to excuse myself in any way for my sins, but to provide a moral context, to build a case for a pattern of my behavior that, until my exposure to POTUS, was as near-exemplary as humanly possible. I say that in all humility, my Lord, but You know it in Your all-encompassing wisdom to be legally accurate. Mother told me that I prayed to You already when I was two weeks old. I knelt as Father preached at home in between haircuts. I didn't drink. I didn't smoke. I went to see You at the Church of Christ. I sold Your Word door to door. I didn't dance. I didn't fornicate. When I married Alice, she taught me to dance. Alice and I didn't fornicate, either—we still don't. We celebrate Your presence in our hearts and loins. I've been true-blue, Lord. I campaigned for Richard Nixon in high school. I've served under Ronald Reagan and George Bush. I've spoken at Pat Robertson College.

I have suffered the slings and arrows of a blasphemous and profane world because of my beliefs and my loyalty to America and You. I have been called Chauncy Gardner and Mister Rodgers. I have suffered calumnies and bogus allegations. I have seen signs that say WHAT'S THE FREQUENCY, KENNETH? as I pass by. I have been called a doofus and a nerd. In my service to You and America on the federal bench and as solicitor general, I have taken courageous and maligned positions against abortion, burning the flag, and homosexuals. I have opined on behalf of school prayer. I have raised in tribute to You, with Alice's help, a beautiful family. *I have never cheated on my wife, Lord!* I have put one cigar into my mouth for a group photograph with my colleagues. I didn't light it.

I have been Your Christian soldier fighting the forces of the Church of Cool. In a world increasingly cool, I have spoken up for family values, for the unborn fetus, for Paula Jones, for the Constitution. I have represented the tobacco companies You need to bring sinners swiftly back to You, the automakers You need to bring broken bodies to repentance. I have gloried in not being cool, proudly using my smarminess, my thick glasses, my baseball cap, my Starbucks mug, my baldness, and my psoriasis as prayer flags for You—a reminder to all Americans of a bygone world when people didn't worship at the altar of cool and weren't focused on the slimness of their bodies, the inarticulation of their speech, the barbarism of their music. Hear me, my Lord! When the tie-dyed hordes befouled the earth in the sixties, I wore a suit and tie to school. My children speak English, not Ebonics; my dear wife is a mate, not a suffragette.

You know, too, surely, that intimately I have violated neither myself nor You. Father taught me the godly nature of an ice-cold shower. Mother never found anything when she examined my sheets. For my entire life, as I've stood at the urinal, I've held myself only with the tips of two fingers. The instant I have felt myself not even attracted, not even tempted, but in the tiniest platonic way curious about a member of the opposite sex, I have fled to Your Scripture. And You have rewarded me with an infinite capacity for work, with an energy impossible to deplete. You have made my psoriasis-scarred flesh as unto the fine, musty-smelling pages of a leather-bound law book. Thanks to You, the briefs I discuss are legal ones; the wildest climaxes I enjoy are in a courtroom at top hourly rates. Thanks to You, my seed is green-backed and collecting interest. *I have never abused myself, my Lord!*

I beg You, then, now that I've defined the moral context, now that I've established my pattern of behavior, to forgive me for what I, a sinner, am about to confess.

In my servitude to America and You, I was asked to read a book in 1993. I regret to say that it wasn't the Good Book. It wasn't Your spirit and Your soul. It was a leprous book—a diary written by a sinner. His name was Robert Packwood. I was asked by a congressional committee. I couldn't refuse. The sinner was a United States senator. I was selected to read it thanks to the probity and decorum that You have granted unto me, oh my God. It was a diary of filth and sexual debauchery. It was a document written in a sewer. I was asked to read every word and form an opinion as to its relevance in a Senate trial. I read every word over and over and over and over and over and over again. It was torture. It was horrifying. Flesh, my Lord! Intimate female flesh that Packwood sniffed like a depraved beast.

Alice woke me one night, screaming, and said that in my sleep I had put my face, sniffing, against her flesh. I had to run to the bathroom because I was wet between my legs, the way I was wet sometimes as a boy.

I tried everything. Ice-cold showers. Ice cubes. Dry ice. Ice cream. Alice and I tried reading the Scripture to each other. I heard her, but my eyes were trapped on her breasts. I read to her, but I was drooling. Packwood, this beast, had immersed his wanton, dripping-wet hands in my brainpan. Images of pink flesh—on a single occasion, even dark-hued, but not black, flesh—were polluting my snow-white, decorous, judicial thoughts. After what seemed a very long time, I felt relieved.

Perhaps it was because I had converted to decaf and abjured eating red meat. Perhaps it was because my daughter's girlfriends stopped visiting our house. I had purged myself of Packwood's poison, but I still felt my recovery tenuous. I was still unexpectedly, joltingly reminded of passages in Packwood's diary by the most nonsensical things: a piece of white chicken meat, the inside of a cantaloupe, the bulb of an angel on our Christmas tree. But I prayed to You, every hour of every day. I bought a desk calendar with Your Word on every hour. And I was better.

I didn't know then that Packwood's diary was only the first step in my ruin, that his frenzied images were nothing but a means to weaken me for POTUS. I knew very well who POTUS was. I had watched him on television and at banquets, displaying his masterful, easy charm. POTUS was everything I wasn't and never wanted to be. He wasn't just cool. He was the Pope of the Church of Cool. POTUS discussed his underwear on television, tooted a horn for the wide-eyed naïfs. POTUS swept through a room like a powerful jolt of electricity. POTUS was good-looking and charming. POTUS wasn't a nerd, didn't wear glasses, wasn't bald, didn't have psoriasis. Nobody called POTUS Chauncy Gardner and Mister Rodgers. I had heard all the talk, too, about how POTUS had always betrayed his wife. *I have never cheated on my wife, Lord!*

POTUS represented everything I was committed to fight against . . . for America and for You, my Lord: Abortion, promiscuity, pornography, suffragettes, homosexuals, AIDS, affirmative action, miscegenation, evolution, the Woodstock Nation, bilingual education, heathenism, communism, globalism, onanism, busing, rutting, flag burning, marijuana, clove cigarettes, herpes, tattoos, graffiti, pierced navels, Boogie boards, skateboards, sushi, Jolt, Brompton's Cocktail, bungee jumping, incense, the spotted owl, the Denim Bible, *The Ultimate Fighting Challenge,* bikinis, yoga, Altoids, protesters, demonstrators, longtime companions, anarchists, surfers, streakers, the Rosenbergs, Teletubbies, Studio 54, professional wrestlers, peace signs, the SDS, the IWW, the SLA, the ADL, the Rainbow Coalition, Nine Inch Nails, STDs, Marilyn Manson, Marilyn Monroe, Charlie Manson, Warhol, Alger Hiss, Henry Reske, Mike Tyson, McGovern, Abbie Hoffman, Allen Ginsberg, Ralph Ginzburg, Al Goldstein, Howard Stern, Jane Fonda, Gus Hall, Che Guevera, Ralph Nader, Mapplethorpe, the Rolling Stones, rap, hip-hop, the Internet, Hollywood, massage parlors, massages, body paint, body parts, birth control, gay marriage, the polls.

I hated POTUS and what he stood for, and when I was asked to replace Fiske as Whitewater independent counsel, I was as happy as on days when Father would cut my hair and preach to me at the same time. I had the cross and the sword in hand now! Thanks to Your help, with Packwood's diary pushed to the back of my mind now, I had my old energy back. I would reveal POTUS as the low and base Borgia Pope that he was. I would force his followers to turn their faces from him in disgust. I would slay POTUS, and abortion and promiscuity and pornography and suffragettes and homosexuals and all the rest of it would die with him. Those who maligned me with their calumnies missed the point: I was *not* Inspector Javert. I was *not* Ahab obsessed with his white whale. I was Your St.

George, facing Lucifer's dragon. I knew POTUS was guilty; all I had to do was to determine of what.

I began in Little Rock, a place built of excrement. I knew the full power of the stench now. It wasn't just POTUS; it was also his suffragette wife, FLOTUS. They were chest-deep in their own slime and corruption. But every time I was about to reach the link that would strip the clothes off both of them and expose their scrofulous nakedness, the link evaded me. Whitewater, Filegate, Travelgate — the link would slip away. I sent Hubbell to jail and the harlot McDougal, but it did no good.

I kept hearing, again and again, about how POTUS had debased himself in pursuit of his fleshly pleasure. There were more stories about his debasement in Arkansas than there were watermelons. The more stories I heard, the more Packwood's diary haunted me all over again. I felt like my brain was a cavern of degradation, my Lord! Flesh danced in my sentence structures and dreams. I found myself confusing what Packwood had done and what POTUS had done. Alice was back in Washington; she couldn't help me. I looked in the mirror and saw an overwrought, overweight nerd with the pouches of sleeplessness beneath his sinner's eyes. I was afraid to fall asleep for fear of wetting the Little Rock Holiday Inn bed. But I did not betray You! I was not an accomplice in the evacuation of my seed.

Two events took place at roughly the same time. They are joined together in my mind. I read the Gennifer Flowers file that Bulldog Bittman and Jackie Bennett and some of my other disciples put together after interviewing her. She has a filthy mouth, my Lord! She has a beautiful filthy mouth, usually painted in hammer and sickle scarlet. I shouldn't have read the file.

I was not prepared — not even after Packwood's diary and the lascivious chitchat in Little Rock and my fevered dreams. How can Your creations do such things? Blindfolds and ropes and food from the refrigerator which they — *ice cubes?* For these purposes! When all of my life I have used ice cubes for the opposite effect! POTUS called her "Pookie."

And I saw the photographs in the file, too. A young Pookie in her full shame! Pookie from every different angle! Pookie in close-ups! Pookie in color! I couldn't stop myself from staring at them, at her. I sat for hours in my office, the door locked and Pookie on the desk in front of me. I was rigid, literally petrified. I couldn't stop looking at her shame. She was disgusting! Pookie was so disgustingly perfect and so perfectly disgusting.

Shortly afterward, I met POTUS and FLOTUS at the White House. We took their depositions. I couldn't keep my eyes off him. He was his smiling, insidious self. I watched him and envisioned the photographs of Pookie in my files. He had done all of those abominable things to her, this smiling sinner sitting here with his betrayed wife. He had debased Pookie, impregnated her, and paid two hundred dollars for her abortion. Two hundred dollars! As I watched him and thought of her body and her shame, I resolved that if I didn't slay him, my life would be proved worthless.

But I was in worse pain than I'd ever been, my dreams filled with Packwood's hands and Pookie's shame and POTUS holding buckets of ice. And sometimes Alice and I would be in there, too. . . . My God, forgive me! I couldn't get it out of my mind! Even Alice wasn't much help to me anymore. She was unexplainably smiling much of the time, talking about our second honeymoon, waking me up at night. Were her lips painted, or was it my imagination? Had my sweet, loving, non-Jewish, baptized, Church of Christ wife now also become part of my infernal dreams? Or was Alice Pookie? Was I POTUS? Were Packwood, POTUS, and I taking turns with—was that Alice touching me or Packwood? Oh, abomination! Lamentation! Shame! Blasphemous ice cubes! *I did not abuse myself, my Lord! I have never cheated on my wife, my Lord!*

Then that woeful pig-nosed woman came to us with her tapes. It was the final straw personally. First Packwood's diary, then Pookie's file, then Pookie's photographs, and now all this splendid new dreck! The ice-cold showers didn't work anymore. Alice didn't want to read Scripture anymore; she wanted to . . . I was now forced to contemplate the horror that took place in the Oval Office hallway and bathroom. Now I had to hear about fellatio and masturbation and that other heinous sin I can't even bring myself to discuss. On top of blindfolds, ropes, food, and ice. And that hideous netherworld cigar. I will never touch a cigar, let alone put it into my mouth, as long as I live.

I was overjoyed and in torment. I knew I had stumbled, thanks to this obscene pig-nosed woman, upon the means to slay POTUS. But at what price to myself? Could I download all this new imagery into my brain and survive—without, minimally, exhausting Alice unto death? I resolved to sacrifice myself and Alice. I would stay within my usual innocent demeanor—my smarminess, my baseball cap, my glasses, my Starbucks mug—while I destroyed him! Even if it meant my dreams and thoughts would be filled with French postcard orgies of sin. No one would know what I had sentenced myself to. No one would know the sacrifice I had made. No one would know that this once-decorous figure of judiciousness and responsibility had become as flesh-obsessed as POTUS.

No one knew, but some became suspicious after I issued my *Report*. Why was it filled with all those many explicit descriptions of sexual debauchery? Because POTUS was engaged in sexual debauchery, that's why. It had nothing to do with *me*. I was merely telling the truth, the whole truth, and nothing but the truth, so help me God. I didn't do those fiendish things; *he* did! I wasn't the degenerate; *he* was! I wasn't the pervert; *he* was! It was true, wasn't it? I didn't have any of those dreams or thoughts until Packwood and Pookie and POTUS forced their disgusting cigars inside me.

I stripped him naked, my Lord, and millions turned their faces away from him in disgust. Not as many millions as I'd hoped, but the idolaters of cool rallied to his side. We knew who'd come to his defense, didn't we? The Jews, the black rabble, and the Kennedys . . . the Ellen Degenerates, the Barney Fags. Never mind, it won't do him much good. POTUS will be impeached anyway—perhaps even removed—if I have to go to Congress and get it done myself. For all practical political purposes, I have accomplished what I set out to do. POTUS is naked and dead, my Lord. I have proven to myself that I am better than he. I am the nerd triumphant! The Church of Christ victorious over the Church of Cool!

I beg Your forgiveness for my thoughts and my dreams. I beg that I be cleansed. I loathe myself for sitting here at my computer in my basement watching the newest naked photographs of Pookie some sinner has posted on the Internet. I sit here rigidly, *but I have not abused myself! I have never cheated on my wife, Lord!*

I hear Alice whimpering upstairs and I regret terribly that she saw me like this. But Alice will get over it. I'll beseech her forgiveness, I'll read from Your Scripture, and Alice and I will celebrate Your presence in our hearts and loins . . . as in my thoughts I recklessly explore Pookie's sinful flesh.

[10]

Sharon and Bill

*"The You Know What of the You Know What found you aw-
fully attractive," Linda Tripp said.*
*"Big fucking deal!" Monica said. "He finds anybody attractive.
I guarantee you that given the opportunity with anyone he'd let
anyone suck his dick."*

Catherine Tramell may have been the bang of the century in *Basic
Instinct*, but that didn't mean Sharon Stone was. Or Bill Clinton, for
that matter. Maybe that's why Sharon was so blasé about his presence
when the president of the United States walked up behind her at that party.
They knew each other already. He had rearranged *his* schedule so he could
meet her in San Francisco. "He was really, really hot for her," Dick Morris
had said. "He has it bad for her." The president of the United States talked
to his golf course buddies a lot about his favorite Sharon Stone scene. Yup,
it was *that* scene! *You* know! The one Sharon was now claiming she'd been
tricked into doing. The one I'd written.

I felt a kind of bemused proprietary interest when I heard about the
friendship between Sharon and Bill. I had created her. I had voted for him.
Her career had gone nowhere until my screenplay made her a global star.
Her accountants had fired her; even her agents had fired her. A producer
who'd seen her at the Deauville Film Festival years before *Basic* told me,
"She came knocking on my door at midnight. There's no way I'd let her in."
One of her former agents said, "We used to have a saying among us at the
agency. Put Sharon in the room alone with the director and she'll close the
deal." She was so unpopular on movie sets that the crew of one of the clinkers she'd done before *Basic* urinated in a bathtub she was supposed to bathe
in. Then she'd read my screenplay, fought to get the part, and the rest was

Hollywood history. The greatest American sex symbol since Marilyn Monroe. Proof positive that Frank Capra was dead wrong when he said, "A nude girl is a nude girl, and that's that—and there is no way you can make a star out of a nude girl."

She was Bill Clinton's ideal woman, the ripest of ripe peaches, apotheosis of the curvy beauty pageant blondes he's always favored—the same physical type as Dolly Kyle, his longtime mistress; as Cathy Cornelius, the young aide who accompanied him on so many government trips; as Kristy Zercher, the flight attendant he'd groped on the campaign plane; as Gennifer and Eleanor Mondale. And Sharon had a lot of Hillary in her, too. She was smart and direct, but not as crude. Those of us who knew Sharon could never imagine her saying, "I need to get fucked more than twice a year, Bill." (It was also true that those of us who knew Sharon couldn't ever imagine her needing to say that.)

And then there was the JFK connection, too. Before he was governor or president or Handsome or the Creep or Butt-head—when he was still Bubba, the fat boy from Arkansas—Bill Clinton had shaken JFK's hand at the White House, and it had changed his life. He emulated JFK to the point where, like JFK, he never carried any money . . . where, like JFK, he changed his shirts three times a day . . . where, like JFK, he had a willard with a zany, serendipitous life of its own. (On the wall in his private office, above the spot where he liked Monica to kneel, was a portrait of JFK.) It was fitting, therefore, maybe even preordained, that if JFK, while he was the president of the United States, had been "really, really, hot" for Marilyn Monroe, the sex goddess of the New Frontier, then Bill Clinton would "have it bad" for Sharon, the sex goddess of the millennium.

Some people who knew her felt that Sharon was as much a politician as he. As many in Hollywood know, a star's career is a lifelong political campaign. Each new movie is an election. Stars have to be as image-conscious as politicians, one of the reasons stars choose heroic (noncomplex) roles, trying to swirl their character's heroism with their own persona, dressing themselves in their character's nobility and goodness. Sharon was especially challenged, since she'd ascended atop her star on the strength of her privates, but she'd handled the challenge well.

Thanks to some advice from Hollywood PR doyen Pat Kingsley, *her* Dick Morris, she'd outgrown her pubes. To begin with, Sharon said she didn't know what the director was doing when he'd gotten *that* shot, that she'd been "tricked"—forgetting that the shot had to be lighted, that the hair and makeup people were between her legs most of that morning. It was

Sharon's way of saying that she didn't inhale. Then she hit the charity circuit, becoming a spokesperson for AIDS, reenacting the all-American tradition: Babe Ruth visiting sick kids, getting his picture taken. Then she stopped taking her clothes off on-camera, the result not only of image making but also of age. ("My ass hangs halfway down to my knees," she told me during the making of *Sliver.*) Then she finally found Jesus, though I worried that it was like one of Jimmy Swaggart's sightings of the ever-fleeting Lord.

She tried to ignore, in the glorious zenith of her stardom, that she'd had only one hit movie—like Bill Clinton, who didn't dwell on the fact that he'd twice been elected as a minority president. There were those of Sharon's friends in Hollywood who worried that she'd wind up as one of those blowzy, loud, has-beens on *Hollywood Squares,* a professional celebrity like Zsa Zsa Gabor, looking a lot like Petula Clark. But then there were also Friends of Bill's who worried he'd wind up getting Steven's decaf each morning.

I remembered something Sharon had said to me late one night, both of us blitzed on Thai hash: "I crawled the hill of broken glass and I sucked and I sucked until I sucked the air right out of my life." Perfect, I thought. Bill Clinton would like her—both for the ineffable Whitmanesque sadness of the thought and for the enticing promise of the action.

She'd like *him,* too, I knew. When we were casting *Sliver* and the studio wanted Billy Baldwin, she said, "He's a boy. Give me a man. Give me Alec. I'd let Alec throw me over a table anytime." She'd be just right for Bill Clinton . . . slam-bang action . . . roaring down the road in Dolly Kyle's turquoise El Dorado convertible, swerving from lane to lane at a hundred miles an hour . . . or going for a walk with Dolly, tripping over a chaise longue on somebody's front lawn, pulling her onto the grass and stripping her with his teeth . . . or running into that groupie, Connie Hamzy, while he was the governor, the one who'd been with Mick Fleetwood and Huey Lewis and Keith Moon and Don Henley. *Hail, hail, rock and roll! Rock and roll is here to stay!*

Such an unadulterated, glorious sixties moment (in 1984). He saw the groupie out by the pool from a hallway at the Little Rock Hilton. She was wearing a bikini. He sent one of his troopers to bring her inside. No small talk, no chitchat. *Alec Baldwin right over the table!* "I'd love to get with you," he said. "Where can we go? Do you have a room here?" She had no room; she was just using the pool. He took her by the hand. He went up and down the hall, opening meeting room doors. *Damn! Goddamn!* Goddamn all these people! *All these people in all these meeting rooms!*

He wanted to get with her so *bad.* "Where can we go?" he said to her.

"Where can we go? Are any of the rooms open? *Where can we go?*" She told him to get an aide to book them a room. "I don't have time for that!" he said. He charged down another hallway, holding her hand, nuzzling her, feeling her breasts, sticking his hand inside her bikini, almost stumbling down the hallways now, trying doors in a vascular frenzy. A door opened! A laundry room . . . *there were more people in it! Damn! Damn!* She kissed him. He squeezed her breasts. *Damn!* He had a meeting! *Damn! Damn! Damn!* He said, "How can I get in touch with you?" She said, "I'm in the book." He started to walk away down the hallway, turned back. She saw the bulge in his pants. "How long you gonna be by the pool?" he asked. She said, "All afternoon." He was gone.

A wild man. Created for Sharon, I thought, who had a boulevard streak of craziness herself. Not long after *Basic's* release, we went out. I picked her up at her house off of Mulholland, overlooking the Valley. We smoked some of her Thai. She brought out two bottles of Cristal, and we wound up on the rug, crawling around her dollhouse. We got hungry and got into the limo and went to a chic Hollywood place to eat, stoned out of our minds. She had scampi sauce dripping down her chin. She looked at the other diners and said, "Who are those fuckers?" They were studio heads and producers and agents, all staring at us. We drank some more Cristal and got back in the limo and smoked some more Thai. We needed music.

Rock and roll! We stopped at Virgin Records and she went running up the steps for James Brown, and then she was running down the steps, her arms wide, playing the diva, saying, "Where *were* you?" very loudly as everyone stared at these two ripped loonies. We paid and tried to leave. A security guard informed us we were trying to leave through the front plate-glass window. He led us to a door.

On the way back to her house, she said, "I wore these brown suede pants just for you. I knew you'd put your hand there." We went back inside her house and watched the twinkling lights. We drank more Cristal and wound up on the rug next to the dollhouse again . . . and then I went back to my hotel, happy that I'd created her.

Right out of *Basic*, that dollhouse scene, I thought as I contemplated Sharon and Bill Clinton. He was a character from that movie, too. He was as jaded, and he even spoke like my Nick Curran: "I stuck it up their ass" (about Republicans) and "He's so stupid, he couldn't get a whore across the bridge" (about Ted Kennedy) and "You know why people go into politics, don't you? Because of their unsatisfied sexual desire" (about himself?) and "She can suck a tennis ball through a garden hose" (about Gennifer). (Hillary, on the other hand, seemed to belong not in *Basic* but in one of my later movies, *Showgirls*. "Where's the goddamn fucking flag?" she said to one of the state troopers in Arkansas. "Put the goddamn fucking flag up!")

Unlike Hillary, I thought, whom he was calling "Hilla the Hun" and "the Warden" and "the Sarge," Sharon would understand his kinks. If he wanted to get *down* at night, smoke a little dope, put her lace nightie on, and play Elvis on his sax, Sharon would be *down* with that. She'd also have her own Thai.

Thinking of kinks, I realized maybe Sharon and Hillary had more in common than being smart blondes. The director Wes Craven told me that Sharon had seduced his wife, Mimi, still one of Sharon's "best friends," and stolen Mimi away from him. When Mimi's divorce from Wes was granted, Sharon had sent Wes a dozen dead roses. Those dead roses, I knew, symbolized Bill Clinton's greatest danger as far as any "meaningful relationship" with Sharon was concerned. Maybe she was his ideal woman, but Sharon was nobody to mess with, or mess around on.

Yes, she had a back rubs and herbal remedies, touchy-feely, warm and fuzzy side, but . . . she *was* the girl who went into the room and *closed the deal*. Paul Verhoeven, the director of *Basic*, said she *was* Catherine Tramell, the devil herself. This was a woman who, when she broke up with Dwight Yoakam, called him "a dirt sandwich," who, when she broke up with producer Bill Macdonald, sent him his mother's heirloom engagement ring back by Federal Express.

She knew at least as much about power as Hillary, but Sharon's knowledge didn't come from committee meetings and 1930s agitprop primers. Sharon's knowledge of power was elemental, primal, learned in modeling sessions (at nineteen) and casting couches and in the back rooms of shadowy black-lighted discos in Milan and Buenos Aires. If Hillary was good with a scalpel and a lethal tongue in a boardroom, Sharon was good with an ice pick and a soft tongue on a couch. Sharon usually got what she wanted on a personal level. Hillary usually got what she wanted on a political level but, at least as far as Bill Clinton was concerned, turned into "Hilla the Hun" and "the Warden" and "the Sarge" on a personal one.

· · ·

I saw Sharon in action with the director Phillip Noyce as we were about to shoot *Sliver*. She thought Noyce was a disastrous choice to direct it. "He's a big goon," she said. "He doesn't know anything about sex." Phillip was a lumbering, talented Aussie who, exactly then, was trying to break a five-pack-a-day smoking habit.

As we approached the shoot, she zeroed in on a scene in the script and said it had to be changed. The scene described a woman masturbating in a tub while gazing at a Calvin Klein magazine ad. Sharon said a woman wouldn't masturbate that way. I'd written the scene, but I wasn't going to fight about it. "Fine," I said to Sharon, "masturbate the way you want." But Phillip decided to draw the line. He wanted her to masturbate as I'd written. He was *the director*. That was the point.

Sharon threatened to walk off the movie and forced a meeting with Noyce in my suite at the Four Seasons. She and I sat next to each other on the couch. Phillip sat on a chair facing us. Sweat streamed down his face and from under his armpits. He was wearing a boxy suit with a black T-shirt. He was pasty-faced, his nerve endings jangling from nicotine withdrawal.

Sharon wore a flimsy, classy white dress. I wore shorts and a tank top. Phillip started talking about the "visual importance" of including the Calvin Klein ad in the masturbation scene. "You don't know what you're talking about," Sharon told Noyce. "It's a male fantasy; women don't do it that way." Phillip kept insisting.

Sharon turned to me. "Does your back hurt?" she asked. I said that it did—I'd pulled a muscle. She started to rub it as Phillip kept talking. "Get down on the rug," she said. I did, my stomach to the carpet. I noticed that Phillip wasn't talking. I noticed that Sharon was straddling my back with her legs, moving up and down. I noticed that she wasn't wearing any underwear.

She kept moving up and down, up and down. I knew she had her back to Phillip, who was watching her from the chair. I could hear Phillip breathing. The room was still. She clenched my sides tightly with her thighs, held them for a long moment, and then we both relaxed. "Better?" she asked, laughing.

I laughed and agreed that my back was much better. She got off of me and I turned. Phillip was gaping at us, his eyes huge, sweat in splotches now on his black T-shirt. He stared at the two of us for a few seconds and said to Sharon in a flat, dull tone, "Do the scene how you want."

She did it *as she wanted* through the entire shoot—not just that scene but every other one, too. *She* was the director of the movie.

She didn't like Billy Baldwin, either—"He's a geek," she said—and did the same eviscerating trip on him. She'd wipe her mouth after kissing him or rinse it with mouthwash. She bit his tongue during a kiss; he sounded cotton-mouthed the next day. Billy was feeling so intimidated about his love scenes that his performance *became* geeky and boyish. According to Billy, Sharon was acting this way toward him in revenge. Billy said Sharon had told a friend when Billy was cast, "I'm going to make that motherfucker fall in love with me so hard, he won't know what hit him." According to Billy, the fact that he wouldn't stray from his mate "really pissed her off."

The worst news for Bill Clinton, as I contemplated a "meaningful relationship" between him and Sharon, was that he wouldn't be able to cheat on her. Hillary might scratch his face, nail him in the head with a Styrofoam cup ("Bad reflexes, Bill," she said), or kick a cabinet door off its hinges . . . but Sharon would kill him. Ice pick or arsenic, he'd be a dead man. The best news for Bill Clinton was probably that his ideal woman knew a whole lot about masturbation and might help.

I suspected that in this "meaningful relationship," Sharon would be Bill and Bill would be Hillary, Sharon would be JFK and Bill would be Marilyn. But maybe Bill Clinton knew that. So that all Sharon and Bill would really do was notch each other like the old gunfighters did. Just another notch (below the belt). Yet another confirmation they were both superstars.

I introduced one of my friends to Sharon Stone once, hoping they'd fall for each other. The reason I made the introduction was because I was in love with my friend's wife. It worked. Sharon and my friend fell in love. They broke up less than a year later. I married my friend's wife and lived happily ever after. On the day I married Naomi, I fought an urge to send Sharon a dozen dead roses, but I didn't want to do that to someone I'd created . . . to someone I'd made a star . . . someone who, thanks to me, didn't even have to turn around when the president of the United States came over to say hello.

[11]

Hillary and Bill

"You know what I was thinking this afternoon?" Monica said to Linda Tripp. "Like, you know, it's so weird that when I was younger, it was such a big deal, like losing your cherry, and who do you lose your cherry to, and my God it's such a big deal. Blah blah blah. And now it's like no big fucking deal."

There was a man, the young Hillary Rodham told her parents, who unzipped himself to her and showed her his willard. There was another man who threatened her with a butcher knife as she played with her friends. There was yet another man who flung her to the ground, got on top of her, and started to kiss her until she flailed at him and he ran away.

Her parents were mystified. Park Ridge, Illinois, was a country club Chicago suburb. The white supremacist, extreme right-wing John Birch Society was strong here, in this bucolic place without Jews, Asians, Hispanics, or blacks. (Many years later, the suburb would become the district of militantly antiabortion congressman Henry Hyde, chairman of the House Judiciary Committee.) The streets were thought to be so safe that Hillary and her two brothers were allowed to walk to school. In winter, the kids ice-skated alone. Yet these things kept happening to Hillary—a willard, a butcher knife, and what sounded like near rape.

Hillary's father, Hugh, who had worked in the Pennsylvania coal mines in his youth, then stacked boxes to put himself through college, ran a mom-and-pop custom drapery company. He was the kind of man who'd never had a credit card in his life. Everything was paid for in cash—the Georgian brick house, the new Cadillac he'd trade in every year. Hugh Rodham chewed tobacco and loved Barry Goldwater. He was gruff and confrontational. When Hillary got straight A's, he said, "You must go to a pretty easy school."

He gave his kids no allowance: "They eat and sleep for free. We're not going to pay them as well." When Hillary asked him over dinner for money to see a movie, he put another potato on her plate instead. He would drive his kids through the slums sometimes to show them how lucky they were. Yet he sat at the kitchen table, helping them with their homework, and he played pinochle with them. He taught her to hit a curve ball. Her brother said she was "daddy's girl."

Her mother, Dorothy, called her husband "Mr. Difficult." (He probably would have gotten along with Monica's father, Dr. No.) Dorothy was the daughter of a fifteen-year-old mother and a seventeen-year-old father who broke up shortly after their marriage. She taught Sunday school now, but Hugh Rodham didn't go to church. Dorothy kept to herself with Hugh and her kids, organizing backyard barbecues for the family, driving the kids to school. When Hillary kept getting beaten up by an older girl in the neighborhood, it was Dorothy who taught her to fight back. It was Dorothy who told smart little Hillary she would grow up to be the first woman member of the Supreme Court. (Monica's ambition for herself was higher.) Neither Dorothy nor Hugh engaged in displays of affection the children could see, but Dorothy had an odd sense of humor. She would show up at one of Hillary's birthday parties, many years later, dressed as a nun.

As Hillary grew into an older girl, she became a jock. She played tennis, soccer, softball, and Ping-Pong. She learned to canoe. She was a pool lifeguard. Hugh Rodham, who had once been a physical education teacher and had been a part of the navy's Gene Tunney program, was pleased. When he heard that she misbehaved in school, he was always the one to spank her. Dorothy, meanwhile, never "gave her advice on clothes and makeup and how to attract boys."

Not interested in boys, Hillary joined every activity in high school. She was a member of the prom committee, the student council, the cultural values committee, the pep club, the debating team, the National Honor Society, the organizations committee, the brotherhood society, the school paper, the spring musical. The school newspaper said she was cold to other students personally, called her "Sister Frigidaire," and said she would become a nun (many years before her mother showed up at her birthday party in a nun's habit). She was known as a "teacher's pet" (as Bill Clinton, in high school, was known as a "brownnose"). She dated a boy briefly, but the relationship ended when she asked him to watch her pet rabbits and he let one of them get away. She punched him in the nose. (Bill Clinton should have taken note.)

Boys in school didn't like her. She was "womanish," they thought, not "girlish." And she had a noticeable overbite. When her girlfriends organized ear-piercing parties, she didn't go. She played Carry Nation in a school skit. Even her girlfriends thought she should "be a little cooler," with all of her many activities. At her high school awards day, her mother said she was "embarrassed" by all the many trips Hillary made up to the stage.

Working-class kids, the few whom she met, disliked her on sight. During a high school soccer game, she said, "Boy it's pretty cold" to the goalie of the opposite team.

"I wish people like you would freeze," the inner-city girl told her.

"You don't even know me," Hillary said.

"I don't have to know you to know I hate you," the girl replied.

A Methodist minister was the first strong male influence in her life besides her tobacco-chewing father. Don Jones was just out of the seminary and drove a red 1959 Chevrolet Impala convertible. He introduced her to the work of Bob Dylan and François Truffaut. He gave her a copy of *Catcher in the Rye*. Don Jones drove Hillary and the other girls in his Bible class to the Mexican migrant-labor camps outside Chicago. The girls served cupcakes and sewed dolls for the workers' kids.

He renamed the Bible class his "University of Life" and took Hillary and the other girls to hear Martin Luther King, Jr., speak. He took them to see legendary Chicago labor organizer Saul Alinsky, who was staging "fart-ins" at various companies' headquarters. He took them to poor black neighborhoods, where he flashed around a Picasso print and asked the ghetto kids what it meant to them.

Hillary loved all of it. "She seemed to be on a quest for transcendence," Pastor Jones said. But she was still urging her classmates to vote for Barry Goldwater. She also applied equal energy to her piano lessons, given at her teacher's house, in rooms filled with the stuffed and mounted dogs that had been the teacher's pets.

She went to college at Wellesley, a school for moneyed kids, one of the East Coast's Seven Sisters, fifteen miles away from Boston. She was elected president of the Young Republicans her freshman year. Wearing demure dresses, she attended the afternoon teas. She buried herself in schoolwork, writing Pastor Jones, "The last two weeks of February were an orgy of decadent indulgence." "*An orgy of decadent indulgence*" meant she was taking it easier and eating three meals a day. As a Young Republican, she was smitten with the movie star–handsome mayor of New York, John Lindsay.

She began dating a Harvard student, whom she would date for three years. It was a relationship he would later define as "romantic but platonic." That meant, in the sexually crazed sixties, that Hillary Rodham was one of the few young women on a college campus not getting laid. (Remember the classmates who said she'd be a nun? Remember her mother attending her party in a nun's habit?) In 1968, when those opposed to the war in Vietnam were flocking to the banners of Eugene McCarthy and Bobby Kennedy, she went to the Republican National Convention in Miami, not as a protester but as a participant.

But while she was still an active Republican, she was already reading things Republicans considered subversive. She neatly filed all of her copies of *motive*, a monthly publication featuring the essays of Carl Oglesby, a Marxist cofounder of Students for a Democratic Society. Besides terrorism and ritualistic witchcraft, the magazine also advocated lesbianism. Hillary amused herself at times by "playing hippie." She wore tie-dyed clothes for a month and painted flowers on her arms.

"My mind exploded at Wellesley," she would later say, but her radicalization began with a local campus issue. All the women at Wellesley signed a "vow," promising to adhere to the student handbook of conduct. Among other things, this meant being in at midnight, wearing dresses for dinner, and being subject to room checks. Hillary began a campus movement to do away with this honor system. She had buttons manufactured at her own cost and wore hers proudly: BREAK THE VOW! the button said. (Bill Clinton would have worn it.)

In her senior year, she was elected president of student government. She was now a chunky young woman with an overbite, and the target of the school newspaper for engaging in corrupt practices. "The habit of appointing friends and members of the in-group should be halted immediately in order that knowing people in power does not become a prerequisite for office holding," the paper said. She was still having her platonic relationship with her Harvard friend, dancing sometimes to the Beatles or the Supremes, but spending endless hours in the dining hall discussing politics. She resigned from the Young Republicans and told her friends she was no longer a Republican. She spoke admiringly of Eleanor Roosevelt, a former First Lady, a social activist, a bisexual, a woman whose husband died in the arms of a longtime mistress.

Hillary felt an overwhelming rage when she heard of the murder of the

Reverend Martin Luther King, Jr. Wellesley's speaker on her commencement day was Massachusetts senator Edward Brooke, a black moderate and prowar Republican, for whom Hillary had campaigned only two years ago. As student government president, she was allowed to say a few words after Brooke's speech. ("His speech was a defense of Richard Nixon," Hillary said later.) "Part of the problem with empathy," said the future First Lady, whose husband would be known for his empathy, "is that empathy doesn't do anything. We've had lots of empathy; we've had lots of sympathy. We're searching for more immediate, ecstatic, and penetrating modes of living." (*"Immediate, ecstatic, and penetrating"* . . . a mother lode for Freudian interpreters.)

Life magazine quoted from her speech and photographed her unflatteringly in oversized glasses and tight striped pants. After the publicity, she was invited to a summer conference organized by the League of Women Voters, where she met a man who would be a great help to her and to her future husband through the years, the head of the NAACP's Voter Education Project, Vernon Jordan. She debated taking a "spiritual journey" to India—the Beatles had just discovered the Maharishi Mahesh Yogi—but decided to go to law school at Yale instead. She immediately got in touch with the leaders of the antiwar movement there—one of them was Gregory Craig, who would one day defend her future husband against impeachment charges. Her dress at Yale was movement chic: an Afghan shearling coat, Levi's bell-bottoms or Vietcong-style black pajama bottoms, sandals, peasant blouses, and wire-rimmed granny glasses. She wore black armbands so often, some people thought it was her sense of style.

Hillary arrived at Yale at a feverishly revolutionary moment. Black Panther leader Bobby Seale, the future barbecue-sauce impresario, was on trial for ordering the murder of another Panther. Movement rock stars were coming to town: Huey Newton, the future cocaine magnate, as well as Tom Hayden and Jane Fonda, who clenched her fist and pumped it into the air as Huey got off his plane. (Fonda and Hayden weren't a couple yet; Fonda was there with Canadian antiwar activist and actor Donald Sutherland.) Fearing police brutality, Hillary organized a group of law students to monitor the protests and Bobby Seale's trial for the ACLU.

Trouble, when it came, didn't come from the cops. It came from the student protesters. Panther David Hilliard told a campus rally, "There ain't nothin' wrong with taking the life of a motherfucking pig." Some students started to boo. Hilliard yelled, "Boo! Boo! Boo! Boo Ho Chi Minh! Boo the Koreans! Boo the African-Americans! Boo all the suffering blacks in this country!" The students' boos got louder and Hilliard yelled, "You're a god-damned fool if you think I'm going to stand up here and let a bunch of so-called pacifists, you violent motherfuckers, boo me without getting violent with you." A foreign-exchange student started to go up onstage to say a few words, and Hilliard bloodily stomped his honky un-American ass.

Movement superstar Jerry Rubin, the future Beverly Hills real estate agent, appeared at another rally and said, "We know what work is—a dirty four-letter word. . . . Things should be free. . . . Fuck rationality; we're irrational and irresponsible. I haven't taken a bath in six months. . . . Arresting us for smoking dope is like arresting Jews for eating matzos. . . . Number one on the program is to kill your parents, who got us into this mess in the first place."

After the movement superstars left town, Hillary became a member of the editorial board of the *Yale Review*. During her term, the review published a long editorial in defense of the Panthers, illustrated with sketches of policemen as pigs. One of the captions read "Seize the time!"—the Panthers' call-to-arms slogan. In the summer of her first year at Yale Law, Hillary worked for the Children's Defense Fund in Washington, assigned to work with Senator Walter Mondale's staffers. (She met Mondale and his family, including his cute little girl, Eleanor, who would one day cause Monica Lewinsky to have a near-epileptic hissy fit when she found out that Eleanor, all grown up, was in the Oval Office with Hillary's husband.)

At the beginning of her second year at Yale, Hillary was sitting in the library, when she saw a young man staring at her. He had a boyish, scraggly beard and long hair. He was more than a little pudgy, but he had the height for it. She thought he looked like a teddy bear. She had seen him in the cafeteria weeks before, talking loudly to a group of people about Arkansas watermelons. When Hillary saw him now, staring at her as he spoke to a male friend, she went up to him. "Look," she said, "if you're going to keep staring at me and I'm going to keep staring back, we should at least introduce ourselves."

He told her about Arkansas, about the Toad Suck Daze Fair and the Hope Watermelon Festival and the Hot Springs Shriners Parade. As they got to know each other, she saw that he mostly subsisted on peanut butter sandwiches. He had a slow southern drawl, read voraciously, and made her laugh. He told outlandish stories, one about Lyndon Johnson on the Oval Office floor having sex with a girl who, at Johnson's insistence, wore a peace symbol around her neck. "Come off it, Bill!" Hillary would say, and "Cut the crap, Clinton!" They got an apartment together and he visited her parents' home, amused that Hugh and Dorothy forced him to sleep separately from Hillary, in another bedroom.

Hillary and Bill went to work for George McGovern in Texas. Bill was in Austin, working phones at party headquarters. Hillary was in San Antonio, registering Hispanic voters. They saw each other on the weekends. She didn't know that during the week he was sleeping with other women—once, three in one week.

Bill made a campaign swing with McGovern and his wife in Arkansas while Hillary stayed in San Antonio. When McGovern gave a speech at a fund-raiser held in a contributor's home, Bill bumped into his old girlfriend Dolly Kyle. They started kissing as McGovern spoke, then went outside when the candidate's speech ended and had sex in the yard.

But Bill was also telling other women how strongly he felt about Hillary and how much he missed her, away from him down there in San Antonio. He started crying to a young woman one night about how much he missed Hillary, and the young woman began consoling him . . . and one thing led to another . . . and soon he was enjoying her on top of the big conference table, with the phones going off at campaign headquarters.

Hillary was getting deeper into feminism, and Bill encouraged and supported her. She was reading a book called *The Female Eunuch* by Germaine Greer, and he flipped through it one weekend when they were together in Austin. He didn't tell Hillary that he had already met Germaine Greer in England. He had attended one of Greer's lectures. Greer said that having sex with middle-class men was always overrated and unsatisfying. When she was finished, Bill Clinton got up and asked a question. "About the overrated orgasm," he said to the future feminist icon, "in case you ever decide to give middle-class men another chance, can I give you my phone number?"

As she spent that weekend, and so many others, with him in Austin, the future First Lady of the United States was happy. Gone was her girlhood, gone the terrifying images of willards and butcher knives flashing at her, of men who forced her to the ground and got on top of her. For the first time in her life, finally, thankfully, after all these years of platonic dates, Hillary, the chubby young woman with the overbite, was in love.

There was a man making his way into her heart who would unzip himself and flash his willard . . . lots of times, to lots of other women—but not very much to her—through the course of her life.

[12]

Monica, Andy,
and Butt-head

"It's more than adequate," Monica said. "It's not, oh my God, like Andy's was, but it's—it's sizable."

"You said it was on the slender side," Linda Tripp said.

"I was comparing it to Andy's," Monica said. "Andy's is huge. Andy's is humongous."

Monica was telling one of the White House stewards, Bayani Nelvis, that she had smoked her first cigar the night before. Nel asked if she'd like one of the president's Davidoffs from his private stash. "Oh my God," she said. "Cool!" Nelvis opened the door into the president's private dining room . . . and there *he* was, standing right at the door, about to come out.

He handed some papers to Nel, asked him to take them to Leon's office, and asked her to come in.

As soon as she was inside, she stuck her hand out and mock-introduced herself.

"Monica Lewinsky," she said, "President Kiddo."

He laughed. "I know your name."

He told her he had tried to call her but had lost her phone number. Then he'd looked in the book, but he couldn't find it.

"I even spelled Lewinsky right."

"I'm unlisted."

He gave her that slow, sexy smile and said, "Well, that explains it."

"What are you doing here anyway?" he asked.

She told him about the cigar she'd smoked the night before and how she had told Nelvis and how Nelvis was going to get her one of the president's.

"I'll give you one." He smiled. He led her to his stash and handed her one.

"It's big," she said.

"I like big cigars."

"So do I," she said, looking into his eyes.

He kissed her and lifted her sweater. He fondled her breasts with his mouth. She put her hands on Willard and empowered him. She knelt down . . . and after a while, he stopped her again. This time, at least, there had been no phone call.

"Happy New Year," he said, buttoning himself up. He gave her a long, soulful kiss.

She gave him her unlisted phone number again.

"This is the last time I'm giving it to you," she said.

He went into the bathroom. She started out. She saw him through the open door. Willard was in his hand. He was bringing Willard to closure over the bathroom sink.

A week later, another Sunday afternoon, her phone rang at home. She picked it up, but there was no one on the line. It rang again minutes later, but her answering machine clicked on. The caller said nothing. She picked the phone up and said, "Hello?"

"Ah. I guess you *are* there."

She thought it was a college friend. "Yeah, I am," she said casually. "How are you? What's goin' on?"

"I don't know. You tell me."

"Holy shit!" she said. "It's you!"

He really laughed.

"Where are you? What are you doing?" she asked.

"Well, I'm going to work in about forty-five minutes."

"You want some company?"

"That'd be great." He laughed. She gave him her office extension number, and he said he'd call her. She drove through a blizzard to get there, then sat at her desk and waited. When he called, he said that she should pass by his office, casually carrying papers. He'd be out there and it would look like they'd bumped into each other.

But when she got to the Oval Office door, he wasn't there. A Secret Service agent was.

"I've got some papers for the president," she said.

The Secret Service agent led her inside. He was sitting behind his desk, smiling.

"You can close the door," he said to the Secret Service agent. "She'll be here awhile."

He asked her if she wanted something to drink. She knew what that meant by now—a move into his bathroom, off the hallway leading from the Oval Office to his private study.

He led her into the bathroom, held her, and kissed her.

"I want to go down on you," he said.

She felt as if she were going into shock. "No," she said. "Please."

"I want to go down on you," he said again, more insistently this time.

Oh my God! Oh my God! This was s-o-o-o unreal! The president of the United States wanted to go down on her! Her! Big Mac and Pig Mac and all the other awful names they had called her. She knew from reading Gennifer Flowers's book how good he was at cunnilingus.

"You can't," she said to him.

"Why not?"

"I've got my period."

"Oh no!" he said.

"I know," she said. She knelt down . . . and after a while, he stopped her.

Afterward, he was chewing on a cigar. Then he had the cigar in his hand and he was holding the wet cigar the way she'd seen him hold Willard when Willard was a little wet.

She looked at the cigar and she looked at him and she said, "We can do that, too, sometime."

He smiled.

Four or five days later, around midnight, he called.

"What are you wearing?" he asked her.

She knew what he wanted. Gennifer's book recounted how much he liked phone sex . . . how much he liked Gennifer talking dirty to him.

She talked dirty to him in her Marilyn Monroe voice. She started touching herself, and she knew he was playing with Willard. His breathing became heavier. She thought they almost came together.

"Sweet dreams," he said, and hung up.

The Sunday after they'd had phone sex for the first time, she bumped into him by the elevator in a West Wing hallway. She was having a bad hair day and wore a black beret. He asked her to join him in the Oval Office.

When they got there, she said, "Is this just about sex? Or do you have some interest in getting to know me as a person? If it's just about sex, it's okay. But you have to let me know."

He said, "What?" and laughed a little bit.

"You never even ask me questions about myself."

He looked deep into her eyes and said, "I cherish the time I have with you."

He put his arm around her and said, "I love your beret. It frames your cute little face so beautifully."

He said, "You have no idea what a gift it is to me to spend time with you and talk to you. I cherish our time together, I really do. It's very lonely here. People don't understand that."

He told her how much pain he was in—his back was hurting again, but worse than that, he said, he had just been informed of the death of the first American serviceman in Bosnia.

She felt suddenly reassured. He was such a caring and sensitive man, so obviously moved that a soldier had been killed as a result of an order he'd given.

As he moved her toward the hallway and the bathroom, she started to tell him that. But he kissed her suddenly and passionately, before she could say anything.

"I feel so stupid standing here in this dumb hat."

"It's not a dumb hat. It's a cute hat. I like it."

She knelt down . . . and then they heard someone in the Oval Office. He shoved Willard inside his pants, zipped up quickly, and hurried into the Oval Office. She had to laugh as she watched him go. Willard looked like the Alien, ready to burst through his clothes.

He ducked back out of the Oval Office and said she had to leave because he had a meeting. He whisked her through a back door to his aide Nancy Hernreich's office and gave her a deep and passionate kiss good-bye. She left and tried to go into the West Wing hallway, but the door was locked. She went back into Nancy Hernreich's office.

She was startled to see him still there, sitting on Nancy Hernreich's couch, alone, staring at nothing. He had Willard in his hand and was clo-suring himself. She watched him with Willard a moment and then she smiled and stepped to her Handsome and kissed him . . . as he kept moving Willard back and forth with his hand.

The next Sunday, February 4, she was sitting at her desk when he called her from the White House residence and told her he'd be going to the Oval Office in an hour and a half.

He said he'd call her when he was leaving the residence upstairs in the White House. She watched the clock. An hour and a half passed, then two, then two and a half . . . and just when she thought he'd blown her off, three hours later, he called.

She suggested they bump into each other "accidentally on purpose," like they had before. They "bumped into each other" in the hall and went through the Rose Garden and into the Oval Office. He walked her right back to his private study and kissed her. She was wearing a long dress that buttoned from neck to ankle. He unbuttoned all the buttons and took the dress off. She took her bra and panties off and was naked for the first time with him. But she still had her black combat boots on.

"They're just like Chelsea's," he said.

He told her how beautiful she was and put his hand between her legs. She had an orgasm and then she knelt down . . . and after a while he stopped her. They got dressed and they went back to the Oval Office.

"Are you sure this isn't just about sex?" she asked him, smiling.

His eyes seemed to her to tear up. He said, "I don't ever want you to feel that way; that's not what this is."

She told him then about Andy Bleiler. She told him that Andy was married and that she sometimes felt he was just using her sexually.

He listened closely as she talked about Andy, and when she was finished, he said, "He's such a jerk."

She felt that he really cared, that he had really listened. Before she left, she went around the side of his desk and gave him a long hug. He kissed her arm and said he'd call her.

She said, "Yeah, well, what's my phone number?"

He rattled off both her home and office numbers perfectly.

"Okay," she said, "you got an A," and left.

When she got back to her desk, her phone rang.

"I just wanted to tell you," he said, "you're a really neat person."

She felt, for the first time, that they had become friends. So she didn't understand, in the days afterward, why he didn't glance at her or smile at her when he saw her. She felt something was wrong. She was hoping he'd call her on Valentine's Day, but he didn't. When he called her at her apartment on the Monday after Valentine's Day, February 19, and she heard his voice, she knew for certain something was wrong.

"Can I come and see you?" she asked.

"I don't know how long I'm going to be here."

She drove to the White House quickly, gathered a bunch of papers at her desk, and headed for the Oval Office. She told the Secret Service agent outside his door that she had papers for the president to sign.

Handsome was sitting behind his desk. He looked pale and depressed.

He said, "Sit down, *dear.*" She hated the word *dear.* It was a word, she thought, that only old people used.

He said he had been thinking and that what was going on between them "wasn't right."

"I'm sorry," he said. "I don't want to hurt Hillary and Chelsea. I want to work on my marriage."

She started to cry and plead with him, telling him how strongly she felt about him, telling him they were good for each other and needed each other.

"No," he repeated, "this isn't right." And then he said, "I don't want to be like that schmuck in Oregon."

Andy Bleiler, she thought. *Here was the president of the United States comparing himself to Andy Bleiler!* She was sorry now she'd ever told him about Andy.

"You know," he said to her, "if I were twenty-five years old and not married, I would have you on the floor back there in three seconds."

"I don't understand!" she cried.

"You'll understand when you're older," he said. "We can still be friends." He gave her a hug and she tried to kiss him.

"We can't do that anymore," he said.

The telephone rang and he picked it up. "I've got to take this call," he said to her.

It was a sugar grower, he whispered to her, and he was about to sign legislation that would hurt the sugar industry.

"When I screw somebody" — he smiled at her — "I like to tell 'em first."

She left then, crying. She'd knelt down for him three times, she'd let him play with her body, and now he'd dumped her. *But she was in love with him!* He was Andy Bleiler all over again, saying he felt guilty about cheating on his wife and child. But that gave her some hope, too. As many times as Andy Bleiler had broken up with her because he felt guilty about cheating, he'd always come back to her to cheat some more. Her only hope now was that the president of the United States would turn out to be like Andy, who'd treated her terribly for years.

She told her mother and her aunt Debra that Handsome had ended their relationship, and, while they could plainly see her pain, they were relieved. She hadn't said a word to them about Willard; all she'd mentioned was the flirting and kissing. But they'd seen the color photograph of the president of the United States next to her bed and were worried for her.

A week after Handsome told her it was over, he called her at home. He had seen her in the hallway, he said.

"You looked so skinny," he said.

She offered to drive down to the White House right away to see him.

"I've got to help Chelsea with her homework," he said.

A week or two later, she saw him again as she was giving a girlfriend a White House tour. He was wearing blue jeans, a denim work shirt, and a baseball cap. He had been in the White House theater with Hillary. She introduced him to her girlfriend and picked pieces of popcorn off his shirt.

In late March, she cut her hand on a file cabinet and went to see the White House doctor. Next morning, she saw the doctor with Handsome, who'd been jogging and was feeling nauseous. The doctor asked her how her hand was and Handsome asked what had happened to it. He called her that night at her desk and said, "I'm sorry you hurt your hand."

He asked her, over the phone, to join him and see a movie in the White House theater. It'd be too risky, she told him. There'd be other people there.

"You're right. It *is* too risky."

"What if I see you this weekend?" she asked.

"I'll see what I can do."

That Sunday, he called her at her desk at lunchtime. The Secret Service agent led her inside the Oval Office. He wasn't there. The agent poked his head into the hallway and they heard the toilet flush. They were embarrassed. Word around the White House was that the president was suffering from an intestinal flu. He came out of the bathroom sweating, wearing blue jeans and a T-shirt. The agent left.

He kissed her as soon as the agent was gone. In his hand, he had an unlit cigar that he'd been chewing.

"I've missed you so much," he said. His fingers were deep inside her. He was still holding the chewed, unlit cigar in his other hand. He put the cigar inside her and began moving it up and down, back and forth. She had an orgasm.

He took the cigar out of her and put it into his mouth.

"It tastes good." He smiled.

He kissed and held her again. When she reached to unzip Willard, he stopped her.

She had the feeling that he "wanted to focus on me sexually." He also, of course, had the intestinal flu. She was elated as she went home that day.

Their breakup had lasted six weeks. His guilt had lasted six weeks . . . until his appetite for her overcame it. The good news was that he was just like Andy Bleiler. The bad news was that he was just like Andy Bleiler.

Five days later, on Friday, April 5, she was called into her boss's office. Timothy Keating was staff director for Legislative Affairs. He told her she was fired. Her last day would be the following Monday.

She would start Monday as an assistant at the Pentagon, writing press releases. Keating didn't use the word *fired*. He said she was merely "being given a different opportunity." But she knew what it meant.

"You're too sexy to be working here," Keating said. "The Pentagon job is much sexier."

She felt as if her world were shattering. She knew why she was being "transferred." She and Handsome had tried to be careful, tried to stay away from the windows in the Oval Office and the study, confining their fooling around to the hallway and the bathroom as much as possible. But word, she knew, always got around the White House quickly. She had been around him too much. Secret Service agents had seen her walking into and leaving his office, sometimes by the back door.

And she knew there were women on the staff, many of them Hillary's friends, some of them his former or present lovers, who were vigilant about observing who was going into his office. They were the women she called "the Meanies." She knew, too, that these women—so unlike her in style and clothing, corporate and unsmiling, religiously professional—were especially vigilant at this moment, April 1996, seven months before the presidential election. She knew the close call he'd had with Gennifer during the last election. The Meanies would make sure there was no "bimbo eruption" this time, while he ran against Bob Dole, her next-door neighbor.

And she knew how much he wanted to win against Bob Dole, who, he said, was "an evil, evil man. He likes cutting food stamps—he likes it. He enjoys cutting Medicare. He relishes slashing education. He loves cutting immigrants. It's how he gets his kicks."

She cried all weekend. He called her Sunday afternoon.

"Can I come see you?" she whimpered.

"Tell me what happened first," he said. She told him.

"I bet this has something to do with me," he said. "Okay. Come on over." He had just come back from attending Easter services with Hillary.

She knew she looked like a wreck, but she went over right away. A Secret Service agent was standing at the door as she arrived with her sheaf of cover-story papers. He wouldn't let her in. He said he'd have to check with a staff member, one of the Meanies. She said, "Please—I'll only be a couple minutes," and he relented.

Handsome looked *s-o-o-o* sad when she saw him. His friend Commerce Secretary Ron Brown had been killed in a plane crash four days earlier. She started to cry. She told him about her "transfer" again and he got angry and upset.

"Why did they have to take you away from me?" he said. "I trust you so much." He got up and hugged her for a long moment and moved her to the hallway.

"If I win in November, you can come back here just like *that!*" he said. He snapped his fingers. She felt a tiny bit better, smiling through her tears.

"Really?" she asked.

"I promise," he said. "You can have any job you want."

"Can I be the special White House assistant for blow jobs?"

He really laughed and she laughed a little bit—she was still crying, feeling "devastated."

He started kissing her and he took her sweater off. He fondled her breasts and took her breasts out of her bra. She took her bra off.

"Mr. President, you have a phone call!" someone in the Oval Office said. He broke away from her quickly and went out into the Oval Office. She put her bra and sweater back on. Then he was back suddenly, and he saw that she'd gotten dressed.

"Damn," he said. "Why did you put your clothes back on?" He was smirking at her.

He led her into the study and took the phone call. It was Dick Morris, his political adviser. As he spoke to Morris, he let his pants drop and pulled his underwear down. Handsome didn't look at her, just gazed off as she knelt down. . . . She didn't know exactly why, but this was the first time that she felt like a whore. Like she was "servicing" him. Handsome hung up and watched her with Willard. He said nothing.

He stopped her and she looked up at him.

"I'm in love with you," she told him. It was the first time she had said it.

"That means a lot to me," he said.

"Mr. President!" Harold Ickes, one of his aides, yelled in the Oval Office.

"Shit! Goddamn it!" Handsome said.

He jumped up, put his pants back on, and went running out into the Oval Office.

She put herself together quickly and went out the back through the dining room. She cried all the way home. She had lost the job she loved. The man she loved had made her feel like a whore. But she loved him still. She loved him s-o-o-o much. She didn't know as she drove home that she wouldn't see this man she loved for nearly a full year.

On the following Monday, April 15, 1996, the first day she stepped into the Pentagon, she knew she'd hate it. The place looked shabby. There were all these uniforms around. Everybody was terminally unhip. In her new job, she mostly transcribed tapes or typed up releases. She'd gone from heaven to hell.

Her world turned to darkness. She'd sit by the phone and wait for him to call. For a while, she didn't even go out, for fear she'd miss a call. He called rarely, telling her once, "Don't worry, I'm going to take care of you. You'll be okay."

Mostly, when he did call, he wanted phone sex—more active now himself, talking dirty as much as she did. He woke her up early one morning when he was at the Olympics in Atlanta and, after he'd climaxed, he said, "Good morning!" And then he said, "What a way to start the day!" From June until October of 1996, he called her eight times for phone sex.

She was having an affair by then with Ted, an older man she'd met at the Pentagon, but she was still telling all of her friends and her mother and Aunt Debra how much she was in love with the president of the United States. She was also going to a weight clinic again and making trips to the White House to take Betty Currie gifts for him: another Zegna tie, a T-shirt.

She attended government and public events, where she'd briefly glimpse him, even as she continued her affair with Ted. She waited on the sidewalk as he and Hillary were driven to church; he saw her and waved at her. She flew to New York to attend a public function at Radio City Music Hall celebrating his fiftieth birthday. She wore a red dress, and as he hurried through a mob of people, campaigning, pressing the flesh, she put her hand on Willard and pressed Willard's flesh.

She positioned herself on the sidewalk outside his hotel the next day so he could see her waving at him. She went to a fund-raiser and saw him hugging another woman at about the same time that she saw him on TV jogging with Eleanor Mondale in L.A. She went to another fund-raiser and he pointed to her as he left the room, and she thought he mouthed *I miss you.* When she wasn't with Ted, and there were no public functions to attend where she could see him, she was at home listening to Billie Holiday singing "I'll Be Seeing You."

During one of his sex calls, she told him how much she missed him and begged to see him. He said he was too busy. During another sex call, she asked him to serenade her with his saxophone over the phone on her birthday. He promised he'd call her on her birthday, but he didn't. During another sex call, she asked him when they would have intercourse.

"Never," he said.

When she asked him why not, he said, "You'll know when you're older."

She got angry at him and he said, "If you don't want me to call you anymore, just say so."

In late September, she broke up with Ted. She had discovered that Ted was sleeping with other women while telling her how much he adored her. In early October, she discovered that she was pregnant. Ted didn't even want to share the abortion cost with her. He didn't even go with her that day. She went alone, using money she'd borrowed from Aunt Debra.

On the day after Handsome was reelected, she went down to the South Lawn to join the crowd that greeted him. She wore her beret. He saw her and gave her what she considered to be a "meaningful" look.

After she saw him on the lawn, she waited for his call. Hadn't he promised that if he won the election, he'd bring her back to the White House—*just like that?* She even got her hair cut, sure that he'd make good now on his promise. She waited by the phone for days. He didn't call. She found herself crying uncontrollably.

She was scheduled to leave for a friend's wedding in Hawaii on December 2, but she postponed her departure for a day when she read that, for the first time since the election, Hillary would be out of town. It will be Handsome's last chance, she said to herself, but she wasn't always calling him Handsome now. Sometimes she called him "the Creep." Sometimes she called him "the Big Creep." Sometimes she called him "Butt-head." If he didn't phone her now, she'd change her phone number. She remembered what Gennifer had called him: "a flat, two-dimensional piece of hardened paper, empty of all feelings."

He called her around 9:30 p.m. It had been six weeks since she'd even heard his voice on the phone.

"Hi," he said. "It's Bill; I've got laryngitis."

He said, "I wish I were there and could put my arms around you." He told her he missed her and asked her to come to see him at the White House the next day. She told him she couldn't—she had to go to her friend's wedding in Hawaii and her ticket wasn't refundable.

He started having phone sex and told her he wanted her to do the talking. She used her Marilyn Monroe voice. She heard a strange noise on the other end. At first, she thought he was climaxing, but then she realized it wasn't *that* sound. She listened. He was *snoring*.

She went to her friend's wedding, got a great tan, and then flew to Portland to see Andy Bleiler. Andy sneaked away from Kate and they shared a day in her motel room. Andy told her that he'd been cheating on his wife with another woman for more than a year.

She'd been worried about pain during intercourse since her abortion two months before and wanted to try sex first with a familiar lover. Her day at the motel with Andy proved to her that she was healed, and she flew back to Washington.

She thought about her relationship with the president of the United States. Interrupted in the hallway and the bathroom by phone calls. Interrupted by aides. Interrupted by knocks on the door. He couldn't go down on her because she was having her period. She couldn't see him because he was out campaigning. She couldn't see him because Hillary was in town. She couldn't see him because Eleanor Mondale was in there. She couldn't see him because her Hawaii ticket wasn't refundable. Then his back hurt. Then he had intestinal flu. Then he broke his leg and was on crutches. Lloyd Bentsen was waiting outside. Asshole Arafat was waiting outside. She couldn't even do him with Altoids. She came in chewing them and they kissed, but he didn't have time. President Zedillo was waiting for dinner.

Some relationship, she thought, "foreplay to the foreplay." The Creep. The Big Creep. Butt-head. She remembered how he'd left Gennifer a T-shirt to hold through the night, after he'd gone hurrying home to Hillary. Monica didn't even have anything to hold. All she had was his photograph on her nightstand.

She was depressed, but she looked forward to seeing the new friend she'd made at the Pentagon. She was sure this was going to be a lifelong friendship. She was convinced her new friend cared about her. Her name was Linda Tripp.

[13]

Monica Feels His Pain

"I would have believed it about any president," Monica said.

"Well, I wouldn't have believed it of George Bush," Linda Tripp said. "He was like a grandfather."

"He had a girlfriend."

"He did not!"

"He did too!"

"Oh, I don't believe that," Linda said. "He was such a—a—old fellow."

The former First Lady was gone and he lived alone in the big house near New York City that they had bought together. He felt himself to be an old man, peeing so many times each day, staring out the living room window sometimes at the snow, with only Monica for company. Who would have thought that at his age he would be spending much of his time with her . . . with Monica, still so young, still in school trying to get her doctorate in . . . foreign affairs. She even summarized the Sunday-morning talk shows for him.

Monica didn't live at the house—he'd had enough of scandal—but she lived close by and came up to the house all the time. Once he even went over to her apartment, and the former president of the United States sat down at the piano with Monica and they sang "Happy Days Are Here Again" together. Sometimes they just talked. He sat in his chair in his study, his foot up on the ottoman, grapefruit juice or white grape juice at his side, pointing his eyeglasses at her or twirling them, biting his pen or clutching his fist to make a point, using the old-time phrases he knew she thought were outdated, things like "Right on" or "Not my bag."

He talked a lot about his mother. "She sacrificed everything for us," he told Monica. "She worked like a dog through pain and tears." He served Monica drinks sometimes—the "Asian martini" he'd first tasted in Singapore, the Chinese mai tai, "so strong it can kill you."

"You're giving me something that can kill me?" Monica laughed.

"You're young," he told her. "You can take it." She knew how consumed he was with the difference in their ages.

"I look damn old," he said to her. "I see how young you are and I— well . . . I see some of my contemporaries and they look so bad."

He told her, "You have your whole life ahead of you. Mine is all past, behind me."

On another occasion he said, "Monica, you need something to live for. Everybody does: countries do, people do. And everyone should maintain a youthful spirit. Sometimes it's hard to do, but, Monica, you must. Otherwise aging will just get you down and defeat you."

Sometimes, when he was in a mood like this, she was able to make him laugh. "I'm in pretty good shape," he admitted to her once. "I don't drink. I don't smoke. I don't play cards anymore. What do I do?"

"Nothing fun," Monica said.

When he was presented with a fortune cookie on an airline flight, he handed it to her and asked her to open it and read it to him. He smiled when she read, " 'Your mentality is alert and analytical.' "

She knew, though, that when she wasn't with him, he was mostly alone, cooking up cans of chili for himself, nibbling his sesame-seed bread sticks, toasting hot dog buns so he could feel himself there at the ballpark as he watched a game on TV. When she joined him for chili, he laid out the fine china himself. He spent most of his days writing his books, worried that he'd been discredited by the scandal, wondering if people still had any respect for him. "I can write op-ed pieces until I'm blue in the face," he told her. When he wasn't working on his books, she helped him. He'd always listened to her ideas; he was reading. Not as much about politics— "It's a dirty and cynical business, always has been and always will be"—as about philosophy.

"I can't find my book!" he said to her once, upset. "I can't believe I'm missing my Nietzsche!" He told her, "Most of the time, I can't make out a goddamn thing in this stuff." He philosophized to her, as well: "I believe that man is both good and bad, light and dark. The evil, though, overrides the good in certain situations because although man has the potential to be good, his inherent evil tends to overwhelm him at times." And: "I think we have to wait until we die to know the answers. I really do. Peace comes with death." She didn't like it when he talked to her like that. "There are so many books left to read," he told her. "My time is running out. You have a lot of time left. I don't." She liked it better when he told her, chuckling, about the philosophers themselves: Rousseau had all kinds of bastard kids; Marx was a drunk who fell down in the gutters. The older he got, Monica noted, he, who'd masterfully worked so many rooms, wanted to have less to do with people. "Why bullshit with people?" he said. "It takes time away from the great books."

Monica loved traveling with him, sitting there and watching him with the leaders of the new world, staying in guest houses and luxury suites provided by the host governments, sleeping just down the hall but always available for his call. When she went to his suite on their trips abroad, he would invariably point to the ceiling and put a finger over his mouth, warning her that they could be listening to or watching them. The two of them occasionally ran into bumps during their travels. The new president of Israel had looked at her suspiciously and said, "Can we trust her?" and the president of Latvia had stood him up for a meeting, and she saw once again her ex-president's old fire-burst of temper. "Goddamn!" he said to her. "I did not come all the way out here to be stood up or to see second-tier people! I am not staying another minute! Let's go! Now!"

But he still had his soft and romantic side, as well. Walking at night in Anchorage together, he stopped and said, "Look how the lights sparkle out here. The colors . . . are just spectacular. Everything up here is either light green or blue. I know people love New York, but after seeing this, we've got to wonder why we go back to the goddamn place." In Moscow, he stooped down and threw a snowball at her. Then he let her decide whether they were going to Prague or Budapest next. She picked Prague, and he said, "It's magical, you'll be overwhelmed." In Saint Petersburg, the mayor asked why Monica wasn't wearing a scarf in the bitter chill. The former president of the United States answered for her: "She's one of those indestructible types." At the Guangzhou market in China, he tapped her on the nose and said, "Be careful of these people approaching you and trying to sell you things. Not everyone out there is nice." And in Tokyo, he told her, "Monica, you must never get tired of these places, even if you come back a thousand times. This is your first time here, so it's all new and exciting. But when you return, you must look at these places as if you were looking at them for the first time."

There was a moment with him in Beijing that Monica would never forget. As soon as they saw him in the street, the crowds were all over him, tugging at him, touching him, adoring him. Watching him basking in it, glorying in it, taking what he later called a "people bath," Monica thought, Just knowing somewhere in the world he is revered absolutely gives him a sense of gratification and vindication. They went from the streets into a teahouse and he swayed to the music. He picked up a tambourine near the stage and started playing it. The former president of the United States, disgraced because of his lies . . . and here he was so many years later, loved by the crowds, with Monica near him, Monica there to share this moment of epiphany.

Sometimes on their trips, it seemed that he just needed to see her. He called her to his suite at midnight, and when she got there, his room was dark except for a small desk lamp. He was in pajamas and a robe. "Oh, hi," he said. "I couldn't sleep." On a plane ride back home, he whispered, "Monica?"

She said, "What's wrong?"

He said, "Oh, nothing. Were you sleeping?"

When she couldn't accompany him on a Moscow trip because of her grad school finals, he called her excitedly, even twice a day. "Monica?" he said. "I can't believe that I got through to you! I just punched in your number and hoped for the best! Well, it's five a.m. here, but I've got insomnia, so I thought I'd call and fill you in." In another call, he said, "I know how much you love this city. I wish you weren't in school. The stopover in London was well worth it. It was beautiful. They are further along in spring than we are. The crocuses and forsythias are out, blooming like mad." He called her, too, when he fell down in the Moscow streets. "I scraped my knee and hit my rib," he said. "It hurts when I breathe. I don't know what happened. I just sort of lost my balance and slipped. . . . I guess the stars just weren't with me this time around."

Back home, she was with him at Halloween, his favorite holiday. She watched as he went out into the yard of the big house, handing candy out and talking to the neighborhood kids, masked there, waiting for him. A father wearing a mask in the likeness of the former president's face came up to him, and he laughed and said to the father, "Well, Mr. President, it's nice to meet you." The father's son got a good laugh out of it, and Monica saw that he was having as much fun being out here with the kids as all the trick-or-treaters.

Monica was with him at Radio City Music Hall for the annual Christmas show. She watched him watch the reenactment of the birth of Christ. The narrator said that Christ died at the hands of His enemies, but every human being had been affected by that "one solitary life." As Monica watched him, she saw that he, who had had so many enemies, whose life had affected hundreds of millions of others, was crying.

Three weeks before he died, he spent the day in New York with the daughter he loved so much. People everywhere were stopping him and asking him for autographs, but what meant so much, he told Monica, was that his daughter was there to see it.

"It was just nice . . . knowing that she was right there to see it all and . . ."

"Share it with you," Monica said.

"That meant a lot," Richard Nixon, eighty years old, told his twenty-two-year-old research and foreign relations assistant, Monica Crowley.

[14]

Kathleen and the Ratwoman

"I said something about Marsha Scott," Monica said. "He said—'She was my girlfriend in like 1968' or something like that, just a stupid thing like that."

"Oh, yes," Linda Tripp said, "he banged her on the canal or something."

"Yeah."

"Oh, how gross!"

U p onstage already were Monica and Paula Jones and Gennifer . . . and now, out of the darkened wings, came not trailer trash or Beverly Hills bimbo but a classy, intelligent, and attractive socialite, Kathleen Willey, doing a "pity me" monologue about yet another unwanted groping in that bordello hallway between the Oval Office and the private study.

Even as the pundits feverishly forecast "the other shoe" that was surely soon to drop, it seemed suddenly that it had. Within weeks, however, Willey's monologue was exposed as a selective and suspect account. The victim of the groping stood revealed as an upscale, scheming, former stewardess trying to make a buck by offering her well-kept body to Bill Clinton, who rarely turned a body down. Backstage, whispering, sharpening her fangs, was Monica's new "lifelong" friend at the Pentagon, Linda Tripp, the Ratwoman.

Kathleen Willey, who enjoyed skiing in Vail and sunning in Bermuda, met Bill Clinton in 1991, with her husband, Ed, a prosperous real estate lawyer. She and Ed set up the state of Virginia's first Clinton campaign headquarters. When the candidate flew into Richmond for a debate with George Bush and Ross Perot, Willey went to greet him at the airport with a group of other Democrats. Nancy Hernreich, then Clinton's office manager in Little Rock, went up to Willey at the airport and told her Clinton wanted her phone number. Willey gave it to her. Moments earlier, news cameras had caught Willey hugging Clinton and Clinton then turning to an aide to ask who she was.

Bill Clinton called her at home that afternoon. He had a bad cold. "It was really good to see you," he said.

"It sounds like you need some chicken soup," she said.

"Would you bring me some?" he asked.

"Well, I don't know about that," Willey said.

Aides came into his hotel room and he told Willey, "I'll have to call you back. I'll call you at six."

When he called at six, Willey had a friend there with her named Julie Hiatt Steele. She asked Julie to listen in on their conversation. Willey told him she couldn't take him his chicken soup. She'd see him at a fund-raiser after the debate that night.

On election night, Willey and her husband, Ed, flew to Little Rock to celebrate Bill Clinton's victory. A few months later, in April 1993, Kathleen Willey became a volunteer at the White House Social Office. She commuted from her home in Richmond three times a week. She organized White House tour groups. She recruited high school bands to play there. She helped plan the White House Jazz Festival.

Kathleen Willey had made her move by then on Bill Clinton, no doubt regretting the chicken soup she hadn't taken him. Like Monica later, she sent him a tie. Like Monica later, she gave him a book—its title as intriguing as *Vox*, the phone-sex book Monica would send him. Willey's book was entitled *Honor Among Thieves*. Like Monica later, she called Bill Clinton to wish him a happy birthday. She sent him a handwritten note inviting him to spend his winter vacation in Vail. She added that she was going to be there in mid-December and offered to help make travel arrangements for him. She never mentioned her husband.

As she was writing her notes and calling Bill Clinton, Kathleen Willey was in the throes of a personal nightmare. Ed had been caught embezzling $340,000. Ed's victims and the law were after him. Kathleen Willey, who knew a lot about living well, was going broke.

The Ratwoman had been watching her by then.

The Ratwoman knew how she felt about Bill Clinton by then.

The Ratwoman had become her friend by then.

Linda Tripp, forty-three years old, was a "floater" in the White House secretarial pool. She had worked for George Bush and had been inherited by Bill Clinton. She was the ex-wife of a career soldier, a lieutenant colonel, who had dumped her and left her with two college-age kids. Thanks to her ex-husband, Linda Tripp had worked the dark side of the Pentagon. She had even been assigned to the supersecret antiterrorist Delta Force. She knew about black-bag operations and had a top secret clearance. She was a creep and a spook.

And here she was now, in the Clinton White House, among people she loathed—people who cussed and wore blue jeans and acted like the White House were a college campus. She was a dumpy, stiffly conservative spy among attractive, sexual young people who had taken over the government. A woman who'd been cruelly dumped by her husband, she seemed to have a special loathing for Bill Clinton, the star of the show. She knew all about the women on the White House staff—"the graduates" who went into his office and did things to him and for him that she would never be called upon to do.

So Linda Tripp began wooing, ingratiating herself with, Kathleen Willey, the volunteer worker who seemed to have a special relationship with Bill Clinton. The former Pentagon black-bagger just happened to be at the right place at the right time, working near Kathleen, just as she'd been at the right place at the right time with Vince Foster, her desk right outside Foster's office, the last person to see him before he drove down to the park to shoot himself. *In the right place at the right time . . .* to later claim that she saw Hillary's Rose Law Firm billing records among Foster's files.

Linda Tripp fawned all over Willey, praising her hairdo, her dresses, even her deep voice. She filled Willey in on her black-bag scoops, pointing out the staffers who were among "the graduates" who were intimately satisfying Bill Clinton's needs. Tripp told Willey how outraged she'd been when she was sent down to McDonald's to get a cheeseburger for the president (a frightening image in retrospect—the Ratwoman, who loathed Bill Clinton, bringing him his fat-poisoned food). She told Willey constantly that the president was romantically interested in her: "Look at him, Kathleen. He's looking right at you and nobody else in the room."

Kathleen Willey's life, meanwhile, was coming apart. She and Ed desperately needed money. She was only a volunteer at the White House; she needed to be paid. On November 29, 1993, she went to see Bill Clinton in the Oval Office. She sat down across from him.

"I've got something I need to talk to you about," she said. He asked if she wanted a cup of coffee and led her . . . into the hallway . . . to his private study. He poured her a cup of coffee in a Starbucks mug. He showed her around the private study and displayed his political button collection (as he would with Monica).

"I've got a really serious problem," she told him. "I need to talk to you. There's something going on in my life. Ed has gotten himself into some financial trouble, and I'm really kind of desperate. The bottom line is, I need a job."

She was crying. Suddenly embarrassed, she turned from him and walked away . . . into the hallway . . . and tried to open the closed hallway door that led back to the Oval Office. Bill Clinton, behind her suddenly, hugged her.

"I'm really sorry this happened to you," he said. He kissed her. They were still in the hallway. She still had the hot Starbucks mug of coffee in one hand. He ran his hands through her hair. She was afraid she'd spill the coffee.

"You have no idea how much I wanted you to bring me that chicken soup," he said.

She said, "Aren't you afraid there are people around here? What if somebody comes in?"

He had his arm above her head. He looked at his watch. He said, "Yeah, I've got a meeting. But I can be late." He took the Starbucks mug out of her hand and put it on a shelf.

"I've wanted to do this since the first time I laid eyes on you," he said.

He kissed her again. He felt her breasts and her back and put his hand up her skirt. He put her hands on Willard. Willard was erect. Bill Clinton's face was beet red.

Then, his nightmare of nightmares—*why did this keep happening again and again?*—some idiot of a damn fool started knocking on the hallway door, yelling, "Mr. President! Mr. President!"

"I've got to go!" Kathleen Willey said. "You've got a meeting." She grabbed the Starbucks mug back off the shelf and walked through the Oval Office and out the door.

She went straight to the Ratwoman's desk. "Where's your lipstick?"

Linda Tripp said. They went outside and sat by a picnic table on the White House lawn. Willey told her what had happened. "I could always tell the president wanted you," Linda Tripp said.

Willey went back to Richmond and told her friend Julie Hiatt Steele what had happened. But she had another, much more critical problem. Ed wasn't at the office and he wasn't home. She and Julie looked everywhere and couldn't find her husband. The next morning, police found Ed's body. He had committed suicide. Kathleen Willey lost it. Julie had to put her in a hospital.

When she got out of the hospital, in dire straits, she got a job as a secretary in the White House counsel's office, working right alongside of Tripp, also in the counsel's office. Kathleen Willey started sending Bill Clinton affectionate and supportive notes again. But now she had another pressing problem — and so did Tripp. A new counsel was coming in, and that meant new secretarial staff could come with him. The Ratwoman and Willey went to see the new counsel, Lloyd Cutler, together. They told Cutler, the most veteran of Washington operatives, that *they* could help *him* maneuver his way around the politics and bureaucracy of the White House.

When Cutler took over, he said he was keeping Willey at her job temporarily but was letting Tripp go. The Ratwoman nearly hemorrhaged! Willey, this inept, spoiled socialite who could barely run a computer, was staying on? Was getting *her* job? *Why?* Because the president of the United States thought Willey was a sexy babe and knew Tripp wasn't? The same old Clinton standards . . . a pair of nice tits and a sweet ass meant more than a woman with job experience, a woman who'd worked with Delta Force.

"Don't you think for one moment I don't know what's going on around here!" Tripp yelled at the inept, spoiled socialite she now hated. "Don't you think I don't know why I'm getting fired and you're getting my job!"

"What are you talking about?" Willey said.

"I know they want you because the president wants you around," Tripp said.

As Linda Tripp walked out of the office on her last day, she turned to Willey and said loudly enough so others could hear it, "I will get you, if it's the last thing I do."

Out of the White House, stuck in a cubicle at the Defense Department, planning celebrity trips to defense bases, Linda Tripp raged and kept tabs on Kathleen Willey. Willey, she learned, was soon out of the White House and was now working for the State Department, flying to glamorous places like

Jakarta and Copenhagen at taxpayers' expense. The State Department! This former stewardess, who'd been organizing White House tours two years ago! Who couldn't even run a computer! But who'd let the president of the United States feel between her legs and had said nothing about it!

In August 1997, the story about the incident in the hallway between the president of the United States and Kathleen Willey made its way into the papers. Willey initially didn't speak to the press. Her story got out through leaks from one of Paula Jones's attorneys. In the beginning, Willey fled from any kind of publicity.

Her story was discredited after she did a nationally traumatic interview with 60 *Minutes*, recounting in low-key, classy, socialite terms what had happened in the hallway leading to the private study. The White House had simply released the affectionate and supportive notes she had sent to Bill Clinton before *and* after the incident.

Her story was discredited in another crucial way . . . by the Ratwoman, who had said, "I will get you, if it's the last thing I do." Yes, Tripp told the press, Willey had come right to her after leaving the Oval Office that day. But Willey, Tripp said, wasn't shaken or upset. She was "excited." Willey had been after Bill Clinton ever since she'd come to the White House. Willey was a "woman on a mission." As they spoke out by the picnic table that day, Tripp said, Willey had wanted her advice on "the next step" in her now-blossoming "relationship" with the president. In no way was this, Linda Tripp said, "sexual harassment." The fact that Linda Tripp was saying this, a person who admitted to an intense dislike of Bill Clinton, was the final factor in the discrediting of Kathleen Willey's story.

What no one at the time knew was that the entire story had been leaked thanks to an anonymous phone call to one of Paula Jones's lawyers. The caller, who sounded like a middle-aged woman, told the lawyer all the details of the incident in the hallway and gave him Kathleen Willey's name. The lawyer leaked the information to a reporter.

Linda Tripp, though no one would ever prove it, had pulled off a black-bag op worthy of the best (or worst) of Delta Force. She began it with an anonymous phone call. She publicly humiliated Bill Clinton with the public revelation of his sleazy sexual behavior, this time with an emotionally distraught woman seeking his aid. She humiliated Kathleen Willey by exposing her as a woman willing to use her body for money. And she made herself look publicly noble by defending the president, whom everyone knew she loathed, against sexual harassment charges.

But by the time the press spoke to her about Kathleen Willey, the Ratwoman was gnawing a bone tastier and more rancid than any of the others. *In the right place at the right time* . . . first with Vince Foster, then with Kathleen Willey . . . and now with a young woman she had met in the office at the Pentagon, a young woman very much Bill Clinton's type. A young woman who had been a White House intern. Linda Tripp crunched her bone and knew that this one came from right under Bill Clinton's soft white underbelly. The Ratwoman smelled roast pig.

[15]

Nixon Impregnates Monica

"The age difference between us," Monica said to Linda Tripp.
"I should tell him I have hearing aids too."

Nixon's Monica—Crowley—didn't go down on him. She took notes and ran to her secret diary after their conversations. But by doing that, by giving us the details of the insomniac Night Creature stewing, plotting, and clenching his fist in his palatial New Jersey crypt, she pleased Nixon at least as thoroughly as Monica Lewinsky had pleased Bill Clinton.

Joyfully turning her loose (or out) on the world was Nixon's former speechwriter, William Safire, clothing himself now in the priestly vestments of the *New York Times*, encouraging her to recount the details of what Nixon had said to her to seduce her into being his trick on posterity. Monica Crowley thanked Safire for "his wise counsel and kind support." Monica Crowley took it all in and Nixon let it all hang out.

But who could ever have imagined a fact as revealing as the Night Creature's admission to his Monica that Halloween was his favorite holiday? Hounds howl, fangs flash in the crepuscular Jersey night on All Soul's Eve . . . and the Night Creature tells Elvira—no, no, Monica!—that he looks *"ghostly"* on TV, that George Bush is a *"bloodless"* Wasp, that Janet Reno is a "partisan *witch."*

In 1992, as the election with George Bush, Bill Clinton, and Ross Perot approached, the Night Creature aimed his acidy venom in frothing, bitter, geyserlike eruptions. At George Bush: "Goddamnit, why isn't he showing some leadership? . . . He's a man consumed with petty crap. . . . He's up there in New Hampshire petting cows and raving about God knows what. . . . He's a mushy moderate. . . . I cannot believe that Bush said, 'We'll kick Saddam's ass,' can you picture Gorbachev saying, 'We'll kick the Republic's ass'? . . . *I think Bush's handlers are on drugs.* . . . I heard him say the other day 'A splash of Tabasco!' 'A splash'? In my day, I heard everyone saying, 'Wait a sec.' What the hell is a sec? . . . He tries too hard to be one of the people, eating pork rinds and the rest, but he's not. . . . Bush was soft on the whole war in Vietnam." Ross Perot, he told his Monica, was "a demagogue, an egomaniac. He doesn't keep his word. He doesn't say what he means." Jesse Jackson "just likes to be around controversy. He's shrewd." Congresswoman Nancy Pelosi was "a jerk," Secretary of State James Baker "an ass," and reporter Bob Woodward "that asshole." Gerry Ford was "Poor Gerry Ford. The pardon was the kiss of death." Lyndon Johnson "invited the press into his bathroom." Republican adviser David Gergen "had no problem prostituting himself. He believes in nothing." Future Secretary of Commerce Ron Brown and Illinois congressman Dan Rostenkowski were "corrupt up to their eyeballs."

The Night Creature's fist shot into the air and he yelled *whamo* when he spoke about Massachusetts senator John Kerry: "Here's a guy who was carrying placards in front of the White House and protesting. *That son of a bitch threw his medal over the fence at the White House.* Here I was trying to end the goddamn war so that his service wouldn't be in vain, and he's throwing his medal back at me!" His fist went *whamo*, too, when he thought about Bush chief of staff John Sununu—"Sununu? For God's sake! Who the hell is he?"—and of his fellow Republicans—"Very few of our goddamn people are any good! *No one stands up to take the bastards on!* They don't have any guts!"

The Night Creature was as bitter now as he had been in the sixties about "all the libs out there" and "the little bastards and assholes in the media" and "the orgy over the Watergate crap." He said, "Look what the press did to me, the Herblock cartoons and whatnot. . . . They put the lies in the headlines but the truth they put back with the corset ads. . . . Seventy-eight percent of the media voted for McGovern." He referred to Watergate as "the Watergate bullshit . . . that silliness . . . that silly, silly thing. . . . I think they just love to wallow in this Watergate crap until they drown . . . who cares about Watergate anymore? It belongs maybe on one of the history channels but not on a major network." He was as scarily paranoid now, it was clear, as he had been in the sixties. "Those who were after me for Watergate were after me for a long time. They weren't interested in Watergate as much as they were interested in getting me on Vietnam. I gave them what they needed, but believe me, Watergate was just the excuse. . . . One of the greatest tragedies of Watergate was that I couldn't build the new conservative majority. And I was going to start with newspaper reporters. I was going to get conservatives in there to take these people on. That's why in '72 they had to bring me down. They knew I was after them and that I'd succeed."

Sitting there, in the fetid darkness of his study, wearing his burgundy dinner jacket, the Night Creature spun furry spiderwebs as explanation for what he had done. The devil may have caused the infamous eighteen-and-a-half-minute gap in the deadliest Watergate tape, but JFK and LBJ had caused Watergate itself: "I never wanted to accept the fact that there is a double standard out there. Democrats survive by it, Republicans get killed by it. Kennedy could be as dirty as they come—and my God! He did some outrageous things in there! But he was protected. Johnson—same thing, although to a lesser degree because he wasn't a Kennedy. Somehow I made the mistake of thinking or maybe not even thinking—maybe it was an unconscious thing—that I could act like them."

Forget his political death; ignore the grimy stake in his heart: The Night Creature knew that he could still run this country. "*Any effective leader has got to be a son of a bitch.* You have to instill the fear of God in your people to get results. . . . *To be credible, you have to bomb the bejesus out of countries.* . . . War has to be cast in idealistic terms or there is no way the people are going to support it. In Korea, we were fighting the Commies. In Vietnam, it was harder to get the message across. . . . The war in the Gulf was well-run, but I'm afraid it was too short and, frankly, even though one casualty is too much, *this one had too few casualties* . . . There is no grand thinking going on. We need more vision stuff, more mountaintop stuff. . . . We should get the CIA to take out Saddam. . . . I don't go for this exporting democracy crap. *Democracy doesn't belong everywhere.* Not all societies or cultures are meant for it."

He knew the swamp rats who could rebuild his America: Newt Gingrich: "He's a bomb thrower and we need him." . . . Dan Quayle: "He's so right on." . . . His former speechwriter Safire: "just a good guy." . . . And former speechwriter Pat Buchanan: "He's a bulldog. He'll go after them." The Night Creature, whose Oval Office meetings had been punctuated with so many racist and anti-Semitic epithets, went out of his way to defend Buchanan: "Buchanan's worried because he has been tagged as anti-semitic, which is totally untrue and unfair. The guy is just not that way."

And he reserved a special slimy passion, which was obviously reciprocal, for Bob Dole: "Damn impressive . . . he is the last great hope for the party in this century."

Over and over again, the Night Creature praised Bob Dole. "He's a class act, simple and honest. . . . Dole is the only one who can lead. He is by far the smartest politician—and Republican—in the country today. . . . Dole is a man of principle, but in an election year he would not be so stupid as to support what he believed was a losing position."

Dole relied on the Night Creature for advice and Nixon became, according to Monica, "Dole's chief, though shadow advisor." "Stay young!" Nixon advised Dole, and he named world leaders who had excelled in their seventies—de Gaulle, Audenauer, Chou En-lai. Nixon wrote a nine-page draft called "The Dole Game Plan" for the 1996 election. He told Dole he had to make "character" the great issue of the campaign. "The character issue will help him tremendously against Clinton," Nixon told Monica, "basically because Clinton has little or no character." The Night Creature saw the war hero from Kansas as his soul brother, even though Nixon had not done much more than play poker during his war. "There is no one but Dole!" Nixon shouted at Monica. At another moment, he said, "Dole is the only one out there swinging."

Bob Dole had always been out there swinging, Richard Nixon knew, agreeing for once with Barry Goldwater's assessment: "Dole's the first man we've had around here in a long time who will grab the other side by the hair and drag them down the hill." *Grab them by the hair and drag them down the hill!* That was Dole all right, who responded to a colleague's proposal to cut the food stamp program by saying, "Do you put in a burial allowance for the ones who starve?" . . . Dole, who told an amputee that he was jealous after the amputee pointed to Dole's mangled arm at a VA hospital and asked, "Why don't you cut the damn thing off?" And it looked, the Night Creature thought, like Dole's wife, Elizabeth, had the same kind of piss and vinegar in her, too.

Small-town boys from Yorba Linda, California, and Russell, Kansas, they went way back together. Nixon appreciated Dole's odd sense of history. Dole liked to point out, for example, that he'd been wounded in combat "eighty years to the day after Abe Lincoln took *his* bullet." Nixon chuckled when Dole told him that the day he was born, the train carrying the disgraced Warren G. Harding's body passed through his hometown.

It was Nixon who'd saved Dole in a difficult race in Kansas by campaigning heavily for him and it was Dole who'd slashed away at the *Washington Post* during Watergate, saying, "The greatest political scandal of this campaign is the brazen manner in which, without benefit of clergy, the *Washington Post* has set up housekeeping with the McGovern campaign. . . . The most intensive journalistic rescue and salvage operation in American politics." Dole added, "There is a cultural and social affinity between the McGovernites and the *Post* executives and editors. They belong to the same elite, they can be found living cheek by jowl in the same neighborhood, and hobnobbing at the same Georgetown parties. . . . The Republican Party has been the victim of a barrage of unfounded and unsubstantiated allegations by George McGovern and his partner in mud-slinging, the *Washington Post*." That was loyalty all right, referring to Watergate as "unfounded" and "unsubstantiated," trying to make Nixon's campaign of lies and illegal acts seem as though he were being victimized by what Nixon called "all the Libs out there." Dole was out there swinging all right, showing the effects of all the DDT he'd inhaled growing up in the farm fields of Kansas.

Years later, when the Night Creature was buried, it was his soul brother who delivered the eulogy, just as he'd delivered Pale Pat's. "How American?" Bob Dole said of Richard Nixon. "A boy who heard the train whistle in the night and dreamed of all the distant places that lay at the end of the track. . . . The grocer's son who got ahead by working harder and longer than anyone else." Bob Dole said, "The second half of the twentieth century will be known as *the Age of Nixon*." And then Bob Dole broke down and sobbed.

As election day 1992 drew closer, the Night Creature was gushing pure bile aimed directly at Bill Clinton: "He's as weak as piss on a rock. . . . He's a goddamned liar. . . . He's a pretty boy who doesn't quite have it together, a waffler and an opportunist. . . . He's a phony baloney. . . . He has little or no character. . . . He's so damned smug. . . . He's a clever bastard. . . . He's Dogpatch. . . . He's damaged merchandise, he's got McGovern's crowd as advisors. . . . He's on media steroids and Bush's people are a bunch of boy scouts. . . . We all have our weaknesses, human nature being what it is. We all succumb to something: Maybe power, maybe money, maybe women or booze or drugs. In Clinton's case, all of the above."

From the Night Creature's shadowy point of view, Bill Clinton seemed his bête noire. Bill Clinton was the symbol and personification of the generation that had driven him from office. "If Bush loses to Clinton, he will have erased my '72 victory because that was a referendum on Vietnam. A Clinton victory will reverse that by saying that it was okay to have actively opposed the war. . . . If Clinton wins, he will have opened up the office to all those who otherwise would have been disqualified, as late as 1988, with Gary Hart. Most in the media, though, are just like him. They are sympathetic with him on Vietnam; they experimented with drugs and casual sex. . . . Clinton is all for recognizing Vietnam. He's just panting to go to Hanoi and walk through the streets, where he'll be welcomed by millions of Vietnamese. Imagine! *The ultimate Vietnam war draft dodger recognizing Vietnam!* Unbelievable! . . . It's not that he was against the war then—almost everyone his age was. It's the fact that he says he's still against it. Clinton still thinks that North Vietnam's cause was more just. . . . I know why he did what he did to dodge the draft; he didn't want to get his ass shot off. As I was out there trying to end the goddamn war, he was running around, claiming privilege, avoiding service, and demonstrating against it. He was a selfish, spoiled brat. He made my job so much harder, and he sent God knows how many men to their death in his place. I'll tell you one thing; if he is elected President, I will know that this country has finally gone to hell."

Only weeks before the election, the Night Creature, architect of so many hellish events, knew hell was fast approaching. The polls were showing Bill Clinton with a sizable lead. "The only things," he told his Monica, "that would be self-destructive to him now would be bombshells, like a letter that showed that he asked to renounce his American citizenship during Vietnam, or an illegitimate child."

Even as he pondered the miraculous October surprise of a bastard child, the Night Creature found himself with mixed feelings about Hillary. He knew he should have hated her—Hillary, who had been part of the House Judiciary Committee that had forced him from office—and in some ways he did. Hillary "was frightening, her ideas way out there. . . . I still can't believe it! She was on the goddamn committee to impeach me! She's a radical! . . . If she gets in, whoa! Everybody had better fasten their seat belts . . . her eyes are ice cold. . . . She really believes this liberal crap. . . . The people around her are all to the radical left. They are going to doom her." But in other moments, he found himself respecting her, admiring her. "How could she sit there next to him on *60 Minutes* knowing what she does about his running around? Humiliating! But she has a higher agenda. She is very sharp, and she just wants to win the goddamn election. Take a little humiliation now and get power later. . . . She's a master behind-the-scenes manipulator. . . . Hillary's so steely. She even *claps* in a controlled way."

When Bill Clinton was elected the forty-second president of the United States, the thirty-seventh president of the United States said to his Monica, "Clinton has vindicated the anti-Vietnam, draft-dodging, drug-taking behavior of the sixties. Most of that generation was bad, really bad. The Silent Majority was a reaction to that moral decay, but who's going to do it now? The Clintons are going to be our moral symbols for four years, maybe eight. Four years, and maybe we can recover. Eight, and the damage will be irreparable."

What he feared had, in his mind, taken place: America had gone to hell. He was talking to Monica about it the day after Bill Clinton's election, when a bird smashed into the window right above his head.

"My God! What the hell was that?" the Night Creature said, throwing his hand over his bestaked heart.

"A bird hit the window, Mr. President," Monica said.

"Oh," he said, "did it fall to the ground?"

"No," Monica said, "it was stunned for a moment but then recovered and flew away."

"That's good," the Night Creature said, searching the squishy caverns of his mind, trying to find Stygian import in the bird's action, and shortly after the inauguration, he sat down and wrote President Bill Clinton a letter. He congratulated him for his victory and went so far as to say that Bill Clinton had "the character to lead America" . . . very far *indeed*, bird or no bird, since he'd called him "as weak as piss on a rock" and "a goddamned liar . . . with little or no character." The Night Creature parsed his letter to Monica: "I know it goes a bit overboard, particularly on the character stuff, but the guy's got a big ego and you've got to flatter the hell out of him if you're going to get anywhere."

President Bill Clinton called Nixon soon after he got his letter. The president spoke to him for forty minutes! The president sought *his* advice about Russia, and the president invited him — *him*, the Night Creature — back into the White House for a meeting. "He was very respectful but with no sickening bullshit," Nixon told his Monica. "In twelve years, neither Reagan nor Bush ever put me on the White House schedule . . . neither Kennedy nor Johnson ever invited Mrs. Nixon and me to the White House. . . . Clinton said things to me that he absolutely would not want made public. *I wonder if his wiretaps are working. . . .* He never brought up Hillary, not once. And I gave him several lead-ins. He didn't respond to any of them. Strange." At dinner with his old Texas politico friend Bob Strauss shortly after his forty-minute chat with the president, Bob Strauss told him that President Clinton had told Bob Strauss that his conversation with Richard Nixon was "the best conversation" he'd had as president.

When the Night Creature returned to the White House for his meeting with the president of the United States, they both drank diet Cokes—Clinton from the can, Nixon from a glass. Bill Clinton told him he had put on weight defending himself against Gennifer's charges in New Hampshire. Bill Clinton used Nixonian words with him: *asshole, son of a bitch, bastard.* Bill Clinton took him up to the residence to meet Hillary and Chelsea: "The kid ran right to him and never once looked at her mother. I could see that she had a warm relationship with him but was almost afraid of her. . . . Hillary is a piece of work. She was very respectful to me and said all the right things. . . . Hillary told me we had done 'great things on the domestic side' although compliments coming from her are like—I don't know what."

There may have been a stake through his black heart, but the Night Creature felt alive after his reentry to the White House. He couldn't stop talking about his visit: "Clinton knows how the game is played . . . the trip was probably the best one I have had to Washington since I left the Presidency . . . it was the best conversation with a president I've had since I was president. Better than with Bush and I've never had such a conversation with Reagan. It was never a dialogue with the others. . . . Clinton is a fast learner and he's not afraid to defer to someone else's expertise. My only concern is that if his numbers are up, he may get cocky and not be as willing to listen to me . . . *as long as he's talking to me, he'll be okay.*" And talking they were. Bill Clinton called him for advice again . . . and again.

The Night Creature's admiration for Hillary was growing, meanwhile, into near infatuation. "Hillary is becoming an icon. . . . He doesn't scare anybody. *Hillary inspires fear!*" He told new Clinton adviser David Gergen: "She's always there, working with him, working apart from him, pushing him to take on more, taking it on herself. No one can control her!" He even gave Gergen advice to make Hillary look better. "Rein in Hillary's sharp sides. She can't continue to appear like those French women at the guillotine during the revolution, just watching, knitting and knitting." He did a scowling imitation of Madame Defarge for Gergen to make sure Gergen got it. After seeing Hillary testify before Congress about her health plan, he said, "Goddamnit! *She has the gift of dazzle!* She knocked them dead up there! They swooned over her and gave her a standing ovation. She takes the gloves off but does it with such sickening sweetness that it makes me want to gag." It was a wonder his Monica didn't raise an eyebrow the way he carried on about Hillary: "She's so clever. . . . She's invisible when the negative stuff erupts. . . . *She's strong and decisive, she's just good.* . . . She's the tower of strength and intellect around there."

But if there was a relationship in the making between the Night Creature and the First Lady, all chances of it ended when the Night Creature's longtime companion, his long-suffering wife, Pale Pat, died. The president of the United States didn't go to Pale Pat's funeral; neither did Hillary; neither did any cabinet member. Bill Clinton sent . . . *a black man* . . . Vernon Jordan, who, a few years later, would try to find Monica Lewinsky a job. The Night Creature, insulted, wounded, horrified, raged! "Vernon Jordan? The Clintons sent Vernon Jordan? Come *on!* Hillary should have been there! He comes to me for advice to save his ass and he can't even send a Cabinet member to Mrs. Nixon's funeral?"

Well fuck them! the Night Creature thought, and immersed himself once again in his vat of bubbling bile, suddenly paying eyebrow-squiggling attention to the developing scandal called Whitewater. "Hillary's up to her ass in it, they are both guilty as hell. . . . It's worse than Watergate. In Watergate, we didn't have profiteering, and *we didn't have a body.* . . . Clinton and Hillary are guilty of obstruction of justice, maybe more. Period. Our people must not be afraid to grab this thing and shake all of the evidence loose. Watergate was wrong; Whitewater is wrong. I paid the price, the Clintons should pay the price. . . . He's pretending not to notice Whitewater. Of course I tried that and it doesn't really work. . . . How dare he bitch about the press coverage? They have treated him with kid gloves. He should be kissing their ass, as Johnson used to say, in Macy's window. . . . To think that Hillary came after me during Watergate! They are making the same goddamn mistakes we made . . . and here was Hillary on the Impeachment Committee, screaming about the eighteen and a half minutes missing from the tape, and now she's in Little Rock, shredding."

As the Night Creature watched the Pope being greeted by the Clintons on television, he snarled, "Well how do you like this? The Pope and the Clintons together! The Saint and the Sinner! What a pair! And Hillary standing there! Oh boy!" *Hell hath no fury like a Night Creature's pale long-time companion's funeral scorned* . . . and in his fury he even called Bob Dole, his soul brother, to tell him to "put someone good" on the select Senate Whitewater Committee—"We can't have a bunch of dumbos asking the questions."

But underneath everything, he was profoundly depressed. A shrewd political operative, he knew Whitewater wasn't going to bring Bill Clinton down, any more than his philandering was. "Maybe it doesn't matter anymore," he glumly told his Monica; "look around—sex, drugs, violence everywhere. Remember when this whole thing got started in the sixties and seventies. Counterculture, they called it. Morals went out the window. Nobody cared about other people, just themselves . . . so you see, the people elected Clinton because they're surrounded by immorality on all sides. It gets to the point where it doesn't affect them anymore. So they sit and listen to what he has to say about health care and saving the spotted owl and are tone-deaf when it comes to his personal character."

The Night Creature was even further dejected by the knowledge that he had no credentials to speak of moral decline. "Watergate took away any chance I have of talking about that stuff credibly. Our critics will say, 'Who is Nixon to talk about this? He contributed to it! He's the Watergate guy, the Vietnam guy. He resigned in disgrace.' "

The Night Creature kept going back to where he felt it had all gone wrong for him—not Watergate, but our protests in the streets in the sixties and seventies. "It was a miserable goddamned time," he told his Monica. "I was the one who had to face down those *hippie hoodlums* who opposed the war . . . those *goddamned protesters* . . . my God, I wasn't just from another generation from these people; it was like I was from a different planet. . . . The pressure of waging the war in Vietnam broke Johnson, but I was damned if it was going to break me. Johnson left a broken man. Me, as President, I always knew that we had a responsibility to leadership no two-bit protesters were going to destroy. I couldn't stop them from destroying our values and our culture, but I could stop them from telling us that we weren't fit to lead." The Night Creature acknowledged that the killing of four student protesters at Kent State in 1970 "wasn't right," and then he added, "Those kids *were* Communists."

What? What, I reflected, was this filth the Night Creature was spewing? *Communists? They* were Communists? The kids at Kent State? I was transfixed by the enormity, the horror of his lie, though it was the very same lie he'd built his entire career on. He'd branded Jerry Voorhis and Helen Gahagan Douglas as Communists when he'd run against them in the beginning in California. And now, the four kids shot to death at Kent State by National Guard kids who were stoned on Nixon's toxic and hateful rhetoric were Communists, too. Bill Schroeder, the apple-cheeked all-American ROTC student . . . a Communist! Allison Krause, the daughter of a Westinghouse executive . . . a Communist! Sandy Sheuer, the pacifist daughter of a Holocaust survivor . . . a Communist! Jeff Miller, with flowers painted everywhere around his apartment . . . a Communist!

He was slandering and violating the dead, whom *he'd* put into their graves. The only word that possibly applied was the word Congressman Dan Burton was calling Bill Clinton now during Bill Clinton's impeachment travail, "Scumbag!"

And when I saw that his Monica—no, no, his *Elvira!*—didn't even question him, didn't say, *Communists, sir? These kids?* I erased all that soft-focus prattle from my mind about the snowball fight they'd had in Moscow and the lights twinkling in Anchorage. His Monica let him do the same thing to her that the other Monica had allowed Bill Clinton to do. Richard Nixon had put words into his Monica's mouth, seeds designed to impregnate the minds of future generations with hate.

Monica Crowley's sin, I decided, was much deadlier than Monica Lewinsky's. What each man had put into his Monica's mouth defined the difference between Bill Clinton and Richard Nixon, between liberals and conservatives, between *us* and *them*.

[Act Two]

MYSTERY TRAIN

Newts, crawling things in slime and mud, poisons,
The barren soil, the evil men, the slag and hideous rot . . .

Do you hear that mocking and laughter?
Do you hear the ironical echoes?

—WALT WHITMAN, *Leaves of Grass*

[1]

The Ratwoman and the Bag Lady of Sleaze

"It was just that he was scared and I enjoyed that," Monica said to Linda Tripp. "Isn't that disgusting? I enjoyed it. I lapped it up that he was so scared. I could just tell in his voice."

G nawing away on Monica's juicy innards, stripping her down to the bone over the phone and in person, the Ratwoman found an ally: a whisky-voiced, chain-smoking, self-styled literary agent to the unseemly likes of Mark Fuhrman, the racist Dirty Harry of O.J. fame, and Gary Aldrich, former FBI man and author of the specious and malevolent anti-Clinton tract, *Unlimited Access*.

Lucianne Goldberg was Linda Tripp's perfect mate. Already handling Dolly Kyle's lubricious account of sex with young Billy Clinton, she was herself the author of soft-porn novels like *Madam Cleo's Girls*. She was in her sixties, tied closely to right-wingers like Al Regnery, the book publisher, and Tony Snow, former Bush speechwriter and now one of Rupert Murdoch's hired guns.

As a literary agent, Goldberg was perhaps best known for representing Judy Chavez, a hooker who specialized in sadism. Chavez became infamous for revealing that Soviet defector Arkady Shevchenko paid her ten thousand dollars a month for five nights of company with money provided by the CIA. Goldberg sold her handcuffs-and-whips account to a publisher and reflected later, "The last time I saw Judy, she was wearing snake from head to toe. How many pythons it took to make that outfit with her five-inch heels, she might as well have had a whip in her hand. With that beautiful white skin and dark hair, what she telegraphs very subtly is pain. 'I'm going to hurt you, tongue-lash you, and cause you pain.' "

To those in Washington who learned of the tight connection between Linda Tripp and Lucianne Goldberg, it made perfect sense, the two of them part of the same sleazy photo: the Ratwoman gnawing on her bone in her bunting-filled gutter and, feeding next to her, the noxious Bag Lady of Sleaze, cigarettes drooping from both their bloodred lips.

Linda Tripp turned to Lucianne Goldberg "for advice and protection" first in the days after she'd been banished from the counsel's office in the White House. She decided, in those first months of rage, that she was going to write an insider's account of the sexual shenanigans at the White House, including Kathleen Willey's magical adventures in the fairy-tale hallway. She called the commentator Tony Snow again, whom she'd met in the Bush White House, and Snow, who would call Bill Clinton "the Caligula of the Ozarks," sent her to the Bag Lady of Sleaze.

Goldberg, naturally, loved Tripp's idea: politics and sex together, her main interests, a book even better maybe than the one she had written called *Purr, Baby, Purr*. Tripp's book was going to be called *Behind Closed Doors* and she was going to write it as "Joan Dean," a cute and barbed reference to John Dean, whose testimony had brought down the Nixon White House. Tripp would bring Bill Clinton down and Joan Dean would be in-joke revenge. Goldberg sent Tripp to an editor at Regnery, a publishing house long devoted to the character assassination of liberals and/or Democrats.

At the last moment, Tripp chickened out, afraid that she just might lose her job at the Defense Department if she wrote the book. "Bubelah," Lucianne Goldberg had said to her, "if you blow the whistle on the big kahuna, you ain't gonna be working for the government." Joan Dean was dead.

Years later, while stripping down Monica, the Ratwoman slipped and told Monica that if she ever lost her government job, she'd write a "tell-all book" about everything she knew. Monica shrugged it off, unaware that her new caring, mothering friend was already at work trying to sell the book. Tony Snow had called the Bag Lady for her and now Goldberg was calling Linda Tripp, who didn't know that Goldberg, no political virgin, was tape-recording *their* conversation.

They talked about the best way to profit off of what the Ratwoman knew. Yes, she could get a book contract, but the best way to maximize both of their profits would be to leak the story first, or to leak "snippets," and while the snippets made their infectious way through the airwaves, walk into a publisher's office with the *whole* story and walk out with millions of dollars. They had to "titillate" the public first, and they picked out *Newsweek* reporter Michael Isikoff to leak the snippets to. They also talked about passing Tripp's slimy knowledge on to Paula Jones's attorneys and blowing the story of the intern and the president wide open through the courts.

Tripp couched her greed in self-righteous tones, saying she was "appalled by" Bill Clinton's behavior. "It's so sickening!" she said. "He has to get his come-uppance." She also portrayed herself as the caring protector of the young woman whose innards she was gnawing. "Enough already. Personally, my opinion is it's time for her . . . she has got to move on. She's right now going through emotional hell. . . . I would very much like to see her leave and just get on with her life."

"Well, have you talked to her about going public with this?" Goldberg asked.

"She refuses."

"Then what can you do with it?"

Tripp told her that she had kept dates and records of meetings, phone calls, and gifts between the intern and Bill Clinton.

"Yeah," Goldberg said, "but you realize the press will destroy her. I mean, I love the idea. I would run with it in a second, but do you want to be the instrument of this kid, um—"

"She's not a kid," Tripp said. "She comes from a very privileged Beverly Hills background. I mean, she's definitely sophisticated . . . she wasn't a victim. When this began, she was every bit a player."

"You have to be ready to lose her as a friend," Goldberg said.

"Oh," Tripp said loftily, "I've already made that decision."

A week later, in their second telephone conversation, allegedly not taped by either of them, Goldberg told Tripp to tape her phone conversations with her young friend, the former White House intern. "You need evidence, you need proof, you need tapes."

Tripp, frightened, said taping her friend would be "unfriendly." Goldberg said, "Well, Bubelah, if you're going to go after the big kahuna, you better kill him."

Tripp started taping Monica and telling Goldberg what she was getting from Monica on her tapes. Monica thought Bill was on drugs because he kept "zoning out." Monica had dates of the phone sex she and Bill were having. Bill had cold sores that Goldberg thought sounded suspiciously like herpes.

They kept trying to figure out how to get the snippets out there to titillate the public. Tripp received an invitation to spend a weekend in Greenwich, Connecticut, from a wealthy woman named Norma Asness, who was known to be a good friend to Hillary Clinton. Tripp had spent time with Asness before, at a Chanukah party at Asness's Georgetown house and also on a civilian tour of the Pentagon, which Tripp had arranged for her.

The invitation from Asness, the former Delta Force associate was certain, was a covert, black-bag op on the part of the White House. She called Goldberg, who agreed with her.

"You're being set up," Goldberg said.

"You don't think they're going to poison me, do you?" Tripp asked.

"Uh, no. They're going to co-opt you. They're going to love-bomb you, show you this is the way you could be living if you stay loyal. . . ."

"All right," Tripp said. "Well, then, I won't worry about it. I just thought, oh good, so they're going to kill me when I'm there or something. . . ."

"No, they're not going to kill you."

They were stewing now in their own witch's brew, furtive, trusting no one except each other (although Goldberg was still secretly taping Tripp's phone calls, just as Tripp was secretly taping Monica's). They decided together that Tripp couldn't trust her lawyer because he sometimes played golf with a lower-level White House attorney, and Tripp fired him. They decided they couldn't trust the *Newsweek* reporter, Isikoff, to whom they were planning to leak their snippets, because he might write a book himself.

They decided to turn, finally, to the one person they felt would be simpatico to Linda Tripp's story about Bill Clinton and Monica Lewinsky, the one person who shared their loathing of Bill Clinton: Kenneth W. Starr. They would use Ken Starr to get them their millions of dollars from the publishers. Tripp would spill him the beans and the preacher's son would scarf them up and disgorge them into the headlines.

Yikes, Lucianne Goldberg just loved it! She hadn't had so much fun since the good old days, back in 1972, when she'd been making a thousand dollars a week as a spy on George McGovern's campaign plane, writing memos that were rushed right into the White House, for the eyes only of Richard Nixon, the man who had hired her. The Bag Lady of Sleaze still thought fondly of Nixon, her dark, political guardian angel.

Through the chain-smoking Goldberg and her friend, the chain-smoking Tripp, the Night Creature was loose in the world again, out of the grave again, smearing, clawing, drawing blood . . . making Bill Clinton pay . . . for sending black Vernon Jordan to the funeral of Pale Pat, his cancer-ravaged wife . . . for the sixties, for the protests, for Watergate, for his resignation, for his disgrace.

[2]

David Geffen Is Angry

"I read," Linda Tripp said, "that he spent the night at Steven Spielberg's partner's house. Castlebaum or Castleman or something."

"Oh, really?" Monica said.

"In LA."

"Huh."

"I don't know," Linda Tripp said. "I don't know who that is. I don't know anything about him."

David Geffen sat alone in the den of his Malibu estate as I walked in. He was watching the House Judiciary Committee's impeachment hearings, although, I noted, *watching* wasn't the right word. He was scowling, glowering, glaring at the set. He looked as if he was ready to kill someone. "Can you believe what these motherfuckers are doing?" he said. "Can you believe these motherfuckers actually think they can get away with this?"

A few days later, actor Alec Baldwin appeared on NBC's *Late Night* with Conan O'Brien and called for the murder of Judiciary Committee Chairman Henry Hyde and his family. Hollywood, I feared, was *tweaking* (as, seemingly, was Alec Baldwin).

It felt odd because Bill Clinton was never Hollywood's first choice to sit in the Oval Office. First, there was war hero Bob Kerrey, the all-American liberal from Nebraska, who'd shared the statehouse in Lincoln with Hollywood's own Debra Winger. Then there was Bill Bradley. When trial balloons floated that Bill Bradley, boring and Ichabod-like, would run for the presidency in 1992, director Sydney Pollack and Robert Redford offered to give the baggy-eyed former basketball star media lessons.

It wasn't until Michael Ovitz invited the already-elected Bill Clinton to his I. M. Pei CAA fortress—souvenir mugs were contemplated with Ovitz's likeness on one side and Bill Clinton's on the other—that the town gave Bill Clinton its blessing. Clinton reciprocated by turning the Lincoln Bedroom into Hollywood's Washington commissary.

The Lincoln Bedroom was a place that other presidents had held sacred, only for the use of a czar like Universal potentate Lew Wasserman (invited there by *both* JFK and Reagan). But now even directors and out-of-favor funnymen like Chevy Chase were enjoying overnight historical dalliances with their wives there. Chevy, who'd become famous by mimicking Gerry Ford, was overnighting at the White House thanks to Bill Clinton, just another wild and funny twist of American politics.

Everyone in town knew that one of Bill Clinton's closest advisers was the TV producer Harry Thomason, who even had his own office in the White House. But anyone who mattered knew that Harry *didn't* matter—at least not in this town. He was a *TV* producer in a town that liked and gladly accepted TV money—but still viewed it pretty much like the minor leagues, a place to work if you were still trying to make it in movies or had busted out.

The town had a long-standing and self-righteous liberal tradition. Jack Valenti, head of the Motion Picture Association of America, the entertainment industry's official Washington lobbying group, was a former LBJ White House aide, who'd begun his career by briefing the cornpone president as he sat on the throne each morning and handing him the presidential toilet paper. Norman Lear, the creator of *All in the Family*, was the founder of People for the American Way, a 250,000-member organization designed to use the medium of television to fight for liberal issues and causes. Warren Beatty and Barbra Streisand and Marlon Brando, among many others, had devoted time, money, and actorly eloquence on behalf of candidates and causes. Esteemed older directors like John Frankenheimer and Norman Jewison had been involved as advisers to Bobby Kennedy's tragically doomed campaign. Most of the studio heads or VPs were sixties graduates with strong liberal leanings.

I'd found it easy, for example, to get a movie made about neo-Nazi right-wingers (*Betrayed*) and the studio was overjoyed when Pat Buchanan attacked it as "un-American." If Buchanan felt that way, we all thought, we must have done something right. The studio's choice to direct it was Costa-Gavras, who'd never even visited the American Midwest but who, thanks to the electrifyingly brilliant Z, was a hero to liberals everywhere.

We were partly united within our liberalism by a belief in free speech. We were convinced that the Nixons and Gingriches of the world, blathering on about the societal impact of screen violence, had their own agenda. First, they disagreed with our politics and were trying to stir the public up to boycott or stay away from our movies and, second, they knew damn well real guns caused violence and not guns on-screen, but they were using the issue of screen violence as a bogeyman so they could keep on getting their contributions from the gun lobby. When I wrote a column for daily *Variety*, pointing out the graphic, over-the-top violence in a Newt Gingrich novel, I received congratulatory notes from many producers in town.

We also shared a loathing for the forces of right-wing repression. Richard Dreyfuss, all these years later, was still trying to get Sinclair Lewis's antifascist tome, *It Can't Happen Here*, made into a movie. There weren't a lot of conservatives in town: David Horowitz, once a New Lefty now a conservative ideologue; screenwriter Lionel Chetwynd (*The Hanoi Hilton*); fallen-star Tom Selleck; the NRA's Charlton Heston; and Arnold Schwarzenegger (he didn't count—he was a Kennedy). While the few conservatives sometimes objected publicly to what they termed "liberal propaganda" on-screen, they couldn't do anything about it. They were having enough problems getting employed. Not that they were completely wrong: The director Betty Thomas succinctly defined nineties comedies to me as "funny moments with liberal inserts."

Hollywood had an umbilical connection—its own "action faction"—to the movement in the sixties and seventies. When the Weatherpeople went underground, the actor Jon Voight supported them. Producer Burt Schneider and director Bob Rafelson financed Huey Newton's ritzy lakeshore apartment in Oakland. Even while the Weatherpeople were on the run, director Emile De Antonio and Oscar-winning cinematographer Haskell Wexler shot a documentary glamorizing them, unconcerned that the latest Weather Underground book was dedicated to Sirhan Sirhan or that Bernardine Dohrn was trying to rally her army in defense of Charles Manson, referring to the people the Manson family murdered as "the Tate Eight," saying, "Dig it. First they killed these pigs, then they ate dinner in the same room with them, they even shoved a fork into a victim's stomach! Wild!" If some people in town liked the Weatherpeople, the Weatherpeople liked Hollywood, too. Sam Peckinpah's *Wild Bunch* was their cinematic bible. Bernardine's storm troopers watched the movie's slow-motion violence over and over again, finding inspiration in the druggie, drunken Peckinpah's fixation on blood.

But no Hollywood figure had a closer tie to the sixties than Jane Fonda . . . even before she met her New Lefty ideologue from the Midwest, Tom Hayden. I met Fonda first when she was busted in Cleveland for bringing a tiny bit of weed over the Canadian border. (Her mug shot went on most of the office walls at the police headquarters on Payne Avenue.) We got to be friends after she read and liked my book about the shootings at Kent State. When I started writing screenplays, we tried and failed to sell MGM a movie about Karen Silkwood, the antinuclear activist. I liked Fonda—her intelligence, her commitment to better society—and the subtle, low-key brilliance of her acting style. But she was getting older—a staggeringly beautiful woman still in a town that discarded actresses ("leftover beef Wellington," a producer said to me) as they approached forty.

I had an idea for a screenplay, which would become the movie *Music Box*, and asked Jane if she was interested in playing the lead. I knew she wasn't getting as many scripts as she'd gotten before. She committed to star before I wrote the script. When she read it, she was overjoyed. "It's a great role," she said; "it's going to be a great movie." The director, Costa-Gavras, was a friend of Jane's and had even stayed at her home. When he got the script, Costa decided Jane was too old for the part. The producer, Irwin Winkler, and I tried to change Costa's mind, but he wouldn't budge. Jane went on a campaign to convince Costa she could play the part. She redid her hair, she put on a sexy dress, and she did an audition tape. Winkler and I thought she was brilliant in the audition tape (no stars ever did audition tapes), but Costa wasn't swayed. He wanted Jessica Lange.

Jane was heartbroken. She had already signed her contract to do the film and the studio was forced to pay over a million dollars to get her *out* of the movie. Not much later, she decided to leave Hollywood. I didn't blame her. It was 1987 . . . a long way away from the sixties. She wrote me a note, thanking me for my efforts to put her into *Music Box*. It was signed, "Power to the People!"

Part of Hollywood's fervently militant liberalism came, too, from media-fueled guilt about the blacklist—a time forty years ago, when a group of screenwriters, directors, actors, and producers were prevented from making a living because of alleged Communist affiliations and their refusal to testify about them before a House congressional committee.

Horrifyingly unjust, the blacklist had been hyped by the mid-nineties to become Hollywood's own holocaust. The Writers Guild, with its own present-day creative issues to fight, seemed to think it was safer and nobler to dwell on the blacklist of the past than fight studios for writers' rights in the present. The Writers Guild was conducting an endless series of seminars and testimonials about the martyrs of forty years ago.

When Elia Kazan, who testified and snitched at the same time the martyred screenwriters didn't, was finally given the Oscar he deserved, the reception he got was as frosty as though he were Leni Riefenstahl, maker of Nazi propaganda films. The iciness of his reception came, interestingly, not just from those few aging producers and directors who were Kazan's peers but also from younger actors like Ed Harris, who wore his liberal social conscience on his tuxedo sleeves.

There were a few people in Hollywood so far out on the radical Left that they smiled when Ronald Reagan was shot. Reagan was shot by the nutcase John Hinckley, who had become obsessed with Jodie Foster in the movie *Taxi Driver*. The screenplay for *Taxi Driver* was written by Paul Schrader, who used the diary of Arthur Bremer as the basis for his script. Bremer was the nutcase who had shot George Wallace. "Two right-wing birds," these twisted Hollywood zealots said—Reagan and Wallace—"with one stone"— Bremer, with an assist from Hollywood in the form of screenwriter Schrader.

Some people in town were professional liberals, singing the political torch songs they knew studio heads (and many critics), upstanding socially committed sixties folks, liked to hear. Oliver Stone was the most successful example. A man of too many personal excesses, Stone seemed as often stoned as he was not. (I once saw him grab a woman by her hair and pull her out of a bar.) Originally the writer of grippingly violent, sometimes farcical, four-letter-word melodramas—*Midnight Express, Scarface, The Hand*—he became a liberal holy man with his two powerful Vietnam dramas—*Platoon* and *Born on the Fourth of July*. Both were antiwar visions, our sixties protester's sensibility blown graphically onto the big screen.

But he outdid himself with *JFK* and *Nixon*. Both movies were utter and absolute lies. Worse, both movies, as far as future generations were concerned, pretended to tell the truth. Yet Stone didn't call himself a liberal propagandist; he called himself "a filmmaker depicting documented reality."

Two different studios made the two different movies, knowing they were whopping, lollapalooza lies that would infect the brains of tomorrow's voters. I knew, though, that the movies were made not because liberal sixties folks ran the studios and believed Stone's lies. They were made because the studio heads believed Stone's lies would make money (*JFK* did; *Nixon* didn't).

I knew, too, from experience that in a head-on collision between shared liberal beliefs and making money, money always won in Hollywood. In 1998, at a time when the energized liberal town was banding around Bill Clinton, I wrote a script for Paramount called *Land of the Free*, about the resurgence of right-wing militias across the country. The studio hoped Mel Gibson would play the militia leader I'd created, a charismatic, falsely appealing man who was, at his core, a racist and anti-Semitic moral monster. Gibson turned the script down and said he didn't want to play "such a bad guy." The studio came to me and asked me to rewrite it so my lead character "wouldn't be such a bad guy." "But these guys *are* bad guys," I told the studio. "They're awful guys. I don't want to do an apologia for the militias." The studio said, "But we really want Mel to do it." I refused to rewrite it; the studio put the project up on the shelf.

I had found myself in the same position in 1987, with *Music Box*. My script ended with the revelation that a benign old grandpa was a Nazi war criminal. Universal, offered a chance to make the movie, said it would be happy to — if I changed the ending and grandpa was shown to be innocent of all war-criminal charges. "It's going to be an apologia for the war criminals being prosecuted by governments all over the world," I said. "It'll wind up being an attack on those agencies prosecuting these people." The studio executive said, "Yeah, but this way we won't sell any tickets." Luckily, producer Irwin Winkler and director Costa-Gavras and I found a studio who made the script as originally written. (We didn't sell any tickets.)

Some people flew in under the political radar and stayed there if they were successful. Who cared if producer-mogul Andy Vajna made enough money to get to Hollywood by being a Hong Kong wig merchant who'd made a deal with the Communist Chinese government to buy the hair that had been shorn off dissidents? Who cared if Mel Gibson made the most awful homophobic comments, until his PR people zipped his lip? Who cared if the guy who directed that Disney movie was a convicted child molester? Who cared if Marlon Brando made anti-Semitic remarks on *Larry King Live* — he was Marlon Brando, and Larry King, who was Jewish, kissed him, didn't he? Who cared if Bruce Willis said, "If I were black, I'd be with Farrakhan, too"? Or: "FDR knew Pearl Harbor was going to be attacked and let it happen anyway"? Bruce Willis was big box office, wasn't he? As opposed to Charlton Heston, who was dead, buried, and mummified at the box office and was also, incidentally, the head of the National Rifle Association.

Hollywood's belief in civil liberties, even sexual privacy, also occasionally broke down. In 1983, when I was writing the movie *Jagged Edge*, my producer was the venerable wild rhino of the business, Martin Ransohoff, tough, smart, no one to trifle with. The studio executive in charge of the project was Craig Baumgarten, who had produced and starred in a porn movie in the seventies. When Ransohoff had a disagreement with Baumgarten and felt Baumgarten wasn't treating him with enough respect, he asked me to intervene and warn Baumgarten that he knew about the porn movie. I warned him, but Baumgarten, young and brash, disregarded my warning. A tape of the porn movie soon made its way to one of the members of the board of Columbia Pictures. Fired days later, Baumgarten sobbed in shocked disbelief.

The studio that fired Baumgarten was then owned by the Coca-Cola company, whose presence in three of America's greatest scandals would be noted by observers: Fatty Arbuckle used a Coca-Cola bottle to bludgeon his young victim internally; Judge Clarence Thomas, Anita Hill would claim, abused her by saying there was pubic hair on his can of diet Coke; Bill Clinton would alibi walking Monica from his Oval Office into his private study by telling his secretary he was going back there "to get her a diet Coke." Coca-Cola, historians also noted, was the cola company of liberal Democrats. Pepsi mostly supported Republicans, especially Richard Nixon, who, true to his deceitful nature, privately drank diet Coke.

While there were occasionally ugly and decidedly unliberal actions, such as Baumgarten's firing, the town followed Hillary's lead and got deeply into New Age psychobabble. Even Hillary's maharishi, Michael Lerner, was invited to a few studio seminars. "Facilitators" became regulars at industry retreats, summoning positive energy like rainmakers.

Superagent Arnold Rifkin was hanging out with walk-on-fiery-coals guru Tony Robbins. Producers Jon Peters and Peter Guber, breaking up their partnership, let it be known they were going to counseling *together*. (I was going through a divorce at the time. "Go to counseling with your ex," Peters told me. "It won't do any good, but she'll think you care. It'll save you at least a million bucks.")

The touchy-feely mood soon found its way to the screen, and when *For-*

rest Gump turned into a smash, all the studios were suddenly looking for "spiritual" or "religious" stories. Sylvester Stallone strutted around my living room one afternoon, trying to talk me into writing a "deeply spiritual" script for him. For years, he said, he had wanted to make a book into a movie in which he'd play Jesus Christ. Now he had a better idea. He wanted to play a televangelist, a modern-day healer who performed miracles. We had a meeting with a roomful of executives at Universal. Sly stalked around the room, waving his arms, pretending to preach the words of the Lord. An executive said, "Guys, listen. Sly, you're a muscle star. Joe, you've just written *Showgirls*. Don't you think this is too harsh a transition for both of you?"

As more and more men on-screen were undergoing sensitivity training, more and more men in Hollywood offices were becoming the targets of sexual harassment suits. The wealthier and more powerful either went to court or made hasty midnight settlements. But some, including mid-level studio executives, were fired. A producer of my acquaintance was not only fired but also, fearing publicity, blackmailed to give up his points in upcoming movies.

Most heterosexual men quickly opted to hire only male assistants. A woman studio executive married to a director had seen so many sexual harassment suits and settlements that she forbid her husband to hire any women on his crew. It was a strategy spreading all over town. Even as that was happening, renowned feminists were spending time in Hollywood trying to make screenwriting or producing deals. Gloria Steinem and I spent a pleasant evening in my home discussing a movie about the young Marilyn Monroe.

As David Geffen watched the House Judiciary Committee hearings, there were deeply underground rumbles at Spago that Warren Beatty, the Mark McGwire of swordsmen, was considering a run for the presidency.

It was a numbing rumor. Here was Clinton, almost out of office for not even having intercourse, and here was Warren, the Hall of Famer, the sleepy-eyed human sex machine, with his eyes on the bestained Oval Office. Rumor was that Gary Hart—*Oh glory, glory hallelujah!*—was advising him. Rumor was that Pat Cadell, wanna-be screenwriter, was unofficially back in the polling business.

I could just hear the dialogue in Robert Evans's screening room, with the fireplace blazing and the Polaroids of naked women on the table . . . preening Warren and bitter Gary and addled Evans in his Bush White House baseball cap and grizzled Pat . . . and the redhead with the cigar in her butt bringing them Perriers as they discussed the ins and outs of seducing the body politic.

Not long after I saw David Geffen, he told reporters he was making House Judiciary Committee member James Rogan of California, a staunch pro-impeachment Republican, his "target number one" in the 2000 elections. David, I knew, had more money than God and was wilier than Satan, and I thought James Rogan would be well advised to beg David's forgiveness . . . *on his knees.*

[3]

Ross Perot on Drugs

Monica said, "I'm like—'I have a mental block on who you really are.'"

"You never ever realized whose dick you were sucking," Linda Tripp said.

"No. I know," Monica said.

The calls for Bill Clinton's impeachment wouldn't cease, the rabid twin gorgons of Scandal and Ruin were running amok . . . and Ross Perot, who had twice come to his aid and made his minority presidency possible, came running in anger to help again. Perot, America's Tin Soldier, accused the president of the United States of doing drugs in the White House.

The charge helped move all of the other charges into the realm of the absurd. The cigar was surreal enough, the twenty-four-hour blow job television fiesta was bizarre enough . . . but *drugs in the White House?* Bill Clinton was now, it seemed, Tony Montana with his head in a silver platter of cocaine. Perot argued that the only way to explain Bill Clinton's recklessness, irresponsibility, and mendacity was to assume that he was on drugs. Perot's was the voice of Carry Nation come pip-squeaking back. Demon alcohol replaced by demon drugs.

We chuckled at the Tin Soldier's argument, but, at the same time, those of us who had truly *experienced* the sixties knew in our secret hearts that the comic book Tin Soldier probably had a tangential point . . . but it was a point most of us thought irrelevant. Marijuana and cocaine, our drugs of choice, didn't make you lie to the nation or make you unzip and say, "Kiss it" . . . though both drugs made the kissing part more enjoyable. Perot kept calling for the president to release his medical records—something other presidents had done — but we knew the reason why Bill Clinton refused. Many of us had damaged our septums through the years.

We knew about the rumors that Bill Clinton, while running for office in Arkansas, had been rushed to an emergency room one night OD'd on coke. Why release records that could be personally embarrassing (George Bush, no surprise, had hemorrhoids), or worse? (JFK, treated for gonorrhea, suffered his whole life from acute postgonococcal urethritis, an inflammation of the genitals that caused a burning sensation when urinating.)

We knew Bill Clinton had done the things we'd done. At Oxford as a student, he'd hung around smoky, pillow-strewn parlors, sipping tea and sherry with the young foxes, smoking hash and dope, trying to learn, as one of those foxes put it, to "inhale." Old girlfriend Sally Perdue described him, as governor in 1983, offering her joints from a cigarette case and coke from a plastic bag. Gennifer described him offering her coke at her apartment before they climbed onto the black satin sheets on her king-size bed. At one of his Arkansas parties for his staff, an aide offered partygoers grass, hash, coke, pills, and syringes. It was a life many of us had learned to live all too well: candles, incense, black satin sheets, zebra drapes, grass, coke, and sex.

In the early eighties, Bubba was on a tear, as were many of us. He was tearing up Little Rock's bars, staying till late, watching the girls dance, never with Hillary, but often with Roger, his little half brother. Roger was snorting coke sixteen times a day and had a four-gram-a-day habit.

Roger was the kind of guy who lit up his own farts. His mother taught him to read from her *Racing Form*. Roger was a sulky loafer who'd grown up doing nothing much more than practicing his guitar, watching his hair grow in the mirror, psychedelic posters all around, and singing "Red Roses for a Blue Lady" to his mother.

Roger loved the man he always called "Big Brother," and he was once videotaped snorting coke and saying, "He was like a father to me growing up, all my life, so that's why we've always been so close." Roger and Big Brother were hanging out in the early eighties while Big Brother was governor, and Roger was living in his "Party Shack," the guest house at the governor's mansion, and invading the mansion's kitchen late at night when he got the munchies.

He and Big Brother were often seen partying together: A waitress at a club called the Bistro later told a grand jury that she sold coke to Roger Clinton, who'd then hand the coke to Big Brother. She said she saw Bill

Clinton snort cocaine "often" and described the night when the governor of Arkansas got so trashed that he slid down a wall and propped himself against a . . . trash can. The manager of an apartment house where Roger lived briefly said she overheard Roger and Big Brother discuss the quality of the cocaine they were doing. A hidden video camera picked Roger up one night as he was trying to score some coke. "Got to get some for my brother," Roger said. "He's got a nose like a vacuum cleaner."

But four grams of coke a day is a lot, a whole lot, a hellacious lot, and Roger's hunger started making him take big risks. He was a dealer now . . . at the same time that Bill Clinton's friends saw a strange listlessness, an unexplainable anomie ravage the governor, who was spending much of his time in the mansion's basement, playing his pinball machine.

Roger was flying up to New York with cocaine strapped to his body, accompanied on one trip by an allegedly unaware Big Brother. Roger was dealing coke on consignment from big-muthah dealers, and his convertible got ripped off one night with the coke inside. His suppliers wanted twenty grand pronto and threatened to kill him.

A later FBI investigation showed that Big Brother went to a business associate, himself later convicted of drug trafficking, and asked him to stash Roger for a while at his Florida farm. The feds were onto Roger by then, though, and he got two years at a federal prison in Texas (prosecuted by a man named Asa Hutchison, who would turn up many years later as a firebrand member of the House Judiciary Committee, calling for Big Brother's impeachment).

Big Brother sat in the courtroom as his little brother was sentenced, his nose red and a little runny. Afterward, on the courthouse steps, the governor of Arkansas, still emotional, said, "I feel more deeply committed than ever before to do everything I can to fight illegal drugs in our state."

Well . . . okay . . . what the hell . . . so what? He wasn't doing smack, was he? He wasn't using a needle, was he? He wasn't nodding out down in the filth of some crack house, was he? (Although that business about sliding down a wall and propping himself against the trash can *was* a little disturbing.)

Cocaine that was snorted wasn't a slum drug; it was definitely white-collar, and maybe even still chic, the drug of choice for the hip and for Hollywood elite, the fabled drug of Sigmund Freud and Sherlock Holmes. Cocaine was our drug, the baby-boomer drug. (The Xers could keep Ecstasy, which put some of us, getting older, into the hospital.)

. . .

As I listened to Ross Perot rant on, I remembered my own fling with cocaine in the seventies, while I was at *Rolling Stone*, which was a buzzing little beehive of cocaine activity. Whenever the dealers in town liked a story in the magazine, especially the stories I wrote exposing corrupt narcotics agents, they showed their appreciation by dropping off a few grams in the office.

I loved the freeing exhilaration cocaine provided, the unself-conscious babbling, and I found it to be the only effective aphrodisiac I'd ever tried. JFK's priapism was allegedly partly caused by the cortisone used to treat his Addison's disease (Bill Clinton took cortisone, too, for his sinuses and knees), but as far as I was concerned, cocaine was the greatest gift to men since the condom. My sexual partners mostly felt the same way — it caused the kind of fireworks that went on explosively and orgasmically for eight hours.

I discovered, though, that not everyone was affected this way. Hunter Thompson, whose breakfast those days consisted of two Bloody Marys, four lines of coke, and half a pack of cigarettes, told me it made him want to write. Jann Wenner told me cocaine made him able to edit Hunter's prose. I concluded that it seemed to energize us for whatever we most liked doing: David Felton, another editor at *Rolling Stone*, liked to talk . . . Hunter liked to write . . . Jann liked to edit . . . and I liked to have sex.

No doubt cocaine was dangerous: It could really mess you up. I watched another of our editors, Grover Lewis, in a bar one night, trying for fifteen minutes to get cigarettes out of a jukebox. Out one night with one of the *Rolling Stone* sweetmeats in a motel, I found myself unable to speak. I could form thoughts, I could perform sexually, but I couldn't form words for about ten hours (a doctor told me later that I'd suffered, at age twenty-eight, a ministroke).

Over the years, most of us who'd abused ourselves with coke stopped doing it. In my case, I was ministroked into it. In other cases, the daily toll of aging did it. But in most cases, the reason was our kids. We didn't want our kids to risk their own health and lives the way we'd risked ours. Some of us adopted Nancy Reagan's "Just Say No!" Others, perhaps knowing more realistically that the apple doesn't fall far from the tree, gave our kids, as they became teenagers, the benefit of our experience: Grass is okay; just make sure it isn't laced with anything, especially angel dust. Coke will burn your sinuses out and put you on Claritin forever. Smack is the monkey you'll never get off your back. Crack is as bad as smack; you'll wind up dead or in jail. Speed kills. Ecstasy can stop your heart. One tab of acid can lobotomize you forever.

And now here was Ross Perot telling us that the president of the United States, whose sinuses were screwed up and who was on Claritin, had a drug problem . . . in addition to his others. Bill Clinton, I was sure, was now as drug-free as I was, and I was immaculate (excepting, like Clinton, nicotine).

But as I listened to the Tin Soldier constantly hammer away at Bill Clinton as "our commander in chief," I thought I knew what was *really* up Perot's craw: It wasn't the blow job or the cigar or the lying. It was the damned draft. Bill Clinton (and I) had successfully and sneakily dodged the damned draft. To the Tin Soldier, that was a hanging offense!

[4]

Bubba and the Burrheads

*"I thought I heard he got two hearing aids," Linda Tripp said.
"It's very unusual because high-frequency loss of hearing you
generally hear about in soldiers who are around ordnance or
weapons."*

*"Well, he's around bands and rallies," Monica said. "I mean,
rock and roll!"*

What Ross Perot didn't understand was that most men of my generation had dodged the draft or tried to. We didn't think going over into those bug-infested rice paddies was cool. We didn't understand—nor would we ever—the reason this war was being fought.

Communists? What sense did it make to fight minor-league Vietnamese Communists while, at the same time, America was playing kissy face with superstar major-league Commies in Moscow and Beijing? As far as going to war because we were being told to go . . . because it was an order . . . because the cornpone or amoral commander in chief had so decided . . . that didn't cut any ice with us.

We didn't believe or respect Lyndon Johnson or Richard Nixon. We didn't want to carry guns; we wanted to carry roach clips. We didn't want to get killed; we wanted to get high and get laid.

And now they were going to kidnap us from our Beatle bootleg albums and incense-scented pads and cut our hair . . . and we'd get reamed by some moronic inbred burrhead in basic training? And then they were going to put guns in our hands and tell us to kill "gooks," whom we sympathized with as fellow freaks shit on by the burrheads of the world? *Bull! Shit!* Hell no, we wouldn't go!

Some of us shot our toes or pinkie fingers off. Some of us stayed in school as long as we could, adjusting career goals to necessitate grad school. Some of us ate pasta ten times a day, turning ourselves into grotesques, hoping to be disqualified for being too fat. Some of us stopped eating, turning ourselves into geeks, hoping to be disqualified for being too thin. Some of us shoved objects in our rectum, hoping to damage ourselves so we'd be disqualified for engaging in anal intercourse. Some of us *engaged* in anal intercourse. Some of us went to Canada.

The burrheads of the world could talk all they wanted about the dishonor of being a draft dodger. We felt no dishonor and no shame. We felt the burrheads were dishonorable and shameful automatons, good Nazis taking orders from higher-up burrheads who were dishonoring the new, loving, peaceful America we were trying to create.

We felt that anybody who didn't do everything to get himself out of this unjust and senseless war was stupid or unprincipled or *cowardly*. We insisted that those in favor of this scurrilous war had been poisoned by listening to Sinatra or Sammy Davis, Jr., or Eddy Arnold, or the gay-hating Anita Bryant.

When Bill Clinton, a graduate student at Oxford, a Rhodes scholar, got his notice to report for induction on May 3, 1969, he literally ran, panicked, to a friend. He was hysterical and hyperventilating. He beat on his friend's door, but his friend wasn't there. He slumped to the floor and sobbed.

He knew, by then, that he was going into politics, and he knew American voters wouldn't elect even a dog catcher who'd gone to Canada or shot his pinkie off or shoved objects into his rectum to avoid the draft. His options were limited by his own ambitions and by his own instinctive understanding of American realpolitik: The burrheads would be electing their "public servants" for a long time . . . until our generation was old enough to instill our values in our young and change America at the ballot box.

Bill Clinton hated this war the way most of us did and knew that he somehow—*somehow!*—had to quash his induction notice. He called his mother and stepfather to ask them if they knew of any strings that could be pulled. He asked his stepfather to see if he could get him into a National Guard or Reserve Officers' Training Corps unit.

Desperate, he flew back from England to Washington to see the most powerful man he knew, Senator J. William Fulbright, the head of the Senate Foreign Relations Committee. Bill Fulbright, who was becoming a public opponent of the war, was a friend and his old boss. As a young man, Bill

Clinton had worked in the senator's Arkansas campaign, driving him at high, reckless speeds around the state, and later, he'd also worked in Fulbright's Washington office. He begged the senator to help him get into a National Guard or ROTC unit immediately so he could avoid induction. The senator said he'd make some calls.

At the end of his wits, scrambled, Bill Clinton went to Little Rock to see another friend, who was working for the executive director of Arkansas's Republican party. Here he was, a young and very liberal Democrat, turning for help to the Republicans, a party even then captive to the forces of segregationist and racist interests, in order to avoid his induction date. Thanks to his friend, the Republican party's director in Arkansas made a trip to see the head of the state of Arkansas's Selective Service, who went to the head of the ROTC program at the University of Arkansas, Col. Eugene Holmes.

Bill Clinton cut his beard and his long hair before he went to see Colonel Holmes, a veteran of World War II POW camps and the Bataan death march. Bill Clinton was a dyed-in-the-wool peacenik, meeting a decorated war hero. Colonel Holmes had two sons who were in Vietnam. Bill Clinton sat with Colonel Holmes for two hours, trying to convince him that he shouldn't be drafted; that he, who loathed the war and everything the burrheads stood for, would make ideal burrhead officer material. He swore that he didn't oppose America's war in Vietnam. The burrheaded Colonel Holmes said he'd think about it. The next day, he was bombarded with phone calls from powerful state and local politicians, who urged him to admit Bill Clinton into the ROTC program. "The general message conveyed to me," Colonel Holmes said later, "was that Senator Fulbright was putting pressure on them and they needed my help."

Colonel Holmes gave them the help they needed and quashed Bill Clinton's notice to report for the induction, which was now only days away. He admitted Bill Clinton into the University of Arkansas ROTC program. But he didn't just admit him into the program; he got him out of the war. Colonel Holmes decided to allow Bill Clinton to finish his year at Oxford *and* to finish two years of law school before he'd have to report. And in three years, everyone knew, this painfully unpopular war would be over.

Back at Oxford, free from the war, Bill Clinton went out on the street for the first time to protest it. He became one of the leaders of Oxford's antiwar movement. He marched on the American embassy in Grosvenor Square with five hundred other protesters. He wore a black armband and carried a placard on which he'd written in Magic Marker the name of a serviceman who'd been killed in Vietnam. He led an antiwar prayer service at a nearby church. Then he marched on the American embassy again, a foot-high wooden cross in his arms. He symbolically placed the cross against the embassy gate.

The newspapers were reporting, meanwhile, that Richard Nixon was withdrawing 35,000 troops from Vietnam. Other reports said the draft would be temporarily suspended shortly—and that when it was resumed, only nineteen-year-olds would be called and "only those draftees who volunteered for service in Vietnam." Nixon was pushing for a lottery system, other accounts said, whereby you'd be eligible for the draft for only one year. Numbers from one to 365 would be randomly selected. If your birthday was picked as a high number, you'd still only be vulnerable for one year. If your birthday was picked as a low number, you'd never be drafted.

When the first draft lottery was held, shortly after the stories appeared, Bill Clinton's birth date was number 311 out of 365. He knew now that if he wasn't a member of the ROTC program, he'd never have to serve in the military at all. Colonel Holmes and the ROTC had been necessary to quash his induction notice, but they were baggage now. He knew that with his low lottery number, he'd never be drafted.

He wrote Colonel Holmes a letter, asking to be reclassified 1-A (for immediate induction), *knowing* he'd never be inducted because of his low lottery number. He knew, too, that this gesture could be made to look good when he ran for future public office. It could be viewed as a patriotic gesture. A young man who *had* a deferment *giving it up* and seemingly making himself, *on paper*, look like he was willing to risk combat. The burrheads would love it.

Knowing that he was off the hook now, he let Colonel Holmes have it with both barrels, as though he couldn't restrain himself. He wrote him a letter. He told Colonel Holmes, almost gleefully, that he'd lied to him. While he had sworn in his meeting with Colonel Holmes that he wasn't against the war in Vietnam, he now wrote that "the admiration [between them] might not have been mutual had you known a little more about me, about my political beliefs and activities." He wrote of "working every day against a war I opposed and despised with a depth of feeling I had reserved solely for racism in America before Vietnam. . . . I have written and spoken and marched against the war." He wrote that he "had no interest in the ROTC program itself and all I seemed to have done was to protect myself against physical harm."

Bill Clinton thanked the burrhead for "saving me from the draft." "No government," he wrote, "really rooted in limited parliamentary democracy should have the power to make its citizens fight and kill and die in a war they may oppose, a war which even possibly may be wrong, a war which, in any case, does not involve immediately the peace and freedom of the nation. The draft was justified in World War II because the life of the people collectively was at stake. Individuals had to fight, if the nation was to survive, for the lives of their countrymen and their way of life. Vietnam is no such case."

His letter, in many ways, was an eloquent presentation of how many of us felt about the war. The way he pulled the whole scam off had rock and roll aspects many of us who'd dodged the draft admired. He hated the war and got inducted. He beat the draft notice by conning a war hero and by squeezing him with political muscle. Then he hit the streets to protest the war he'd already gotten out of. Then he got out of . . . what he'd gotten into, the reserves . . . to get out of the draft. Then he told the war hero the details of how he'd conned him. Then he lectured the war hero about war.

It almost caught up with him six years later, when he ran for Congress in Arkansas against a Republican World War II veteran who started asking questions about how Bill Clinton had gotten out of the draft. Bill Clinton knew that his letter to Colonel Holmes might prove especially embarrassing to him. He wanted it back.

He'd squeezed Colonel Holmes once before through his friend Senator Fulbright, and now he squeezed him again through friends who were administrators at the University of Arkansas. The war hero called an aide to say "he wanted the Clinton letter out of the files." The aide sent the letter to Colonel Holmes, who sent it back to Bill Clinton.

Sixteen years later, in 1991, that same aide, Ed Howard, started getting questions from reporters about a letter that Bill Clinton had allegedly once written to Colonel Holmes. Ed Howard ran into Bill Clinton in Little Rock and told him about the reporters' questions.

"Don't worry about that," Bill Clinton said. "I've put that one to bed."

No one knew that another copy of the letter existed, allegedly made by another aide to Colonel Holmes. It was leaked to the press during the New Hampshire primary in 1992, and for a few days Bill Clinton and his advisers went into shock. There were those who saw it as that conned and lectured old war hero's perfectly timed revenge. What would America think about a letter from a presidential candidate that was a flat-out admission of dodging the draft?

As it turned out, America thought nothing much at all. My generation had grown up now. We had taught our values to our young. The burrheads were dead or dying or certainly out of touch, like Ross Perot. Without a doubt, they were outnumbered.

In the America we had created, dodging the draft was no reason not to vote for a man . . . no more reason not to vote for a man than a blow job or a good-tasting cigar. In both instances, Bill Clinton thought there was no evidence of what he had done. He denied everything. One lie was exposed by a letter, the other by a blue dress.

[5]

Mark Fuhrman and the Navy Blue Dress

"Can I ask you a question?" Linda Tripp said. "I have a lot of fear. Do you? I mean I have a lot of fear!"

"Do you want the honest truth?" Monica said. "Do you want me to tell you the honest truth? I have fear about one thing, and that's you saying something."

I t was a navy blue dress without décolletage—buttons to the top—that cost $49.95 at the Gap. It was not, as one of Kenneth W. Starr's prosecutors referred to it, "a cocktail dress." It was a dress whose color and style made Monica, always paranoid about her weight, look slimmer.

It would become one of the most famous dresses in American history, better known than Scarlett's red dress in *Gone With the Wind*, its impact upon America's government nearly as deadly as the blood-splattered pink suit Jackie Kennedy wore as LBJ was being sworn in on *Air Force One*.

This simple "work dress," as Monica called it, would also become known as one of the sexiest dresses in recent popular culture—sexier than Barbra's nearly see-through Oscar pantsuit, sexier than Marilyn's sewn-on white sequins, sexier than the black safety-pin number that got Elizabeth Hurley a modeling contract. Monica's navy blue work dress was certainly the Gap's biggest fashion statement since Sharon Stone, Handsome's other friend, had worn her black Gap turtleneck to the Oscars.

On February 28, 1997, Monica Lewinsky hadn't seen Bill Clinton for eleven months, although they'd had phone sex half a dozen times as he crisscrossed the country campaigning against Bob Dole and the Tin Soldier. The day before, Betty Currie had invited Monica to Bill Clinton's weekly radio address. Monica watched him give the speech with six other guests, then had her photograph taken once again with the Handsome she'd been intimate with for nearly a year only on the phone.

They were a blue couple. He wore a navy blue blazer and a denim button-down shirt; she wore the navy blue dress she'd recently had dry-cleaned. She liked the way it fit her. After the photo was taken—"I was really nervous," Monica said—Bill Clinton told her to go up to Betty Currie's office because he wanted to give her something.

She chatted with Betty as Bill Clinton spoke to the other guests at the radio address, and when Bill Clinton came into Betty's office, Betty walked them both into the Oval Office. She walked the two of them into the private study and left.

"Come here," Monica said to Bill Clinton. "Just kiss me."

"Wait, just wait," he said. "Be patient. Be patient," and he handed her a little box decorated with gold stars. She opened it and found a glass pin that was the color of her dress. As she admired it, he almost sheepishly slipped something into her purse and quietly said, "This is for you."

Monica reached into her purse and found a gorgeous leather-embossed volume of Walt Whitman's *Leaves of Grass*. It was, she thought, the most "meaningful" and "beautiful" gift he had given her. She felt he was telling her, through Whitman's words, of the depth of his affection for her.

Bill Clinton told her he'd seen the message she'd sent him on Valentine's Day in the *Washington Post*'s classified section, a note addressed to "Handsome," quoting *Romeo and Juliet*: "With love's light wings did I o'er-perch these walls/For stony limits cannot hold love out/And what love can do, that dares love attempt." Bill Clinton told her how much he loved *Romeo and Juliet*.

He kissed her then and they moved to the hallway she'd missed so much. She unbuttoned his denim blue shirt. He said, "Listen, I've got to tell you something really important. We have to be really careful." He kissed her again and unbuttoned the top buttons of her navy blue dress. They did what they had done before and she knelt down. He froze suddenly. He thought he'd heard someone in the Oval Office.

They moved into the bathroom off the hallway and she knelt down again. After a while, he stopped her and started to push her away. She stood up and put her arms around him and whispered, "I care about you so much. I don't understand why you won't let me make you come. I mean, it's important to me. I mean, it just doesn't feel complete, you know? It doesn't seem right."

He whispered, "I don't want to get addicted to you. I don't want you to get addicted to me."

They looked at each other for a moment. "I don't want to disappoint you," he said.

She knelt down again and, for the first time, she felt Willard find closure in her mouth.

"I was sick after it was over," he would say later.

"You've got to put yourself together again," he told her now. She buttoned her dress up and put her lipstick on, and Betty Currie magically reappeared and was suddenly knocking on the door of the private study. Betty walked them both into the Oval Office and then walked her out.

Though her departure had been abrupt, Monica was sky-high. She had gained his trust. He had allowed her to finish what he'd never allowed before. They hadn't had intercourse, but until this day, he hadn't really allowed her to do fellatio, either.

They had moved now from fellatio interruptus to fellatio. She dreamed of the day they would move from fellatio to coitus . . . or at least to coitus interruptus. This was the best day, Monica thought, they'd ever had. He had given her *Leaves of Grass* and seeds of himself. She was grateful for both.

She went straight to dinner with some friends at McCormick and Schmidt's and then went home to her apartment. She threw the blue dress into her closet. Weeks later, she saw the dress there before going out with her friends. She tried to put it on, but she'd gained some weight and it didn't fit.

She noticed two "tiny dots" on it—stains in the area of her chest and lower hip. She wondered if they were the president's stains. She also wondered if it was either the guacamole or the spinach dip she'd had at McCormick and Schmidt's that night. She threw the dress back into her closet. She told two of her girlfriends about it, though, saying that Bill Clinton "should pay the dry-cleaning bill."

She also told the Ratwoman about it. Linda Tripp had been on a diet, with Monica's help, and, as a reward, Monica invited her over to her apartment to pick out clothes Monica wasn't wearing. And there in the closet was the navy blue dress. Monica told Tripp the story and showed her the stains.

The Ratwoman went into a frenzy. She called *Newsweek* reporter Michael Isikoff and told him about the stained navy blue dress.

"Should I take it?" Tripp asked.

"And do what with it?" Isikoff asked.

"Give it to you."

"What am I supposed to do with it?"

"Have it tested," Tripp said.

"What in God's name are you talking about?" Isikoff yelled.

"DNA?"

"Where the fuck am I supposed to get a sample of the president's DNA?" Isikoff said, and hung up quickly afterward.

When Tripp called her, Lucianne Goldberg had the answer. Staying with her at her New York apartment—*in the right place at the right time*—was a man who knew all about stains and DNA. From out of the O. J. Simpson case's toxic sewers came the ex-cop known as "Führer Man" and "Fuhrman the German," to become an accomplice now to the plot to bring down the president of the United States.

The former Los Angeles detective, Mark Fuhrman, was ungodly perfect casting to be teaming with Tripp, the former Delta Force black-bagger, and Goldberg, the former Nixon spy. Once a marine, the collector of Nazi memorabilia, Führer Man, an author now, had been accused of planting evidence at the Simpson trial. He had once told a police psychiatrist that he tired of the Marine Corps "because a bunch of Mexicans and niggers were telling me what to do." A witness claimed to have overheard him rant about "burning all the niggers." He was living now in a small Idaho town not far from the headquarters of the Aryan Nation, a town filled with other ex-LAPD retirees.

Führer Man knew just what the Ratwoman and the Bag Lady of Sleaze could do with Monica's navy blue dress. A Q-tip would do it. A plastic bag. Sterile water. But they somehow had to get the dress.

Tripp and Goldberg knew very well what the dress meant. With a DNA-tested dress with his semen on it, Bill Clinton couldn't "deny, deny, deny" (as he'd suggested to Gennifer). The White House spin doctors wouldn't be able to turn this into another he said/she said. And if Bill Clinton should deny in court his encounters with Monica Lewinsky, he could go to jail. They somehow had to get a hold of that navy blue dress!

Together in the office at the Pentagon one day, Tripp turned to Monica and said she was running out of money. She was so broke, she said, that she was selling her clothes. That morning, someone had seen the suit she was wearing and wanted to buy it. Right now. Literally off her back. So could she go over to Monica's apartment, the Ratwoman asked, and borrow something out of her closet? *Right now?* So she could sell the suit she was wearing? Monica said okay, she'd go to her apartment with Tripp.

Oh no, Tripp said, she didn't want to put Monica to all that trouble. Couldn't Monica just give her the key to her apartment? Monica thought about it, then said she didn't really feel comfortable having anybody in her apartment alone. The Ratwoman foamed and accused Monica of not trusting her.

If Tripp and Goldberg couldn't physically get the dress, they had to try to make sure that Monica wouldn't send it to the dry cleaner. They decided to try to frighten her out of doing that.

"I want you to think about this," Tripp said to Monica. "And don't just dis what I say, okay?"

"I don't always dis what you say," Monica said.

"You're very stubborn," Tripp said. "You're very stubborn." She sighed. "The navy blue dress. Now, all I would say to you is I know how you feel today, and I know why you feel the way you do today, but you have a very long life ahead of you, and I don't know what's going to happen to you. Neither do you. I don't know anything, and you don't know anything. I mean, the future is a blank slate. I don't know what will happen. I would rather you had that dress in your possession if you need it years from now. That's all I'm gonna say."

Monica said, "You think I can hold on to a dress for ten or fifteen years with semen from—"

"Hey, listen," Tripp said. "My cousin is a genetic whatchamacallit—" It was a lie. The cousin she was referring to was the Bag Lady's houseguest, Führer Man.

"—and during O. J. Simpson I questioned all the DNA and do you know what he told me? I will never forget this. And he's like a Ph.D. and blah blah blah. And he said that on a rape victim now—they couldn't do this, you know, even five years ago. On a rape victim now, if she had preserved a pinprick size of crusted semen, ten years from that time, if she takes a wet Q-tip and blobs it on there and has a pinprick size on the Q-tip, they can match the DNA with absolutely—with certainty."

Monica said, "So why can't I scratch that crap off and put it in a plastic bag?"

Tripp said, "You can't scratch it off. You would have to use a Q-tip. And I feel that this is what I'd tell my own daughter. That's why I'm saying this to you. I would say it to my own daughter: For your own ultimate protection, which, mea culpa, I hope you never need it. But I don't want you to take the dress away, either. I'm telling you, I would say this to my own daughter, who would tell me to fuck off, but—"

"Well, I'll think about it," Monica said.

Tripp said, "Believe me, I know how you feel now. I just don't want to take away your options down the road, should you need them. And believe me, I know better than anybody, probably, other than your own mother, that you would never, ever use the dress if you didn't have to. I know this. Believe me. I just don't trust the people around him [Clinton] and I just want you to have that dress for *you*. Put it in a Baggie, put it in a Ziploc bag, and you pack it in with your treasures, for all I care. I mean, whatever. Put it in one of your little antiques."

"What for, though?" Monica asked. "What do you think—"

"I don't know, Monica," Tripp said, picking her frightening words carefully. "It's just this nagging awful feeling I have in the back of my head."

"What if I don't have the dress?" Monica asked.

"I think it's a blessing you do," Tripp said. "And it could be your only insurance policy down the road. Or it could never be needed, and you can throw it away. But I—I never ever want to read about you going off the deep end because someone comes out and calls you a 'stalker' or something . . . and in this day and age . . . I don't trust anybody. Maybe I'm being paranoid. If I am, indulge me. I'm not saying you should do it if you don't want to. I'm just saying it would be a smart thing to do. And then put it somewhere where no one knows where it is but you. . . ."

Fear . . . Paranoia . . . Motherly Concern . . . Using Monica's own mother in her arguments . . . pretending to speak to her as though she were her own daughter . . . at the same time taping her and conferring daily with the Bag Lady, whose houseguest was Führer Man. A conspiracy of scum. But a successful one. In a later conversation, Monica talked about not betraying her Handsome or the White House: "I would not—for fear of my life—I would not cross these—these people—*for fear of my life*. . . ." She did exactly what the Ratwoman had told her to do. She put the navy blue dress in a Ziploc bag with her "treasures" (tapes of his messages left on her machine) and hung the bag in the closet of her mother's New York apartment.

· · ·

When Tripp blew the whistle by calling Kenneth W. Starr's deputy, Jackie Bennett, Tripp told the prosecutors about the navy blue dress, which Monica would never have told them about. Starr's prosecutors knew they had Clinton *and* Monica by their short hairs, thanks to what Tripp had told them about the existence of the dress.

If Clinton denied under oath that he had sex with Lewinsky, the stains on the dress would prove him guilty of perjury. If Monica denied having the dress or if she dry-cleaned it, she would be guilty of perjury or obstruction of justice, destroying evidence. They even had a witness—Tripp—who had not only *seen* the stains but who had discussed with Monica on tapes (that they now possessed) the blue dress's importance.

When Monica finally got her immunity deal, the prosecutors immediately asked for the dress and she had to turn it over or go to jail. She had no choice. The Ratwoman had taken all of her choices away. The navy blue dress was tagged as item number Q3243 and taken to an FBI lab. The president of the United States was forced to provide a blood sample. The stains on the blue dress were revealed to be neither guacamole nor spinach dip.

[6]

Jay Leno and the Cigar

"Oh," Linda Tripp said, "I'm beginning to think he's a huge moron, but that's my opinion."

"And I'm beginning to think he's an asshole more than a moron," Monica said.

"How about a combination, a moron and an asshole?" Linda Tripp said.

H e had played his sax on Arsenio Hall's show, had nearly flashed his underwear on MTV, and now, as all the scurrilous rumors and charges inundated America, he tried to be hip again. He gave it the Bart Simpson response: "I didn't do it. Nobody saw me do it. You can't prove anything." But Bart Simpson wasn't working. More and more newspapers were calling for his resignation.

Fellow Democrat Bob Kerrey's old quote—"Clinton's an unusually good liar. Unusually good. Do you realize that?"—had been pulled out of the newspaper morgues and was reappearing everywhere. A column in the *Washington Times* called him "a lying, thieving hick in Allen Edmonds wingtips." A former Reagan aide said he was "as full of shit as a fertilizer bomb and he might go off in the White House." The same aide, Lyn Nofziger, gleefully pointed out, "With all his legal bills, Clinton can no longer afford $200 haircuts." The chairman of the Republican party in Ohio said Bill Clinton "operated with a rectal-cranial inversion." A columnist asked, "Do we really need the CIA to answer to a guy whose main interest is uncovering Victoria's Secret?" And fellow Democratic senator Fritz Hollings, of South Carolina, said, "Clinton is as popular in South Carolina as AIDS."

Even the shrine he had ordered constructed for himself in the Pentagon was suddenly under fire. The Pentagon's third-floor corridor, known as the "Commander in Chief's Corridor," was filled with wall-size photographs of Bill Clinton alongside top-rank military brass. Never a popular project, because of his actions to dodge the draft in the Vietnam War, the picture collection and the corridor were now being avoided by those Defense Department officials whose offices were near it. A janitorial worker had been assigned to wash the glass in which the photos were mounted every morning . . . to remove the spit that had been left there the day before.

But doing the most incendiary damage to the Clinton presidency, some of his aides felt, was the nightly evisceration of Bill Clinton seen by 70 million Americans. Jay Leno was America's cynical conscience in the nineties and his nightly machine-gunning Clinton jokes were not in the relatively gentle spirit he had shown toward senators Bob Packwood and Bob Dole.

The jokes Jay Leno lacerated Bill Clinton with each night and which much of America was repeating the next day were, Bill Clinton felt, belittling him, making him look like "the dumb hick" and the "Caligula of the Ozarks" that the columnists accused him of being. "It came out today that Clinton once tried to have phone sex with Hillary, but she said, 'Not tonight, I have an earache.' " Or "Al Gore is just an orgasm away from the presidency." Or "Monica is considering suing the president. She wants a million dollars for pain and suffering and $2.50 for dry cleaning."

The Leno joke that Bill Clinton told a friend he really hated was this: "Former president Jimmy Carter has been hospitalized for the treatment of a skin rash. He's going to be fine, but if any Democratic president came down with a skin rash, I'd think it'd be Clinton."

Leno's jokes spawned thousands of Internet imitators, E-mailed to offices all over America: "Why does Bill Clinton wear boxer shorts? To keep his ankles warm." . . . "What's the most popular game in the White House? Swallow the leader." . . . "What's Bill's definition of safe sex? When Hillary's out of town." . . . "What's the only election promise Clinton has kept? Reuniting Fleetwood Mac." . . . "What's the difference between Bill Clinton and a gangbanger? A gangbanger screws in turn; Bill Clinton screws interns." . . . "Why is Bill Clinton always losing his voice? He keeps eating his words." . . . "Why is Bill Clinton not circumcised? It would have been throwing away the best part." . . . "What are the two worst things about Bill Clinton? His face." . . . "What's Bill Clinton's favorite instrument? The strumpet." . . . "What's Bill Clinton's idea of foreplay? 'Yo, look at this, bitch!' "

Even more humiliating to the president of the United States were the jokes about the First Lady: "What would happen if Hillary got shot? Bill Clinton would become president." . . . "Hillary is the only woman to stand by her man. All the rest had to kneel." . . . "How did Bill and Hillary meet? They were dating the same girl in high school." . . . "Why does Chelsea look so ugly? Heredity." . . . "What kind of jewelry does Hillary look best in? Handcuffs." . . . "When will there be a woman in the White House? As soon as Hillary leaves." . . . "What happened when Bill Clinton was given a shot of testosterone? He turned into Hillary." . . . "Why are female White House staff annoyed with Hillary? She keeps leaving the toilet seat up." . . . "What's Hillary's new nickname? Oldielocks." . . . "Why does Hillary wear turtleneck sweaters? So we can't see her Adam's apple move when Bill talks." . . . "Why doesn't Hillary wear short skirts in the White House? She doesn't want people to see her balls." . . . "What's the difference between Hillary and the West Texas oil fields? The oil fields get drilled once in a while."

As if the proliferation of the jokes, windblown pollen, wasn't bad enough, graffiti was found scrawled into the Executive Office Building's toilet stalls: MUTE NEWT . . . KEN STARR DOES IT IN HIS UNDERWEAR . . . CLINTON IS A POTATOE HEAD . . . BUDDY SNIFFS BUTTS. And bumper stickers were flooding the land: HILLARY HAPPENS . . . FIRST HILLARY, THEN GENNIFER, NOW US . . . THE JOKE'S OVER, BRING BACK BUSH . . . IF SHE DIDN'T SPIT, YOU MUST ACQUIT . . . HEY, HILLARY, SHUT UP AND FUMIGATE . . . THE SEX EDUCATION PRESIDENT . . . ABORT CLINTON . . . I VOTED FOR BUSH IN THE LAST ELECTION . . . WHERE THE HELL IS LEE HARVEY OSWALD WHEN WE NEED HIM? . . . I FEEL YOUR TONSILS . . . I LIKE A JUICY CIGAR.

His cigar! His beloved cigar! The cigar he'd always enjoyed so much and which he couldn't have anymore. Hillary was bad enough, with her hardheaded declaration that the White House was a no-smoking zone, but now Dick Morris was telling him, "Do not be seen with a cigar again! Ever! Not in your hand! Not in your mouth!" Bill Clinton knew well enough the reasons why. He knew Dick Morris, as always, was right, but he had enjoyed his cigars so much and he and Monica had had so much fun . . . just talking about cigars. She had even given him a standing antique sterling silver cigar holder. He even had two books about cigars in his private study—*The Ulti-*

mate Cigar Book by Richard Carlton Hacker and *The Cigar Companion* by Anwar Bati and Simon Chase—right next to a book Monica had given him—*Oy Vey! The Things They Say!*—and Wally Piper's *The Little Engine That Could.*

No more cigars. Gone, along with Monica. Her oral fixation wound up robbing him of his. He felt like one of those Arabs, the subjects of that sultan from the Middle Ages, who were in danger of having their noses lopped off if they were caught with a cigar. A cigar was "a lone man's companion, a bachelor's friend, a hungry man's food, a sad man's cordial, a wakeful man's sleep, a chilly man's fire." There were two things a man never forgot: "his first love and his first cigar." A cigar "numbed sorrow and filled the solitary hours with a million gracious images."

Was that cigar with Monica in the private study the best cigar Bill Clinton had ever had? Well, in some ways, maybe. Was that the worst cigar Bill Clinton had ever had? Well, in some ways, maybe. It angered him, though, that he couldn't smoke them anymore, couldn't even put them into his mouth anymore. JFK had enjoyed his cigars; Churchill had enjoyed a quarter million of them in his ninety-one years.

All this national soul-searching over a wet, half-chewed Davidoff, and what none of the learned historical whizzes on television pointed out was that a cigar was a patriotic object, as all-American as apple pie. Benjamin Franklin paid for the Continental Congress by getting a loan on tobacco futures. With the money he got for "the royal leaf" for cigars, Franklin financed the American Revolution. And the Union won the Civil War thanks to three cigars. Two Union soldiers found the three cigars with some papers wrapped around them. The papers were discovered to be Robert E. Lee's battle plans.

No, it just wasn't right, Bill Clinton thought, all these scumbags calling *him* names, all these jokesters humiliating him, all these damn bumper stickers and people decking themselves in cigar costumes, as if the whole country was celebrating an impromptu, unscheduled Halloween. And he couldn't even have a damn cigar. He sat alone in the dark on Nancy Hernreich's couch, nostalgically contemplating his lost royal leaves, their meat, their structural stability, their lack of protruding veins, their seedlings . . . and the careful, hands-on tending his royal leaves needed.

As he settled back comfortably on Nancy Hernreich's couch, the tending of his royal leaves still foremost in his mind, he thought unexpectedly, in this period of jokes, of a joke Monica had told him. "Why do Jewish men like to watch porno films backward? So that they can see the hooker give back the money." Bill Clinton thought, too, of the joke he had told her. "What do you get when you cross a Jewish American Princess with an Apple? A computer that won't go down on you."

Bill Clinton remembered sadly how they'd laughed. He closed his eyes in the dark room . . . on his way to a few moments of sweet solitary solace during this nightmarish time . . . and he unzipped his . . .

[7]

Billy Can't Help It

"I brought my mom and my aunt to an arrival ceremony,"
Monica said. "The Big Creep said, 'I saw them. They're cute.' And
I said, 'Shut up.' Not that cute, not cuter than me."
"I wonder what he was thinking?" Linda Tripp said.
"How he could do them too."

In an America increasingly in search of repressed memories and primal traumas and childhood violations, there was one other way to defend Bill Clinton's actions. The commander in chief was the victim in chief, and the real culprit was that hoary bugaboo from the sixties: society. Or, in this case, the family. Specifically, Bill Clinton's "dysfunctional" family.

Pro-Clinton teams of shrinks swept down on the talk shows to put the blame for the pickle the president was in on his mother, his father, his step-father, his grandmother, and his grandfather. It seemed like a familial scorched-earth plan. The president stood by without comment as the shrinks euphemistically told us mom was a slut; dad a slut and a drunk; step-dad a slut, a drunk, and a wife-beater; grandma a slut and a grandpa-beater; and poor old doddering grandpa a plain old-fashioned drunk. It was a family depiction worse than any Erskine Caldwell could have drawn.

Bill Clinton, the shrinks said, had even recently, after many years of child abuse and a lifetime of abandonment, been cruelly abandoned by three important figures in his life. His beloved mother, Virginia, died in 1994. His important "father figure," Israeli prime minister Yitzhak Rabin, died in 1995. His close friend, Commerce Secretary Ron Brown, died in 1996.

In discussing these recent personal "traumas," the shrinks did not say that two days after Ron Brown's death, Bill Clinton invited Monica into the

Oval Office for a blow job; nor did they say that the videotape of the president going into Ron Brown's funeral had caught him laughing and joking with a friend.

They did say that Ron Brown's plane crash probably reminded Bill Clinton of the car crash that killed his father when he was still in the womb. They talked about how Bill Clinton had nearly lost his composure at Rabin's funeral, but they did not say that public display was probably good for a few million Jewish votes in the 1996 election. (As Hillary prepared a few years later to run for the Senate in New York, she suddenly uncovered "Jewish relatives" deep within the Methodist foliage of her family tree.)

We were to believe that Bill Clinton's problems all began with the drunken father who died in that car crash, Bill Blythe, and with his mother, Virginia. The shrinks described Virginia as flamboyant, flirty, extroverted, a "lady about town," who wore a skunk stripe in her dark hair and heavy makeup with thick, sweeping, painted-on eyebrows. Bill Blythe, they said, was a "womanizer" who "lived a life of lies."

When Bill Clinton was a year old, his mother left him with her mother and father so that she could work out of town. Virginia's mother, Edith, was like her daughter: a high-energy, razzmatazz, "let it all hang out" kind of flirty woman. She, too, wore painted, thick, sweeping eyebrows. She, too, had dark hair with a skunk stripe in it. Edith threw temper tantrums and kitchen utensils and beat her husband, who stuck increasingly close to his bottle.

The little boy called Edith "Mamaw" and the shrinks said Mamaw was a "rage-aholic," while "Papaw" was an alcoholic. Mamaw enabled his drinking, they said, and Papaw enabled her rages. (The shrinks also said both Bill's mother and grandmother looked like a skunk-stripeless Monica.) As an infant, little Billy watched Mamaw beat on the hapless Papaw, and the shrinks said this caused Billy to "bury his fear" of women deep inside himself.

Billy's mother came back from out of town when he was three years old, and the family was reunited, but the shrinks didn't see this as good news at all. This is where they thought Billy's problems had really begun. Both his mother and grandmother loved him very much, but this wasn't good. This was bad, because it meant there was a "highly pathological" struggle over him by the two flirty, skunk-striped women.

Some shrinks thought that since Mamaw had a no-account helpless drunk for a husband, she was in love with little Billy. No fool, Billy realized he had two "overtly sexual" painted women fighting for his attention. The shrinks said he learned to be "exploitative" and "manipulative," explaining something that he said to a friend many years later at the governor's mansion in Little Rock: "What am I supposed to do about these women who throw themselves at me?"

Although there was no evidence the infant Billy was the victim of incest or sexual abuse, the shrinks said the home he lived in was *"sexually charged"* and inhabited by two women with *"flashy lifestyles."* Both the home conditions and the nature of the two women meant there was "a certain amount of *emotional incest"* in his childhood. These sensual women were *"overly seductive,"* even though they only touched Billy with affection, never sexually.

Nothing had happened, but the shrinks said something bad had happened—because he was adored and worshiped by his mother and grandmother. It didn't mean he was just another little boy badly spoiled by an adoring mom and grandma; it meant he was "traumatized" and "abused." They violated poor little Billy as surely as if they had violated him. Poor little Billy was the victim of *nonincest incest.*

Mom and grandma were unwitting pedophiles who inappropriately exposed poor little Billy to "prematurely associate sex with excitement and intense arousal," which explained why he went gaga trying to find a room with rock groupie Connie Hamzy at the Hilton in Little Rock many years later. Nothing really happened sexually in poor little Billy's infanthood, the shrinks emphasized, but that didn't mean a lot of lifelong sexual damage hadn't been done.

Onto the scene when Billy was four years old came his stepfather, Roger Clinton, a womanizer like Bill Blythe, sharp dresser, high-stepper, and a drunk like him, too. Billy's mother, Virginia, the shrinks said, went for the same kind of man, or for a male counterpart of herself, and Virginia was a "flirt" (substitute the unshrunk word *slut*).

Roger was a Buick dealer, and he beat his new wife because he thought she was cheating on him. Or because he was cheating on her and figured if he was cheating, then she had to be, too. Roger Clinton was, the shrinks said, an "alcoholic rage-aholic."

Virginia, who took his beatings and ignored his drinking, was now enabling him the way Papaw was enabling Mamaw and Mamaw was enabling (and still beating) Papaw. The shrinks said Virginia didn't leave Roger because she had seen Mamaw beat Papaw so much, the violence felt like home to her. It was "normal." Little boy Billy saw Roger beat his mother, but it felt normal to him, too, since he had seen Mamaw beat Papaw and had seen his mother and Mamaw yelling at each other all the time (over him).

Roger Clinton then moved his wife and stepson from Hope to Hot Springs, Arkansas, and the shrinks had a lot of fun with this one. He was a drunk cheating on her and she was a slut cheating on him, and now they moved to Sin City, the Vegas of the Ozarks, where they both started to gamble heavily, too.

Hot Springs was a round-the-clock whorehouse and the shrinks saw three things wrong with the move for little Billy: First, the smell of sex was in the air and the little boy caught rushlike whiffs of it. The smell would stay inside the tissue linings of his nostrils for the rest of his life. Second, Hot Springs was a place of hypocrisy, where everyone denied the shenanigans going on and the little boy learned to deny and lie for the rest of his life. And third, the racetrack and the casinos were the centerpiece of the place, and while the little boy certainly didn't gamble, he caught a subconscious dose of gambling fever from his parents. He'd get aroused, take risks, and try to beat the odds (of discovery, in his case) for the rest of his life.

Other shrinks saw other imports and parallels: Virginia and Mamaw and Roger Clinton were all *"sensation seekers,"* and little Billy was always around them. . . . Bill Blythe and Virginia and Mamaw formed little Billy's *"neurological composition,"* to which Roger Clinton contributed only indirectly, which sounded like a fancy way for the shrinks to make a hodgepodge of the theories of nature and nurture.

Hot Springs certainly turned up the heat underneath little Billy's abuse levels. Now Virginia and Roger were yelling at each other all the time, drinking more than ever, cheating more than ever. Billy, meanwhile, was pretending to the outside world that everything was fine at home. He was learning that lying was *necessary* to preserve his family's *reputation.*

He was lying for *them,* in their interest, a twofold explanation of why he'd jab his finger at us years later and lie into our faces. First, to preserve the reputation of his family, of Hillary and Chelsea; second, to preserve *our* reputation, of America in the community of nations, so our country wouldn't be embarrassed around the world.

Little Billy Clinton was learning, right there in Hot Springs, thanks to Roger and Virginia's mutual abuse, *to lie for us* as he was lying for them. His lies were protecting Roger and Virginia's respectability as his lies would one day protect Hillary and Chelsea's . . . as well as ours. Little Billy Clinton, even back then, was a *heroic* liar.

As Roger's drinking worsened—he even took a shot at Virginia while the boy was looking on—Billy tried to counteract Roger's abuse of his mother by ignoring his *own* abuse and trying to please his mother. She praised Billy and told him he could be anything he wanted in life. He didn't want to let her down. He became ambitious and worked hard to realize her dreams for him.

But the shrinks said trying to inspire her beloved son to be something in life wasn't good. It was as damaging as the affection she'd showered on him when he was smaller. Virginia was violating Billy again. He was trying to be a hero for her and that made him feel "terminally unique."

I am special, Bill Clinton may have been saying to himself as he began accomplishing the success his mother so awfully much wanted for him. But he would have been better off as a loser. Because by being a loser, the shrinks said, he would have been recognizing his common lot with most of humanity. He wouldn't be weighed down by all the stress his hard work and ambition were placing on him.

Virginia's attempt to inspire her son was further abuse. Winning and trying to win was losing. Losing and not trying anything was winning. By trying so awfully hard to please his mother, by trying to make something out of himself, Bill Clinton was letting his mother violate him again. To be unviolated meant not being her hero, not being the rescuer of her (and his) self-esteem.

When Billy was sixteen, after twelve years of yelling, screaming, drinking, cheating, and gambling, Virginia divorced Roger. Billy even testified against his stepfather in court, against the man he called "Daddy," the man whose last name he had legally taken. Then, after the divorce, after Billy had gathered all his gumption and spoken ill of his stepfather in court, Virginia decided to marry Roger again.

Talk about abandoned, the shrinks tsk-tsked. Oh, Sigmund! Oh, Carl! Oh, Art Janov, screaming his shrink soul out somewhere in the Malibu hills! Billy had stood up for her in court and she turned her back on him and went back to her worthless Good Time Charlie . . . as the betrayed and abandoned teenage boy watched. It was the best explanation, the shrinks said, for why Bill Clinton had "problems" with women. Why he carried within him a "*hidden hostility*" that caused him to treat women for the rest of his life as objects to penetrate or observe as they knelt in front of him. He was getting back at his mother for the way she'd betrayed him with his stepfather.

After she remarried him, Roger Clinton, impotent, his liver the size of a cantaloupe, sank deeper than ever into the black lagoon of his alcoholism. He stayed in his room much of the time, his bottle between his legs. And now Bill Clinton, nearly a young man, became, the shrinks said, "husband" to his mother, the painted, skunk-striped, flirty woman who had had non-incestuous incest with him in his infancy, the woman who had so recently betrayed him by remarrying the semicomatose, semihuman, boozy sponge lying down in the other room.

Husband to the wife who was his mother . . . and in gratitude for his love, his forgiveness of her betrayal, Virginia built Bill a shrine in their home of all his high school trophies. As he went off to college, the shrinks said, and began the penetration and rug burning of one woman after another, all Bill Clinton was trying to do was to "reconnect" with his mother, a husband in search of his unfaithful wife, not certain what would happen if he found her. Would he want to love her or kill her? Make love to her or sodomize her? Please her or humiliate her? Nurture her or rape her?

The shrinks were able to explain everything: Bill Clinton was sex-obsessed because of his mother and Mamaw. He had the sex that was or wasn't sex with Monica because she looked like his mother and Mamaw. He was sexually insatiable because of the incest that wasn't incest with his mother and Mamaw. He lied all the time because of hypocritical Hot Springs and because he had had to lie about his parents' drinking and abuse. He liked threesomes because his mother and Mamaw had fought over him. He was ambitious because he was protecting his mother's self-esteem. He flew into rages because he'd seen his stepfather beat up his mother. He allowed Hillary to hit him because he'd seen Mamaw beat Papaw.

A modern president, Bill Clinton was allegedly the victim of incest, pedophilia, child abuse, erotomania, sexual addiction, gambling addiction, alcohol addiction, rage addiction, wife beating, husband beating, grand-father beating, low self-esteem, jealousy, and poverty.

Bill Clinton was the abused, real-life punching bag available as "exhibit A" for many of the nineties liberal causes. The president of the United States was the personification of the nightmare that many liberals felt was repressed and regressed deep within the national psyche. He was the living victim of the horrors we were trying so hard to eliminate for our children and grandchildren.

If the shrinks were right about it all, then Bill Clinton himself was responsible for none of his own actions. He was a nice-looking stage upon which two sluts and two drunks had acted out a psychodrama that opened in

Hope, played in Hot Springs, and became an international sensation at the White House. If the shrinks were right, Bill Clinton wasn't just a victim; he was a casualty. But if the shrinks were right, it also meant there was one hellaciously screwed-up human being with his finger on the nuclear button.

There he was on television, this victim in chief, asking to be forgiven for something he wouldn't admit to having done. How hard it was not to shed empathic tears over abandoned Bill Clinton!

Bill Blythe abandoned him by dying. His mother abandoned him for a job out of town. His stepfather abandoned him for his bottle. His mother abandoned him by remarrying his stepfather. His grandmother abandoned him by dying. His grandfather abandoned him by dying. His stepfather abandoned him by dying. His mother abandoned him by marrying two more stepfathers after Roger Clinton finally died. Gennifer abandoned him for a book, as did Dolly Kyle. His mother, Vince Foster, Ron Brown, and Rabin all abandoned him by dying. Stephanopoulos abandoned him for a book and for Sam and Cokie. Dick Morris abandoned him for a book and for Rupert Murdoch and Trent Lott. Barbra abandoned him for a TV actor. Monica abandoned him for a book and Ken Starr. Hillary and Chelsea were on the fence. Which pretty well meant only Buddy was left. As Harry Truman had said, "If you want a friend in Washington, get a dog."

Buddy was certainly an improvement over Zeke, Chelsea's crazed cocker spaniel, killed, finally, outside the governor's mansion in Little Rock while chasing a car. Zeke had barked nonstop, clawed at doors, had even caused a political uproar by constantly violating Little Rock's leash laws. Even dog psychiatrists couldn't silence the demented Zeke; only a car could.

While Buddy didn't seem to be as politically PR-savvy as previous presidential dogs like Fala (FDR) and Yuki (LBJ), he probably wouldn't splat the Great Wall of China, like Bush's C. Fred. Although Buddy still wasn't house-trained, thus limiting the photo ops. Plus, he had gone right up to Monica as she sat in the private study and had instantly shoved his nose right between her legs. "Buddy," Monica had said, "you're better at this than your daddy."

As the shrinks kept shrinking Bill Clinton on the talk shows in an effort to save him, White House spin doctors were concerned that some friendly liberal shrink would start saying that . . . judging by his behavior . . . Buddy was a victim of abuse, too. Just like his master.

(8)

Bob Dole's Johnhenry

Who knew? Right? Nobody knew. During the campaign. Against Clinton. For the enchilada. I was on message. Character, character, character. Who would you leave your kids with? And all that time. He was getting his johnhenry blown. By our next-door neighbor. Jiminy! By this girl. Lipinski. Kaczynsky. Whatever.

Bob Dole didn't know, and neither did Elizabeth Dole. We knew she was our next-door neighbor. We'd seen her at the elevator. But we didn't know she knew his johnhenry.

Funny, isn't it? How things work out? Yeah, right here at the Watergate. All three of us. Bob Dole. Elizabeth Dole. Monica Lipinski. And our neighbor, Lipinski, gets bigger than Watergate! Dorothy had it right. Right? In that movie about Kansas. "We're way out of Kansas now, Tonto."

I was gonna win the election. "There are doers and there are stewers." Dad said that. Three times is a charm. Somebody said that. Eighty and '88; this was three. Had it set up right to stay on message, on message, on message. Told 'em some jokes. Got grasshoppers so big in Kansas, they eat pigs' noses. Got cabbage leaves we use for circus tents. Use cornstalks to build bridges. Then back to message—Character! Character! Character!

Didn't have to mention the war stuff. The shoulder. The cigar box. The pen in my right hand. Bob Dole took a lickin' but keeps on tickin'! Everybody knew about it. Wasn't like back in Kansas. Hadda run those TV ads. A picture of me and a picture of my shoulder. It wasn't there. Didn't even have to talk about the war. Everybody knew. Like they knew about his draft dodging.

The great silent issue of the campaign. World War II against Vietnam. Years in the hospital against his years at Oxford. A Purple Heart against his deferment. NASA against *Sputnik*. The NFL against the NLF. Kansas against Hollywood. Dead against Red. Love it against leave it. Leaded against unleaded.

The other big issue besides the war to end all wars—isn't that what Eisenhower called it? That issue was his johnhenry. We called it character. Everybody knew about him, and his johnhenry, too. Bob and Elizabeth Dole were happily married. Everybody knew that, too. The war stuff worked into that. Bob Dole was physically challenged, not the kind of man who *had* a johnhenry. It was *my* character against his. Apple pie against cherry pie. Maturity against his saxophone. Bifocals against his sunglasses. My missing shoulder against his johnhenry. Bob Dole tells the truth! Bob Dole loves America!

Knew going in that we had just the tiniest amount of exposure there, too. On johnhenry. It was my divorce. Batted it around with my guys. With George Will's wife and Rudman and David Keene. But it was so many years ago, back in '72, we thought Bob Dole would be okay.

Reagan was divorced. And Phyllis, my ex, had come back aboard. She sold DOLE FOR PRESIDENT buttons in '88. And our daughter, Robin, who was a kid in her forties now, had been a part of every campaign.

So Bob Dole had mended the bridges. He'd pork-barreled the home district. Plus, the guys all felt Elizabeth's presence would get us over this. Elizabeth looking radiant up on the platform. Her arms around Bob and Robin Dole. Most voters wouldn't even know that Phyllis was still alive.

Jiminy, we got off to a bang-up start, didn't we? Bob Dole on message: Character! Character! Character! And right during the Democratic National Convention, johnhenry was the issue that came up. Like a hand grenade had landed in the middle of their party. Blown all of their shoulders off. Philip Morris, the little weasel, caught with a pro. Morris, Clinton's pimp, caught paying two hundred dollars an hour. So he could suck her toes. So he could get down on the rug naked and bark like a dog. Bob Dole had to laugh. It was too good to be true. Even though Trent and Jesse Helms were a little itchy. Morris worked for them, too.

But I laughed. Morris even told the pro he wanted to have at it with Hillary. He told her there was bacteria on Mars. That was top secret. He let her listen in as he spoke to Clinton. While the pro did what our neighbor girl was doing. All they could do was let Morris resign. Though I know he still gave Trent advice afterward. And somebody at the White House called him an "externality." Yeah, that was a good one. He was an externality all right. Like the kind men have. Character! Character! Character! And then this happens. And Morris's externality reminds the voters of Clinton's externality. On message. On message. On message. I'll say!

Bob Dole said not a word about it, of course. Bob Dole stayed on the high road. He remembered the advice from President Nixon he'd gotten in '72. When Bob Dole was getting divorced. Bob Dole went to the Old Man and offered to resign as chairman of the Republican National Committee. And the Old Man told me that a politician had to be judged on his public behavior. Not his private one. He gave me a book that Bob Dole read carefully. It was about Israeli, the Hall of Fame English prime minister. Very big, Israeli. Bigger than Churchill. Bigger than Thatcher. Babe Ruth big. Dempsey. Sam Rayburn. And the book said Israeli was married half a dozen times. Jumped around more bedrooms than the clowns jumping around at Ringling and Bailey. So Bob Dole said not a word about the weasel down on the floor. Barking like a dog. But the voters all heard very clearly. What Bob Dole wasn't saying.

What a start! A landslide start! A mandate start! And after that start . . . *I fell down.* In Kansas. In California. You probably saw the pictures. I couldn't help it. Bob Dole tells the truth! Bob Dole loves America! I'm not young. I'm mature. I tried to stay on message. But they started firing their poison gas. The libs, as the Old Man said, are like that. They wanted to get back at us for Morris, the weasel naked on the floor.

Jiminy, they called *me* the hatchet man! Accused me of writing the mother of a candidate I was running against in Kansas. Telling her he was an alcoholic! Accused me of calling another opponent an abortionist! Accused me of saying the Democrats caused 1.8 million American deaths in World War II! Accused me of using my missing shoulder to get my votes! Accused me of being a snarling attack dog! And now here *they* came!

Accusing me of choosing a running mate, Jack Kemp, who they said was a homosexual. And a draft dodger. They didn't do it directly. They *denied* doing it. To give the story more play. To take the voters' minds off the weasel on the rug. The weasel denied doing it himself. Like the weasel he was. The weasel said reports were untrue. That he and the president's campaign were "tracking" rumors. That Jack was a homosexual. And had gotten out of the draft due to a pro football injury.

Bob Dole knew how slimy this was. A slander upon a fine, upstanding NFL family man. The veteran of countless linebackers. Roughings of the passer. An effort to character-assassinate Bob Dole's missing shoulder. The weasel was denying. Done to obscure un-American activities. Of the two johnhenrys. Kennedy's—I mean Clinton's. And Philip Morris's. Bob Dole tells the truth! Bob Dole loves America! This was wrong. Wrong, wrong, wrong.

The next shot they took came even closer to me. Roger Stone. One of my campaign aides. A good man. A fine Republican. A patriotic American. Director of

President Reagan's Political Affairs. Even kept close touch with the Old Man in his final years. Visiting him at his New Jersey house. Whispering him political gossip. Keeping the Old Man in the loop. And now the rags were showing pictures of Roger. Bare-chested and wearing a mask. Pictures of his wife on a bed. Not wearing a whole lot. Pictures that were a part of ads Roger had run. In sex magazines. Looking for group sex. They were seen at a sex club. At an orgy. One of the ads run by Roger's wife said something about a hot babe. Who needed real men.

Bob Dole didn't believe a word of it. I didn't care *what* the pictures showed. They wanted to get Roger because of Reagan. Because of the Old Man. Because of Bob Dole. Because Roger was the best man we had for negative advertising. Because the sex maniac I was running against for president had hit on Roger's wife. At the Old Man's funeral. The same wife whose picture was in the ads. Who said she was 40DD-24-36.

Think about that. President Nixon is barely in the ground. I'm giving the eulogy. (Bob Dole cried.) And the president of the United States—at the funeral of one of the greatest presidents in history—is thinking about his johnhenry. They wanted to get Roger. And they got him. As I say, I didn't believe a word of it. But I asked him to resign.

Then they got Arthur Finkelstein. A bullet to the spine. Arthur was Roger's mentor. One of the best consultants on the Republican side. A little to the right. Working for the antihomosexual guys. Helms. Don Nickles. Lech. Faircloth. A lot of Arthur's guys were now working for Bob Dole. And it just happens to come out now—after Morris—after Roger—that Arthur is—*aarg!*—homosexual. That Arthur is living with his—*aarg!*—homosexual husband. Or wife. Or whatever. I don't know about that stuff. We didn't have that stuff in Kansas. And they're raising two boys. Yup. That's what I said. Arthur's a homosexual. Getting paid by those guys who don't like that stuff. And he and his whatever have two boys.

I struck back at the bastards. Never let it be said that Bob Dole doesn't return fire. That he doesn't spear with his helmet when they spear him. "Can't never not do anything." Mom said that. I went after the bastards' supply line. Their money supply. Hollywood. Bob Dole told them they made money from music that voted for the "raping, torturing, and mutilation of women." From movies that cast their ballot for "nightmares of depravity."

I laid it on real good. The Old Man would have been proud of me. It was like one of my speeches back in the old days. About the longhaired vermin in our streets. Bob Dole got their attention. Bob Dole burst at them with machine-gun fire. George Will's wife and my other guys thought the bullets were ricocheting all over Clinton.

I tried to stay on message. Character! Character! Character! But some of my guys were worrying. Maybe the message was turning into a double-edged sword. A plague of Kansas locusts. A game of Russian roulette. I felt like we were dodging bullets. That Bob Dole was back there with the Tenth Mountain Division. At the Pra del Bianco. Or wherever.

The troops—Roger, Arthur—were taking hits. I was weary. Stumbling. But if I could just slog through the mud. For a little while longer. I'd plant Old Glory on election day. Atop this heap of dirt and slime. And win the Super Bowl. I didn't pay attention to the polls. The polls were sniper fire. Bad calls made by the refs. Polls had to be ignored. I had to keep plowing up the middle. On a cold day in Green Bay. Through the shrapnel. Sniper fire. Win one for the USA. The Gipper. FDR. Ike. The Brooklyn Dodgers. Whatever.

Almost did it, too. Almost planted that flag. Almost won my championship ring. Took my bullet in the middle of October. Just a few weeks before election day. It was the divorce. Phyllis! Phyllis and Robin!

First the rags wrote that I met Phyllis at the hospital. When I was in rehab after the war. That she helped me walk again. Cut my meat for me. Helped me go back to school. Took notes for me there. Helped me pass my bar exam. Always took dictation for me. Sewed my clothes. Sewed campaign workers' clothes. That in the final year of our marriage, I was sleeping in the basement. *Alone.* That I had dinner with Phyllis and Robin twice—on Christmas and New Year's. That after twenty-three years of marriage, I dumped her. By just saying, "I want out."

Making me look as bad as Gingrich. Asking his wife for a divorce settlement while she was in the hospital. Diagnosed with cancer. It sounded bad. A woman who'd helped me to walk again and cut my meat. Dumping her like that. I couldn't deny any of it. Bob Dole tells the truth. Bob Dole loves America.

But that first bullet just grazed me. They quoted Phyllis as saying I was a workaholic. That's what broke us up. I was working too hard for America. If you need a reason for dumping somebody who's helped you walk again, America's not bad. Plus, there was no hostility. She made money selling her Bob Dole buttons, right? Robin was being paid by the Dole for President campaign, right? So far not too bad.

Then I caught one in my missing shoulder. A piece of shrapnel the size of a big fat lie. Wounded in the campaign for Europe. Wounded again now in the campaign against Clinton. Wasn't even sure if Phyllis knew about this stuff. Workaholic, huh? *Yeah, right.* A week before the election, after staying on message:

Character! Character! Character! After my Hollywood speech about values. And they nailed Bob Dole on character. On his johnhenry. Because he couldn't keep it zipped. Equating Bob Dole with the sex maniac he was running against.

It was a long time ago. The early seventies. But I knew that wouldn't matter. The whole country was sexually bats then. But I knew that wouldn't wash, either. Bob Dole was Bob Dole. Bob Dole had the Purple Heart. Bob Dole had the missing shoulder. Bob Dole wasn't supposed to have a johnhenry.

Her name was Meredith Roberts. She was thirty-five at the time. A secretary at George Washington University. I was forty-five. A senator. The rags had found her now. She was sixty-three. Still single. Living with a bunch of cats. She was still mad at me, too. She told about how she used to call Bob Dole "Bobby D." How everybody thought Bob Dole walked on water. But she knew Bob Dole wasn't squeaky-clean. How we were supposedly madly in love.

Jiminy! I wasn't surprised she was still mad at me. She thought I dumped her for Phyllis. She thought I was going back to my wife. Wrong, wrong, wrong. I did go to Phyllis, but it was a different Phyllis. It wasn't my wife. It was Phyllis *Wells*. A model. Character! Character! Character! And now Bob Dole was Bobby D.

Bob Dole tells the truth! Bob Dole loves America! But Bob Dole wanted to be president! We tried to stop the bleeding from this hit. It wasn't easy. It was clear now that I'd dumped the woman who'd helped me to walk again for the sake of my johnhenry. Then, for the sake of my johnhenry again, I dumped the woman who was taking care of my johnhenry. For a model who took *better* care of my johnhenry.

I told the voters. Don't read that stuff. Don't watch television. You make up your own mind. Don't let 'em make up your mind for you. We tried to keep it out of the mainstream press. Some of my guys who'd worked with Finkelstein talked to the *Washington Post*. I had Elizabeth talk to the publisher of the *Post*. I felt funny about that. My wife was asking that a story about cheating on my ex-wife be kept out of the papers.

Some papers kept it out. Some didn't. But I'd bled to death anyway by then. Bob Dole was old. Bob Dole fell down. Bob Dole had only one thing going for him with the voters. Character! Character! Character! And now character had come back. And bitten Bob Dole on his johnhenry.

Bob Dole's shoulder had been forgotten. Bob Dole was the joke now. "A candidate for the glue factory. At his best when the memorial service isn't for him. He always sees the glass of Metamucil half-full. The woman involved was Wanda Flintstone. To appear more presidential, he's been smoking pot and hailing hookers."

I died in the mud. Impaled by my flag. Slick Willy beat Bobby D. My championship ring was out of my reach by the length of my johnhenry. My right hand couldn't grasp it. Stuff like this can happen in any given war. On any given Sunday. Read S. L. Marshall. Listen to John Madden. See *Private Ryan.*

And then, when it was all over, when Bob Dole was dead and buried, I discovered that this Lipinski girl was our next-door neighbor. Bill Clinton and Bob Dole were veterans of the same campaign. He had Hillary. And Gennifer. And Lipinski. I had Phyllis. And Meredith. And the other Phyllis.

Then I took another bullet. Bob Dole was six feet under politically. But it still hurt. A doctor in Kansas said I'd taken a young woman to him. For an abortion. In 1972. One of my former campaign aides backed him up. But it wasn't true! Bob Dole tells the truth! Bob Dole does not believe in abortion! Bob Dole believes abortion is wrong. Wrong, wrong, wrong. Bob Dole is not Bobby D. Bob Dole is not Bill Clinton.

Bob Dole loves America, not his johnhenry. He's got one, though. Just like everybody else. Not everybody, I guess. Just men. I don't mean that to sound sexist. Bob Dole is not sexist. Sexism is wrong. Wrong, wrong, wrong. What? What's that? It does what? Really? Jiminy! What's it called? *Niagara?*

[9]

Billy Likes Doing It

"I did such a naughty thing yesterday," Monica said to Linda Tripp, "but I couldn't resist. Egon Schiele — he's one of my favorite artists. It's like a lot of naked women and stuff. It's very erotic. So I picked this one postcard and it's like of this — like naked — total fucking naked girl. She's butt naked. I sent him the card."

More than anything else, what seemed to distress some people — like the Reverend Donald Wildmon, head of the American Family Association, and James Dobson, head of Focus on the Family — was that the president of the United States played with himself.

"Should this man who is seen in Starr's report masturbating in the West Wing," wrote the conservative columnist George Will, whose wife, Mari, was the former speechwriter for the formerly impotent Bob Dole, "be seen for 28 more months in the Presidency?"

It was as though some people were waving that old yellow-stained book about hair and warts growing on boys' palms: *Onania, Or the Heinous Sin of Self-Pollution and All Its Frightening Consequences, with Spiritual and Physical Advice to Those Who Have Already Injured Themselves by This Abominable Practice, to Which Is Subjoined a Letter from a Lady to the Author, Concerning the Use and Abuse of the Marriage Bed, with the Author's Answer* (4th ed., London, 1726).

Congressman Bob Barr was talking about "the flames of hedonism, the flames of narcissism, the flames of self-centered morality," reminding observers of what Senator Orrin Hatch had said about now Supreme Court Justice Clarence Thomas — "that anybody could be that perverted — I'm sure there are people like that, but they're generally in insane asylums."

Flames of hedonism . . . insane asylums . . . George Will, in another column, scoffed at a psychologist who said, "Masturbation cannot hurt you and it will make you feel more relaxed" . . . scoffing about playing with yourself . . . which the psychologist said 99 percent of Americans did but that only 1 percent admitted.

Did George Will never play with himself, when Mari was off with the impotent Dole, or when a good-looking young Chicago Cub hit one over the fence, or when he considered the tightly fitting white dress Cokie wore on the show last Sunday? Did Bob Barr, in between his three marriages, never play with himself? Or Orrin Hatch, remembering the ex–porn queen who'd once worked in his office? Or after a tour of that part of Mormon country where men had seven wives?

Masturbation, it seemed, was still the sin that turned out the freaks with pitchforks spewing fire and brimstone. It was still the "original sin" that made us all sinners. When Joycelyn Elders, Bill Clinton's Surgeon General said, "I think masturbation is a part of human sexuality and a part of something that perhaps should be taught," the "high-tech lynching" Clarence Thomas had talked about really took place and Elders had to resign. ("If President Clinton had followed Joycelyn Elders's advice," Jay Leno wisecracked, before the *Starr Report* revealed the president's onanistic inclinations, "he wouldn't be in trouble now.")

But Bill Clinton *was* in trouble now and he couldn't deny this one. He had a pattern of playing with his willard; he'd done it with Gennifer and he'd done it twice with Monica. Michael Isikoff, the *Newsweek* reporter, even got an anonymous phone call, *before* the *Starr Report* came out, from a woman who was groped by Clinton in his private study and who'd then had to watch as the president took Willard out and "finished the job himself."

White House spin doctors didn't want to deal with whacking directly, although Clintonista theologians talked about Jesus' admonition to "love thy neighbor as thyself." The head of America's solosexual movement, Harold Litten, asked, "Did Jesus masturbate or did He have nocturnal emissions, wet dreams? Now, if you believe the Bible that Jesus was a human being in every way—it must be one or the other." Other religious scholars pointed to Saint Teresa and John of the Cross as examples of saintly onanists (although John also flagellated himself, which no one so far had accused Bill Clinton of doing). Saint Bernard was quoted as having written, "If anyone once receives the spiritual kiss of Christ's mouth, he seeks eagerly to have it again."

Secular scholars, meanwhile, pointed to famous pud pullers like Tolstoy,

Nietzsche, de Maupassant, Wagner, Jack London, and Shakespeare, even quoting from one of the Bard's sonnets: "Sin of self-love possesseth all mine eye / And all my soul and all my every part / And for this sin there is no remedy / It is so grounded in word in my heart."

Some thought in the White House was given (allegedly, it was a James Carville idea) to presenting the president's onanism in a political context: The world was overpopulated; hunger was everywhere. What the president was doing was good for the whole world.

Howard Stern offered up, on the air, what could have been an onanistic race-card defense: "The closest I ever came to making love to a black woman was masturbating to a picture of Aunt Jemima on a pancake box." A generation of white boys who'd grown up assiduously reading every issue of *National Geographic* knew what he meant.

The spin doctors ultimately presented no defense, because Bill Clinton, even upon cursory examination, was the classic whacker. Onanists love Jacuzzis for obvious reasons, and the first thing Bill Clinton had installed at the White House was a Jacuzzi. Onanists love to jog, love the feeling of their stiff willards flapping against themselves, and Bill Clinton was a lifelong jogger.

Some people pointed, too, to his red face. Why was he so often red-faced? What had he been doing? That he loved Willard, no one could deny, a modern-day example of Leonardo da Vinci's dictum: "The penis has often a life and intelligence separate from the man, and it would appear that the man is in the wrong by being ashamed of giving it a name or to exhibit it, seeking rather to cover and conceal what he ought to adorn and display with ceremony as a ministrant." Bill Clinton wasn't ashamed of his; he named it and exhibited it—"Kiss it"—he adorned and displayed it to Flowers, Monica, et al. And he had his own ceremony on Nancy Hernreich's couch or over the sink.

He also fit the classic profile of the onanist in his relationship with Monica, as defined by the respected Dr. Karl Menninger: "They are very proud of their sexual organs, and, indeed, it is not inaccurate to say that such persons prefer masturbation to sexual intercourse. Such intercourse as they perform is frequently only a kind of intravaginal masturbation." In Monica's case, the masturbation wasn't even that—it was intra-oral. The first time she took Willard in her mouth, he didn't even know her name. (His eagerness to display Willard did seem to put the lie to conservative writer Ann Coulter's theory that Willard suffered from Peyronie's disease, curvature of the penis, known henceforth inside the Beltway as "Ann Coulter disease.")

Militant onanists everywhere, seeking empowerment, like other forgotten Americans, an awesome and vast silent majority, claimed Bill Clinton as one of their own.

They were hoping, naturally, that Bill Clinton would do for them what Martin Luther King, Jr., had done for blacks, Harvey Milk for gays, Cesar Chavez for Hispanics, Gloria Steinem and Lorena Bobbitt for women. Only Pee-wee Herman had had this chance, and he'd gone skulking off like he was ashamed of what he'd been caught doing—what most of us had sometimes done—in that theater.

By saying, Yes, I masturbate, like most of you, and, like most of you, I love it! Bill Clinton could have freed men and women everywhere from the disdain and prejudice they were victims of. Homosexuality had already been transformed into a mainstream all-American trait on the sitcoms; couldn't Bill Clinton do the same for solosexuality? Lincoln had freed a couple of hundred thousand blacks—what was that compared to freeing hundreds of millions of blacks, whites, browns, yellows, reds, albinos, and so on? Bill Clinton could have been Mandela, Walesa, Gandhi, and Yeltsin combined.

They had their hearts broken, though, those militant onanists who stuck it into eggplants and melons and avocados and the tail pipes of cars. Bill Clinton *was* Bill Clinton, who said he hadn't inhaled, who hadn't dodged the draft, who hadn't had sex with Gennifer and Monica, who even denied *smoking* his cigars—"I admit that I did do it when Captain Scott O'Grady was found in Bosnia, because I was so happy. It was a form of celebration."

Even the onanists got angry at him, as angry as George Will and Bob Barr. Here was this titaholic solosexual in the perfect position—the Oval Office—to help them, and he was letting them down. He was jacking off all over the White House (certainly in the new Jacuzzi, and on the new jogging track, too), probably using feather dusters and Vicks VapoRub and flower vases and scrotal straps and napkin rings and vibrators . . . and he was acting just like Pee-wee Herman, skulking off and hoping Americans would forget about it . . . instead of putting them up on the cross for their hypocrisy. There was no doubt he used a Sears pistol-whip vibrator; Gennifer had told us about that.

What an opportunity Bill Clinton had for the kind of breakthrough Nixon had achieved with China, Reagan had achieved with Gorbachev's

Evil Empire, Jimmah had achieved with Hugh Hefner's *Playboy*. Like the rest of us of his generation, Bill Clinton had whacked in joyful teenage circle jerks, whacked while watching strippers in burlesque houses, whacked while playing pocket pool in school, whacked while reading the Sears catalog, whacked while watching Cecil B. DeMille's biblical epics, whacked while listening to Claudine Longet's voice. Whacking, whacking, whacking (DeSalvo, the Boston Strangler, whacked eight times a day), and now he blew it. He didn't have the balls to tell America how he loved playing with his balls.

He was an aficionado of onanism. He even liked different kinds of phone sex. He liked the kind where Monica was kneeling in front of him and he was on the phone conducting the nation's business with that sugarcane magnate or the congressman about Bosnia or with Dick Morris.

The Morris phone-sex conversation was a kind of telephonic orgy, a four-way disembodiment of intimacy. Here Bill Clinton was with a phone to his ear and Monica on Willard at the White House, talking to Morris, who had a phone to his ear and a hooker on *his* willard at the Jefferson Hotel.

But that wasn't even the real thing. The real thing was with Monica, whom he turned into his "phone whore," as the 900 operators called themselves. Monica could do that silky Marilyn imitation and she had a natural Valley Girl voice, which is what the 900 operators all try to fake. Monica was so out there, he could get her to do *anything*.

After he'd put the cigar inside her, after he'd given her the leather-bound Whitman book, she'd sent him a note that said, "Whitman is so rich that one must read him like one tastes . . . a good cigar—take it in, roll it in your mouth, and savor it." Monica, who'd described phone sex to Vernon Jordan by saying, "He's taking care of business on one end and I'm taking care of business on the other." Monica was a sensational phone whore, as opposed to Gennifer, who'd never liked it and had re-created one of their sessions in her book.

> Bill would never come out and say, "Let's have phone sex." Instead, it usually went something like this. We'd be having a nice conversation. Suddenly, Bill would lower his voice, and I knew he was about to start getting into it.
> "What are you wearing?" he would ask.

"Nothing, except for the black teddy you bought me," I'd answer. "I've got my hand on the girls [her breasts] and I'm about to rub them very softly."

"Do you know what I wish?" Bill would ask breathlessly.

"No, what?"

"God, I wish you were here, and could do the same to the boys [his testicles]."

We would go on like that for a while until, finally, Bill would come.

He loved having sex with Monica by phone. They had phone sex fifteen times and only had "real" in-person sex ten times. He initiated all the phone calls. He'd be in the middle of a conversation, lower his voice, and say, "I want to talk about something else."

Monica knew what she was doing, like the Tiffanys, the Vanessas, the Porsches, and the Mercedes at the 900 numbers who moaned and screamed and pushed their callers' "dick buttons." Like the best of phone actors, Monica the phone whore knew how to make slurping noises. She sucked her fingers and smacked her lips. She jiggled her fingers up and down in front of her teeth and between her lips, getting into the saliva, making a slushing sound, which, overdone, could sound like a waterfall or a washing machine. She knew how to use the four basic dirty words creatively. Phone sex with Monica really was "the next best thing to being there."

And what was the big deal in calling her for a little phone sex? Two hundred fifty thousand Americans called the phone-sex 900 numbers every night. Bill Clinton wasn't calling the 900 numbers, was he? He knew it would be unseemly for the president of the United States to do that. He had his own private, devoted, and starstruck phone whore. He wasn't part of that shady army of faceless men who called the 900 whores each night and said things like "Beg for it. . . . Let me hear you scream. . . . Be my pig fuck. . . . Crawl. . . . Scratch me harder."

No phone whore would ever be able to say about Bill Clinton what one 900 actress said about her clients: "They hate the women they lust after and need to degrade women during sex. They view women as physical bodies without names. They adore their cocks and love to talk about them." Thanks to having Monica, no phone whore could ever say about him: "They need to call me a degrading name as soon as possible. It not only helps them to get off, but it releases a knot of pent-up desire to verbally debase and abuse the woman."

. . .

While masturbation and phone sex became a part of the national debate over the blow jobs and the cigar (a debate that had begun years before, during the Clarence Thomas and Anita Hill hearings, with Long Dong Silver and the pubic hair on that Coke can), no one had the stomach, it seemed, not even Kenneth W. Starr, to explore the most sexually incendiary revelation of the *Starr Report*. It was a simple short sentence, footnote 209. "*Lewinsky. 8/26/98 depo. at 20. They engaged in oral-anal contact as well.*" Blow jobs, a cigar, whacking, and . . . *anilingus?*

Rimming? What the textbooks describe as "kissing or licking in the anal area," in the Oval Office? "Some people have a strong, perhaps even exclusive preference for either rimming or being rimmed," one textbook states. "Others enjoy both, either taking turns or else experimenting with positions that allow simultaneous rimming . . . of all forms of anal stimulation, rimming is most likely to trigger strong revulsion and disgust. Most of us learned early in life that when something is dirty we should definitely avoid putting it in or near our mouths. . . . Those who decide to explore rimming usually want to try it during or immediately after showering or bathing. This can lower discomfort with the odors commonly found in the anal area and also reduce the possibility of encountering feces." Most doctors strongly advised using a latex dental dam during rimming.

The rimming that took place in the Oval Office survived as the greatest unsolved mystery of the *Starr Report*. No newspaper account mentioned it; the talk shows didn't present anal experts to pontificate about it; Jay Leno made no jokes about it. The children of America, who'd already learned about penis size, pubic hair on Coke cans, blow jobs, masturbation, and an interuterine cigar, were spared.

Even Starr and his prosecutors didn't ask Monica more detailed questions, such as: Who was doing the rimming? Those Washington insiders who knew *everything* said it had to be the president who was *being* rimmed, but they were guessing. Was it possible that Bill Clinton, who wanted to perform cunnilingus on Monica but couldn't because she had her period, turned to anilingus instead?

It was obvious from the *Starr Report* that no dental dam had been used and that neither Clinton nor Monica had showered beforehand. Had either of them been infected? Had the president of the United States risked the nation's interest by engaging—*if* he engaged—as the rimmer?

The debate over presidential whacking did have one healthy effect upon the body politic. It pushed the Oval Office *blow jobs* into the background. As more facts came out, it appeared that a lot of people, besides Monica, agreed with Bill Clinton that a blow job wasn't sex. One of the state troopers guarding Governor Clinton in Arkansas said the governor told him way back then that the Bible said a blow job wasn't sex. A governor who attended a conference with Governor Clinton heard him make the same claim. Other public figures, it developed, had drawn the same distinction.

Speaker Newt Gingrich, twenty years earlier, had let a campaign worker go down on him but not have intercourse with him, so he could say, "I never slept with you." Virginia senator Chuck Robb had allowed mistresses to massage him and go down on him but not sleep with him, so he could issue a statement that said, "I haven't done anything that *I* regard as being unfaithful to my wife." Even Sammy Davis, Jr., had allowed Linda Lovelace to go down on him but not sleep with him.

The 1994 movie *Clerks* featured a character who'd had three lovers but had gone down on thirty-seven men. "Oral sex isn't really sex," she'd said. A 1996 *Playboy* survey of young men and women at twelve colleges showed approximately 50 percent of the students didn't believe oral sex was "real sex." Three-fourths of those surveyed said they hadn't included in their list of partners those with whom they'd had only oral sex. Oral sex, it seemed, at least among the young and hip, had become just a friendly step beyond a kiss on both cheeks or a handshake, a kind of "good pals," very personal . . . *manicure*. Women like Liz Phair and Alanis Morissette were good-naturedly singing, "I want to be your blow job queen" and "Would she go down on you in a theater?"

There was more bad news for the Messrs. Wildmon, Dobson, Will, and Barr in the rest of that *Playboy* survey. Almost half of the students surveyed had masturbated in front of one another, more than two-thirds had performed phone sex, a third had tried bondage, one in five had used a blindfold during sex, four in ten women had had sex in front of others, and the vast majority had watched X-rated videos with a partner.

While the reverends and their cohorts fulminated about masturbation, Americans had spent $8 billion in 1996 alone for hard-core videos and live sex acts and sex devices; the *fans* at a Cincinnati Reds baseball game cheered when they heard their museum director had been found not guilty of indecency for showing Robert Mapplethorpe's photos; and Howard Stern was on the radio, not only talking about how much he wanted to have sex with Lamb Chop but also featuring one guest who put his willard into a mousetrap and another who played the piano with it.

In Los Angeles, Hugh Hefner claimed the president for himself, too. Not only was Bill Clinton the first rock and roll president (Jann Wenner), the first black president (Toni Morrison); Hefner said he was "the first *Playboy* president." Hefner, as most men of his generation in L.A., had discovered the wonders of Viagra, gotten divorced, and, as his magazine said, "restored the rep of the *Playboy* Mansion as party central." A well-known movie producer, not so lucky, discovered Viagra and promptly suffered two strokes. Viagra, as *Playboy* said, "offered a return to phallic-centered sex, *the great god Cock.*"

For some fundamentalists and their allies, waving their crosses like brooms to "Clean up America," it was just too much. Blow jobs, masturbation, the cigar, and anilingus . . . Mapplethorpe, Viagra, and now the great god Cock.

Most Americans shrugged, maybe grinned a little, and went off to buy or rent their X-rated videos. Judiciary chairman Henry Hyde sounded frightened: "I wonder if after this culture war is over, an America will survive that's worth fighting to defend."

Firebrand Paul Weyrich, president of the conservative Free Congress Foundation, threw the towel in: "I no longer believe there's a moral majority. I do not believe that a majority of Americans actually shares our values. The culture we are living in becomes an even wider sewer. In truth, I think we are caught up in a cultural collapse of historic proportions, a collapse so great that it simply overwhelms politics."

Who could blame the president of the United States if, on occasion, even in his time of crisis, even as we all approached the promised biblical Armageddon, he displayed for the cameras . . . a great big Christ-kissed, solosexual, rapturous, red-faced (and possibly shit-eating) grin?

[10]

Better Than a Lava Lamp

"I don't know, you know?" Monica said. "I can understand that there's the issue of truth, you know. We're all God's children, God is synonymous with good, truth and kindness and happiness and all sorts of good things."

"I don't care about all that right now," Linda Tripp said.

A week before he and Monica tried his cigar, Bill Clinton sat on the dais with Hillary at the National Radio and Television Correspondents Dinner and glared stone-faced as Don Imus, a bad-boy gunslinger from the Old West, made jokes about his philandering. "Remember the AstroTurf in the back of the pickup truck?" Imus said, looking right at him, leering.

When Bill and Hillary got home to the White House, there waiting to comfort them was Hillary's guru, Jean Houston, the self-styled secular spiritualist and the reincarnation of the goddess Athena. The president drifted away to watch the Arkansas Razorbacks on television, but Jeanie stayed with Hillary to make her feel better. Hillary liked and trusted her. Jean Houston had arranged Hillary's chats with Mahatma Gandhi and Jesus Christ and, most important, with Hillary's role model, Eleanor Roosevelt, whose oil portrait hung above Hillary's desk in her office.

The First Lady's relationship with Jean Houston was an outgrowth of Hillary's desire when she graduated from Wellesley to take the summer off and tour the holy places of India. She had always been spiritual—drawn to Rod McKuen's verse and *Jonathan Livingston Seagull*; for a while she even wore a mood ring and lighted her dorm room with a lava lamp. She wanted to get into the swami thing a lot of sixties people, led by the Beatles' discovery of the Maharishi Mahesh Yogi, were doing. A touch of acid or hash, a swim in the sacred Ganges, some soulful empathy with the beggars, and the discovery of God in a land full of gods and shrines and horseflies.

Hillary opted not to do that, opted to work for a Black Panther lawyer in Berkeley instead, but the urge was there, as it was there for many of us in the sixties who went to places like Esalen in Big Sur and smeared chicken gravy over our faces as we ate roast chicken, the better to communicate with the bird we were eating.

Then, in the seventies and eighties, as we grew older, our spirituality found more convenient forms of expression than trekking halfway around the world to catch amebic dysentery. We started carrying chunks of crystal embedded in sterling silver, using our sacred objects as magic wands. We made treks to more hygienic spiritual places like the Vortex on Kauai, with a McDonald's just down the road. We started listening to Yanni and John Tesh and, at Christmas, Mannheim Steamroller. Tony Robbins and Marianne Williamson and Jean Houston, daughter of a Hollywood gag writer, became our secular gurus and worldly theologians, the Pat Robertsons and Jerry Falwells and Jimmy Swaggarts of the posthippie, New Age Left.

Hillary arrived at Jean Houston through her brief dalliance with Michael Lerner, author of "The Politics of Meaning" and editor of *tikkun* magazine, the kind of obscure journal that Hillary, who had neatly filed Carl Oglesby's articles in her student days, liked to discover. What Lerner had to say, viewed especially as a mirror-image description of her husband, the president of the United States, must have struck her heart.

"If our world needs to be healed," Lerner wrote, "it will be done by wounded healers; people who themselves are in need of healing. Once we realize this, we have every right to insist that the media stop caring about the personal inadequacies of political figures and refocus on the content of their ideas. . . . The insistence in American politics that our leaders be on a higher moral plain than anyone else has not led to a new level of morality in politics. Instead it has ensured that our leaders are liars, since they are forced to pretend that they have magically avoided the seductions and distortions that have helped morally flaw the rest of us."

Even the Night Creature, flawed and distorted as he was, saw something significant in the dalliance between Hillary and Lerner. While sometimes dismissing it as "gushy shit," "Hillary's way-out sappy sentimentality," and "Hillary gassing around about the Michael Lerner crap—the politics of meaning or whatever the hell it is," Nixon also said, "Hillary's on to something. There is a spiritual vacuum out there."

"Wounded healers" must have been the phrase that especially got

Hillary's attention, not just because of her husband but also because of her-self . . . wounded by the health-care crusade, which had so ruthlessly been defeated . . . wounded by the polls, which showed her approval rating at an all-time low (pre-Monica) . . . wounded by Whitewater and the endless slew of stories that implied she was a crook . . . wounded by ever-present and continuing allegations that her husband was and had been betraying her with anything that jiggled from the time they were engaged.

If Bill Clinton was a wounded healer, so was Mrs. President Clinton, and she sought help from the Genie who specialized in healing the wounded, Jeanie Houston, who, in her youth, had once been offered a seven-year Hollywood deal as an actress. And what was wrong with that? Could anyone really say that Jimmy Swaggart, for example, couldn't act?

It wasn't the first time that a First Lady had gone to a guru for help. "Mommy," which was what Ronald Reagan called Nancy, had gone to San Francisco astrologer Joan Quigley, who had achieved fame on *The Merv Griffin Show*. (To Republicans of a previous generation, who used Billy Graham for photo-op counseling, turning to an astrologer made as much sense as turning to a secular healer did for posthippies.)

Merv introduced Mommy to Joan Quigley, and for seven years, Joan Quigley ran Ronald Reagan's life. If Mommy was Ronnie's president, then Quigley was Mommy's. "If Ronnie was going someplace," Joan Quigley said, "I'd have to look at all the location charts — the chart of the country, the chart of the premier of the country. I had to look at Ronnie's charts. I did more than fifty or sixty charts for him every year. I was not only ahead of my time in possession of knowledge of when Ronnie would do things, but I was actually *setting the times* for those movements. There were very few things that were restricted — I could do anything that I wanted."

Quigley analyzed Gorbachev's charts and told Mommy he and Reagan "would share a vision." Quigley told Mommy when the president shouldn't be making public statements and when he shouldn't be in crowds. Quigley picked the time of the presidential debates and claimed Reagan's election was her accomplishment. "I take the credit for the fact that Carter lost. What I did was pick a time when Carter would get careless and misspeak himself." Quigley planned the trips to Bitburg and Bergen-Belsen, making sure that the Bergen-Belsen trip would be "most prominent." Quigley decided Reagan shouldn't go out on a speaking tour defending Iran-Contra.

"I gave a great deal of advice on the relationship between the super pow-

ers," Quigley said, saying she thought she'd even be able to keep Ronald
Reagan safe from assassination. "The assassination had to do with the
Jupiter star in conjunction. It's called the great mutation. At the time Reagan was elected, it fell on Libra. While I felt it was dangerous . . . I thought I
could do it, that if I really concentrated, I could keep him safe."

Mommy went to Quigley for a solution to another problem, too, the
same problem with which Hillary would turn to the born-again goddess
Athena. Mommy had been wounded, too. She was having trouble with her
image. Her approval ratings were down. "I knew exactly what to do,"
Quigley said. "Nancy was the most glamorous woman since Jackie to
occupy the position of First Lady. She expected to be treated like a fashion
symbol—as Jackie had been—but the situation in the United States was
very different from what it had been when the Kennedys were in office. At
that time, people had wanted royalty figures; by the time the Reagans had
come to Washington, we had double-digit inflation . . . things like getting
extra china, though it was being donated privately, seemed extravagant, and
her social connections, her playing that up, was not sympathetic to the average person. Also, being a fashion plate wasn't appropriate at the time. So I
said to Nancy, 'No fashion magazines. You can go to parties if you want to,
but the only things that should be talked about should be official functions.
In order to be more sympathetic, you must play up *children in trouble,* and
small people.' "

"*Children in trouble,* and small people": It would seem, years later, that
Hillary Clinton had overheard Quigley's advice. Interestingly, the book she
called *It Takes a Village* was unofficially cowritten by her own guru, Jean
Houston.

Jean Houston claims as her ancestors Sam Houston, Robert E. Lee, Thomas
Jefferson, and the Todados of Sicily. She was born in L.A. as her dad, the
joke meister, was creating this joke in the hallway: "What do you get when
you cross a melon, a collie, and a baby? A melancholy baby." She was
named after the baptizing priest's favorite actress, Janet Gaynor, but her parents decided they liked "Jeanie" better. Her father wrote jokes and gags for
Ed Wynn, Eddie Cantor, Henny Youngman, Jack Benny, and George
Burns. She was traumatized as a little girl by an actor who fell in love with
her puppy dog, Chickie, and finally offered to buy it for $450. Her dad,
always broke, badly wanted to sell the puppy for such a high price, but her

mom prevented this and told the nasty actor off. (It was Ronald Reagan. No wonder she and Hillary would become friends.)

The little girl saw the secular Lord in the shape of the wooden dummy Charlie McCarthy when she was eight years old. She was with her dad, who was delivering jokes for Edgar Bergen, and they walked into a room where Edgar Bergen had his back to them. Edgar was talking to Charlie, conversing with the dummy the way you'd converse with people. Charlie was offering his own opinions. She got goose bumps and "an electric hand" seemed to touch her. Jean Houston had a realization that human beings "contain so much more than we think we do."

She was a terrible student, and when she wanted to go to college, her SAT scores were disastrous. A teacher noted she "wasn't suited for intellectual work." She somehow got into Columbia University and, a striking-looking, tall young woman with jet black hair, she was soon in the drama department. She was a talented actress, playing opposite Peter Falk in a play, winning Off-Broadway awards, asked by a Hollywood studio to audition for a part in *Jane Eyre*.

After miraculously recovering from what should have been a near-fatal bout of typhoid fever, she began to study religion. She met some psychiatrists doing a study of LSD and they asked her to help them with their research. One of the few people in New York with a legal supply of acid, she took acid only three times herself, but she became a "psychedelic guide" to more than three hundred people who took acid trips. "I would open a door into the glorious cathedral within a green pepper or I would surround my subjects with a cornucopia of fruits and vegetables and ask then to enter into a friendly relationship with them. I would slowly peel back the husks of an ear of corn and my subjects would know that they had witnessed a mystery."

Done with acid, she moved on to studies involving a sensory-deprivation chamber, an audiovisual-overload chamber, and something called "the witch's broomstick," a metal swing on which subjects stood, wearing blindfold goggles. Thanks to a pendant her Sicilian mother gave her, she realized that Athena was her "archetype," made trips to the Acropolis, and never took the pendant off. "Like Athena," she wrote, "I seek to reweave the world, bringing technology, culture, knowledge, and spirit into a more beautiful pattern and a more possible society. I am always rescuing people who have been cast aside, the deviants, the mavericks, the wounded and the unseen." She described herself as "a hierophant of innerspace" and a "traveler in outward spaces."

While Genie claimed Athena as her archetype, others saw something positively Christ-like in her behavior. She claimed to have performed miracles, ridding herself of an orange-sized breast tumor in four days, "gifting" those who couldn't have children with babies. She miraculously saved herself from gangrene brought on by the bite of jellyfish. "I seem to show up in many peoples' dreams," she wrote. She often spoke about the time in India when some little boys had seen her with her long hair at a shrine and pointed to her and yelled, "Jesus Christ! Jesus Christ!" "I feel that I can embrace and therefore help redress the pain of others and, because of my own diminished ego, be able to appreciate not only the pain they are feeling, but also the deep inner truth, the absolute worth of their lives"—which sounded to some like Bill Clinton saying, "I can feel your pain" or Jesus of Nazareth saying, "Rise and ye shall walk."

Her description of her mother sounded as if she was describing a supernatural being: "My mother has always been fey, an inhabitant of several worlds, a woman who sees angels, is prescient about the future, intuits deeply, and operates on many levels simultaneously." Her Nights of Gifting sounded like Jesus performing miracles. Genie would bless 180 people in a single night. They'd walk up to her and she'd hold their hands. They'd meet in a "circle of communion," with Bach blasting in the background, and Jean Houston would "gift" them with whatever they wanted.

People were paying big bucks for the gifting and for Jean Houston's books and videos, since secular religion is not a nonprofit vocation. They were hearing her say such things as "Most nights when I am home, I turn on my computer and modem and tune in to the world. Through the Internet and several other networks, I am wired through the music of frequency to the planetary mind." *The goddess Athena in cyberspace? The miracle worker named after Janet Gaynor and traumatized by Ronald Reagan . . . surfing the Net?*

"All systems, both personal and social, are in transition. Whenever psychological energy no longer binds to social forces, many people and institutions embark on quests for the green world within to help re-seed the wasteland without."

"The green world within"? *But wasn't there a green world without that Genie was tapping hungrily into?*

"The patterns in the weather, the turbulence in the winds, the rhythm pounded out by an African drummer, the rituals performed by queens and shamans and celebrants of the new year, the courtship habits of peacocks and prairie dogs, the landscapes of nature and the inscapes of dreams—all embody fractal phenomena."

Huh? Say what? "Fractal"? "The courtship habits of peacocks and prairie dogs"? *Who was she talking about? The Donald and Bill Clinton? What had that idiot savant dummy in the tuxedo, Charlie McCarthy, done to her at the age of eight?* She had written, "I can speak of the most abstruse intellectual subjects and make them sound like a hopped-up tent-meeting sermon." She had described a vision of her dead father. By her own account, the old joke meister told her to visit some comedy clubs and "then you can quit this scam you're into."

The first time Jean Houston met Hillary was in the company of competing gurus like Tony Robbins, "the Firewalker," and Marianne Williamson, "the Love Guru to Hollywood Stars." It was at a Camp David get-together.

Jean Houston told Hillary that, as a woman, Hillary was on the front line of the battle for women's equality. Maybe getting just a tad carried away, just a centimeter too theatrical, Jean Houston also told Hillary that she was, at the same time, Joan of Arc, Mozart with his hands cut off, and a female Christ crucified.

Hillary liked her insight. Genie told Hillary about her theory of wounding, a theory that fit oh so perfectly with the pillorying Hillary felt she was suffering in the media. "The wounding of our lives can cause the withdrawal of our substance, the leaching of our spirits. Or we can choose to see them as the slings and arrows that fortune provides to gouge us sufficiently full of holes that we may yet become holy."

Jean Houston also put the thought a different way: "I continually joke that Christ must have his crucifixion—otherwise there's no upsy-daisy." And, just to make sure that Hillary understood she was dealing with a serious, soulful, and herself *wounded* healer here: "When they go through the dark night of the soul that precedes transformation, I find myself experiencing it with them, sharing their pain and grief as if it were my own. My hypersensitive availability to others' wounding makes for a constancy of inner pain that belies the outer merry face that I present to the world."

The two women had some things in common. While Hillary had carried on a three-year platonic relationship with a man in college, Jean Houston had once carried on a nine-year platonic relationship with a man who was having "romantic entanglements" with other women. Like Hillary, Jean

Houston was the extracurricular queen in school, a member of the student senate, the president of as many clubs as she could join, "the girl in class that everyone hated." And they both shared a reverence for Eleanor Roosevelt, pioneer for children's rights and social progress and the first bisexual First Lady in the White House.

When she was a young girl, Jeanie had actually met Eleanor through her dad, the joke meister. Her father had once posed as a waiter at Mrs. Roosevelt's favorite restaurant and had squirted her with ice cream as a publicity stunt. He had later written jokes for some of FDR's speeches. Hillary had long admired Eleanor and had even spoken publicly, shortly after Bill Clinton's election, about "talking to her sometimes and asking for help," the way that other women in the past had spoken to Saint Teresa of Avila or the Little Flower or the Blessed Virgin Mary.

When Hillary and Genie next met, they spoke right away about Eleanor Roosevelt. Jean Houston was certain that Eleanor was Hillary's "archetype." She had a technique she called "docking with your angel," a kind of actor's exercise where the actor improvises *both sides* of a dialogue to get a better fix on his or her "character." Jean Houston encouraged her subjects to chat with their spiritual soul mates, their "angels," improvising both sides of the dialogue.

Jeanie proposed that Hillary develop her relationship with the long-departed First Lady, and they went up to the solarium perched atop the White House. Some of Hillary's aides joined them. Somebody ordered popcorn, pretzels, and fruit.

Pretty soon, with Jean Houston's encouragement, Hillary started docking away with Eleanor, asking her how she'd overcome her own wounding. Hillary talked to Eleanor about how lonely she felt. Then Hillary became Eleanor and spoke to herself in her Eleanor voice. "You have to do what you think is right," Hillary as Eleanor told herself.

Genie told Hillary that she had to understand that Eleanor had been badly wounded, too, but had worked through it. Hillary had to dock with her archetype and keep on docking until she could call upon Eleanor's strength to work through her own wounding.

Then Jeanie suggested that Hillary speak to Gandhi, and Hillary did, telling the little man how very much she admired him. Then Genie suggested Hillary speak to Jesus Christ. The others in the room kept munching their popcorn. Hillary, drained after her discussions with Eleanor and the Mahatma, demurred about speaking to Jesus Christ. She said this was too personal and she had to check on Chelsea, who had a tummy ache.

In subsequent sessions, Jean Houston told Hillary that "as baby-making occurs through the wounding of the ovum by the sperm, so soul-making occurs through the wounding of the psyche." She spoke to Hillary about food and drink that would help heal her wounding: macadamia nuts, "so possessed of their macadamiality"; sun-dried tomatoes, "memory and desire, earthbound, sun-kissed, crossed into something ethereal"; caviar—"You do not chew, but press it on the roof of your mouth like a holy word"; and truffles—"This is no mere ecstasy; it is love that exceeds all human understanding."

As Jeanie worked on the book that she had originally suggested that Hillary write, she noticed that Bill Clinton did not seem comfortable when she was in the room. She asked Hillary about it, and Hillary said, "My husband is a very conservative man." Well, maybe, as far as docking with archetypes or truffles being the love that exceeds all human understanding was concerned, Bill Clinton *was* a conservative man, who'd rather sit down and watch the Razorbacks lose, eat a burger, and grumble about the trash that stone-crazy Imus had said than listen to Jean Houston's blissed-out way-outitudes. Or maybe Slick Willy just knew a scam when he saw one.

But with a fine half-chewed Davidoff cigar in his hand, Bill Clinton was capable of doing radical, creatively unconservative things no hierophant would ever be able to archetype. And as far as his own wounding was concerned—those red scratches and bruises that showed up on his face sometimes after a shouting match in the family quarters—Bill Clinton knew he'd always be able to find someone whose silky, soothing breasts, pressed hotly against his wounded, handsome face, would heal him.

[11]

Bubba in Pig Heaven

TO: Bubba
FR: Joe
RE: Hooray for Hollywood!

Dear Bubba,

The producer Rob Fried told me that he was playing golf with you one day at Burning Tree and on the way back to the White House in the limo you started bitching about Paula Jones. Her lawsuit had just been filed and you said, "Jesus Christ, one of these days someone's gonna accuse me of fucking a cow." This was before Monica.

And Rob said to you, "Mr. President, Joe Eszterhas has already written a script about that." He was referring to a screenplay I'd written in 1989 called *Sacred Cows*, about a fictional president who, nostalgic about his farm-boy adolescence, does just that. Rob got back out here and sent you my script, but he never heard a word from you about it.

The only indirect response I got was from Steven Spielberg, who was going to produce *Sacred Cows* but suddenly dropped out, telling a roomful of executives at United Artists that he didn't feel "comfortable" producing it anymore because of his new "friendship" with you.

Well, that's okay, Bubba. I lost Steven Spielberg because of you, but I guess I know why. What the hell, it's only a movie, and *Basic Instinct, Showgirls, Sliver, Jade, Flashdance, Jagged Edge* . . . I *know* you've seen all of those. I know you're a fan. Not just from what Dick Morris said about *Basic*, but from what Gennifer said, too. If I have a core audience for those movies, I know you're hard-on hard-core, Bubba.

This is what Gennifer said: "One night Bill asked me to put on a short skirt with no underwear, then sit in a chair and cross and uncross my legs while he watched. He became so aroused just watching me, it was a thrill.

He said he read about that move in a magazine, long before Sharon Stone wowed audiences with it in *Basic Instinct*. His fantasy was to have that scenario actually take place in a meeting someday."

Of course you liked that movie, Bubba. It's about you and Gennifer, isn't it? Some of it is a direct homage to your relationship. You had Gennifer tie you to the bedpost with silk scarves—the opening scene of my movie. "Bill loved to talk dirty," Gennifer said, and so does Michael Douglas in *Basic*. Come to think of it, Monica could have been describing Michael in *Basic* when she described you: "That raw, intense sexuality that I saw a few times—watching your mouth on my breast or looking in your eyes while you explored the depth of my sex." That business about dripping ice on Gennifer took place after Gennifer broke up the ice with an ice pick. The mad urgency of wanting to have sex with Pookie—in a phone booth, a men's room, on a desktop, a bed in the window of a furniture store—that drive to "fuck like minks" is the urgency that drives every scene of *Basic*.

Gennifer describing her relationship with you is Gennifer describing the subtext of not only *Basic* but also *Sliver* and *Jade*: "All I could think about was our sex games! What we had done to each other the night before and what we might do the next day. I spent my days in a trance, pretending to work and function like a normal person, but all the while being obsessed with what we were doing. In looking back, I believe we were addicted to the sexual excitement. It was almost like being addicted to a drug. As the addiction increased, we craved more and more sex at a higher intensity."

You've got to move out here, Bubba. You don't belong in Washington or Little Rock or Chappaquiddick: Hollywood is the place for you. "Addicted to the sexual excitement. . . . more and more sex at a higher intensity." This place reeks sex from its celluloid pores.

Everybody uses Altoids here and all the women carry breath mints in their Chanel and Prada bags. Show business people use Gold Bond medicated powder for that tingling sensation and Fiesta glow-in-the-dark condoms for comic relief. And the women here, Bubba! "Jell-O on springs," to use Billy Wilder's words.

A townful of nuts and sluts on the make, wanna-be stars, willard-friendly and experimental, bored with ham and egg, Al Gore orgasms. Hooked on crush videos, facial aerobics, and Kegel exercises. Women with just the right amount of saliva and sculpted flesh.

They do *everything* to stay in shape. They swallow tapeworms. They make trips to Costa Rica to drink the local water and pick up the chicest intestinal bug. They gobble Ritalin and Dexedrine. They drink lemon juice with cayenne pepper. They eat cotton balls soaked in orange juice for breakfast.

Ripe-peach women with ba-ba-booms and jungle drums . . . "I think the whole obsession with the size of a girl's breasts is a perversion," Jane Fonda said, and then went and got implants.

There are no pizza butts in Hollywood, Bubba, and you don't have to have a Jurassic willard to make it here, either. Everybody appreciates a knowledgeable and sensitive willard that is not dysfunctionally enormous, especially at a time when a lot of the young studs are getting theirs pierced. You can become a human paranometer here, Bubba, measuring the tightness of vaginal walls.

Remember that card Monica sent you? The one that said, "Nothing would make me happier than seeing you again, except to see you naked with a lottery ticket in one hand and a can of whipped cream in the other"? Forget seeing her again, Bubba, but move out here. That's what Hollywood would mean to you: being naked, with a lottery ticket in one hand and whipped cream in the other.

I know you've spent your whole life in politics, not show business, but Reagan became president only after he'd learned about politics here. Hollywood was his training ground to make it in Washington. Washington will have been your training ground to make it in Hollywood. As you'll see, there's little difference between the two. Maybe I can convince you to move out here. Maybe, if I take you behind the scenes . . .

Sexual Harassment

It's an old Hollywood joke, Bubba: "Did you hear about the Polish starlet who slept with the screenwriter to try to get the part?" When I sold the script of *Basic Instinct* for a record amount of money, newspapers across the country ran the story on the front page. The Hollywood trades ran banner headlines.

I noticed something different after the sale. Every time I went down to L.A., the hotel concierge handed me a stack of envelopes. They were filled with glossy photographs of starlets, their home numbers enclosed. Some had handwritten and scented notes. *I'll bet Monica scented her notes.*

Some of the women in the photographs were topless. Some were naked. One envelope contained a pair of strawberry-scented black panties. *Gennifer?*

And I'm just a schmuck with a manual typewriter, Bubba. Imagine what would happen to you, the former president of the United States?

Role Models

At the time that I was rewriting screenwriter Tom Hedley's original screenplay, *Flashdance,* the director, Adrian Lyne, kept carrying on . . . and on . . . and on about *Last Tango in Paris.*

It was one of his favorite movies, Adrian said, and he wanted to give *Flashdance* a *Last Tango* kind of edge.

"The trouble with that, Adrian," I said, "is that this movie is a fairy tale, a piece of cotton candy, about a young dancer and a group of kids trying to make it."

In other words, I was saying to Adrian that there was no place for the stick of butter in this movie. *Gennifer said you love butter.*

But Adrian kept fretting and fretting, and shortly before the shoot was to begin, he asked for a story meeting—at Caesar's Palace in Las Vegas, of all places. The story meeting would be combined with a casting call. *You'd love those, Bubba.* We would also audition hundreds of the most beautiful young nubile dancers in Vegas. When I checked in, I found myself in a bordello red suite. Even the ceiling was red. Even the glowing neon outside the window was red. *No zebra stripes, though.*

Don Simpson, one of the producers, had a suite with a Jacuzzi in the middle of the living room—*Beats Camp David, doesn't it?*—and this is where most of the creative action took place. Simpson was in the Jacuzzi, a cigar in his mouth, a bottle of Tanqueray at the side, and a tray with lines of white powder on the floor. The rest of us sat in chairs on the side.

After a busy casting day, Simpson decided to throw a party for the dancers we'd auditioned in his suite. There were a hundred gorgeous women and four of us men—Don, his coproducer Jerry Bruckheimer, Adrian, and me. *This is turning you on, isn't it?*

The party went late, we were all exhausted, and I wanted to say good night to Don. "He's in there," Jerry said, jerking his thumb at a bedroom. I opened the door and saw Simpson, in the buff, holding a young woman up against a wall. He was inside her. I said, "Good night, Don," and he waved, without interrupting his movements or turning, and said, "Eight-thirty tomorrow, okay?" *I'm glad Betty Currie never saw anything like that.*

At 8:30 the next morning, Don was back in the Jacuzzi, and we continued the story meeting. Adrian chose this bleary-eyed moment to go back to *Last Tango in Paris.*

"I've got it figured out," he said. He took out some scrawled penciled notes. "This is what we do." He paused for dramatic effect. "At the age of eight, our girl, Alex, is raped by her father."

Jerry Bruckheimer, good at being inscrutable, said nothing. Simpson looked at me from the Jacuzzi, an impish grin on his grayish face.

I said, "Adrian, are you out of your mind! Have you lost your marbles! You're going to have our girl . . . *raped* . . . by her dad? In this little fairy-tale, feel-good movie? You're going to put in your stick of butter? That's it for me! I'm out of here! I'm gone!"

I stormed out, threw my stuff in a bag, grabbed a cab, and flew home.

Adrian went looking for me, realized I'd checked out, and went back to Don's suite, apoplectic.

"He's gone!" he said. "Can you believe the bloody bastard's gone?"

But he changed his mind. When *Flashdance* was released, there was no stick of butter in it, no incest, no rape.

When we were working on *Jade,* director Billy Friedkin had a similar fixation on *Belle de Jour.*

"This isn't *Belle de Jour,* Billy," I kept saying. Billy kept saying, "You're right, you're right."

But when I saw the rough cut, there was a lengthy sex scene (later shortened) involving dark shenanigans—*I'll send it to you, Bubba*—with a woman wearing a nylon mask and stiletto-heel shoes, who, some people mistakenly thought, looked like Billy's wife, studio head Sherry Lansing. *No nylon masks for Hillary, right?* The scene wasn't in the script.

"What's all that?" I said to Billy. "What's it doing there? What does it do for us?"

Billy smiled. "Just a little bit of *Belle de Jour,*" he said. *How many times have you seen that movie?*

Kiss It!

Richard Gere had something he wanted to pitch me, my agents told me. I met him in midafternoon in his suite at the Chateau Marmont. He welcomed me warmly and asked me to sit down. He sat across from me in a chair. He was wearing jeans and a blue work shirt. **Your sense of style, Bubba.**

What he had in mind, he said, was a movie about the blues scene in Chicago in the fifties. Muddy Waters, Howlin' Wolf—

"Jimmy Reed," I said.

"You know it?" he said.

I talked to him about Memphis Minnie and Mance Lipscomb and we both talked a lot about Robert Johnson.

"Excuse me," he said suddenly. "I've got a photo shoot. You don't mind if I change, do you?"

I said, "Of course not." He disappeared into a bedroom. I sat there, thinking about doing a movie about the blues. It sounded like fun.

Richard reappeared. He was still wearing the jeans and the work shirt, but now he was carrying a fresh pair of jeans and a fresh work shirt.

"Memphis Slim," I said. "He's always fascinated me. I love that boogie-woogie sound, and then the guy becomes an exile and lives like the lord mayor of Paris for twenty years." **The same thing would happen to you here.**

"No Chicago connection, though," Richard said. He stood ten feet from me. He started to take his clothes off.

"No, I guess not," I said.

His shirt was off. He was unbuckling his belt and unzipping his fly.

"Big Bill Broonzy," Richard said, "he was a Chicago guy."

His jeans were off. He wasn't wearing underwear. **Forget the boxers— you should do that.**

"Big Joe Turner?" I asked.

"Kansas City."

Richard was snuggling into the fresh pair of tight jeans.

"Big Mama Thornton?" I asked.

"Maybe. I know she did some things on Chess."

Richard buckled his belt and started putting on his fresh work shirt. His fly was still unzipped. **You've been there, Bubba.**

"What I'd like to do," I said, "is research it first. Spend a couple months in Chicago and do the research."

"Sounds great," Richard said. "I think it could be a helluva movie, don't you?"

He zipped his fly up.

"Fun," I said.

"Yeah," he said. "A lot of fun."

He asked me to walk him down to the parking lot.

"I hate photo shoots," Richard said. We shook hands. "I'll call you next week," he said. "We'll work up a deal."

I thanked him. We smiled at each other. He got into a hot little Porsche and roared away.

I never heard from him again. *Don't you wish you would never again have heard from Paula Jones?*

The Saturday Night Massacre

The first time I met Gina Gershon, standing a few feet away from a naked and sweat-soaked Elizabeth Berkley on the *Showgirls* set—*Easy, Bubba! You'll get bursitis in your hand!*—she told me how much she admired my screenplay. "I know you were inspired by the story of Zeus and Aphrodite," she said; "it's one of my favorite stories."

Well, I didn't know about *that*, but I liked her performance. I had a script called *Original Sin*, a story of past-life romance, over at Morgan Creek Productions, and I convinced the company head, Jim Robinson, to see her performance in *Showgirls*. *He's a stand-up guy, always appreciative of a great performance.*

Robinson liked what he saw, but he said, "She's not a star. She's a starlet." I told him that with the right part, I thought Gina could become a star. *You'd like Gina a lot!* Robinson wasn't certain, but I talked him into it. Morgan Creek signed Gina for the lead in *Original Sin*. I knew she wasn't getting any star offers. "I just love this script," she said; "it's the perfect script." She said she, like her character, had also had a past-life romance. *You and Cleopatra?*

She said, "Thank you, thank you, thank you."

We needed a director. I had seen and admired the English director Nick Broomfield's documentaries and asked to meet with him. I asked him if he was interested in directing a fictional feature. He was. I gave him *Original Sin*. He liked the script "very much," he said, but had "thoughts." We spent an afternoon discussing his "thoughts." I liked them and told Jim Robinson I'd found the perfect director. He wasn't overwhelmed.

"He does documentaries, for Christ's sake," Robinson said; "plus, he's a Brit. This piece takes place down south. What the fuck does he know about the South?" *Robinson's got a little bit of Carville and Ickes in him.* I talked him into meeting Broomfield and I rewrote the script, including Nick's "thoughts." Robinson liked Broomfield, liked the script, signed a deal with Nick, and we had a go movie.

A month later, Robinson called me and said, "What the fuck's going on?"

Broomfield, he said, wasn't out scouting locations, wasn't doing casting, wasn't hiring a crew.

I said, "What's he doing?"

Robinson said, "He's working on the fucking script."

I said, "Whaaaat?"

When I calmed down, I said, "I thought you liked the script?"

"*I* like the script," he said. "Broomfield doesn't like it. Gina Gershon doesn't like it."

I said, "Whaaaat?"

When I calmed down, I said, "Gina Gershon is lucky to be in the movie. Nick Broomfield is lucky to direct the movie. *I* convinced you to bring them into the movie." ***How would you feel if Al Gore gave you lip?***

Robinson laughed. "That's right," he said, "call 'em."

I called Gina and said I'd heard she had script problems. "Not really," she said. "I mean, I love the script. It's really the perfect script. But Nick and I have been talking. I'm just worried about my motivation in some scenes. I don't understand why I'm doing what I'm doing. Nick and I have some ideas where I do things that are different."

I called Broomfield. "Gina's really gotten into her part," he said. "She is *becoming* her character. She's got some insights we should listen to."

"She's '*becoming*' her character?" I said. "She didn't create her character; *I* did. If she wants to *become* her character, all she has to do is what's in the script." ***Does Al Gore improvise? Hell no!*** "I see your point," Broomfield said. "But I think we should talk."

I didn't want to talk. My script and I had gotten both these people their jobs. Now they were conspiring to change what I'd written?

At exactly this delicate moment, Jon Bon Jovi, who loved *Original Sin* and wanted to play a leading part, flew across the country for a meeting at my home in Malibu. Robinson and Bon Jovi arrived together and, moments later, Nick and Gina arrived together.

As we talked, it became obvious to Robinson and me that Bon Jovi was more excited about the script than either Nick or Gina. While Jim and I thought Bon Jovi would be perfect in the movie, Broomfield and Gina condescended to him.

"Yes, perhaps I'd have time to audition you tomorrow," Broomfield said, his English accent becoming buttery-crusted. *Blumenthal would like him.*

"Have you taken acting lessons?" Gina asked Jon. *You're fine — Harry Thomason is better than Stanislavsky.* Nick and Gina excused themselves, leaving Jim and Jon and me to mull over the evening.

"That guy's an asshole," Robinson said of Broomfield. "I think he's afraid to direct. That's why he's not scouting or casting. That's why he's still dicking with the script. He's afraid to go out and do it."

I could see Robinson was angry at the way Nick and Gina had treated Bon Jovi, who'd gone to great effort to have this meeting.

"You told me to hire Broomfield," Robinson said to me.

"Fire him," I said.

The next morning when Nick Broomfield arrived at Morgan Creek to audition Jon Bon Jovi, Jon wasn't there. There were security people there who, at Jim Robinson's behest, escorted Nick Broomfield off the lot. A settlement was reached with Nick and, sometime later, a settlement was also reached with Gina. *You'd still like her a lot, Bubba.*

Sensitivity Training

A few years after the success of *Jagged Edge*, its director, Richard Marquand, died of a stroke in England at the age of forty-eight, leaving behind his wife and two small children.

He was my good friend. Crushed, I informed those who'd worked with him on the production. When I reached Glenn Close in New York, I was still in shock. She said not a word as I gave her the details: In seemingly perfect health, Richard had been vacationing with his wife in Greece, and so on. There was a pause when I finished.

I said, "Glenn?"

"Yes, I'm here," she said.

There was another pause, and then Glenn said, "Well, you know, he didn't do anything for me in that movie. My ass looked too big." *Politics ain't beanbag, either, right?*

High Noon

Frank Price was the head of Columbia when I wrote *Jagged Edge*. He was a former television writer and was known as a smart executive. He hated the ending of my script and insisted the movie end with Jeff Bridges innocent and with a hug between Jeff and Glenn Close. I told him I thought that was a silly television idea.

He told me he'd produced *McCloud* and *Columbo*.

"I know your credits, Frank, and your credits are a good part of the problem," I said. *Frank passed on* **E.T.**

The producer, the veteran Martin Ransohoff, agreed with me. We didn't know what to do. The studio president had given me a direct order to change the ending and I'd said no.

Ransohoff called his friend Herbert Allen, a member of Columbia's board of directors—*You'll never be as powerful as he is, Bubba*—and discovered that Frank Price's job was shaky.

We decided to outwait his firing. Every other week, Frank Price wanted to know where the new ending was, and every other week, Marty Ransohoff said, "Joe's still working on it." We dodged for three months . . . until Frank Price was finally fired.

Three days after his ouster, I turned in my new ending—which was the same ending I'd written before. The new president liked my new old ending and the movie was shot that way. It didn't hurt that the new president was my former agent.

It doesn't hurt to have Janet Reno as attorney general, does it? . . .

Negative Advertising

You remember Ryan O'Neal, don't you, Bubba? He played Al Gore in *Love Story*, which Al says is the story of Al and Tipper. (I guess Tipper, a formidable woman, came back from the dead somehow.)

I wrote a script a couple years ago called *An Alan Smithee Film: Burn Hollywood Burn*, which featured a character named James Edmunds, a cynical, deceitful, low-life Hollywood producer. *You know him—he stayed in the Lincoln Bedroom three times.* We had trouble casting the part, and then my wife thought of Ryan O'Neal. Once a big star, Ryan wasn't getting big parts anymore. He was appearing not in films but in *People* magazine, in stories about his relationship with his daughter, Tatum, or his longtime love, Farrah Fawcett. He was washed up in Hollywood and had ballooned physically. His spare tires were approaching the size of Alec Baldwin's. *How's Kim?*

I thought it was a great idea. Who better in a Hollywood satire to play a Hollywood animal than a Hollywood animal whom the town had discarded? I sent the script to his agents, and within a day, Ryan accepted the part.

Within a week, he was at my house having lunch, telling me very loudly that this was the best script he'd ever read. He gave me a hug at the end of the lunch, then asked that my wife join the hug, and gave her a hug that was a little too close for my comfort (and hers). *Your kind of hug, Bubba.*

The shoot began and we made plans for Ryan and Farrah to come to dinner at our home. The day before the dinner, I asked my assistant to cancel it. A week of rain in Malibu had caused mud slides and Malibu was nearly isolated. On the night of the scheduled dinner, our gate bell rang and our housekeeper informed us that Ryan and Farrah had arrived. Naomi and I were both in our frumpies, containers of Chinese food all over the floor, which was wet from a leaking window. We were in no shape to entertain, and we told the housekeeper to inform Ryan and Farrah that we were not at home. I called my assistant, who confessed that he had forgotten to cancel the dinner. I called Ryan the next day, apologized, and sent flowers to Farrah, which she never acknowledged. *No! Don't! Take my advice—stay away from Farrah!*

As the shoot went on, it became obvious to those of us on the set that Ryan was having an affair with our female lead, Leslie Stephenson, young, sultry-eyed, and playing a hooker. Then Ryan informed me one day that he and Leslie were living together out in Malibu and that he had left Farrah. "It's all thanks to you," he said. "If you wouldn't have written this script, I never would have met Leslie. And after you stood us up for dinner that night, my relationship with Farrah was never the same. She was nuts. She got all dolled up—it took her two hours—we drove out there through the rain, and you guys weren't there."

He seemed in love and happy, although he was still Ryan. We shared a limo on the way to a screening and he talked about Leslie, but as he talked, he kept touching my wife's bare leg, until I finally said, "Ryan, if you touch her again, I'm going to break your arm." *You never told Vince that, did you?* When we got to the screening, Ryan hovered in a corner to get away from the public, although, from what I could tell, no one even approached him for an autograph.

When the movie was about to be released, the studio organized a press day at the Four Seasons Hotel. Ryan was supposed to be there, but the night before, I heard he wasn't coming. He hated these things, I was told. He'd done too many of them through the years. I called his agents and said, "Come on. The guy was unemployable. I had to convince the director to give him the part. What do you mean, 'he's not coming'?" Ryan called me later that night and said there had been a misunderstanding . . . of course he'd be there.

When I got to the Four Seasons the next morning, a studio publicist informed me Ryan was there, getting ready to do interviews in the suite the studio had arranged for him. Everything looked under control until . . . a producer came to tell me he had just seen Ryan in his suite and the suite reeked of marijuana. Then the producer came to tell me he had just seen Ryan's first interview and Ryan had said he "didn't really like" the movie, that he didn't even want to talk about the movie. He wanted to talk about another independently made movie in which he had a smaller part. *Forget Hillary's health-care plan; let's talk about the spotted owl.*

I called his agent and his agent started screaming, "Get him out of there! Right now! You gotta get him out of there right now!" Moments later, Ryan left, leaving a note for me saying he was sorry but that he wasn't feeling well. He thought he had the flu and had to go home. *You, too, can be a Hollywood animal, Bubba!*

Don't Ask, Don't Tell

Studios and producers sometimes have trouble deciding how they feel about a script and sometimes have even more trouble articulating it.

I rewrote a script called *Other Men's Wives*, about wives cheating on their husbands. *Why should the talk always be about us, right?* The head of the studio was Sherry Lansing—*You'd like her, too*—and the producers were Wendy Finerman (*Forrest Gump*)—*Too skinny for you*—and Mario Kassar, the once-legendary head of Carolco.

I sent the three of them the script by messenger on a Friday afternoon. On Sunday morning, Sherry called me and said, "I didn't really like it, but don't say anything about my reaction to Wendy or Mario. I want to hear their reactions first. I also want to think about it. I could be wrong."

Wendy called me Sunday night. "I didn't really like it," she said. "Have you heard anything from Sherry or Mario?"

I said I hadn't.

"Well, I could be wrong," Wendy said. "I want to reread it and think about it. Don't say anything to Sherry or Mario about what I think; I'll talk to them myself."

I heard nothing from Mario on Monday, and neither Sherry nor Wendy called me back.

Mario called me at noon on Tuesday. He sounded scrambled.

"Joe," he said, "we've been friends. I need you to tell me the truth. Did you hear from Sherry about what she thinks of the script?"

"Wait a minute, Mario," I said. "Tell me what *you* think of the script first."

"Look, Joe, it doesn't matter what I think. I don't run a studio anymore. I'm just a producer. I want to be in agreement with what Sherry thinks." **You should bring Dick Morris out here with you.**

I told him Sherry didn't like it.

He called me back two hours later, irate. "How could you tell me she doesn't like it when she likes it?"

I said, "She does?"

"There are some things *in* it she doesn't like, but she likes it."

"Are you sure?"

"Well, we had a pretty bad connection—she's on her way to a corporate retreat in the Bahamas—but—"

"Maybe you should call her back."

"No," he said. "I've got a better idea. I'm going to make some calls over to Paramount—to Goldwyn and Manning and some of the others—to see what Sherry told them."

"You mean she might have said something different to them?"

"We'll find out," he said.

He called the next day to say that on the basis of his conversations with studio executives John Goldwyn and Michelle Manning, he didn't think Sherry liked the script.

"Did Goldwyn and Manning like it?"

"They need more time to think about it."

Wendy called me to schedule a meeting with her and Mario.

"What are we going to talk about?" I asked.

"We've got to figure out how we feel about the script."

"Well, *I* like it," I said.

"You don't count; you wrote it."

"Then why don't you and Mario have the meeting without me?"

"You're right," Wendy said. "Good idea."

You didn't have Hillary at most cabinet meetings, did you?

The Politics of Personal Destruction

• When I learned that a Columbia executive named Robert Lawrence had bad-mouthed one of my scripts to a star, I called him to say, "I'm gonna come down there tomorrow and kick the living shit out of you!" I went down the next day on other business with Columbia and Lawrence had called in sick. ***F-word Milošević!***

• Years later, the same Lawrence turned up as an executive at United Artists, where I'd just made a three-picture deal. I told studio head Jerry Weintraub I didn't want to work with Lawrence, and Jerry summoned him to his office. "If you fuck with Joe," Weintraub said, "I'm going to throw you out this fucking window." Lawrence nodded, smiled, and left. ***F-word Saddam!***

• While at an airport pay phone, producer Marty Ransohoff learned that Jane Fonda didn't like my script of *Jagged Edge*. "The sleazy fucking stupid cunt!" Ransohoff screamed into the phone. "What does she know? Jane Fonda went down on the Vietcong." ***His mom used to work for Goldwater.***

• Robert Evans heard that a condition of Sharon Stone's contract for *Sliver* was that Evans could never be on the set when Sharon was there. Sharon had a girlfriend who claimed that Evans had kept her in his house, naked and wearing a dog collar, for months. Evans's response: "Sharon Stone is a lying dumb cunt who's had all the brains in her head fucked out. I wouldn't fuck her for all the money that I've pissed away. I've never kept a girl in a dog collar in my life." ***"I did not have sexual relations with that woman, Miss—"***

• When I publicly objected to the "citizen's arrests" of gay people by *Basic Instinct* producer Alan Marshall during the filming of the movie in San Francisco, Carolco head Mario Kassar called my agent, Guy McElwaine. Mario was apoplectic.

"What is Joe doing? He's making assholes out of us!" Mario yelled.

"He doesn't like you arresting protesters," Guy said.

"I'm going to sue him!" Mario yelled.

"If you do that," my agent said, "you're going to have every gay person between San Francisco and Paris protesting the movie."

"Fuck him!" Mario screamed. "I'm going to put out a contract on him." ***Kathleen Willey's dead cat?***

• Thinking that producer Irwin Winkler had leaked a script before he was ready to sell it, my agent, Guy McElwaine, called him and said, "If you're walking down the street and you see me driving by, run! Because I'm going to put you through a store window. If you're in a restaurant and I walk in, run! Because I'm going to drag you out by your neck. If you're in a rest room and I see you, pray! Because I'm going to stick your head in a toilet." ***F-word Linda Tripp!***

• Knowing that he'd conspired against me as I tried to convince Jean-Claude Van Damme to stick to my script, I called his agent, Jack Gilardi. "I'll tell you what I'm going to do, Jack," I said. "I'm going to come down there with a baseball bat and bust your knees so you can't walk. Then I'm going to bust your ribs so you can't breathe. Then I'm going to bust your ears so you can't hear. I'd bust your head, but you can't think anyway. So I'm going to bust your balls so you can't fuck." *You'd feel at home here, pal.*

I saw him about a year later with his wife and some friends by a pool in Maui. I went over and apologized and we shook hands.

"It was a helluva speech, though," Jack said. "I remember it almost word for word. You oughta put it in one of Jean-Claude's movies." *Camp David Accords?*

Talking Points

Jagged Edge was about a celebrity figure, the editor of a San Francisco newspaper, Jack Forester, who kills his wife and gets away with it. *Don't even think about it!*

Part of his alibi is the public's reluctance to believe that a respected figure and husband could kill his wife in such a heinous, vicious way. *They'd suspect you immediately.*

Crucial to Jack Forester's defense is that the murder weapon, a knife with a jagged edge, is never found. *The Rose Law Firm billing records?*

In the summer of 1993, Naomi and I spent an afternoon around the pool of the Ritz-Carlton on Maui with O. J. Simpson and his wife, Nicole. O.J. talked about how much he wanted to be in one of my movies and told me how much he admired *Basic Instinct* and, especially, *Jagged Edge.*

A year later, as Naomi and I heard the shocking details of Nicole Simpson's and Ron Goldman's killing, we thought about our pleasant afternoon at the Ritz with O.J. and Nicole. We had a peripheral connection to the case. Days before he joined the defense team, attorney Bob Shapiro was representing me in my divorce trial in Marin County.

As the O.J. trial proceeded, I was struck by the similarities to *Jagged Edge.* Here was a celebrity figure accused of killing his wife. Those defending him argued that he was a good father and that he loved Nicole—that a husband who loved his wife couldn't kill her in such a heinous, vicious way. Then there was the murder weapon, a knife, as in *Jagged Edge,* a knife never found. There was even a spooky coincidence of a knife, not the murder weapon, but like the murder weapon, shown to the court during O.J.'s trial.

"This thing's like *Jagged Edge*," I kiddingly said to Bob Shapiro.

He looked me dead in the eye and said, "You have no idea."

I hadn't seen *Jagged Edge* for a long time—it was released in 1985—and I put it on again. I stopped it suddenly, rewound it, and played it again. I felt chills down my back.

The date of the murders was the same. The night of June 12 in the movie, the night of June 12 in real life.

I asked Shapiro later what his international fame meant to him. "It means," he said, "that I can get a blow job anywhere in the world." **Fire Bob Bennett; hire Bob Shapiro.**

Vernon Jordan Recommended Her

Charles Evans, Bob's brother, the executive producer of *Showgirls*, called director Paul Verhoeven and said he had just auditioned the perfect lead for *Showgirls* . . . in his New York hotel room. **I told you you'd like show business!**

Verhoeven went ballistic with the mild-mannered Evans. "*You* don't audition!" he yelled. "*I* audition! Are you crazy? You're auditioning girls in your hotel room? Do you want to get us sued before we roll any film?" **It's okay. Everybody does it. Don't worry.**

Charlie Evans argued that this girl was striking and talented. "Please," he said, "just audition her."

Paul said, "Forget it! I don't even want to know her name."

Paul continued auditioning actresses in L.A., and one day he auditioned a young woman named Elizabeth Berkley, a minor TV starlet. Those who saw the audition said Elizabeth was uninhibited and visibly impressed Paul with the size and shape of her bared breasts. **Maybe you should direct.** When the shoot began, Paul and Elizabeth began a steamy and public affair, not unusual behavior for directors during a shoot.

You would have loved the set of *Basic*, the movie Paul and I previously did. Paul outdoes most directors, who view their sets during a shoot the way you view your windowless hallway. He told me once that his best sexual experience was with a woman who defecated on the bed when she climaxed. **No, not Farrah.** His Rabelaisian attitude was perfect for *Basic*, whose set was a barrel of libido and testosterone squeezed into a sardine can.

To get ready for the shoot, Michael Douglas went down to Mexico to lose weight and get some sun "so I can look beautiful." The shoot began and Michael had a fling with Jeanne Tripplehorn; then Sharon and Michael had a confrontation, which ended with the kind of ego standoff where each insisted the other be the one to move closer before they embraced.

Then Paul and Sharon developed a fixation on each other. *You know how Sharon is: "I'm naked at the drop of a hat," she told* People *magazine.* But Sharon insisted Paul move out on his wife—which Paul refused to do—before the fixation was consummated. *You didn't have to do that, did you?* Then Paul burst an artery in his nose—which was or wasn't the result of a Michael Douglas punch—I couldn't ever get it clear. **The various accounts at various times were as carefully parsed as your grand jury testimony.**

Anyway, back to *Showgirls.* . . . Elizabeth continued her uninhibited antics all through the shoot. "I'm trying to help her get through a scene," Gina Gershon told me, "and she's telling me what she's going to do to Paul's dick that night." *Elizabeth is your dream girl! Beat your bongo drums! Call her! Send her* Leaves of Grass! *Now!*

Not until the end of the shoot did Charlie Evans tell Paul that the young woman he'd auditioned in his hotel room that day was Elizabeth Berkley.

I hope I've convinced you, Bubba, and thanks for being a fan. O.J. is a fan, too; the first thing he did after his acquittal was to see *Showgirls* and *Jade* back to back.

I feel your pain,

[signature]

P.S. Steven's chickenshit. You'd be great in *Sacred Cows,* too.

(12)

The President's
Piece of Cake

Goddamn! Talk about a spoiled Jewish American Princess! Shaking me down for her bullshit job! What was wrong with working at the Pentagon anyway? She had a chance to travel, didn't she? London. Hong Kong. Brussels. Well, okay, maybe she didn't like damn Brussels. . . .

And then I work it so she can go to the UN and live in New York, and she doesn't want to do it. The deal is almost done, and then she decides, she and her Beverly Hills mother, that there are too many *Arabs* in New York! It's the Jewish capital of America, and she thinks there are too many *Arabs* there! Well, what about Beverly Hills? The Arabs have taken over Beverly Hills. Don't they bother her there?

Christ, I should have my head examined just for letting her start all this. She had that come-hither look the first time I saw her. Snapping her underwear at me so I could see the crack of her ass. You talk about come hither—*mama!* Hot little bitch. Big snow-white titties popping out of her dress. Shaking that ass at me every time she walked by, like it had a fun life of its own. Well, maybe it was a little big, yeah, but a little big never bothers me.

What was I supposed to do? What the hell was I supposed to do? She was putting it right out there like her own oven-warm angel food cake, and I was hungry. I'm always hungry. Was I supposed to say no and deny myself even this little reward?

I was busting my butt at this job, up till three, four hours of sleep, always on the plane, jet-lagged all the time. My sinuses were driving me nuts. My back hurt. My knee ached. A little *reward*. Just a *little* reward. A piece of angel food cake to recharge my batteries. I didn't even pop her. I didn't even do that.

All I did, really, except for a couple times at the end, was let her kiss me there. She wanted more. She always wanted more. She had her hands all over dumb Willard the first time I kissed her. She knew the deal. She told me right away she'd been with that married guy. What did she think was going to happen? I was going to leave Hillary for a piece of cake?

I made such a mistake! God, oh God, *such* a mistake! I knew there were dangers right off the top. She had to be a little nuts, following me around, showing up everywhere I went, even on that sidewalk in New York as the car went by. And the chatter, the constant, endless chatter. Motormouth. All those da da da da das. All those blah blah blah blah blahs. I kissed her as soon as I saw her sometimes, just to shut her the fuck up. Trying to stop her motor before she got cranked. Goddamn, didn't she get it? She was supposed to kiss me there, not talk to me. She was supposed to unbutton herself, not tell me her ideas about education. Even when she wasn't talking, the noise that she made! When I had my fingers there and she was making those dolphin noises? Can't she even moan quietly? I was afraid the Secret Service would burst through the door, thinking I'd cardiacked. I had to put my hand over her mouth. My hand got all wet. She was roaring down her track like that steam locomotive I used to watch in Hot Springs.

Then she started putting her little dramas into play, talking to me about her mother's dimwit book about Pavarotti, about her father cheating on her mother and marrying his nurse. Was I supposed to care? Why did she think I'd care? I didn't even know her name the first time. She knew that; she even made a joke about it.

Now she was telling me about this loser, Andy, up in Oregon, cheating on his wife. I'm the president of the United States and I have to hear about *Andy?* My head is full of budgets and bills and battle plans and I have to hear about how mean Andy's been to her?

What did she think I was? Her friend? Her lover? Her father? Her shrink? Why did she think I gave a shit? How could she not know that she was nothing more than a piece of cake? Is she *that* stupid? The whole country—the whole world—knows how I feel about cake! Books have been written about it. She *had* to know whom she was dealing with. That had to be the reason why she'd snapped her underwear at me.

So why was she acting like she was a human being to me now? Didn't she know I'm always busy? I'd certainly *let* her know. I was on the phone, taking care of America's business even as she was kneeling there. Talking about Bosnia, about the sugar subsidy. Her ears and her mouth were wide open. What is she—deaf *and* dumb?

What a drama queen! All those crock-a-shit tears when she lost her job at the White House. It was an election year, for Christ's sake! I didn't have any room for any more Gennifer stories. Didn't she get it? People talked. Nancy and Marsha and Debbie and Cathy watched her like hawks. They know if I have new cake. They know me too well. They get jealous. They don't want any other cake around. They take my new cake away.

People talk. The stewards talk and the residence staff talks and the Secret Service agents talk, and Hillary's damn spies are everywhere, listening to everybody talk. She lost her job so I wouldn't lose the presidency. She lost her job so Nancy and Marsha and Debbie and Cathy wouldn't have to compete with her. But no—she didn't understand that! She didn't think it was fair that she lost her job because of me. Her focus wasn't on the presidency, on America—her focus was on herself, on her bullshit job.

It was as if she took herself seriously when she told me she wanted to be secretary of blow jobs. She had somehow elevated her crummy White House job into a cabinet-level position. She actually expected me to do something about it, to get her White House job back for her. Was she really that self-involved . . . to think that the president of the United States would personally issue an order to bring a twenty-three-year-old former intern back into my work space? *After* all these people had already talked about her coming in to see me in the Oval Office?

I could just see the story breaking during the campaign, putting the White House back into the hands of those motherfucking bastards I've fought my whole life to take it from. But she didn't see these things. All she talked about was getting her bullshit job back and how unfair it was that she'd lost it because of me. This little ditz was trying to make *me* feel guilty?

Even when I called her from the campaign trail at the end of a long day . . . I've got Willard in one hand, the phone in the other. I just want a moment of peace. I've got flashes of her tits running through my head. Even then she wants to talk about her job. I couldn't fucking believe it! She knew I liked her talking dirty to me. All day long, I'm out on the stump, up on the platform with Hillary, sound bites and photo ops . . . and I get back to the privacy of my hotel bedroom and call her, and she badgers me about what I'm doing to get her White House job back.

I shine her on. I have her see some staff people, including Marsha, who shines her on, too. But that leads to a whole other drama. Now she's angry that I sent her to Marsha. She knows that Marsha and I . . . And now she's saying that Marsha's never going to help her get a job at the White House because Marsha's jealous. She's telling me that it isn't fair that Nancy and Marsha and Debbie and

Cathy can see me and she can't. Come on—I've got Willard in my hand at the end of a brutal day and I have to hear *this?*

I was getting a little afraid of her, too. I couldn't afford to make her angry. I couldn't afford her flipping out somehow. If she told—a young White House intern and dumb Willard in the Oval Office—well that, plain and simple, goddamn it, would be the end of the world. I felt trapped. I couldn't afford to piss her off or freak her out, but I couldn't afford to let her back inside the White House, either.

I was trapped in another way, too. I didn't want to see her—and I didn't see her through the whole campaign. But I did want to see her with her mouth there and her tits sticking out of her bra, glowing white in that dark hallway. I was *afraid* to see her because I knew my hunger was gonna force me to lead her into that hallway or into the bathroom.

In my more paranoid moments, I wondered if it was possible that this babbling idiot had set me up. *Of course* she knew about my hunger for cake. *That's* why she snapped her damn underwear at me. *That's* why she followed me around. *That's* why she knelt down before I knew her damn name. She *wanted* to compromise me. She wanted to have the president of the United States by his willard.

She kept crying over the phone, telling me how unhappy she was in her Pentagon job, how much she missed me. "I don't wanna talk about your job tonight!" I finally said to her once. "I wanna talk about other things." She knew what that meant. She did the dirty talk and that led her to talk about how much she wanted to sleep with me.

And that sent her on another crying jag, until I asked if she wanted me to stop calling her. She said no. She started showing up again at campaign events. At one of them, I'm reaching across a rope line to grip and grin with somebody, and she reaches out and grabs Willard. Man, that spooked me! I thought she was flipping out. *Grabbing Willard in public?* Willard shrunk!

When I saw her damn Valentine's Day ad in the *Washington Post,* it spooked me even more. What had I done to myself? How could I have done this to myself? I'd allowed my fate to be held hostage by a piece of cake? Was this *Fatal Attraction?* I was scared shitless. So I agreed to see her. I hadn't seen her alone in ten months. *Ten months,* and she was hanging all over me.

What could I do? If I dumped her, she could flip and talk. I shined her on. I gave her some Christmas presents and then I took her into the hallway and allowed her, for the first time, to make Willard happy. I'm not sure why I let her do that. Either it was my hunger for cake or it was part of my strategy of shining her on so she wouldn't flip out or talk. Or it was a combination of the two reasons. Or it was just hardheaded, dumb Willard.

Then I heard from Marsha that the idiot had told her mother about our "friendship." Her mother told Walter Kaye, that old moneybags who keeps sending me shirts, who then told Marsha. It was my worst nightmare. Who else had she told? Who else had her gossipy damn mother told? Who else had kiss-ass Walter told? I cursed myself out. How could I have ever trusted Motormouth not to tell anyone? I knew I had to end this and end it now and try to do it as gently and diplomatically as possible, so she wouldn't turn on me and do the fuck knew what. She'd betrayed me.

I invited her down to the Oval Office. I told her I was trying to be faithful to Hillary. But I also told her that I was very attracted to *her*. I said she was a great person. I told her how skinny she looked. I wanted us to stay friends. I said I could do a lot to help her. She started to sob. I hugged and kissed her good-bye. I clenched my jaw a couple of times. I let my eyes well up. I could hear violins.

I hoped to God this stupidity I'd allowed with this babbling piece of cake wouldn't blow up in my face. A few days later, the Supreme Court ruled that Paula Jones's sexual-harassment suit against me could proceed. *I prayed to God* Jones's lawyers wouldn't find out about her.

She kept trying to call me. I didn't take her calls. She was still trying to get her White House job back, seeing Marsha and Bob Nash. She was under the impression that I was trying to help her get the job indirectly. There was no way I wanted her in the White House. I didn't want to see her. I didn't want to hear from her. She wrote me a letter, angry that I wasn't taking her calls. "Please do not do this to me," she wrote. "I feel disposable, used, and insignificant. I understand your hands are tied, but I want to talk to you and look at some options." No way! I ignored her letter and kept refusing to take her calls.

"Disposable," "used," and "insignificant." Well, she was finally getting it. She wrote me another letter. "Dear Sir," it began. She told me I'd broken my promise to help her find another job. She threatened to disclose our "friendship" to her parents. I knew she had already told her mother—now she was threatening to tell her father. The bitch had brought it out into the open now between us. Blackmail! The president of the United States was being shaken down to find a piece of cake a job.

.　.　.

I was enraged. I had to stop this somehow. I had to soothe her, stop her from telling anyone else. I invited her down to the Oval Office again. I told her it was illegal to threaten the president of the United States. She said that I'd done nothing to help her find a job. She started to cry. I hugged her. I stroked her arm. I played with her hair. I kissed her on the neck. I told her how smart and beautiful she was. I told her how skinny she looked. I clenched my jaw a couple times. I let my eyes well up. *I aced it.* She wasn't going to tell her father or anyone else. It was under control. When she left, the moron was convinced I was in love with her.

When she called to tell me she'd decided to work in New York, it was music to my ears. New York would be easy. New York would get her away from Washington. New York would get her away from me. I'd get her a job at the UN through Bill Richardson. Bill's cool. He doesn't ask questions; he knows the score. It was *done.* She met with Bill. She went to New York. And then the spoiled, pampered bitch came back and said she didn't want to work at the UN. *Because of the Arabs!* I couldn't believe it! She wanted to work in *the private sector.* She wanted *me* to find her a job in the private sector!

Well, la-dee-fucking-dah! I'm the president of the United States, and now I was assigned by a piece of cake to find her not a government job but some job where her damn employer would be doing the president of the United States *a favor* to hire her. She told me that I owed it to her. Because she'd been transferred out of the White House as a result of her "friendship" with me. Because I said I'd help her find a job and so far I hadn't found her one. Because she'd left the White House "quietly" and hadn't told anyone she had lost her job thanks to me.

In other words, it was all my fault and I *owed* it to her to make it right and find her a job. Not just any job, because the UN job wasn't good enough. But some private-sector job that Miss Hoity-Toity Blow Job Cabinet Member considered acceptable. That, of course, meant money. A salary, probably in six figures, that mommy and her new sugar daddy approved of. *I . . . wished . . . she'd . . . just . . . fuck off and die!*

I put Vernon on it. Vernon was on the board of so many companies, he could find something. Vernon was in the process of hunting a job for her when she was subpoenaed in the Paula Jones case. She really had me now. The bitch! The miserable babbling bitch! If she told the truth, it would be all over. But she'd have to lie under oath now and commit perjury to save me. She'd have to break the law for me. I was screwed, blewed, and tattooed.

I invited her down to the Oval Office again. I gave her a bunch of shit: a marble bear's head, a Rockettes blanket, a Black Dog stuffed animal, a small box of chocolates, a pair of joke sunglasses, and a pin with a New York skyline on it. I let her play with Buddy. I gave her a long and passionate kiss. I told her how skinny she looked. I clenched my jaw a couple times. I let my eyes well up. She fell for it like the big sack of blubber that she is.

A week later, she signed a false affidavit saying she had never had "a sexual relationship" with me. Two days after that, Vernon got her a job at Revlon in New York. She was happy. Her damn mommy was happy. The damn sugar daddy was happy. It was finally over. I was free of her.

And then . . . and then . . . *Tape recordings?* That prick Starr had—*tape recordings?* The world was ending! My first thought was that she'd taped me, just like Gennifer—oh my good merciful God! *The phone sex!* I could just hear myself moaning on the NBC nightly news, Brokaw scowling, more mush-mouthed than usual. But no, it was tapes of her and that toxic garbage dump who'd befriended her. Motormouth babbling on and on about God knew what.

The cigar? No! No! *Oh, no, no!* Please God, not the cigar! It was her idea. *Her idea!* She was the one who said, "And if you want to do that sometime, we can do that, too," looking at my cigar like a ten-dollar whore, telling me to put it there, just about *ordering me* to do it. My hand was nothing but the instrument of *her* filthy fantasies. What happened happened between her privates and my cigar. *I* had little to do with it.

There was nothing to do but trash her now. Charlie Rangel was already doing it anyway, saying, "That poor child has some serious emotional problems"; saying, "I haven't heard that she played with a full deck"; saying, "She's fantasizing." It wouldn't be that much of a stretch, either—slice and dice one more time. Hey, this *was Fatal Attraction*! She *was* a nut and a slut! She *was* a stalker! Beverly Hills trailer park trash! Forget her damn age! She was porking that married guy up in Portland—but wait, wait, wait! Get Carville back here! Hold the nuts and sluts! Tell Begala and Blumenthal and Barney's sister to cool it! Hold the slice and dice!

There was a report on ABC that said she had a navy blue dress with my . . . Then there was another report that denied it. Even if she had a dress, was she gonna turn it over to that prick? What if she didn't turn it over? Then it was a he said/she said. No proof. Shit, I couldn't trash her if she had that dress. If I trashed her, she'd turn it over for sure. No, I had to be nice to the stupid, scheming, fat-ass, blackmailing bitch. Being nice had worked before. The piece of cake was in love with me, wasn't she? But what could I do to be nice to her? I couldn't see her or talk to her. Yes! *Yes!* I had it! It was brilliant! It was beautiful!

She'd see me on TV . . . and I'd be wearing one of the ties that she'd given me. A private little love message . . . which the whole world would be watching and missing . . . except her. She'd never give the dress to that prick! She'd fall for it just like she fell for me. Hey, pieces of cake always fall for me. I'm the man! I'm the dude! I'm the motherfucker! I'm the mack! I'm the shit! I'm the president of the United States!

[13]

Bob Packwood's
Reptile Tongue

"He's a creep," Monica said to Linda Tripp. "He's a piece of shit. I hate him."

As the Lewinsky headlines gathered sexually steamy steam, those kinky miscreants interested in recent tawdry parallels considered the disgraced and banished former senator from the do-good state of Oregon . . . the sometime dinner companion of that great pro-choice feminist icon, Gloria Steinem . . . *ta-dah* . . . Reptile Tongue, the Man with the Horny Hands, Bob Packwood!

In 1992, when Bill Clinton went to the White House, Bob Packwood, elected in 1968 on the length of the Night Creature's fingernails, was the most powerful feminist advocate, the most prominent male feminist, in America. Bob Packwood had introduced the first abortion bill in the Senate in 1970 and had always been the leading Republican advocate for the Equal Rights Amendment. Bob Packwood had written groundbreaking proposals on pregnancy leave, insurance-industry reform to end discrimination against women, and child care.

Way back in 1962, Bob Packwood had told a campaign aide that "women's talents are the greatest wasted resource in the country." About his friend Gloria Steinem, Bob Packwood said, "On women's issues, she regards me as almost a hundred percenter. She appreciates the fact that women predominate in the upper echelons of my office, and are paid accordingly." It was true that almost all of Bob Packwood's staff was composed of women, although there were whispers that Packwood liked to hire divorced women or unhappily married women, so they'd have no relation-

ship that competed with "the job." High turnover was always a staff problem. Others pointed out that some of the women who worked for Bob Packwood, though uniformly attractive, weren't all that smart or political or
libertarian, citing as example a conversation between Packwood chief of
staff Mimi Weyforth and another aide. The aide asked Weyforth why Packwood, who wasn't Jewish, took militantly pro-Israeli positions.

"Don't you know the senator went to N.Y. Jew Law School?" Weyforth
said.

The aide, insulted, told Weyforth he was Jewish.

"You mean I hired Jew and I didn't even know it?" Weyforth said.

Hurt and shocked, the aide turned away, and Weyforth said, "Weyforth is
a German name; don't you ever forget that!"

There were cynical longtime Oregon political observers who, looking at
Bob Packwood as the number-one feminist in America, said that Packwood's
feminism was a sham—just another example of the political opportunism
that got him elected to office as a longhair-bashing Nixonite. "If we're talking about people carrying signs," Packwood had said in the sixties, "walking
barefoot, bead-wearing guys, they're not my cup of tea. When I saw that
crazy kid [Mark Rudd] at Columbia University sitting in the president's
chair with his feet on his desk and smoking a cigar, I got mad."

As Watergate exploded, Bob Packwood quickly abandoned the Night
Creature, whose landslide had gotten him elected by three-tenths of 1 percent. Packwood lectured Nixon with words that would come back to haunt
him. "Some politicians have a weakness for alcohol. For others, it's gambling. For others, it's women. Your weakness is credibility." Packwood told
Nixon he had to "disclose everything."

The most startling example Oregon political observers gave of Bob Packwood's political opportunism was his attitude toward gay people. Speaking
at a women's rights forum, Packwood was asked, "Do you support antidis-
crimination legislation for gay people?" Packwood blurted, "No. I think
homosexuals are disgusting." Booed and condemned by the women who
constituted his core constituency, Bob Packwood quickly agreed to cospon-
sor a federal gay rights law.

Packwood's fellow Republican senator from Oregon, the esteemed Mark
Hatfield, Packwood's college government professor, loathed him. He
refused to attend any Senate meetings to which Packwood was also invited.
"Packwood is an unscrupulous son of a bitch," the usually decorous and
understated Senator Hatfield said.

A nerd who wore thick glasses in school, Bob Packwood wanted to be a mechanical engineer. He won an award as "the ugliest guy" in his fraternity and his college friends joked, "Every time he asked a girl out, she said she was doing her hair." When he was thirty-three, Packwood married a divorcée two years older, Georgie Oberteuffer Crockett, the daughter of the founder of the National Camp Fire Girls, a longtime leading figure in the Boy Scouts of America.

Georgie liked blue skies and horses and Bob Packwood liked smoke-filled rooms and leather-boothed cocktail lounges. Shortly after she married him, Georgie said, "He was the first man I'd ever met who didn't know how to flirt and didn't even try." They adopted two children and a year after their marriage Packwood's Camp Fire girl noted in a calendar: "Bob got drunk and wants a divorce. Well, we almost made it through one year." Bob Packwood started calling Georgie his "albatross," went off on a drunken binge three or four times a year, and told her, "I want a divorce. We should never have married. I want to be a bachelor." But they stayed together.

Reporters covering Packwood's campaigns were hearing rumors. A reporter who covered a political conference noted, "Some mornings Bob came in bleary-eyed and everyone suspected he had been sleeping with some Republican babe. He was playing close to the edge for someone recruiting women for key roles in his campaign." Packwood was often seen at a place called the Black Anvil Tavern in the Hells Canyon National Recreation Area near the Idaho border. "Packwood always seemed to have five or six real good-looking women on his staff," said a drinking partner at the Black Anvil, "and he'd figure out which one it was for the night."

A new campaign scheduler was quickly educated by other staff members about Oregon towns and cities to keep the candidate away from. "There was Susie in Salem, Judy in Eugene, Elizabeth in Coos Bay," making it sometimes difficult for the scheduler to mount a real statewide campaign. Georgie heard the rumors, too, and asked Packwood why he always traveled with an attractive female aide. "People would call me a homosexual if I traveled with men," Packwood said.

Georgie knew what was going on and knew, too, that Packwood had a lot of straying colleagues in the Senate. At a luncheon for senators' wives, she looked around the room and thought it "a whole get-together of enablers." The Camp Fire girl saw that her husband was behaving increasingly oddly. Trying to stop a Democrat-sponsored bill to control campaign spending, Packwood refused to go to the Senate floor, so that there wouldn't be a quorum to hold a vote. The majority leader, Robert Byrd, sent the sergeant at arms for him. Packwood locked his office door and blocked the inner door with heavy furniture. Deputies broke down the doors and Packwood broke his finger resisting them. They had to carry Packwood to the Senate floor.

In 1989, the Camp Fire girl became convinced that Packwood was having an affair with his chief of staff, a woman who was often seen "conferring" with the militantly feminist senator in her bikini while they enjoyed a hot tub. "Senator Packwood is fond of hot tubs and does a lot of his thinking in them," his comely chief of staff said. The Camp Fire girl pressed ahead with her divorce, and, ultimately, Packwood didn't fight it. "I don't want a wife. I don't want a house. I just want to be a senator," Packwood told Georgie and his two now-grown children. "But Dad," his son said to him, "someday you're going to get defeated, and we're the best friends you have." Best friends or not, the divorce was granted and once again Packwood was the bachelor that he wanted to be.

In 1990, Senator Bob Packwood, the darling of feminists everywhere, public symbol of the sensitive, selfless, gender-blind man of the New Age future, was the star of the show at a Senate workshop on sexual assault. The room was filled with women Senate staffers learning how to defend themselves against sexual assault. Packwood was up onstage, having been asked by the organizers to play the role of the sexual predator. He was grabbing women by the butt, squeezing their breasts, reaching between their legs. He got a rousing round of applause.

Two years later, newspapers in Washington and Oregon started writing stories about a pattern of Packwood behavior that stretched back thirty years. It was behavior that wasn't run-of-the-mill Senate philandering. It was behavior that amounted to sexual harassment, intimidation, humiliation.

It wasn't Mick Jagger sixties behavior; it was "dirty old man" behavior from the fifties: kisses and copped feels in harmony with the Sinatra songs that Packwood sang to his aides, behavior in sync with the card he sent to one of his sexually abused staffers: "Were you the girl I met under the clock at the Biltmore in 1954?" Forty-eight women eventually came forward to tell their stories, most of them former staffers or aides, who said the unstated rule in the great feminist's office was "Put out or get out."

There was the high school summer intern at his Senate office who asked him for a college recommendation. Packwood showed up at her home. "He seemed a little heated," she said. "He laid a juicy kiss on my lips. I could feel the tongue coming." . . . There was the sixty-four-year-old newspaper reporter who had just interviewed him. Packwood came around the desk and forced a kiss on her lips. . . . A woman who responded to a letter from Gloria Steinem asking for volunteers to help him. Packwood "turned and pulled me toward him and sensually kissed me in a way that was very inappropriate." . . . A woman who worked on his 1986 reelection campaign. Packwood "leered at me, pushed his body toward me, smacked his lips suggestively, and asked for my measurements. I felt like some kind of beef steak." . . .

A visiting twenty-three-year-old woman from a politically prominent family in Oregon, who had a drink with Packwood and her family members. Sitting next to her, Packwood put his hand up her skirt. . . . A woman being considered for a campaign job. "He asked me to dance at a restaurant. He kissed me on the neck. His hands were all over my back, my sides, my buttocks. He made suggestive movements." . . . Another senator's aide, who went to his office to deliver a package. Georgie was there. Packwood introduced the aide to the Camp Fire girl, who immediately asked the aide if she could baby-sit their kids that night. The aide, somewhat taken aback, agreed. As Packwood walked her to her car from their home, he held the baby-sitter by the shoulders and tried to shove his tongue through her closed mouth while touching her legs. . . .

A local campaign worker who drove Packwood and his chief of staff, with whom he was having an affair, to a Eugene hotel. When the chief of staff got out of the car, Packwood "quickly gave me a French kiss." . . . A twenty-one-year-old receptionist whom Packwood asked into his inner Senate office. "I sat down, he walked over to me and pulled me out of my chair, put his arms around me, and tried to kiss me. He stuck his tongue into my mouth." . . . A twenty-one-year-old mail clerk, also summoned into Packwood's inner office. "He locked the doors. He ran his fingers through my hair and kissed me on the lips. I could feel my skin crawl. I was paralyzed and trying to push him away." She quit her job with Packwood and went to work for others on Capitol Hill. Six years later, she met Packwood again in the Capitol's underground corridor. Packwood asked where she was working now. "He stopped at an unmarked office and said, 'Step in and we'll finish the conversation.' " Packwood grabbed her by the hand, kissed her, and started pushing pillows off a sofa. "I resisted, but he had a tight grip, and I pushed him away until he stopped. I kept saying to myself, How could you be so stupid?" . . .

A twenty-eight-year-old aide who had dinner with her husband and Packwood. When her husband went to the bathroom, Packwood kissed her. Packwood went up behind her at the office the next day and kissed the back of her neck. "Don't ever do that again!" she told him. She walked into another room and he followed her. He grabbed her by her ponytail and stood on her toes. "He reached his hand up my skirt to pull my underpants down. I struggled to free my feet. I freed one and began kicking him hard in the shins. It made him stop." Packwood told her, "Not today, but someday." She confronted Packwood a week later and said, "What was supposed to happen next? Were we just going to lie down on the rug? Like animals in the zoo?" Packwood told her, "I guess you're the type that wants a motel." . . .

A twenty-seven-year-old elevator operator whom Packwood grabbed by the shoulders and kissed on the lips as soon as she closed the elevator doors. "What do you want from me?" she asked, frightened. Packwood said, "Two things. First thing is, I want to make love to you. Second thing is, you have a job where you hear things, and I want to hear what you hear." . . . A thirteen-year-old hostess at a political gathering in Oregon. Packwood grabbed her buttocks. "I wasn't even dating yet," she said. "I was so excited about getting the job. I got to wear a black dress and black panty hose. It was the first time I'd ever gotten to wear black panty hose."

America's foremost male feminist was politically dead pig meat. The newspaper stories led to a formal Senate investigation. Jay Leno was at work on him: "President Clinton wants to give vaccination shots to all kids. Not to be outdone today, Senator Packwood promised free breast exams to all women." And: "Boy, did you hear what happened to Packwood today? Broke three fingers when he tried to grab the rear end of a woman who used that *Buns of Steel* workout tape." Gloria Steinem told reporters that, yes, she and Packwood had had dinner, then added, "Please don't say we had dinner alone."

Packwood vowed to fight the charges. He got vanity plates for his car that said MASADA and explained that he had selected the name to honor the heroic band of Jewish patriots who had committed suicide rather than surrender. But it was all over when he was forced to turn over to the Senate an eight-thousand-page diary detailing many of his sexual misadventures. His diary was Packwood's Watergate tapes, his "Monkey Business" photo, his stained blue dress.

At the end, the Night Creature, whose electoral loins spawned Packwood, was one of the few still defending him. "Packwood must be scared shitless," Richard Nixon said, also describing Packwood as someone who could be "mean." "If they force Packwood to resign, they should force Teddy Kennedy and everyone else with a problem to resign, which means we'll have almost no Senate left! I know those people! How many women has Teddy chased around desks? And Clinton? Oh, my God, more than you know! And what about the other Democrats guilty of the same thing? There are so many of them down there that do this sort of thing—and have for years—that you wouldn't believe it!"

Bob Packwood tried to put the blame on alcohol, but it didn't get him off the hook. He checked himself into the Hazelden Clinic in Minnesota. He told interviewers his father was an alcoholic who drank potent vanilla extract during Prohibition. Sympathetic journalists—William Safire was one, his son an intern in Packwood's office—recounted how Packwood had always ordered two drinks at a time. "I drink immense quantities of liquid," Packwood said. "It doesn't matter what it is. I will, on occasion, drink a gallon of milk at dinner, or two or three pitchers of water, and when I drank alcohol I would go through beer and wine the same way." The more malicious wondered if Packwood was suffering from Minamata disease, whose symptoms include loss of muscular control, slurred speech, and brain damage.

Packwood tried apologizing, but that didn't work, either. He called his actions toward women "unwelcome and insensitive." He said, "My past actions were not just inappropriate. What I did was not just stupid or boorish. My actions were just plain wrong." He talked, finally, in his banishment from the Senate, about the Book of Job. "Although I'm not a particularly religious man, I take solace from time to time in reading the Book of Job. Some people think they've got problems. That poor devil *really* had problems."

A few years after Packwood's banishment, as Bill Clinton contemplated the expansive and humiliating apology the media wanted him to make, Packwood's fate gave him food for thought. Packwood, the feminist Galahad, had apologized fully and wide-rangingly.

Packwood hadn't seized the word *inappropriate* as his fraying lifeline. Packwood had foolishly swum past it into shark-infested waters, and the op-ed sharks and the feminists had eaten him alive.

And all Packwood had done was play a lot of grab-ass and dumb-ass kissy face. Packwood hadn't serially undraped the gross enormity or the enormous grossness of *his* willard to anyone. Packwood's mortal sins had the texture of acne and the smell of starched, callow pubescence. Packwood's excesses *were* those of the nerd with thick glasses who wanted to be a mechanical engineer.

Packwood's willard may have been out of control, but his reptile tongue and his soft white hands were acting it out. Unlike Bill Clinton, who'd always let Willard do the talking. No public blow jobs for Packwood, no juicy cigar. And still the feminists and their shock troops, the soccer moms and the PTA activists, had turned on him.

As he thought about Packwood, Bill Clinton knew he had a huge and sharp edge: Hillary. He had Hillary to help him, unlike the demented Packwood, who'd divorced his un-Hillary-like, Camp Fire girl wife. Would the feminists really go after Bill Clinton, knowing that going after him would damage their own icon, who just happened to be his wife? They'd gone after their icon Packwood, but Packwood was a man (sort of). Would the women really go after Saint Hillary, the first woman copresident of the United States?

Bill Clinton didn't think so. He smiled to himself about the righteous and wicked ironies of his life. Bob Packwood, seeing the Lewinsky headlines and hearing the new Jay Leno jokes, smiled, too. He announced in Portland that he was considering running for the Senate again.

[14]

The Scavenger
from Cyberspace

"The last time I saw the Creep," Monica said to Linda Tripp, "he said, 'I have an empty life except for my work and my work is a fucking obsession.'"

As Linda Tripp and Lucianne Goldberg plotted . . . first about Kathleen Willey and now about Monica . . . they knew they had to convince the Beast to trumpet their stories to the world. They didn't trust the Beast's hypocritical, self-righteous posturing. They hoped that the Beast's greed for a big moneymaking story would overcome its liberal biases and Tourette's-like seizures of sanctimony.

They sucked *Newsweek* reporter Michael Isikoff, known as an uncompromising investigative reporter, into their web. But they still felt themselves on shaky ground. What if Isikoff couldn't convince his editors to run the story? How could the Ratwoman and the Bag Lady of Sleaze *force* the media to headline the ingredients of their witch's brew? And then they found an ally even more helpful than Mark Fuhrman. He, too, was a Californian, working out of a dingy apartment above the seedy Hollywood Boulevard strip . . . the Scavenger from Cyberspace, Matt Drudge.

While manipulating Monica was Linda Tripp's unholy gig, manipulating the media was Goldberg's. She who had spied on the media at the Night Creature's behest had learned Nixon's lessons about the media well. "Seventy-five percent of the media voted for McGovern," Nixon had said. "They protected Kennedy and sometimes they pimped for him." And about those reporters covering Clinton: "They're draft dodgers just like he was. They share his immorality and lack of values. They take care of their own." Goldberg didn't have to be convinced. She was a woman who had been good friends with Nixon's notorious Red-baiting hatchet man, Murray Chotiner, and with Victor Lasky, a right-wing backalley slasher who had bloodied JFK in several scurrilous volumes.

Isikoff, Lucianne Goldberg thought, was probably just like those other liberal reporters Nixon had talked about. The Reverend Pat Robertson had called Isikoff "one of the most vicious, anti-Christian bigots in the entire world. He is absolutely unbalanced and he is, uh, emotionally in my opinion, uh, uh, stunted." But Isikoff was also a steel-nosed reporter; he had once called an editor at the *Washington Post* a "fucking asshole" for not running a detailed, lengthy account of Paula Jones's claims. He had been suspended from the *Post*, then joined *Newsweek* shortly afterward.

Goldberg's experience working for Nixon had prepared her well for what she was doing with the Ratwoman now. "The Nixon people were looking for really dirty stuff," she said. "Who was sleeping with whom, what the Secret Servicemen were doing with the stewardesses, who was smoking pot on the plane—that kind of thing." The Bag Lady of Sleaze knew all about "the dirty stuff." One of her novels, *People Will Talk*, focused on a gossip columnist who "can unzip a fly with her toes." In another novel, *Purr, Baby, Purr*, she suggested that women should view themselves as "a switchboard with all sorts of lovely buttons and plug-ins for lighting up and making connections."

She had made connections when she came to Washington as a young woman by sleeping with a lot of men. "Lucy would claim that her entire social life took place Monday through Friday because she only went out with married men," a friend said. Another friend said, "She had those tight skirts, kind of bouncy blouses, and blond hair piled on top of her head. She'd clack across the room in her high heels." Goldberg practiced an English accent, had herself paged in fancy restaurants, and had pictures taken with politicians like Hubert Humphrey by pretending she was "an old friend from the past."

She had told other lies through the years, too. One book jacket claimed "she started her journalistic career at the *Washington Post*" (she was a clerk). Another book jacket said she "was appointed to the White House staff" after JFK was sworn in. (There is no record of her employment at the Kennedy White House.) As a literary agent, she had been sued by author client Kitty Kelley for stealing her foreign royalties, and the court awarded Kelley sixty thousand dollars.

Now, at sixty-two, as she loaded her gold Dunhill holder with a cigarette and took yet another sip of vodka, the Bag Lady of Sleaze knew that the sordid nature of her experience in Washington would be a great help to her in putting this sordid story out there.

She had to laugh. Here Monica was telling Linda about using Altoids before she went down on Bill Clinton, and right there in one of Lucianne Goldberg's novels—*Madam Cleo's Girls*—was the same scene, not with Altoids but with Life Savers. The Bag Lady knew what she was talking about and, more importantly, whom she was dealing with.

Michael Isikoff got a tip one day about the Oval Office encounter between Kathleen Willey and Bill Clinton from one of Paula Jones's lawyers who had been tipped off by Linda Tripp. Isikoff tracked Willey down and she told him off the record what had happened. She pointed to Linda Tripp as a witness—the first person Willey had spoken to when she left the Oval Office. Isikoff tracked the Ratwoman down and told her he was working on the story. Tripp confirmed that something had happened, but she told him that Willey hadn't seemed unhappy about it. Isikoff couldn't run the story until Willey went on the record and until he straightened out the conflicts in the Willey and Tripp accounts. But now Tripp and Goldberg knew that *Newsweek* had it and, as weeks went by, that *Newsweek* was sitting on it.

Enter then at this moment, from cyberspace, the Scavenger, Matt Drudge, whom Lucianne Goldberg would call "a fellow spirit." Drudge was the thirty-year-old author of the *Drudge Report,* a Web site gossip sheet that he had started in 1994, devoted, in the beginning, mostly to Hollywood items. He had reported correctly that Jerry Seinfeld was demanding $1 million per episode and that there were money-costing problems during the shoot of *Titanic.* His biggest political exclusive was that Jack Kemp would be Bob Dole's running mate. When he started running gossip about the Clintons, Rush Limbaugh knighted him as "the Rush Limbaugh of the Internet."

Lucianne Goldberg was impressed with Rush's endorsement and didn't care that some people saw Drudge as a "slanderer" and "king of the junk media." She liked, too, Drudge's view of himself: "All truths begin as hearsay. . . . I'm not a journalist, I'm a kangaroo. . . . I've got a gotcha sheet in a town where nobody's playing gotcha. . . . I go where the stink is." She especially liked "There are no filters and editors between me and the media." It meant that if Drudge wanted to post an item on his Web site, no one could stop him, and hundreds of thousands, even millions, would see it, never mind whether it was true or not. Drudge had no staff, no fact-checkers, no suspicious liberal-leaning editors. Drudge had none of the drawbacks Isikoff had.

While Drudge didn't have *Newsweek* behind him to give him credibility, the Bag Lady of Sleaze knew that the Scavenger could get it out there. She also knew that, besides sharing her political philosophy, Drudge was hungry. He had gotten a tiny taste of minifame with his items about Seinfeld and Jack Kemp, but he was broke, making hardly anything from America Online. His Web site itself was tacky, featuring a red police siren that wailed when Drudge's "word of mouse" informants and "E-mail tipsters" provided him with breaking news.

That the Scavenger was a queer creature, no one could deny. He drove a dented Geo and lived with his cat in his ninth-floor Hollywood apartment near Musso and Frank's, once one of L.A.'s premiere show business hangouts, now a place frequented by more hookers and chicken hawks than agents or writers.

The son of "liberal hippie parents," Drudge had grown up in the Washington, D.C., suburb of Takoma Park. His mother had undergone treatment for schizophrenia. His parents were now divorced—his father a social worker, his mother a lawyer. In grade school, Drudge was diagnosed with an attention-span disorder, cut classes, sneaked off to art museums, and threw rocks at the other kids. In high school, he was a poor student (*D* in current events) who listened for long hours to talk radio in his room, then pretended with a tape recorder that he was conducting his own show. He recited the Pledge of Allegiance over the school loudspeaker every morning. When he graduated—"I barely got out of high school"—he left a "Last Will and Testament" for his classmates: "To my only true friend Ms. Thing, Vicky B, I leave a night in Paris, a bottle of Chaps cologne and hope you find a school with original people. And to everyone else who has helped and hindred [*sic*] whether it be staff or students, I leave a penny for each days [*sic*] I've been here and cried here. A penny rich in worthless memories, for worthless memories is what I have endured."

Drudge went to Europe for a month after he graduated, lived in New York for a year working in a grocery store, then went back home to Takoma

Park. He became a night manager for 7-Eleven stores in other Washington suburbs. He moved to L.A. and got a job as a grunt at the CBS gift shop in Studio City. He folded T-shirts, cleaned shelves, and stacked boxes. He did that for *seven years*. He also gossiped with the technicians who filmed TV shows in the same complex. He put the technicians' gossip he heard onto a home page he had created with a computer his father bought him. He E-mailed the gift shop gossip to friends, who passed the word to others. He started scavenging the trash of studio executives at CBS and other places and put what he found in the garbage on his Web site, too. Word spread. The Scavenger had taken his first baby steps on the way to becoming a cyberstar.

As Lucianne Goldberg waited for Isikoff's editors to run the story about Bill Clinton and Kathleen Willey, she seethed. What was taking *Newsweek* so long? Would this story be deep-sixed by the liberal Washington media, like all the JFK stories her friend Victor Lasky had told her about? Would *Newsweek*, owned by the liberal *Washington Post*, really publish this story? She knew that Vernon Jordan, Bill Clinton's close friend, was a frequent dinner guest at *Post* grande dame Katharine Graham's house. She knew that Ben Bradlee, the former *Post* editor, was one of those journalists who'd partied with JFK, instead of exposing him. And she knew all the problems Isikoff had had trying to publish his Paula Jones story with the *Post*. Enough already! It was time for the Bag Lady of Sleaze to take matters into her own hands. She called Matt Drudge.

The Scavenger put it right out there. His headline read WILLEY'S DECISION: WHITE HOUSE EMPLOYEE TELLS REPORTER THAT PRESIDENT MADE SEX PASS. WORLD EXCLUSIVE! Drudge's item ended: "Isikoff has held back on the exclusive story because the woman has refused to go on the record with her allegation. Nevertheless, the events surrounding Willey have become the talk of the Washington underground and threatened to undermine President Clinton's defense in the ongoing Paula Jones sexual harassment case." Isikoff was furious, but the Bag Lady realized that going to the Scavenger was a double whammy. Because *Newsweek* decided *after Drudge's item* that since the story was already out there, the magazine would also run its account. It was as though Drudge had freed *Newsweek*. Now the story was really out there, with *Newsweek's* credibility behind it. Drudge was delighted, too. The Scavenger had *scooped Newsweek*. And *Newsweek's* story strengthened *the Scavenger's* credibility. The number of hits on Drudge's Web site shot up like a Fourth of July rocket.

. . .

When Isikoff had first spoken to Linda Tripp about Kathleen Willey, Tripp had told him that Bill Clinton was having an affair with a White House intern she wouldn't identify. Now, after Isikoff's story on Willey had run thanks to Drudge, Tripp invited Isikoff to a rendezvous to discuss the young intern.

When Isikoff showed up, Lucianne Goldberg was there as well, along with her son, who worked for a video production company. What Isikoff didn't know was that the Bag Lady and the Ratwoman had decided to set him up again. It had worked beautifully the first time—the Willey stuff was out there—why couldn't it work the same way again? With a much bigger story?

They told Isikoff the intern's name and told him that Linda had secretly taped her. Isikoff wrote all the details down and went to his editors at *Newsweek*. The editors decided that the magazine didn't want to run this kind of salacious story about the president's private life. Not much later, Isikoff got a tip—he never revealed the source—telling him that Linda Tripp had gone to Kenneth W. Starr and that Starr was investigating the relationship between Monica and Bill Clinton. Isikoff went to his editors again. He thought this was a huge story: The special prosecutor was investigating the president's private sex life. After a lot of hand-wringing, *Newsweek* editors decided once again not to run the story. "There are times it's just not worth being first," an editor told Isikoff. "Sometimes it's just not the right thing to do."

Lucianne Goldberg was by now literally bursting with the news of Bill Clinton and Monica. For months, she had been telling her novelist friend Dominick Dunne the skinny, referring to Linda Tripp as "the woman who served Vince Foster his last hamburger." Dominick Dunne knew all about it before Kenneth W. Starr did. He even knew Tripp was taping Monica. "I never picked up on the seriousness of what I was hearing," Dunne would say later. He even saw Vernon Jordan, an old friend, at a dinner and thought about warning him. "I've known Vernon for a long time and like him very much," Dunne would say. "As I was leaving, he came over to my table to say hello. I was going to say to him there's a kid in the Oval Office who's being taped. I knew all that stuff—the stained dress, the oral sex. That's what I was going to say to him, but it seemed so absurd, a made-up thing. Instead I said to him 'Give my love to the President.' I blew it."

When Isikoff told the Bag Lady that *Newsweek* wasn't running the story, she called Matt Drudge. The siren went off at his Web site: NEWSWEEK KILLS STORY ON WHITE HOUSE INTERN—BLOCKBUSTER REPORT: 23-YEAR-OLD, FORMER WHITE HOUSE INTERN, SEX RELATIONSHIP WITH PRESIDENT—*WORLD EXCLUSIVE—*MUST CREDIT THE *DRUDGE REPORT*. His story said, "At the last minute, at six p.m. on Saturday evening, *Newsweek* killed a story that was destined to shake official Washington to its foundation: A White House intern carried on a sexual affair with the President of the United States! The *Drudge Report* has learned that reporter Michael Isikoff developed the story of his career, only to have it spiked by top *Newsweek* suits hours before publication. A young woman, 23, sexually involved with the love of her life, the President of the United States, since she was a 21-year-old intern at the White House. She was a frequent visitor to a small study just off the Oval Office where she claims to have indulged the President's sexual preference. Reports of the relations spread in White House quarters and she was moved to a job at the Pentagon, where she worked until last month. . . . The *Drudge Report* has learned that tapes of intimate phone conversations exist. . . . *Newsweek* and Isikoff were planning to name the woman. . . ." Within days, the *Washington Post* published its own bannered front-page account. And within days, *Newsweek* ran Isikoff's story—not in the magazine, but on Drudge's turf, the Internet.

Lucianne Goldberg's ploy had worked perfectly again in precisely the same way. Isikoff had been screwed again. He had been turned loose, *Newsweek* had refused to publish his story, and Drudge had written a story about *Newsweek*'s refusal. Then *Newsweek* followed Drudge's story with its own account . . . which had been stolen by Drudge. It was the story that rocked the world and the presidency, and the Scavenger, thanks to the Bag Lady and the Ratwoman, had gotten it.

First Willey and then Lewinsky, and as fevered weeks went by, Drudge exclusively ran new details, ones that only Linda Tripp and Kenneth W. Starr's prosecutors knew. Drudge's siren sounded about the blow jobs, the semen-stained dress, and the cigar. All of America was checking out the *Drudge Report* now. A million clicks a day—as many scrollers as the *New York Times* had readers.

Thanks to Drudge, Goldberg and Tripp hadn't just *forced* the media into running their toxic brew; they had taken the media over. The media was *following* their hungry Scavenger, *covering* him. Matt Drudge was an event. There was an additional benefit Goldberg and Tripp hadn't expected. Jay

Leno and Don Imus were taking Drudge's most salacious items . . . and joking about the blow jobs, the cigar, and the blue dress day after day. Goldberg and Tripp were reaching not just a million Internet scrollers but also tens of millions of television viewers. They were doing what Victor Lasky had tried and failed to do with JFK: going for Bill Clinton's jugular.

The Scavenger, once dismissed as a sleazeball, was being hailed as "the town crier for a new age." He did a *Playboy* interview. He became a regular on *Politically Incorrect. Time* picked him as one of the most intriguing people of 1998. Drudge was on magazine covers. Drudge was a highly sought-after lecturer. Drudge did a radio show on New York's WABC. Drudge got a complimentary suite from Washington's Mayflower Hotel. And certainly most painfully for Michael Isikoff, Drudge was picked by *Newsweek—Newsweek!*—as one of the magazine's "new media stars."

One after another, meanwhile, the stories he kept breaking on his siren-blasting Web site were proved to be bogus. Drudge said Hillary would be imminently indicted. Drudge said Paula Jones saw an American eagle tattooed on Willard. Drudge said Kenneth W. Starr had seventy-five compromising photos of Bill and Monica. Drudge broke three straight false items about NBC political reporter Tim Russert. Drudge said Clinton aide Sidney Blumenthal was a wife-beater. Then Drudge pulled the item. Then Drudge apologized. Blumenthal sued him for $30 million anyway.

His biggest goof—*the rock on the playground that came back and hit him in the face*—was, ironically, also a tip from the Bag Lady of Sleaze. One of Lucianne Goldberg's few admirers was the *Star* tabloid's political pooper-scooper Richard Gooding, who thought Lucianne "a delightful person." When the *Star* financed a DNA hunt, led by Gooding, trying to match Bill Clinton's DNA with that of a black teenager named Danny Williams, who was allegedly his illegitimate child, Drudge was all over it. WHITE HOUSE HIT WITH DNA TERROR; TEEN TESTED FOR CLINTON PATERNITY.

At a conservative conference in Arizona, filling in as a late substitute for Henry Hyde, Drudge said, "It's a huge story if it comes together. It's a story of worldwide impact. People have been moved into safe houses today awaiting medical results. Stay tuned to the *Drudge Report*." Rupert Murdoch's newspapers in America and abroad splashed the story all over front pages, quoting Drudge, who then quoted their stories about him in his Internet follow-ups. When the rock hit him in the face—when the DNA didn't match—all the Scavenger said was that it had been "a cruel hoax" perpetrated by the boy's mother.

By then even tabloid journalists were criticizing him as "an informational sucker fish on the body of journalism," claiming that Drudge had somehow acquired passwords that got him access into computerized files, where he scavenged for stories they were still working on. Steve Coz, the editor of the *National Enquirer*, said, "He rips off our advances! He's so quick he can have things up in five minutes." Many journalists said he was a plain and simple thief, gathering headlines from what they were still in the process of writing or researching . . . stealing as surely as the Bag Lady of Sleaze had stolen Kitty Kelley's foreign advances.

It didn't seem to matter, though, somehow. Drudge was quite the celebrity seen about Washington, where he was described as "the man with the Dickensian name." There was talk that he was about to market his own T-shirt line, that Wall Street investors said an Internet public company featuring Drudge would be valued at $4.5 billion. Dustin Hoffman, professional liberal, went up to him at a party and said he'd like to play him in a movie. Drudge took Paula Jones to a dinner for White House correspondents. He was seen with chic conservative writer Ann Coulter, who described him as "larger than life and sort of childish. It's hard to find anyone who knows the whole Matt, there may not be one." Coulter described Drudge driving around in his battered Geo, which he now called the "Drudgemobile," and listening to tapes of himself on his radio talk show. Drudge, she said, laughed uproariously as he listened. He was now making $400,000 a year, handing Coulter hundred-dollar bills "for the cab" and telling her to keep the change.

The Scavenger was a TV star, "the mod muckraker, the citizen journalist," speaking in a Joe Friday voice, fedora on his head, Fox Television's biggest Saturday draw, reaching over 250,000 households a show. At the same time, he was photographed in an alley near his Hollywood apartment, wearing boxer shorts, his pants down around his ankles, holding a laptop. He was quoted as saying things like "Those Supreme Journalism types seem to think the news has to be terribly boring. I don't." And declaring, "I got the president of the United States saying on videotape in front of the grand jury that I gave him anxiety. Me! Five times!"

One of the frequent guests on his new TV show was Lucianne Goldberg, who sat there smoking, cackling, and sipping vodka. She called herself a "facilitator" in the investigation now. "I wanted to keep the Beast alive," she said. She was critical of the fact that the Ratwoman had taken her tapes to Kenneth W. Starr. " 'Here's the deal,' I said to her. I had offers of sixty million dollars—up!—for those tapes. I could have sold them. But Linda would have gone to jail for about three months for illegal taping and contempt. 'Okay,' I told her. 'Sixty million for three months! Do it!' It wouldn't be so bad. With that kind of money, she could buy off any lesbian who made an advance, could order in food from the best restaurant in town. What's the problem? But she didn't have the strength for it." Goldberg said she'd been spat on in the street on Manhattan's Upper West Side, cursed, and manhandled. "Actually," she said, "both times I was pushed by gay guys and I flipped them over and left them on the floor." She cackled when she said it. She thought it was funny.

As Lucianne Goldberg cackled away, planning her own radio talk show, Michael Isikoff wrote a book and described how he felt. "As a general rule, we don't give our sources moral litmus tests—nor should we. Sometimes the best stuff comes from the most unpleasant people."

The Scavenger enjoyed the increased exposure that his new TV show was giving him. His boss was Roger Ailes, the head of Fox News, who had once masterminded Richard Nixon's campaigns. And when a camera crew tried to shoot into his apartment from across the street, Matt Drudge put on . . . a Nixon mask.

(15)

Hillary Loves Eleanor

Why couldn't her asshole husband pay more attention to her *that* way—more than twice a year?

Even the Trumans, Ma and Pa Kettle in the White House, had broken the slats of their White House bed. Even JFK, busy with so many other women, including his nympho secretaries, Fiddle and Faddle, had visited Jackie every afternoon in her boudoir while the kids were napping. Jackie had even had leopard-skin rugs in her bedroom, like Gennifer's zebra-skin bedspread, but Hillary knew that wasn't *her* style. Her style was to eat fried chicken in the backseat of the limo with Bill when he was governor and to leave the chewed bones on the limo floor.

All she could do was yell at him when she heard about somebody new. "Come back here, you asshole!" she yelled, so loudly the Secret Service heard her. "Where the fuck do you think you're going?"

Hillary knew his behavior was not uncommon for a president in the White House. She knew there was no intimate relationship between Franklin and Eleanor or Nixon and Pat or LBJ and Lady Bird. . . . She knew Nixon once walked a nine-hole golf course with Pale Pat and his daughters without saying one word to them, knew that LBJ would lock himself into his stateroom on *Air Force One* with a nearly illiterate secretary while Lady Bird sat outside. But that didn't make Hillary feel any better. She got so angry at her asshole husband, she threw a briefing book at him—not a lamp, as the press reported it—a briefing book, the policy wonk's weapon. Her old friend Brooke Shearer, who'd been a private eye before joining her staff, filled her in on what Hillary occasionally didn't know.

And Hillary knew most everything. She knew her husband had his own White House staffers for his own intimate use, in addition to celebrity guests like Markie Post, photographed bouncing up and down on Lincoln's bed; Eleanor Mondale, *such* a good and loyal Democrat; or Barbra, with her libidinous social conscience, so committed, with her hundreds of millions, to talking to Bill about improving the lives of the poor.

Hillary was the First Lady of the United States, but she didn't see herself that way. Hillary ran her husband's life for him is what she did . . . what she had *always* done . . . and if he happened to be the president of the United States and if she told *him* what to do, that meant Hillary was . . . "Vote for one, you get two," he had said in New Hampshire, but Hillary wondered sometimes where he got "two" from. He knew how to smile—she'd give him that. He was sensational at a fund-raiser.

She hated it, trapped here in this place Truman had called a "jail" and FDR had said was "a goldfish bowl made out of magnifying glass." Eleanor Roosevelt had called the White House "a splendid prison" and her own asshole husband had said it was "the crown jewel of the federal prison system." The only time she really had fun, Hillary sometimes thought, was on Saturday, when she stayed in bed until noon with Earth, Wind, and Fire blasting.

She felt her privacy violated on the most intimate level: One of the maids told her that while she and her husband were out of town, butlers and staff aides sneaked their girlfriends into the family quarters and had sex on the floor and in their beds, then went downstairs to the mess to swill champagne and gobble caviar.

She understood now what Eleanor Roosevelt had meant when she said that the Secret Service had looked at her as if she "was about to hatch anarchists." They hated her, Hillary felt, because she was an intelligent and independent woman, unlike any First Lady they had ever seen.

What did the staff *expect* her to do? Introduce them to heads of state like Bess Truman had? Bring them back jade from China like Pale Pat had? She wasn't like them, wasn't like other First Ladies . . . not like Ida McKinley, whose husband would put a handkerchief over her face at state dinners because she'd nodded off and was snoring loudly; nor Nancy Reagan, shopping Rodeo Drive and staying in the Steve McQueen suite at the Beverly Wilshire; nor Margaret Taylor, wife of Zachary, who rarely left the second floor and smoked a pipe; nor Barbara Bush, cooking her own spaghetti and serving it on paper plates.

Some staff members, Hillary knew, compared her to Nancy, who once told an usher, "Don't you ever point your finger at my dog!" after the dog had bitten him. But they were wrong, as were those sarcastic guttersnipes who pointed out that Martha Washington had liked to be called "the Presidentess" or "Lady President." Hillary wasn't like Jackie Kennedy, either, although she had the greatest respect for her and although their husbands had some obvious things in common. All Jackie had done was to redecorate the White House—a wifely, *wifey* function—but Hillary did agree with Jackie's feeling that "the only thing I do not want to be called is First Lady. It sounds like a saddle horse."

The First Lady whose example Hillary loathed, whom she ridiculed when she was with her friends, was Mamie Eisenhower, who did nothing much except lie around in bed smoking and playing the organ in duet with her mother, who played the harmonica. Mamie dressed in pink and decorated as much of the White House as she could in pink—pink headboards and pink curtains and a king-size pink bedspread and upholstered pink chairs. She spent much of the day smoking and watching *As The World Turns* and other soaps as she sat on a pink couch. She bragged that the only exercise she needed was her daily massage, and she always wore a jingly gold charm bracelet with "Ike charms" on it—a tank, five stars, a map of Africa, and a helmet.

Hillary's role model was Eleanor Roosevelt, a First Lady of many firsts—first to drive her own car, first to board a plane, first to make official trips by herself, first to hold press conferences. Eleanor had been shy as a child, "always afraid of something . . . an ugly duckling," whose mother told her, "You have no looks, so see to it that you have manners." As an adult, Eleanor was tall, gawky, and athletic. Martha Gellhorn, a strong, independent woman herself, who had the brains to dump Ernest Hemingway, said, "Eleanor gave off light. I cannot describe it better."

Eleanor Roosevelt was an inspiration for Hillary Rodham Clinton, who thought that they had many things in common. Like Hillary, Eleanor was militantly outspoken in her efforts to better the lot of the poor, the disadvantaged, and the black. Like Hillary, Eleanor did not shy from controversy. When the army wanted to paint the White House black during the war, it was Eleanor who stopped it. When Winston Churchill paraded around naked in the White House residence, it was Eleanor who told him to put something on.

Like Hillary, Eleanor was a campaign trooper—as Will Rogers described her, "out at every stop, standing for photographers by the hour, being interviewed, talking over the radio, no sleep. And yet they say she shows no sign of weakness or annoyance of any kind." Like Hillary, Eleanor wrote a newspaper column. Like Hillary, Eleanor had a close black educator friend, Mary McLeod Bethune. Like Hillary, Eleanor disliked the Secret Service and sometimes refused its protection. Like Hillary, Eleanor drove off by herself sometimes without the Secret Service knowing.

Maybe most importantly, like Hillary, Eleanor was in a marriage that was not the usual marriage. "We never saw Eleanor and Franklin Roosevelt in the same room alone together," wrote White House chief usher J. B. West in *Upstairs at the White House*. "They had the most separate relationship I've ever seen between man and wife and the most equal." Like Hillary, Eleanor was married to a charismatic, charming man who cheated on her. Like Hillary's husband, Eleanor's husband saw his mistresses when she was out of town. Like Hillary, Eleanor had her own Vince Foster, Joe Lash, a future historian, who lived in a room near her at the White House. Like Hillary, Eleanor had close friendships with other women . . . like the fan dancer, Mayris Chaney, her frequent White House visitor . . . and Lorena Hickok, her mannish former-reporter lover.

Hillary understood Eleanor's loneliness and pain. Franklin was off with Lucy Mercer, formerly *Eleanor's* social secretary, and with his own secretary, Missy LeHand, and Eleanor, before she found her beloved Hick, threw herself into her public activities and into raising her kids. Hillary envied the joy Eleanor must have felt when she finally found Hick, driving through the New England countryside with Hick, giving her lacy underwear, writing Hick love letters: "I love you deeply and tenderly. My arms feel very empty. I love you beyond words and long for you . . . it was a lovely weekend, I shall have to think about it for a long, long time. Each time we have together *that* way—brings us closer, doesn't it?" Hick was pensive, explosive, a big, skittish cat—"I wonder what is happening with you tonight. I feel restless, unable to settle down to anything." Eleanor to Hick: "Oh how I wanted to put my arms around you in reality instead of in spirit. I went and kissed your photograph instead and there were tears in my eyes. . . . Darling, I feel very happy because every day brings you nearer." Hick wrote to Eleanor: "I've been trying today to bring back your face—to remember just *how* you look. Funny how even the dearest face will fade away in time. Most clearly I remember your eyes, with a kind of teasing smile in them, and the feeling of that soft spot northeast of the corner of your mouth against my lips. . . . I want to put my arms around you and kiss you at the corner of your mouth. And in a little more than a week now, I shall."

Even as Hillary contemplated the sadness of what happened at the end to Franklin and Eleanor—he died with Lucy Mercer at his bedside, summoned there by Eleanor's daughter, Anna—Hillary Rodham Clinton knew how much she had grown to love Eleanor Roosevelt—her voice shrill and falsetto, her hair back in a bun . . . Eleanor in jodhpurs and boots and with a riding crop . . . Eleanor moist, sweaty, smelling of horse.

Some people thought Hillary's love for Eleanor was tied to her love of Chelsea—gawky and tall like Eleanor, a child cruel classmates teased about her looks. Hillary was proud of Chelsea. She knew she had been away from her maybe too much—"Mommy went to give a peach," the little girl told friends—helping Chelsea with her homework by fax, maybe not the best way to do it. And she knew that her husband wasn't all that focused sometimes on Chelsea when she wasn't there. She'd heard Gennifer's story of Bill interrupting phone sex because Chelsea had fallen out of her bed.

Hillary was proud of Chelsea. She wasn't a brat like Amy Carter, breaking crackers on *Air Force One* so she could watch the help pick the pieces up. She wasn't smoking dope with the marines at Camp David like Chip Carter had. No Secret Service agent had accused her, as they'd accused Michael Reagan, of shoplifting. Chelsea wasn't catting around Georgetown bars with a fake ID or sneaking around the parking lot with Secret Service agents like Susan Ford had.

When they got to the White House, Hillary knew what the deal would be. Her husband had gotten them there with all of his glitzy, glib, seductive, telegenic talents. Now it was time to buckle down to the serious business of governing. *Vote for one, get two!* It was going to be no different from the way it had been in Arkansas. As John Robert Starr, the editor of the *Arkansas Gazette* put it, "The indications are that she was Bill Clinton's number one advisor throughout the time he was governor. He kept saying, 'Well, Hillary thinks . . .' "

Her husband's first order of business was to change the White House phone system so he wouldn't have to go through the operator to make a personal (top secret) phone call. Hillary's first order of business was to provide Americans with a decent health plan. Hillary told a reporter, "I suppose I could have stayed home, baked cookies and had teas, but what I decided was to fulfill my profession, which I entered before my husband was in public life."

All White House employees had to be approved by Hillary. She wanted all incoming and outgoing mail from the office of his chief of staff routed through *her* office. *She* oversaw his schedule. *She* hand-picked Zoe Baird, Kimba Wood, and finally Janet Reno—whose specialty was child abuse—as attorney general. *She* hired Donna Shalala as secretary of Health and Human Services. *She* hired her former Watergate boss, Bernie Nussbaum, as White House counsel. *She* hired her Rose Law Firm senior partner, Vince Foster, as deputy White House counsel. *She* made her personal aide in Little Rock, Carol Rasco, chief domestic policy adviser. *She* made Maggie Williams, her chief of staff, also a special assistant to the president—a post that would ensure that Williams (and Rasco) would attend all high-level meetings and see key memos.

She attended White House staff meetings and acted as the summarizer of all positions. *She* said her Health Care Task Force would cost $100,000—and it wound up costing $13.4 million. *She* had an affirmative-action agenda that guaranteed the hiring of as many minority and lesbian women and minority and gay men as possible. *She* made sure that *her* portrait and not Al Gore's went up all over the White House.

Those who'd worked with her in Arkansas or on the campaign trail weren't surprised by how the First Lady took charge. *She* had always handled the family finances. *She* had turned to George Stephanopoulos during a bimbo eruption and said, "We've got to destroy her." Her husband, meanwhile, had gotten the phone system redesigned and was busily dialing away without any operator possibly overhearing any phone sex. (It was the biggest White House telephone crisis since Caroline Kennedy had wanted to call Santa Claus directly.)

In the year of Bill Clinton's impeachment crisis, many Americans— especially women—had come to the conclusion that Hillary was ventriloquist Edgar Bergen and her asshole husband the smiling wooden dummy Charlie McCarthy . . . the same wooden dummy who had changed Jean Houston's life.

Some men, in their impotent frustration, set up a Web site showing pictures of the occasional cuts and bruises on Bill Clinton's handsome face. Her asshole husband, these men claimed, was Hillary's battered wife.

[16]

The Sorceress from Hell

"Just because you wear a red sweater does not mean you have to wear red lipstick," Linda Tripp said.

"I understand that," Monica said. "I would never wear red lipstick to see him."

She had made a cynical deal with a sexually troubled man, those who loathed her said. She knew what their marriage would be like but married him anyway. What she was really interested in was power, not sex. She was smart, articulate, and politically involved, a star already in college, a fierce debater, an intellectual. She had depth and lofty spiritual inclinations, even suffering the media's arrows when it was revealed she was devoted to a New Age guru. She was tough and resilient, and knew how to play political hardball. She knew how to play personal hardball, too. When the decision was finally made between them to divorce . . . she told those close to her husband . . . that he was . . . gay.

As I watched Arianna Huffington trash Bill Clinton during his impeachment crisis, I was certain she was the unwanted result of a thirty-second coupling between Joe McCarthy and Zsa Zsa Gabor. She was everywhere, in print and on the air, dagger in hand, carving him up with her nasal Mediterranean accent, looking elegant in her Carolina Herrera suits and fiery auburn hair. She was "dizzy and nauseated," she said, by Bill Clinton's actions. "His DNA has been spilled in more places than Starbucks coffee. . . . Leave office he must—prolonging the nation's nightmare is the worst possible thing for the nation. . . . Clinton first vulgarized political leadership and then made the vulgarization respectable. . . . He emptied

American politics of all principle and, with the help of his wife and his minions, refined the art of scapegoating. . . . Like a drowning man grabbing on to his rescuer, the president is willing to take the nation down with him. We must not let him. . . . There is nothing wrong with this poor soul [Clinton] that cannot be cured by standing him upside down and shaking him gently until whatever is inside his head—all the bloodless, calculating, truth-twisting equivocations that have worked for him in the past—fall out."

She set up a Web site called Resignation.com and said, "Take responsibility, Mr. President, for what you have done to your party, your office, and your country." Arianna made jokes, too: "If Hillary is indicted, can Al Gore become First Lady?" and "Taft kept cows on the White House lawn. Clinton considered having cows there, but Hillary vetoed it. She was afraid Bill would eat them." Arianna drew up a Christmas gift list for the first family: for Bill, AstroTurf for "the Rumpus Room" at the Clinton library; for Hillary, a Deana Carter CD—"Did I Shave My Legs for This?"; for Chelsea, "Her freshman face book from her father, who has had it since Parents Weekend at Stanford."

Arianna Huffington? I pondered. *Arianna Huffington* was saying these morally outraged, judgmental things? The same Arianna Huffington who'd hired private eyes to research Maureen Orth, about to do a magazine profile of her? The *same* Arianna Huffington who'd offered to find campaign manager Ed Rollins "companionship" if things weren't right between him and his wife?

This was the same Arianna Huffington who, through the years, had been called "craven and beyond contempt"; "a dangerous Greek Rasputin determined to ride her husband's wealth to political glory at any cost"; "one of the most unprincipled political creatures I've ever encountered"; "a spectacularly dedicated and shameless social climber"; "scheming, indefatigably ruthless"; the most upwardly mobile Greek since Icarus"; "the Sir Edmund Hillary of social climbers." Ed Rollins, the warhorse Republican campaign manager said, "She was the most ruthless, unscrupulous, and ambitious person I'd met in thirty years in national politics—not to mention that she sometimes seemed truly pathological. Her allure and style were only a veneer: The soul of a wily sorceress lurked beneath."

The Sorceress was born Arianna Stassinopoulos in 1950 in Athens, Greece, the daughter of the publisher of a financial newspaper. She was born into the Greek Orthodox faith and was praying to the Virgin Mary at the age of three. Her parents divorced. At sixteen, she went to Shantaniketah University outside Calcutta to study comparative religion. At seventeen, she moved with her mother to England to prepare for English university exams. They had little money. She got into Cambridge and distinguished herself quickly. She became president of the Cambridge Union, the university's debating society. She was the first foreigner and the third woman to head the university's internationally known debating team. She was brilliant and beautiful — her build was statuesque and her hair fiery red. In her farewell debate, she attacked late seventies feminism for ignoring "a woman's special needs for children and family." The debate was televised and, with her own quick wit and sexy looks, Arianna became a celebrity in England. George Weidenfeld, her new publisher, gave her some advice: "Don't bother with the men. You'll only make the wives jealous. Concentrate on the key women, and if you play your cards right, you'll be a success." Her new friend Werner Erhard, the founder of est, also gave her advice: "If you say it, you *are* it."

Arianna wrote her first book, *The Female Woman*, an answer to Germaine Greer's *The Female Eunuch*, and went out on her first book tour. "Everything went wrong one day. I was on my own. I got to the hotel and there was a line of two hundred GIs checking in, so I had to wait. Then I got into my room, and it was the tiniest little room, a postage stamp that smelled of cigarette smoke, and there I was. I had nothing to do that night, and I had to leave at five in the morning to go on an early morning talk show." The Sorceress didn't like being alone. The Sorceress didn't like waiting in line to check in. The Sorceress didn't like tiny rooms or cigarette smoke. She didn't like having nothing to do at night or having to get up at five in the morning. The Sorceress was "depressed and in despair," so she went back to England and went on a water fast. "I wanted to touch the spirit, to be filled by it, that anything that was not spirit or about spirit was an encumbrance." When she finally stopped fasting, "I could tell the difference between sips full of the various brands of bottled water I had in my flat," she said.

Taking Weidenfeld's advice, she sought out the company of socially prominent English women and became known for sending flowers after a first meeting. She began a relationship with an elderly columnist for the London *Times*. They went to the opera a lot. She did a BBC television talk show, *Saturday Night at the Mill*, which quickly failed. She explained the failure by saying, "Britain is too conscious of accents." She was, meanwhile, working on another book — this one about Greek opera diva Maria Callas.

When she went to New York to promote her Callas book, the Sorceress "felt right at home." The book made a little money—Ari Onassis, she wrote, considered Jackie "cold-hearted and shallow" and was about to divorce her before he died—but she was sued for plagiarism and her publisher had to pay a five-figure amount to settle it. She met and befriended society figures like Barbara Walters and Lucky Roosevelt, President Reagan's chief of protocol. Through Weidenfeld, she met San Francisco social queen Ann Getty. She dated real estate tycoon Mort Zuckerman. She was the Sorceress— charming, smart, witty, beautiful, and sexy. "She's a great, great flatterer and we've all been seduced by it," Bob Colocello would write in *Vanity Fair*. He also said she was "relentless . . . with the discipline of a religious zealot." She met Kathleen Brown, the California governor's sister, and did a brief lecture tour with her. She did a piece on Jerry Brown for *People* magazine and then started dating him. The Sorceress who didn't have any money was a socialite. "They gave me the sobriquet of socialite and I earned it," she would say later.

Arianna was also a minister by then in MSIA, known on the West Coast, where it was centered, as "the Cadillac of cults." She had met John-Roger, its Christ figure, in 1973 in London. John-Roger, who had once been a night orderly at a psychiatric hospital in Salt Lake City, was inhabited by a spirit named John the Beloved while in a coma after surgery for a kidney stone in 1963. John-Roger said that John the Beloved told him that John-Roger was "the Mystical Traveler Consciousness," which inhabited the earth once every 25,000 years. The Sorceress liked John-Roger and believed in the Mystical Traveler Consciousness. "He dealt in the only thing that I was really interested in," she wrote in *Interview*. "Helping people wake up to the spirit inside themselves, to their natural knowing and inner wisdom. I bought his books, I subscribed to his monthly discourses, I went to meditation retreats." She also tried to help John-Roger find new disciples among her celebrity friends. "I had him thrust upon me by her," columnist Liz Smith said. "He really sort of gave me the creeps. He wanted to lay hands on me because I had a headache and it was very dismaying and embarrassing to me. And I also thought he was a fake."

Partly to be closer to John-Roger and partly to be closer to Ann Getty, the Sorceress moved to Beverly Hills in 1984. She was planning another book by then, too, on Pablo Picasso, and Picasso's longtime mistress, Françoise Gilot, now the wife of Jonas Salk, who lived part-time in Southern California. Her friend Ann Getty, meanwhile, wanted to find a husband for her.

She even drew up a list of possibilities. In Tokyo one day at a meeting of the Aspen Institute, a nonpartisan think tank, Ann Getty met a man who said to her, "You're so wonderful, do you have any daughters?" And Ann said to him, "I don't have any daughters, but I have a great friend."

Ann called the Sorceress from Tokyo and told her she'd found the perfect husband for her. His name was Michael Huffington. He was the son of one of the wealthiest men in America. The Sorceress smiled.

Big Roy Huffington was Michael's dad, oilman, wildcatter, hard-drinking, hard-living, larger than life, as Texas as they come, big, macho, cussing up a storm: John Wayne magnified! And Michael was his only son, his one eye so bad, he had to wear a patch over it when he was a kid, scrawny, packing none of the beef that Big Roy had in excess. When Michael was seven years old and Big Roy caught him playing with matches, he took Michael out into the backyard and made him light matches until he'd burned both of his hands. Big Roy did it to him with cigarettes and alcohol, too. You want to smoke a cigarette, kid? Here you go, partner. . . . Until Michael was green . . . until Michael threw up from all the booze. By the time he was fourteen, all he did much of the time was watch TV with his mother, Phyllis, once a beauty queen, now stoking herself constantly with nicotine. Phyllis was such a die-hard Republican, she'd rant and rave at the set if any of those goddamn Commie-loving liberal turkeys said something biased, East Coast, and critical.

Big Roy sent Michael to the Culver Military Academy in Indiana that year, and he was pleased about how Michael did: near the top of his class, a marksman, letters in crew and swimming. The other cadets hated him. He was in charge of busting them for reading *Playboy* and for being late to their barracks. "I even turned in my roommate for being five minutes late to our room. Two days later, he moved out on me. But the point is, I was abiding by the rules."

After graduation, Michael went to Stanford. He joined the Young Americans for Freedom and stood defending the administration building against antiwar protesters. Big Roy was proud of him. He was drafted but rejected — he was legally blind — in the summer of 1968. As most of Michael's generation was smoking dope and getting high, Big Roy got him a job as a gofer in George Bush's congressional office. Michael had his own apartment and decked it out with NIXON'S THE ONE posters. He wore a Spiro Agnew watch; its face showed Agnew flashing the peace sign with each hand. One day, as he was walking with George Bush, the congressman casually put his arm around this nice clean-cut kid . . . and Bush's casual, meaningless gesture moved Michael Huffington like he'd never been moved before. His parents had rarely hugged him.

He went to grad school at Harvard Business. He'd had sex with a woman at Stanford, and in his senior year, he became friends with a guy who told him he was gay. A year later, in the banking business in Chicago, Michael Huffington had sex with a man for the first time. He went back home to Houston and founded an investment bank, and his mother asked him to join the family oil business, Huffco. Michael couldn't say no to his mother, though he saw her only once a month, at a formally scheduled dinner.

He became a vice president of Huffco. A competing oilman said, "He was the typical rich kid who was playing with his father's money. Almost everything he put his hands on failed. He had a refinery and a drilling company that failed. The banks ended up holding the bag. He made a lot of promises to the banks and ruined his reputation." Michael irritated many employees by banning coffee, which he felt to be unhealthy, from the office. A commercial banker said, "There are a lot of guys who had run-ins with him during negotiations. Some people have the smooth touch and others the bludgeon. He had the bludgeon."

He converted from Presbyterianism and became an Episcopalian. A friend said Michael talked to him for hours about the existence of God. When his friend wanted to play golf, Michael insisted they keep talking about God. At the same time, he was taking clients to lunch at a topless bar, where they'd paint the women with their fingers. He was also having sex with men, mostly one-night stands, but he had one serious relationship with a man, whose photograph he kept hidden in his apartment. He prayed to God that he not be attracted to men. When he saw a gay man on TV who claimed that he had given up homosexual sex, Michael started to sob. He promised God that he'd never have sex with a man again.

He was sitting in Ann Getty's magnificent mansion one night, when Arianna Stassinopoulos walked into the parlor. They were introduced and Michael Huffington asked her what the most important thing in her life was. The Sorceress said, "God."

He went to New Year's dinner at Arianna's house in Beverly Hills. Shirley MacLaine and Arianna's mother were there with a group of others. The Sorceress passed a crystal magic wand around the table. Everyone had to make a wish. The Sorceress said she wished to be pregnant within the year. Michael Huffington wished that her wish come true. When they were alone, he told her that he had had sex with men. The Sorceress said it made her love him even more.

They were married in New York. "We'd almost given up on you, Michael!" Big Roy toasted. Her bridesmaids were Barbara Walters and Lucky Roosevelt. Everything was paid for by Ann Getty, including Arianna's eighteen-thousand-dollar wedding gown. Among those at the wedding were Henry Kissinger, Norman Mailer, Helen Gurley Brown, and Shirley MacLaine. Kissinger said the wedding "had everything except an Aztec sacrificial fire dance." She spent her wedding night not with her husband but with John-Roger, giving a moving speech at an MSIA fund-raiser. In an interview shortly after the wedding, Arianna said, "I always knew I would be taken care of. I always felt I wouldn't have to worry about money."

They honeymooned in the Caribbean and in Europe. Michael was hurt that even during the honeymoon, Arianna was working on her Picasso book. They moved to Washington, where, through Big Roy's influence, George Bush had appointed Michael as his deputy assistant secretary of defense for negotiations policy. His immediate supervisor at the Pentagon, Frank J. Gaffney, would say, "It was a favor from George Bush to the Huffingtons, but it was no favor to the rest of us. The organization continued to toil away under him and in some cases in spite of him. It didn't matter who he was or what he was doing as long as he wasn't doing any damage. His schedule would typically have a lunch on it—and that would sort of be it." Michael lasted a year at the Pentagon. Arianna worked on her Picasso book. Michael went to the movies a lot alone.

Their son was stillborn and Michael went to an Episcopal monastery for three days with a close male friend. When he got home, he told Arianna he wanted them to move to California. He bought a $4.3 million house in Santa Barbara, but he only saw her there on rare weekends. He was back working for Big Roy at Huffco. Arianna got pregnant again after they saw *Wings of Desire* together. She gave birth to a daughter, Christina. "We put her in a crib next to my bed," Arianna would later write. "A few moments later, after everyone had left the room, I began trembling convulsively . . . and then my body was no longer shaking. I had left it. I was looking down at myself, at Christina, at the tuberoses on the night stand, at the entire room. I had no fear at all. . . . I knew I would return, and I was being washed in a sense of enormous well-being and strength. It was as if the curtain of heaven had been pulled back to give me a glimpse of wholeness: Birth, life, and death—and seeing them all at once, I could accept them all."

She published her Picasso book. She was accused of plagiarism again; *Time* magazine called the book "mere fluff . . . best suited for talk show hosts and gossip columnists." Picasso's daughter Paloma said, "She uses cheap psychology. At a party she looks you right in the eye and asks you questions about your personal life, then tells you it's so interesting you should write a book. Next day she'll send a little present, so you don't forget her."

In 1990, Big Roy Huffington sold his company for $500 million. Michael's share came to $80 million. In 1991, Arianna gave birth to another daughter, Isabella. She had gotten pregnant after they saw *Jesus of Montreal* together. In Santa Barbara, they started getting involved in California politics. They hosted parties for Pete Wilson and for Bill Bennett. Six months after coming to California, Michael announced he was running for Congress. He was a terrible speaker. He shook and sweated. But he spent $5.6 million of his own money and beat an eighteen-year incumbent.

They bought another home for $4 million in Washington. On the wall of his congressional office, Michael kept a picture of Jimmy Stewart. He told reporters that he cried when he saw *Mr. Smith Goes to Washington*. "There's a lot in me similar to what the movie represented," he said. But he hated being a congressman. "There is nothing to do but deal with constituents," he said. Representative Barney Frank said of his performance as a congressman, "Even when he's around, he isn't." Michael really wasn't around much of the time. Scheduled to be at an embassy party or at a banquet, he'd sneak off alone to see a movie. He began to hug his male staffers so often that one of them quit. He talked about Washington as a "black hole."

But the Sorceress prospered. She spent $130,000 of his money to buy a talk show for herself on a conservative television network. She organized celebrity "Critical Mass" dinners. Each dinner had a theme that each guest had to address. "Critical Mass" meant, according to Arianna, "a critical mass of spiritually-inclined citizens who would succeed where the government failed, volunteering time and money en masse to care for the tired and the poor."

Very rich but sick and tired of being a congressman, Michael went to Greece for a vacation with Arianna and the girls. She was at work on a new book and he climbed a mountain to get to a Greek Orthodox monastery on Mount Athos. He stayed there for three days. He spent the time "praying and just looking over the sea and enjoying the monks." When he came back off the mountain, he told Arianna he was going to run for the Senate, even though he was only halfway through his congressional term. "I think that's when he had a great sense about the crisis we are facing as a nation," Arianna said. "We could say—wait!—but these are not normal times."

"I should have decked her," Michael Huffington's campaign manager in his Senate race against Diane Feinstein would say later. "And if she were a man, maybe I would have." The Sorceress's motto, she told Ed Rollins, whom *she* hired, was "Strike first! Strike fast! Strike hard!" Her campaign would cost Michael Huffington $28 million, more than twice the amount previously spent on a Senate seat ($10 million by Senator Jay Rockefeller of West Virginia).

It became quickly obvious to political insiders (and to many outsiders) who the *real* candidate was. *She* debated Michael's primary opponent six times; Michael debated him not once. After two campaign appearances, Michael went to vacation in Hawaii for two weeks while *she* kept hitting the stump. "I'm running against a missing person," his primary opponent said. "His wife is the one with the ambition, who wants to buy the Senate seat on the way to the White House. Hillary wants to be in the White House for the purpose of making policy for the country. Arianna wants to be in the White House as a way of making a social life." When it was time for a photo op at a forest fire, Arianna flew in with bottles of Evian water. Barney Klueger, a prominent Santa Barbara Republican, said, "It's his wife who's running, not him. You can call his office with any request, it has to be filtered through his wife." A columnist for the *San Francisco Examiner* wrote, "Never mind Michael Huffington debating Diane Feinstein on Larry King—I'm waiting for Arianna versus Diane. Eliminate the front man." A friend of the Huffingtons said, "I think of that thing inside John Hurt in *Alien*. But with better hair. In Michael, she's found a host." Rollins, the campaign manager, concluded, "The campaign I'd been hired to run was the obsession of his upwardly-mobile wife, not his. . . . When she wasn't seducing me, she was bossing him around. He sat there for the most part like a bump on a log."

The media tagged Michael "Perot West" when they got wind of how much of his own money he was spending for the campaign, although Rollins said, "Compared to Arianna and Michael, Perot is St. Francis of Assisi." Rollins concluded that Michael "couldn't relate to average people or their problems. He is awkward, shy, also painfully poor at small talk and public speaking. He is as much of an oddity among the moneyed set as in the political water." Pete Wilson's press secretary said, "There was a suspicion that Michael was not able to give a speech while Arianna was drinking a glass of water." Another campaign observer said, "You look into his eyes and you see the back of her head." A headline read, HER BRAINS, HIS MONEY. Michael was described as "a complete cipher who gives empty suits a bad name. . . . A tabula rasa, a man who stands for nothing. . . . A virtual candidate." Rollins would write that he soon realized "this poor bastard wants to be a senator about as bad as I want to be the Pope. I thought to myself—he hates all of this, he hates fund raising, he hates giving speeches, he hates campaigns, he hates meeting constituents, and if he gets elected, he's going to hate being a senator."

When Michael wouldn't release his tax records or his personal financial worth, the media attacked him. Rollins told him he had to release the information. "I can't do that," Huffington told him. Rollins pressed him, but Michael was adamant. "If Arianna knows how much money I have, she'll spend all of it," Huffington said. The records were never released.

There were constant rumors that Michael was gay, journalistic descriptions like "secretive, strange, elusive, troubled." Ed Rollins got a case of condoms from a friend with a note that said, "Remember when you're around Mike, protect your ass at all times." When Rollins asked him if he was gay, Michael didn't deny it. "I'm not going to answer questions like that from you or anybody else," he said. His response to Vanity Fair was, "I'm sorry, I have no comment." But Arianna denied it vehemently, saying, "That's like saying that Michael is Chinese." When asked by the Los Angeles Times about the congressional staff members he'd hugged, Michael said, "I'm a hugger, so is Bill Clinton." To himself, he raged at Arianna and John-Roger. He was certain Arianna had told John-Roger that he had slept with men, and he considered John-Roger, as David Brock would later write in Esquire, "a spooky man who had a hold on his wife."

It was John-Roger who gave the campaign its first serious bump. The media not only uncovered Arianna's special closeness to the MSIA messiah but also found male ex-members who said John-Roger had used "spiritual threats and promises" to elicit sexual favors from them. Other ex-members said that those who complied with J-R's sexual advances were promoted to positions of authority and praised for their spiritual qualities. Two former members claimed they had been subjected to hate mail, vandalism, and death threats. The Sorceress said she didn't believe any of it and called John-Roger "an old good friend," downplaying her ministry in MSIA.

Yet, amazingly, even with John-Roger exposed as a badly tarnished messiah, Arianna's determination and Michael's $28 million almost pulled it off, thanks largely to a barrage of negative television ads designed by the man who'd created George Bush's racist Willie Horton commercials. The fact that Arianna and Michael lost the election finally by two points was due, ironically, to Arianna's own actions. Arianna had hired a nanny in the late eighties, over Michael's objections, who was an illegal alien. When the *Los Angeles Times* broke the story, Michael immediately dropped six points in the polls.

According to Ed Rollins, "Arianna was hysterical. She began babbling about the need for a counterattack." When Rollins discovered what she meant by counterattack, he almost quit the campaign. She assembled a team of a dozen private eyes to find any illegal immigrant who'd ever worked for Feinstein. Rollins knew by then that she had also hired private eyes to investigate Orth, the *Vanity Fair* writer, and Peter McWilliams, an ex–MSIA member who was writing a tell-all book. "Arianna was utterly out of control," Rollins would later write, "incapable of listening to me or anyone."

The Sorceress lost her Senate seat. Michael Huffington told David Brock years later that he was hoping that he would lose.

Back in Washington, Arianna asked Michael to double her monthly allowance for two years so that she could launch a career as a political commentator. He agreed. She began appearing in print, in radio, and on television. She became a director of the Progress and Freedom Foundation, a conservative think tank closely tied to Newt Gingrich. She appeared at fund-raisers with Gingrich and urged him in articles to run for the presidency. "Arianna wants to be famous," a California Republican said. "Her first plan was getting her husband elected. That didn't work. So now she's working the Gingrich crowd. She'll hitch her star to anyone that will help her to get attention." Newt Gingrich, meanwhile, kept a copy of Arianna's latest book—*The Fourth Instinct*—on a bookshelf in his office, next to his copy of Dr. Seuss's *If I Ran the Circus*.

The Sorceress was becoming known in Washington as a lavish hostess, "the Imelda Marcos wanna-be of the New Republican plutocracy." Michael was seen at these parties, which he was paying for, flicking the lights on and off when he wanted guests to leave. He was meeting gay men at these parties, too, and asking them out to private dinners. When his two-year arrangement with Arianna was up, he told her he wanted them to move back to California.

But the Sorceress wasn't going anywhere. She said she wanted a divorce. She called Michael's mother, his sister, and some of his friends and told them Michael was gay and that she was getting a divorce. Michael went back to California, became a movie producer, and had sex with gay men. He had a lot less money now, but Arianna was out of his life and Big Roy was dead.

As Arianna appeared on more and more talk shows, trashing Bill Clinton, she began working with the voice coach for *Forrest Gump*, trying to get rid of her accent. She was the Sorceress of all of Washington now, impressively wealthy, still throwing her lavish parties for her spellbound conservative followers. Her research assistant was Matt Drudge's best friend. She even threw one big bash where Drudge was the guest of honor. Drudge came walking in with Lucianne Goldberg and all the guests started to applaud. The Scavenger, the Bag Lady of Sleaze, and the Sorceress had a fiendishly good time!

[Act Three]

SUSPICIOUS MINDS

To taste the savage taste of blood—to be so devilish!
To gloat so over the wounds and deaths of the enemy . . .

To make the people rage, weep, hate, desire, with yourself,
To lead America—to quell America with a great tongue.

—WALT WHITMAN, *Leaves of Grass*

[1]

The President Is Black

"He must feel as though everybody potentially can turn,"
Linda Tripp said. "Do you know what I mean?"
"But that's his own fault."
"Why?"
"Because if you fuck people over," Monica said, "they're going
to turn around and fuck you."

While Republicans in Congress formed into a posse riding full gallop to a lynching, it was those who had the most experience with lynchings who became Bill Clinton's staunchest defenders: African-Americans. Republicans didn't much want to be seen messing with *them*. Racism in the nineties had become the media's hanging offense. And those black people who were putting their bodies on the line in defense of Bill Clinton knew a thing or two about damagingly playing the race card against their adversaries.

Feeling themselves all too vulnerable anyway to charges of racism, Republicans found themselves outfoxed, outshouted, and, in the mid-term November elections, which they insisted on turning into a referendum on Bill Clinton, outvoted. When it came to their moment of no return—calling the president's devoted black secretary, Betty Currie, the woman at the epicenter of all the parsings and contradictions, as a live witness—they chickened out, fearing that if they called her, they would publicly cast themselves in the racist role too many of them privately played so well. The irony was enormous: Had Betty Currie and, to a lesser extent, Vernon Jordan been white, Bill Clinton very possibly would have been convicted and removed from office.

Bill Clinton, as Toni Morrison put it so well, was "the first black presi-

dent of the United States"—one reason why the Republican posse hated
him so much. But black people knew in their bones what this posse was
about. The posse's spiritual ancestor was J. Edgar Hoover, the FBI icon who
liked to wear red dresses and feather boas, who had one teenage boy read to
him from the Bible while another diddled him wearing a rubber glove. The
rheumy-eyed old queen had tried to do to Martin Luther King, Jr., what the
posse was now forming to do to Bill Clinton.

Hoover, described as looking like "a remarkably ugly woman" when
dressed in a short, flounced black dress with lace stockings, high heels, a
curly black wig, pancake makeup, and false eyelashes, wasn't in good shape
at the end of his reign. He hated people with moist palms or pimples or people who were bald or had their ears sticking out. He hated germs and flies,
keeping on his staff a black servant whose duty was to swat them.

More than anything or anyone else, he hated Martin Luther King, Jr.,
especially after Dr. King won the Nobel Prize in 1964. Ferreting into Dr.
King's private life, the kiddy-porn lover assigned his agents to tape-record
Dr. King in flagrante delicto with a woman other than his wife. Hoover sent
the tapes in an unmarked box to Coretta King, with an anonymous note that
urged Dr. King to kill himself as "the honorable way out." Dr. King didn't
know, as he tried to keep his marriage together, that he was *still* being
taped—that Hoover was giggling every evening as he listened to Dr. King's
tortured discussions with his wife. But Dr. King didn't allow the tapes to stop
the crusade that would transform America. When he was assassinated several years later, an FBI agent in Atlanta shouted, "We finally got the son of a
bitch!"

As the posse formed for the lynching of Bill Clinton, African-Americans
made it clear they were not going to allow the political assassination of "the
first black president of the United States." "Let us not be confused," Jesse
Jackson's son, Jesse Jackson, Jr., said. "The Republicans are impeaching
Social Security, they are impeaching affirmative action, they are impeaching women's right to choose, they are impeaching Medicare, Medicaid,
Supreme Court justices who believe in equal protection under the law for
all Americans. Something deeper in history is happening than sex, lying
about sex, and perjury." Representative Maxine Waters, Democratic congresswoman from California, said, "This is indeed a Republican coup
d'état. The Republicans will couch this extremist radical anarchy in pious

language which distorts the Constitution and the rule of law. Bill and Hillary Clinton are the real targets, and the Republicans are the vehicles being used by the right-wing Christian Coalition extremists to direct and control our culture." John Conyers, Democrat from Michigan, chairman of the congressional Black Caucus, said, "Impeachment was designed to rid this nation of tyrants and traitors, not attempts to cover up extramarital affairs." Perhaps John Lewis, the venerable veteran of so many street-fought civil rights battles, put it most powerfully: "America is sick. Her heart is heavy. Her soul is aching. Who among us has not sinned?"

Black people heard the Republican rhetoric about raising the flag at Iwo Jima and the Founding Fathers and the incessant waving of the Constitution (which some Republicans kept in their pockets) and they knew damn well what they were hearing: It was the same old cracker bullshit. It had red-white-and-blue sparkles on top, but it still smelled to high heaven. More specifically, it was the same old *Republican* cracker bullshit . . . the party of Lincoln still mutated as the party of whippin', the party of lynchin'. Earl Butz was a Republican, wasn't he? He'd said, "All a black man needs is a new Cadillac, a tight pussy, and a warm place to shit." And James Watt was a Republican, too, Reagan's secretary of the interior. And he'd said, talking about a commission he'd appointed, "We have every kind of mix you can have. I have a black. I have a woman, two Jews, and a cripple." And George Bush was a Republican, scaring all the white folks with that ad about bad Willie Horton, who just happened to be black, raising the specter of black people out there robbin', rapin', maraudin'. George Bush didn't even bother to make a trip to L.A. after the Rodney King explosion. And Nixon or Reagan—how many black faces had anyone seen around them? Eartha Kitt? Sammy Davis, Jr., with his Nehru jacket, love beads, and mile-long cigar? And James "Go for the Green" Brown? And what about right now—which black faces were in there among the Republicans? J.C. "Couldn't Make It to the NFL" Watt? Or Clarence "Long Dong Silver" Thomas, who liked to go fishing with that sexual-harassing cracker from Texas, Dick Armey? The truth, black people sensed, was not subtly hidden in lifelong Republican Linda Tripp's words. The Ratwoman said she didn't want to get her hair done during the Million Man March because she "didn't want to see all those—all those *bodies.*" (Chris Rock made the same point in reverse at the Republican National Convention: "I feel like I'm at the Million White Boy March.")

Even among Democrats, black people had never felt like they had one of their *own*. Everybody knew LBJ was a cracker, him and his cowboy hats, talking about "nigger" this and "nigger" that among his cronies. . . . JFK believed it, he talked the talk, but did he walk off into the night with *black* women? Did he sit down and do some ribs with Jackie? . . . McGovern had as much soul as a Kiwanis Club president in a one-horse town. . . . Jimmah was okay, but he was a damned old fool when he was still a young man. . . . Dukakis or Du-who? or Du-whatever, aw, man, who *was* that chump? Somebody gonna do his woman and the chump says he gonna . . . *aw, man!*

But now Bill—President Bill Clinton—he was different. No wonder he'd been called "Niggerhead" and "Nigger Lips" his whole life. No broomstick up his white ass. None of this "I share your concern" crap, a stiff shake of the hand and I'll see you next election. Bill Clinton could get down. In all kinds of ways. With the sax. With the ribs. With his shades. With the bitches. *Down, man,* human. Real. It was in his eyes and the way he hugged you if you were black. He meant it. He walked the walk in all *kinds* of ways. And Hillary. Maybe *she* wasn't black like he was black, but at least she tried. For a white bitch from the lily white suburbs, she *really* tried. Didn't she always say the greatest moment of her life was meeting Martin Luther King, Jr.? When she was up there in her private fancy Yankee school, didn't she try to make sure the brothers weren't done over by the *po-lice?* Didn't she even work for a Black Panther lawyer one summer? Didn't she go into the *ghet-to* when she was a girl, even if it *was* like a class trip to the zoo? Not bad. Not bad at all for someone from Park Ridge, Illinois, the same place that white-haired cracker with the sore ass was from . . . Hyde, Mr. Henry . . . *that fool gonna put the flag up on Iwo Jima again?* . . . Mr. Henry Hyde.

Bill Clinton knew and liked black people as much as he liked his fellow whites; didn't see an ounce of difference between them. Not even at first at the integrated convenience store his Papaw used to run. Played with black people, hugged them, cussed them, fought them, dated them, seduced them, passed legislation for them, tried to help them . . . and black people recognized that, relative to all the other white politicians, there was something special about him. Hillary didn't have his *flow*, and there was talk about how Hillary had dissed the only black man in the Senate when she was in college, but even that didn't matter, because lots of people thought Edward Brooke was more white than black, and anyway, he was a Republican. But Bill Clinton had *flow, ease, soul,* and when he ran for president, black voters responded to him. He'd kept his promises, too, just as he had in

Arkansas, where he'd appointed an unprecedented number of black people to state boards and commissions. He appointed Ron Brown secretary of commerce, Mike Espy secretary of agriculture, Hazel O'Leary secretary of energy, Jesse Brown secretary of veterans' affairs, Clifton Wharton, Jr., deputy secretary of state, and Dr. Joycelyn Elders surgeon general. And he saved affirmative action and welfare from the planned cross-burning by Newt Gingrich and his "Contract with America" Republicans.

There was one other relatively hidden factor, too, which indicated the absolute lack of a smidgen of racism on Bill Clinton's part. Clearly a man who enjoyed intimate contact with women, he enjoyed intimate contact with *black* women, too. No wonder his name was William *Jefferson* Clinton. He may have been a sexual predator or he may have been a satyr, but he didn't discriminate. His willard was an equal opportunity predator, his satyriasis was integrated. The point was that he enjoyed contact with black flesh. No president since Thomas Jefferson had been known to enjoy that. JFK and LBJ had enjoyed contact with thousands of women and no one ever implied that even one of them was black. Bill Clinton, meanwhile, was being linked with a black Little Rock newswoman, with a black former Miss America, with former Commerce Secretary Ron Brown's daughter, with a black prostitute who claimed to have given birth to his child, linked even in Joe Klein's fictional *Primary Colors* to a black teenager whom he impregnates. The president of the United States was making love to black women in an America that had been suffering racial strife for forty years. Perhaps not the Great Emancipator, the Great Masturbator was also the Great Integrator. No wonder black people loved him and white racists hated him: Bill Clinton understood black people from the inside.

It drove the racists to their usual excess: Some claimed that the only reason Bill Clinton liked black women was because he was black himself. They pointed to the fullness of his lower lip, his mother's flirtatious nature, and his birth father's death while he was still in the womb. But if the racists thought they were damaging him by making their charges on the Internet and in faxed sheets, they were wrong. It only strengthened Bill Clinton's already-massive black support. Maybe he really *was* the first black president of the United States. Fine! Dig it! About damned time!

As the unyielding, adamantine nature of the president's black support became apparent, the same old polarization became apparent, too, the same deep electoral chasm we had seen during the Night Creature's reign between the Silent Majority and the rest of us. The Silent Majority then and now was made up of Christian Conservatives, Republicans, strict Constitutionalists, and nonrelative moralists screaming for Bill Clinton's lynching. They also included, as they always had, those people who simply didn't like "niggers."

But there was a difference this time, as the November elections showed. There were more of us than them. They were no longer a majority. Those of us who had grown up in the sixties respected and, in some cases, revered black people. The unyielding nature of their support for Bill Clinton influenced those soccer moms and Little League dads who were maybe wavering in their support of the president who had dropped his wet, half-chewed cigar on their dinner tables. We were struck by the *steel* in the black response to the charges. We were reminded in our preretirement years that the battle for equality among whites and blacks in the sixties was still being fought by some people. We saw that the police batons now were in the hands of Gingrich and DeLay and Armey and Hyde, et al. We realized that black people felt if Bill Clinton was removed from office, they'd be back where they were before . . . because he was *one of them.* Were we, the white generation that had fought alongside our black brothers for civil rights, now going to let people like John Lewis, a hero to us in the sixties, down?

We had aged since then, too, and there was another element to this black anger that we found deeply troublesome. There was an anger at play here that we recognized from the sixties, its last manifestation the reaction to the Rodney King verdict not too many years ago. We remembered all too well the urban riots and racial conflagrations in Watts and Detroit and Cleveland and Newark and so many other cities. We remembered our cities burning and occupied by National Guardsmen. We remembered the explosion of black rage following Martin Luther King, Jr.'s assassination as we remembered the more recent images of snipers on rooftops on Sunset Boulevard. But crime was down now.

Bill Clinton, thanks to his special relationship with black people, had accomplished the tentative beginnings of a racial peace in America. If things weren't exactly cool, they certainly weren't hot anymore, either. We didn't have to worry about driving down certain streets after certain hours. We could walk by a group of black people on a street corner without hearing trash. Bill Clinton, the first black president of the United States, had done that.

Were we going to risk our welcome and relative sense of peace by letting him be removed from office? Were we going to risk an explosion of black rage once again in our cities? Ross Perot may have been talking about caravans of trucks coming from everywhere, carrying petitions for Bill Clinton's resignation, but we were more concerned about National Guard half-tracks coming from everywhere to invade our cities again. If we thought there was going to be a riot in L.A. upon O. J. Simpson's conviction, what did we think was going to happen across America if Bill Clinton was removed from office?

It was Bill Clinton's race card and, Slick Willy poker player that he was, he played it brilliantly. He was photographed with black leaders every chance he got. The Reverend Jesse Jackson seemed to shuttle between appearing on *Larry King Live* and counseling the first family at the White House. When the president arrived at Martha's Vineyard after his admission that he had "misled the American people," there to greet him with a bear hug was Vernon Jordan, one of the most prominent black men in America, the former head of the NAACP, his old friend, and Monica's job hunter. During his "I Ask Your Forgiveness" tour, Bill Clinton's first heavily televised event was at a small black Baptist church.

We were receiving a subliminal White House message that no one would ever articulate. These are my beloved and loving constituents, Bill Clinton was telling America. They will go to the wall for me. They will be extremely unhappy if I am removed from office. Do you *really* want them to be extremely unhappy? Do you want that to happen *now*, when the economy is booming and you don't have a whole lot of worries in your life? Do you want to have to worry about *that* again?

Just as the race card was being played, a joker fell on the table in the form of Danny Williams, Bill Clinton's alleged black child. It was an old story, one that had been around since the mid-eighties, but reintroduced now within a fevered impeachment context, Danny Williams's reappearance was explosive. Drudge had broken the story that the *Star* was financing DNA tests comparing Danny's blood type to the analysis of Bill Clinton's DNA published in the *Starr Report*. Alongside Drudge's story was the photograph of a freckled, light-skinned, pudgy black teenager who looked, to many Americans, like the spittin' image of young Billy Clinton. I was sitting in a meeting at Paramount Studios the day the *Drudge Report* came out, and no one at the meeting was discussing the script we were supposed to be discussing.

Danny Williams was in the air. "That's it," said Sherry Lansing, the studio head. "If the DNA matches, Clinton's gone."

The details were certainly Clintonesque. He was jogging outside the governor's mansion in 1983, said a black hooker named Bobbie Ann Williams. He pulled her behind a hedge and asked her for a blow job. He talked all through it. He pulled his pants up and jogged off. He came back two weeks later in a white Lincoln driven by a state trooper. He picked up Bobbie Ann and two of her hooker friends. They drove to a house in Hot Springs owned by his mother. He got into bed with all three of them. When Bobbie Ann, still hooking, ran into him on the street next, she told him she was four months pregnant. "He laughed," Bobbie Ann said. "He was rubbing my big belly and said, 'Girl, that can't be my baby.' "

Shortly after Danny was born, Bobbie Ann went to jail for prostitution and possession of drugs. Lucille Bolton, Bobbie Ann's sister, became Danny's legal guardian. "He started to look more and more like the governor," Lucille said. Lucille went to the governor's mansion and confronted Clinton aides, trying to get child support for Danny. She got nowhere. Bill Clinton refused to supply a blood sample.

The story of Danny Williams got out into the local black tabloid press. Bobbie Ann and Lucille both took lie-detector tests and passed them. Don Williams, Bobbie Ann's husband, drove up alongside the governor as he was jogging one fine sunshiny morning and confronted him about Danny. The governor kept jogging, but he threw all the cash he had in his pockets into the car. Gossip about Danny made its way around the state and even into a governors' conference in Chicago. "Listen, I don't have a black baby!" Bill Clinton told some of his fellow Democratic bigwigs.

When Drudge, in the midst of the impeachment crisis, broke his story about the *Star*'s DNA analysis, Danny Williams rocked America, appearing on the front page of the *New York Post*, although few other newspapers. Danny Williams was as much a firestorm underground story as the cigar had been before Starr issued his report. That's all anyone in Hollywood and in much of the rest of the country was talking about.

Some people thought it suspicious that Clinton supporters had released a DNA study only weeks before showing that Thomas Jefferson had fathered a black child by Sally Hemmings. Were the Clintonistas anticipating a matching Danny Williams DNA? Was Thomas Jefferson being outed as an alibi for Bill Clinton? That is, if Thomas Jefferson had done it, had William *Jefferson* Clinton done anything that was wrong?

Days later, when Drudge reported that the DNAs didn't match, that the spittin' image of young Billy Clinton wasn't Bill Clinton's son, I thought I heard DeLay and Armey and Barr and Henry Hyde and Rogan and the rest of them groaning all the way out in Malibu. I could hear them sputtering: You can't match DNA without actual DNA! You can't match DNA on the basis of "information" in a report! The experts said, though, that they were wrong: That freckled-faced and pudgy Danny still didn't have a daddy.

Then it was crunch time for the Republican posse that had formed for the lynching. They had been Mack-trucked in the November election. Angry blacks were massing on the Capitol steps. The DNA had gone to hell. Vernon Jordan was too sharp and could handle himself, but Betty Currie was a different matter. She had contradicted herself in her previous testimony. She had been vague. She had looked rattled. And she knew *every-thing*! But as the Ratwoman had said, she "had this hero worship shit" for Bill Clinton. As a black woman, Betty Currie admired him and was deeply loyal to him.

They'd have to cajole, threaten, force the truth out of Betty Currie. They'd have to beat her up in public. With millions of angry black people watching. With millions of angry black people watching a group of white men, many with southern accents, do that to a hardworking, responsible, deeply religious black woman.

Without calling Betty Currie as a live witness, the posse wouldn't get its lynching. But calling Betty Currie might mean that the whole damn courthouse would burn down.

They forgot about raising the flag at Iwo Jima again. They rode out of town muttering "Oh Danny Boy" under their breath. The race card lay on the hallowed Senate floor . . . Bill Clinton's lucky but well-earned *ace of spades*.

[2]

Al Gore and I
Want to Be Black

H unky" and "Greenhorn" and "D.P." were the names I was called by many white Americans as I, a gawky, freckled-faced refugee from Hungary, grew up on Cleveland's near West Side. They were names that gave me a lifelong understanding of another word that was a wound to others and, later, to me: *nigger.*

There weren't a lot of black kids in my neighborhood, but there were some, and from the time I could barely speak the English language, I sought them out and played with them. I didn't know why then, didn't understand that I was naturally gravitating to other refugees, those who had fled the American South, fellow outsiders who knew in their hearts, as did I, that too many white Americans viewed us equally as trash. These black kids, too, wore clothes their moms had scrounged at the Salvation Army. Their moms, too, were down at the West Side Market early in the morning, seeking deals on fruit and vegetables that were almost but not quite spoiled. There was a line, though, drawn in the playground sand. We'd shoot hoops or play baseball together with our falling-apart balls, but we never saw the inside of one another's homes. It was always, "Yeah, later" at the end of a game, never "Hey, you wanna come over and watch *American Bandstand* at my house?"

I went back to the upstairs apartment I shared with my parents, who spoke little English, and I turned my battered green portable radio on and listened nonstop to what my father, who wore a beret even inside the house, called "jungle music." It was music that moved me like nothing had, music that seemed to reach into my core and upend my heart and soul. My parents were religious and told me stories about Jesus. I didn't want to hear about Jesus. I wanted to hear Chuck Berry telling me about "Sweet Little Sixteen" and "Johnny B. Goode" and "Maybellene." I wanted to hear Little Richard shriek about "Good Golly, Miss Molly" and "Tutti-Frutti." I wanted to hear Jackie Wilson and Fats Domino and Sam Cooke and the Drifters, the Platters, and the Flamingos. I felt that the black music I loved so much had a rawness, a *burn*, that Elvis and Jerry Lee and Bill Haley and Carl Perkins and the other white rockers couldn't match. I felt an inner turbulence, which only this music could soothe. My little green radio was a shelter from the juvenile trouble I was getting into in the alleys at night, where some of us carried zip guns and knives rubber-banded to our wrists, where others threw lighter fluid on cats, rolled bums, broke into grocery stores, and played games with neighborhood girls that they didn't necessarily want to play.

Sports provided a shelter, too. I rooted for Larry Doby and Al Smith and Luke Easter and Minnie Minoso of the Indians and Marion Motley and Bobby Mitchell and, later, Jim Brown, whom *Time* magazine called "Supernigger" of the Browns. I prayed that the old mongoose, Archie Moore, would finally finish off Yvon Durelle and cried when my radio told me that Ingo's thunderous right hand had put Floyd Patterson to sleep.

I went to high school on Cleveland's predominantly black East Side and, although I hated this upper crust, nearly lily white Catholic school (it was the only scholarship I could get), I loved the neighborhood it was in. I prowled the coffee shops around 105th and Euclid, playing Stevie Wonder's "Fingertips" and Cozy Cole's "Topsy II" and Gary U.S. Bonds's "Quarter to Three" and Ray Charles, the Marvelettes, and Ben E. King on the jukeboxes. One afternoon, heading for the bus that would take me back to the West Side, I heard a sound coming from a bar and it stopped me in my tracks. The door was open and I saw a young black woman on stage rehearsing with her band. She had a voice that was at the same time bluesy and operatic. A small sign on the door said TONIGHT! ARETHA FRANKLIN.

In my freshman year of college at Ohio University, I realized I was finally at a school where there were lots of black people. Many of them hung out at the Student Union at Baker Center, which is where I hung out, too. That's where I first heard the Contours do "Do You Love Me" . . . and that's where I met Delia. She was from Cleveland, too, a freshman, too, an English major, too, and she, too, loved Gary U.S. Bonds. She was black and I was white, she was from the East Side and I was from the West, her family had come from Mississippi and I had come from Hungary.

It was 1962 in southern Ohio and interracial relationships, even on a college campus, were taboo. Delia and I saw the looks in bartenders' eyes when we bought the beers we'd saved our pennies for. We saw the grins and leers on the fancily dressed fraternity boys' faces when we walked down the street holding hands. We didn't care. We had fun. She was living in a dorm and had to be in by eleven each night, and as I kissed her outside the dorm doors, we pretended those gaping white faces around us weren't there.

We talked a lot. I told her about Attila the Hun and how the Magyars fought the Turks, and she told me about her great-grandfather, who'd been a slave, and about the uncle whose eyes were beaten out because some white woman said he'd looked at her "in a dirty way." She introduced me to Ellison and Richard Wright and Chester Himes and to W. E. B. Du Bois. We both loved Faulkner, although Delia felt he made her nervous sometimes: "He hits the nail on the head a little too much."

Our initial sexual intimacies were more comic than passionate—we were both nervous kids—but we liked each other very much and nature took its course. We went back to Cleveland together. I went to her house in Cleveland's Glenville District and she came to mine in the Hungarian "Strudel Ghetto" off Buckeye Road where my parents had moved. Her parents looked at me as if I were a Martian. But they were polite. My parents just stared at this beautiful, vibrant young black woman. But they were polite. We went to black clubs on the East Side to see Roland Kirk and Cannonball Adderley and an upstart white blues band with a wild keyboardist named Al Kooper. Delia loved the blues, and we spent hours listening to it.

But there was an increasing tension to our relationship. Her parents didn't understand what she was doing with this white boy, and her older brother, she told me, was telling her this "honky" had no place in her life. (I smiled when she told me that. I'd been called a "hunky" as a kid; here was the same word, different spelling.) When her parents told her they couldn't afford to send her to Ohio University anymore, that she'd have to go to school in the Cleveland area somewhere, both of us cried. We knew what it meant. We were young and adventurous and our burgeoning relationship wouldn't withstand the distance.

It didn't. We started dating others, still seeing each other occasionally, and then drifted apart. Years later, when I drove alone from Athens to Columbus to see the Muhammad Ali–Sonny Liston fight on a theater screen, I thought about how much Delia would have loved Ali, how we would have rejoiced together in the magnificence of Ali's triumph. Suddenly missing her a lot, I called her parents' home after the fight. Her mother told me Delia was married and living in Buffalo and had a little boy. She had married one of her brother's friends.

My first job as a journalist was in Dayton, Ohio, which had the words CLEANEST TOWN IN AMERICA painted on its trash bins. It was also a racist town (though there was a bar owner there named Larry Flynt, who would shake things up a bit).

One day, my city editor wanted me to do a feature on a black man named "Hospital" Stewart, who had just died. The angle was that Stewart had gotten his nickname because most of the hospitals in Dayton knew him on sight. They knew him because his penis was allegedly so massive that it often got stuck inside his mates and both partners would have to be taken to the hospital to ease it out.

On another occasion, I wrote a human-interest feature about a little black kid who survived after being struck by lightning. The kid was articulate and cute and the story was the kind of heartwarming fluff that usually got special play on the front page. I was surprised when I saw my story about Casey Popo Jones, Jr., badly truncated and hidden on the obit page. I asked my city editor about it. "If you want front page," he said, "find a white kid who gets hit by lightning."

When Stokely Carmichael came to town, I was the only white face at a black Baptist church listening to him. "Black Power!" was the cry across the land, and during an interview with him, I was struck by Carmichael's charisma and dynamism, and wrote a story about him. It, too, was buried, truncated, in the back pages. The same thing happened when I interviewed one of my early rock and roll heroes, Fats Domino.

I got to the *Cleveland Plain Dealer* not long after the city's first racial upheaval—what became known as Cleveland's "Hough Riots." When I got there, the city's East Side, made up of white ethnic "islands" scattered among mostly poor black neighborhoods, was a raw racial nerve. I was assigned to the late shift at the police beat, which meant sitting in a tiny office on the first floor of Central Police Station and waiting for something awful to happen.

When things were slow, there were always interesting people to share an illegal six-pack of beer with. One of my favorites was a big, beefy, friendly cop named Elmer Joseph, who'd always come by. He, too, was Hungarian, and we'd kibitz about the Indians or the quality of the chicken paprikas at Elizabeth's restaurant on Buckeye Road or some tear-jerking story I'd written that Elmer decided to make fun of. Another of my favorites was Ahmed Evans, a dashiki-wearing black nationalist who led a houseful of young black militants who lived in the Glenville District, not far from where Delia had lived. Ahmed would come by my office late at night and go into a riff that included UFOs coming from Mars, murderous white police pigs, and the history of slavery in America. He quoted Marcus Garvey and Malcolm X, as well as Edgar Cayce and Nostradamus. He'd always refuse my beer at first and then drink most of the six-pack. I asked one night if I could try his dashiki on, and when I put it over myself, Ahmed laughed so hard, I thought he'd burst.

I had just gotten home from vacation one summer night, when my city editor called to tell me to go to Glenville, where a "disturbance" had broken out. I drove straight from my home in my rusted, beat-up old car, and as I approached Glenville, I saw that it was a war zone. Smoke was everywhere. Houses were burning. Police cars and fire trucks, sirens screaming, screeched by me. I parked my car and, waving my press pass, dodged around police cars and through hundreds of policemen, their guns drawn. It was chaos. I heard heavy gunfire now, and as I ran toward it, crouched, policemen screamed at me to get down. One of them almost knocked me down, shoving me onto my back against a car tire.

As I huddled there, I heard the roar of automatic weapons. Bullets were zinging off and going through the car behind which I was huddled. I could hear someone moaning and screaming, "Help me!" I was shaking so badly, I couldn't hold on to my press pass. I felt my pants wet between my legs. I peered around the tire as the gunfire continued. I saw a policeman out in the street, no more than twenty yards from me. I recognized him. It was my friend Elmer Joseph from the police beat. A pool of blood was around him as he screamed for help. He was caught in the cross fire, I saw. No one could get to him.

The automatic weapons' fire was coming from a building across the street. Inside was my friend Ahmed Evans and his houseful of black militants. I was trapped behind that tire for more than an hour. When it was over, a lot of people were dead, including Elmer Joseph. Ahmed Evans would be sent to prison for life. Glenville burned for three days. Delia's father's house, I saw the next day, had survived.

· · ·

The holocaust in Glenville led, finally, to a thorough investigation of Cleveland's police department. Too many times had policemen claimed to see a "gleaming object" before they pulled the trigger on a young black man. Too many times had politicians blamed poor peoples' rage on "outside agitators." Martin Luther King, Jr., an outside peacemaker, came to town, and as I followed him around, I noted the man's serenity, his sense of inner peace, as he worked with all sides to try to prevent yet another racial explosion.

The newspaper I worked for, the *Plain Dealer,* tried its best to serve as a responsible and progressive voice of the community. My feature stories about black people were on the front page here. I did a front-page series that showed statistically that the greatest victims of crime were black people. I went to Mississippi to do a follow-up on the Goodman, Chaney, and Schwerner civil rights killings and found myself with a shotgun stuck into my gut by Deputy Sheriff Cecil Price, one of those accused of the killings. I was escorted by his deputies to the Neshoba County line.

Not that the newspaper staff itself was free of racism. An older investigative reporter, citing unnamed FBI sources, kept trying to talk the editors into digging dirt on Cleveland's (and the nation's) first black mayor, Carl Stokes. She first claimed that Carl had taken payoffs as a liquor agent. The story didn't pan out. Then she claimed that Carl had fathered an illegitimate child in Tennessee. The story didn't pan out. Then she claimed that Carl, married to a black woman, was having affairs with white women. (Shades of Kenneth W. Starr . . . that story *did* pan out and ultimately cost Carl reelection.)

The *Plain Dealer* gave me the freedom to cover civil rights rallies, racist and corrupt police unions, even Hungarian vigilantes who "patrolled" the Buckeye Road ethnic neighborhood where my parents lived. Hungarian vigilantes who drove or walked up and down the street carrying saps and Saturday Night Specials and who attacked or harassed black people in the old-world Nazi ways. Only the butcher store owners on Buckeye Road welcomed the influx of blacks into this old Hungarian neighborhood, happily noting that black people loved smoked paprikaed bacon and peppery sausage and head cheese, putting big signs on their windows that said SOUL FOOD. My stories about the Hungarian vigilantes put them out of business. Many Hungarians on Buckeye hated me. I didn't care about these honky, racist, anti-Semitic, anti-American, anti–jungle music, antediluvian Hungarians.

I took my newfound friend Jimi Hendrix into a Hungarian restaurant on

Buckeye for some liver dumpling soup and smiled as the Hungarian owner and staff bug-eyed this astral cowboy with his Afro, his beads, and his flashing silver jewelry. I did the last interview with Otis Redding hours before his plane crashed. I tried James Brown's cape on backstage after a show. (It fit.) I saw Chuck Berry before a concert, demanding his money in brown paper bags before he went onstage.

When I got to *Rolling Stone* magazine, I discovered that an awful lot of young white people felt as deeply about black people and black culture as I did. With most of us, it really had begun with the music. We had grown up listening to Chuck and Little Richard and Jackie and so had the Stones and the Beatles and the Doors and the Jefferson Airplane. That music, which my father had called "jungle music," had changed us. We wanted to be black. The irony was that in the sixties and seventies, we were listening to white versions of that black sound—Janis and Mick and the Beatles—much more than to Muddy himself or Chuck himself.

We may have wanted to be black, but we couldn't go all the way with it. It was our kids, fittingly, who'd come much closer to it. By the nineties, rock and roll was aging like we were and our kids were captive to the lacerating, hypnotizing beat of hip-hop and rap and to lyrics so raw that many rock and roll parents, forgetting their own enjoyment of songs like the Stones' "Starfucker" and much of Prince's oeuvre, were demanding warnings on CD labels. Our kids weren't interested in white artists knocking the real thing off—no Mick doing Muddy for them—they listened to the real, nonwhite-washed ebony black sound itself: to Tupac and Snoop and Dr. Dre and Wyclef Jean. My own son, in his early twenties, who'd grown up on Dylan and the Stones, was a hip-hop deejay calling himself D. J. Rogue. He listened only to black music, surrounded himself with black friends, and knew how to spin as well as some black deejays. He even turned his nose up at the Beastie Boys.

When I got to Hollywood, I found it easy to write about racial equality and the forces of white racism, and I wrote two movies from differing points of view—*Big Shots*, about a friendship between a white kid and a black one, and *Betrayed*, about the "mud-hunting" neo-Nazis.

I also found Hollywood frightened of certain *areas* as they related to black and white relations. Hollywood had never done a movie about the urban riots of the sixties, ideal and historically significant dramatic subject matter. Love stories between blacks and whites, especially movies showing sexual intimacy between black men and white women, were still taboo.

(Although the love scenes between Richard Pryor and Margot Kidder in *Some Kind of Hero*, left on the cutting room floor, had become a collector's item.) Some executives, I discovered, had a particular problem with Spike Lee. Spike, who wanted to direct a script of mine called *Reliable Sources*, never had a chance. An executive at Paramount sent other executives a Xerox copy of an article accusing Spike of making anti-Semitic remarks. When Spike showed up for a studio meeting with his Nation of Islam driver, the studio execs smiled, jived him, and then made him a financial offer so low, they knew he'd have to refuse.

Months after Bill Clinton's impeachment, Al Gore appeared at a black Baptist church and, working hard to empathize, told his audience that he, too, understood prejudice. When he came back from Vietnam, he said, with his short hair and his uniform, all the longhairs made fun of him and looked at him with scorn. "It was a Ralph Ellison moment for me," the vice president told his black audience. *Well . . . why not?* Good old stick-in-the-mud, party-pooping Al Gore. *Even him!* Private schools, Harvard, a senator's son. *Just another white boy who wanted to be black.*

[3]

James Carville Kicks Ass

"Okay, he has a problem," Monica said to Linda Tripp. "And we, the American people, elected him. So let him do his stupid job."

It was one of those urban legends, like the one that said singer John Denver had been our best sniper in Vietnam, always waiting for the sun to blind his targets before pulling the trigger. But this "legend," my unimpeachable sources in Washington told me, was "Put your hand on the Bible and bet the whole wad" true—censored out of the press only because it was, really, a sticky family matter in the era of family values. I'd heard it first in 1992 and now I was hearing it again as Kenneth W. Starr and his congressional allies were unsheathing their long knives to slit Bill Clinton's throat.

James Carville was Hunter S. Thompson's bastard little brother.

They had found each other during the 1992 campaign and determined for themselves that they were suffering from the same inherited disorder that made them abuse themselves (no, not that way!), foam at the mouth, mumble, cuss, stutter, and twitch. I considered, as I watched the approaching sharpened long knives, that two Carvilles, two Thompsons, *two* crazy people at a crucial moment like this were better than one.

What I really hoped was that Hunter, up in Woody Creek on his Colorado mountain, a lunatic dervish watching CNN twenty-four hours a day, was once again advising his bastard little brother . . . like he'd advised him in 1992 in a series of strategy memos that won Clinton the election and made his little brother famous. On the Bush strategy: "They [Bush and James Baker III] would torture the Queen of England for three days and nights to make her say that Bill Clinton raped her repeatedly, while he was a student at Oxford, and she has many crazed love letters to prove it." On an October surprise: "They might hire Bill's daughter to say he abused her. Like Woody Allen." On the Clinton strategy: "Don't deny anything, especially if they accuse you of fucking pigs. Just stand up in front of the mike and smile like a champion." On Clinton's vulnerability: "By the way, where was Bill Clinton on the night James Dean died? Drunk and naked on some teenage golf course in Arkansas? Ripping lust-hardened tire tracks across the 18th green? Chasing a naked young girl into the woods?" On Ross Perot: "Why did you let the goddamn little weasel into the debates in the first place? Fuck Ross Perot! He is an evil, dangerous tar baby and the willing creature of James Baker III, who wants to bury us all. Especially you and me, James." On the nature of the enemy: "Take my word for it, James, these lying, whoring swine will stop at nothing. How many points do you think James Baker III believes it might be worth if he could strut out on the South Lawn of the White House on October 15th and display the still-bleeding head of Saddam Hussein. . . . Beware James, beware. Baker III is so mean that he makes *you* look like a garden snake. He would serve up the head of Barbara Bush on a platter if he thought it would win the election." Big brotherly advice: "You're lucky you ain't running against me. I would have that degenerate [Clinton] locked up for his own good."

This was the kind of spirit needed right now, I reflected—no, not locking the president up as a degenerate, but the old sixties, Notre Dame fighting spirit. Off the pigs! Win one for Abbie Hoffman! Acid into their water supplies! Tear-gas masks and shattering glass and the time to set the night on F-I-R-E! The stuff Hunter was infused with and reeked of like a sixties political wino up there in his mountainous fortress in Woody Creek, still using his phone and his fax machine, his anger and his wit, like laser-guided missiles fueled by nicotine, alcohol, various medications, and an unyielding and unbroken hope for a better America. I knew that his bastard little brother seemed to be just like him, without the nicotine and the medications, and I knew James had talked a good game, even to Hunter, whom he affectionately called "Doc": "The Bible says everyone will eat a pound of dirt before we die," James told Hunter. And: "Elections are about fucking your enemies, winning is about fucking your friends." And: "You think God is mean? Shit, you ought to see my scorecard! Richard Nixon never even thought about keeping an enemies list like the one I keep." Nice words. Good, tough talk. Perfect for the time when the long knives were flashing in darkened congressional offices lighted only by a bloodred moon. But still . . . *talk*. James, I felt, needed his big brother at his side.

I knew the two had had a nasty familial falling-out, which Hunter described in *Better Than Sex:*

> I stood up suddenly and whacked him on the side of his head with my open hand, right on his ear. He never saw it coming. He staggered sideways and dropped to his knees as the crowd parted, trying to get away from the violence and jabbering hysterically as James scrambled around on the floor and went into a snakelike crouch, snarling and hissing at me. I tried to back away, but it was too late. He hurled himself at my knees, in the style of a crazed Sumo wrestler. I would have gone down, but there were too many people in the way. I tried to stomp him, but he slithered away and cursed me. People were yelling, and I tried to stomp him again. I felt hands grasping at me, and then I was seized from behind in a chokehold and dragged off balance. I swung wildly and hit somebody, just as James lunged at me again.

But then I reread Hunter's description and reconsidered . . . James on the floor in a snakelike crouch, "snarling and hissing" . . . James as "a crazed Sumo wrestler" . . . James slithering away and cursing . . . James lunging. Maybe, I thought, little brother would be just fine. Crouching, snarling, hissing, slithering, cursing, sumo-wrestling the men in the dark suits with the long knives, the values-stoned posse of Christian vigilantes. Maybe he *could* do it without Doc's help. Maybe James Carville was crazier even than Hunter Thompson, James breathing his own evangelical fire in defense of the Americans he loved, the guys at the diner, the women at the Kmart. I hoped "Serpent Head," as his wife called him, had told Hunter the truth. Gaga little brother, at this particular moment, had to be meaner than God . . . meaner than Richard Nixon . . . meaner than Hunter . . . meaner than all of them combined . . . to get the first rock and roll president of the United States out of this mess.

"Meaner than a junkyard dog!" was what an aide to a candidate James Carville had defeated called him. And the *Washington Post* had even cartooned him as a Doberman. James was described as "a malignant John Malkovich on speed," and "Anthony Perkins playing Fidel Castro on acid." He was called Attila the Hun and Rasputin, but he objected to the Rasputin part, pointing out that Rasputin ended up raped, castrated, and thrown in the river. His enemies said he was as subtle as a clenched fist and accused him of kneecapping his opponents. James didn't deny it. He called himself "Corporal Cueball" and said, "It's hard for someone to hit you when you have your fist in their face . . . when I'm running a campaign, I always say I want the people I'm running against to catch the clap and die."

He was fifty-three years old the year the long knives came for Bill Clinton. He was tall and muscular, favored jeans and high-tops and T-shirts. He grinned, giggled, cackled. "My mother," James said, "used to say I was like a toaster. I popped up all the time." He spoke a peculiar, jabbering, mumbling tongue with a coonass accent. Cal Ripken wondered what language James spoke. His wife called him "the King of Ramble" and said she thought a third of what James spoke was Ebonics.

The foreign tongue was the outer manifestation, no doubt, of a congenital inner dementia. James urinated blood sometimes during his campaigns. He refused to change his underwear in the final week of a campaign, so he wouldn't somehow hurt his candidate's momentum. On election day, James curled up in the fetal position in a darkened room. He got up on the alternate side of the bed each day for good luck. He wore black mittens for better luck. James kept eleven jars of Chef Dan's barbecue sauce on his desk for no discernible reason. He watched the Weather Channel all the time. He watched reruns of *The Andy Griffith Show* whenever he could. He stopped his stress headaches by cracking raw eggs on staffers' heads. James thought Marcella Hazan, a priestess of gastronomy, was the Second Coming. James spoke to his mother every day. He had an office in the basement of a Capitol Hill row house he called "the Bat Cave," obvious homage to Hunter's Owl Farm. James appeared on television with a glass of Wild Turkey in his hand. James shot beer bottles and Coke cans in his backyard.

James went off on jazzy, primeval riffs, which were dangerous to the sensibilities and composure of millions of unfortunates who had corncobs up their butts. Ranting, raving, mumbling, twitching, jabbering, yammering, mesmerizing, lacerating, intimidating, humiliating . . . *real scary.* "I'm sort of a political goon," the King of Ramble rambled. "I'm a little like a piano player in a whorehouse. Somebody out there hears something, I try to pick it up. . . . I'm weird. I'm a disconnect. Yet my whole ability to earn a living depends on my ability to connect with other people's everyday lives. . . . I relish and like political combat. This era of everyone sitting at the table of commonality is not my moment of history. . . . When I pick a candidate, I've got to live in the same foxhole with him for a year. You've got to smell their breath a lot. . . . I'll die before I turn into one of those guys in a tie, down at the Gucci Gulch, testifying before some congressional committee. . . . I need a villain. I stay pretty mad during the whole campaign. I'm like uranium 235, not quite stable. . . . If your guy is in trouble, throw water. If the other guy is in trouble, throw kerosene. . . . You pick up the snake, you're going to get bit. . . . Fightin's fightin'."

Those who knew both Thompson and Carville were amazed by how influenced James was by the gonzo-political doctrines Dr. Thompson had formulated, which James had not read until recently. "I gotta catch myself from lapsing into slang and cusswords. . . . I have a weakness for bourbon whiskey, scotch whiskey, gin, red wine, and beer. . . . Do you think I never bounced a check or made a forward remark to a subordinate? Or inhaled? . . . What we need in this campaign is more McDonald's thinking," James said. "For the raw practice of political art, George Wallace was something to behold. . . . All the V-chip does is let parents program their TV so their kids can't watch certain programs. Shit, I may not want my child to watch Jerry Falwell on TV. Well, now I can V-chip him right out. . . . If you want to see the whiningest, complainingest bunch of do-good weenies, look at the liberals. My message is: Quit complaining, get off your butts, and organize. Get out your checkbook. Write letters to the editor. Do the things Republicans do. . . . Republicans are the party of big money and sex rumors, that's all they're good at. . . . I wonder if there's any Republican in the United States that's actually read the Constitution." James's definition of "the enemy" sounded like a listing of his big brother's lifelong political targets: "Republicans, the media, the opposition, the sharpies, the quote sluts [independent analysts], the ole thirty-second hit guys [experts]."

How sad, I thought. James and Hunter seemed more than brothers; they seemed like physical and ideological twins. And now, as the long knives approached, they weren't next to each other, where they belonged. One was on his Owl Farm; the other was in his Bat Cave. They weren't sharing their Wild Turkey; they were tilting their gallon jugs in different places, shooting up different backyards. And all because of a family dispute in a Little Rock dump. Two tough guys who, at a triumphant moment—Bill Clinton's election—didn't know how to stop fighting and so turned their lifelong fury on each other.

While Hunter was the ideologue, spewing his fax tracts off the mountain, James was the grunt, trying to gouge out eyes. "I only represent Democrats, not crooks, not racists," James said. That was mumbled Ebonic Cajun rationalization for gouging out eyes, busting kneecaps, slitting throats . . . but only for the good guys: Democrats, not crooks, not racists.

Observe James meeting with a pollster. "He was glowering and scowling," the pollster said. "He stands up and walks around and then on top of the furniture and then he starts screaming as he paces up and down and I think—Oh my God, I am in the presence of a lunatic! I think he needs immediate hospitalization."

Observe James meeting a possible candidate/client. The candidate asks him about his staff. James says, "There was once a sheriff in a small Texas town that was having a riot. So the sheriff calls in the Texas Rangers. And the train rolls up to the station, where the sheriff is anxiously waiting. And out walks one Texas Ranger leading his horse. And the sheriff says, 'Look, we got a hell of a riot going on! Where are the rest of you?' And the ranger says, 'Lookee here, Sheriff. One riot, one ranger.' " And James says to the candidate/client, "I ain't got no staff."

Observe James in 1983, a part of Gary Hart's campaign. Hart drops out of the race due to Donna Rice. "I was heading back to my motel in Maryland. I was standing on a curb on Massachusetts Avenue in the middle of a rainstorm. My garment bag broke, and everything I owned spilled into the street. I had six dollars in my wallet. That was everything I had in the world. I felt like a stone-ass loser. I sat down on the curb and cried."

Observe James in 1984, managing Lloyd Dogett's campaign for the senate in Texas. James is living in his car. Dogett not only loses; he suffers the biggest defeat ever sustained in Texas by a Democrat. James holes up in a dumpy apartment in Austin. "I'd cry a lot. I was scared I was a failure. I was 40 years old. I didn't have any money. I didn't have any health insurance. My life insurance policy was worth $2,500 cash value and I had to get the money to keep the Visa people from coming to lynch me. Did you ever look at a telephone and hope it rings? Believe me, I've stared at a phone for weeks, months, just kind of staring at it. I thought, I got to get out of this business. I can't win."

He decided in that dump of an Austin apartment that he loved what he did too much. He decided he wasn't going to lose again. It was do or die. No more sobs on the curbs. No more living out of his car. No more waiting for the phone to ring. No more Mr. Nice Guy. Go for the jugular! Get the dirt! Run the negative ads! Slice and dice! Trash and bash!

Campaigning against Bill Scranton II in Pennsylvania, he ran ads show-

ing Scranton in a Nehru jacket and talking about transcendental meditation. Even though James enjoys a nice fat joint on occasion, he leaked
details about Scranton's pot smoking to the press. Scranton lost; Carville
won. Campaigning against former Rhodes scholar and Heisman Trophy
winner Pete Dawkins in New Jersey: "I needed to cut Dawkins off at the
knees. If he ever established credibility, we'd be in for a rough fight." James
ran ads saying Dawkins was a carpetbagger, ending with the line "Come on,
Pete, be real." Dawkins lost; Carville won. Campaigning against former
Reagan attorney general Dick Thornburg in Pennsylvania, he personally
attacked Thornburg: "The idea of Dick Thornburg coming back to Pennsylvania and saying 'Send me to the corridors of power because I know Washington' is like running on a pro-leprosy ticket against Jesus." Thornburg lost;
Carville won.

By now, James had also taken to spooking his opposition candidates personally by using his physical presence, showing up in the back as they held a
press conference, smiling his evil smile. "We spent too much time waiting
and ducking James Carville," a Thornburg aide said. Thornburg's campaign
manager said, "What Carville is best at is *not* doing something, but making
you believe he's going to do something. It's mind psych. We spent a lot of
energy trying to anticipate something that ultimately never happened."

James was on the road to stardom by then, though he was also picking up
a reputation as the Democratic Lee Atwater, the Reagan and George Bush
puppet master who was the founding father of negative, personally destructive, scorched-earth campaigning. A national political analyst said, "Carville
is what a lot of Democrats have been looking for. Somebody who not only
matches fire with fire but isn't afraid to use a blowtorch." Occasionally, the
blowtorch misfired. In a Democratic primary against Governor Ann
Richards of Texas, James, who inhaled often, ran ads accusing her of drug
abuse. Richards won; Carville lost.

It didn't matter. As the 1992 election approached, Bob Kerrey, Tom
Harkin, and Bill Clinton all wanted him to handle them. He was a winner
now, a wunderkind, a killer, a star. "This is one of the few businesses where
it's actually of some benefit for people to think you're half a quart low,"
James said. "Sometimes clients as well as opponents." His newfound young
partner, Paul Begala, told prospective clients, "We all know that James isn't
playing with a full deck. But I'm the only one who knows which cards are
missing."

He picked Bill Clinton because he liked him personally, liked his ideas,
liked Hillary, and thought he could get him elected president. "You know,

you pay for my head, but I throw in my heart for free," James told Bill Clinton. He did the opposition research he believed in so much, not just on George Bush but also on Bill Clinton, so he could defend him. He issued orders that he wanted as little as possible in writing. He worked twenty-four hours a day, a demonic figure in jeans and T-shirt, always telling his staff, "Run! Don't walk!"

On the morning Bill and Hillary did their *60 Minutes* interview about Gennifer Flowers, James woke up at dawn "wrenched and drenched" and sobbing. After the interview, he hugged Bill Clinton and was crying again. Those who saw the extraordinary bond between the two men pointed to what they called James's "Kmart life." Inside his head, some felt, James Carville lived in a Kmart from somewhere out of his childhood. And as Jack Kennedy was the candidate from Camelot, Bill Clinton was the candidate from Kmart.

On election night, James sobbed again . . . and then got into his vicious barroom brawl with Hunter, who'd come down from Woody Creek to see his little brother. And the two comrades and brothers got off the grimy, beer-coated sawdust floor and went their separate ways. (Well, shit, every revolution ate its own.)

James didn't become a cabinet member or a spokesperson. "I wouldn't want to be part of a government that would have me in it," he said. He moved on to other campaigns, but he stayed personally close to Bill Clinton. "I can't think of anybody who has been better to me, nicer to me, or has given me more of a chance to be at the top of the world than President Clinton and I hope I don't let him down," James said.

He didn't seem to change much at his moment of greatest triumph. "I didn't go into the lobbying business," he said. "I didn't show up at the Georgetown dinner parties. I didn't get a new circle of friends." At times, he seemed overwhelmed by his fame. "I was in New York up on this dais. I don't know if it was everybody who was anybody in New York, but it was everybody I ever heard of. For forty-five minutes I'm sitting in front of all these people and all I'm thinking is—Is my fly open?" He still wore the jeans people expected him to wear. "When I started campaigning," he said, "I'd always wear jeans and a T-shirt. Then I bought a suit to go out and speak in. People come up and say 'Well, that's it! You elect a president and you got a nice expensive suit now. You've changed!' I get requests—'Tell him to wear his jeans!' In Georgia, I went out and wore khakis. People were very disappointed. People said, 'Where are your jeans, man?' "

A part of him expected his glory to end. "It's the splat ceremony," he said.

"They run you up the flagpole and then you fall and everyone goes, 'Gee, what a shame!' There seems to be a cycle. You get built up and you crash." James had no great ambitions. He wanted to keep doing what he liked doing. "They used to say about Ted Williams that all he looked forward to was the next time at bat. All I look forward to is the next campaign. I'm a campaign guy. I like the smell of headquarters."

He bought himself a cabin in the Blue Ridge Mountains. James sat on the porch in his underwear and took potshots at rabbits. His friend Burt Reynolds visited him there, as Johnny Depp and John Cusack visited his big brother on *his* mountains, and said, "Man, I'm having a *Deliverance* flashback." James just smiled his spooky smile, scratched the nuts he scratched so often, and kept blasting away.

That the draft-dodging Bill Clinton's most lethal defender was born at Fort Benning and spent two years in the Marine Corps was the kind of kingfish irony that James loved.

James grew up in Carville, population 1,020, deep in inbred Louisiana, where creatures who resembled him slithered horizontally through the ooze, where the stop signs looked like Swiss cheese, thanks to shotguns. His father and grandmother both served as postmasters, so the town was named after them. "I was a mama's boy," James said. His mother, whom he called "Miss Nippy," meant everything to him. "I had a very happy childhood," he said. "I just assumed everybody else did, too. I cannot remember an unhappy moment as a child. I was lucky. I had a horse when I was six years old. My grandparents lived down the road. I could stay with them if I wanted to. I was loved and never wanting for anything. When my daddy broke it to me that there was no Santa Claus, it was nothing compared with the glee of being the one who knew something that my younger brothers and sisters didn't know. Plus, I got to help my father put the stuff under the tree."

His most cathartic moments as a child occurred when his mother taught him about politics and when Harper Lee taught him about racism. His mother taught him about politics by taking him along as she sold the *World Book Encyclopedia*. James was six. "She was a great salesman, the best. We would look for any yard that had bicycles. Prime suspect. Any yard that had a bicycle and a bass boat was 100 percent. She would go in and pitch educational materials for children. And, inevitably, the man of the house would say, 'I can't afford it.' And she would make the point that he was able to afford a bass boat for himself, but it struck her as odd that he can't afford educational materials for his children. It was the guilt approach. The deal was done by then."

He was sixteen when he read *To Kill a Mockingbird.* "I had never really thought about things like race. I mean, you had white folks and you had black folks. And white folks got things and black folks didn't. Thus it was, thus it is, thus it shall be. And I didn't question it—it was sort of a benign world I lived in. I didn't pay attention to the fact that some people are robbed of their dignity. But then I read *Mockingbird* and what happened to Tom Robinson and I knew instinctively that—A. It happened to a lot of other people, and B. It probably happened to people right around where I grew up. And that it would happen again. And that caused me to question what I'd always accepted. It started a process that changed my view of the world."

James played football, ran track, and rode horses. He went to college at LSU. "I drank, chased a lot of coeds, and got into a lot of fights. I made John Belushi look like a scholar." He was thrown out of school and spent two years in the Marine Corps as a regimental food-supply corporal. He went back to LSU, graduated, got a law degree, and put out his shingle. "He was the worst lawyer in the world," his mother said.

A nearby car dealer was running for the state legislature and he asked James to help him. The car dealer campaigned by stretching his arms wide and imitating Elvis: "I want you, I need you, I love you!" The car dealer lost; Elvis lost; James Carville lost.

It was his first losing political campaign, though he had taken his first political action many years earlier. When he was seventeen, still in high school, James went around town tearing down the campaign posters of a local politician he didn't like.

If James was the Ragin' Cajun, then his wife, Mary Matalin, was the Ragin' Croatian, a woman who worked in a steel mill and a beauty parlor before she got into politics, a striking Debra Winger look-alike who described herself as a "chick," who cussed like James and wore blue jeans like James, but who also sported the kind of bloodred nails that James didn't dare to wear in public.

Her voice was deep and raspy and she used it to call Bill Clinton a "philandering, pot-smoking draft dodger" who suffered from what she termed, what she first defined, as "bimbo eruptions." Mary Matalin was, unbelievably as far as James was concerned, not only a Republican but the head of the Republican National Committee when they met. She ran George Bush's campaign while he ran Bill Clinton's. Their marriage was Marilyn Chambers mating with Pat Robertson, Warren Beatty with Phyllis Schlafly, Barney Frank with Pat Buchanan.

An unlikely mating, too, because James had the same problem with his willard as Bill Clinton had with his. And few who knew James thought he could be faithful, even though he was always saying that Mary was "very cute" and "real sassy" and looked at her on a stage once and said, "My God, honey, you got a great figure!" James was the man who said, "Whoo boy! You think Gary Hart had a problem?" . . . Who admitted, "I think the double standard, I act the double standard, I live the double standard." A friend said, "James littered the American landscape with broken hearts," adding, "I met fifteen Marys before I saw James with Mary." And James denied that during the 1992 campaign he'd shown his willard to a female campaign worker and said, "Hey, lookee here!" prompting her to say, "Gee, I've never seen one that old." James said he had unzipped himself, yeah, okay, so what, but it was only his *shirttail* that was peeking out of there.

James didn't care what anybody said about his willard; he knew that he adored Mary, convincing even her friends, one of whom said, "If Marilyn Monroe was reincarnated and walked through the room naked, he wouldn't notice now." Mary just said, "He excites me beyond compare—his brain does and other things do too," although he teased her, saying, "Marrying a Republican means getting used to celibacy most of the time."

Mary knew her man, though. "I don't care if you wear it in your nose," she said, "but I want you to wear a wedding ring." The ultimate political junkies, politics itself was sex to them, too. As James defined it, "A political campaign builds itself up, explodes, and then ends. That's the aphrodisiac of it."

James knew how sharp she was, and while he said, "The only thing I do with Republicans is beat 'em and date 'em," what got him were her brains, her balls, and her irreverence.

In some ways, Mary Matalin was James not as a slithering bayou creature but as a normal human being. She was smart enough to have been part of the team (led by the wicked Lee Atwater, her mentor) that transformed George Bush from an East Coast preppy into a country music–loving, pork rind–eating Texan who went down to JCPenney to buy himself socks.

That, James knew better than anyone else, was no small feat. Mary was irreverent enough to talk about how while Bush was campaigning in Ohio on a train, an entire family bent over and mooned him. She called George W. Bush "Joooooooonior," said Bush White House Chief of Staff John Sununu had "the political acumen of a doorknob," and allowed that Pat Buchanan was a gnat—"Let's just take out the fly swatter and squash him."

Mary had the balls to tell James to his face and publicly what she thought of him: "He's learning-disabled and his mind works like a Ping-Pong ball. . . . He takes it as a point of honor that everyone thinks he's a wack job. . . . The guy is a nutcake. James could get on and beat Ross Perot. . . . Is James a sensitive man? He's sensitive to pain. . . . He looks to have been sired from a love scene in *Deliverance*."

She liked him right away. "He is, simply, unequivocally, the most brilliant political strategist, the most brilliant man, period. He scares me. . . . We agreed on practically nothing but we had a good time barking at each other. It didn't take long before we were fighting. We'd known each other for a half hour and we were screaming at each other in public. . . . When I met him, he owned one thing—a Schwinn. It wasn't even a ten-speed. And when someone broke into his apartment, they stole a bottle of Wild Turkey 'cause that was the only thing worth stealing. . . . The first thing I loved about him is that he loves his mama. He reveres his mama."

She proposed for him. "We were at a stock car race sitting on the hood of a pickup truck," she said. "And he admitted that he didn't know how to propose. So I said, 'Repeat after me.' And I did the proposal, then I said yes." They got married in New Orleans, their wedding attended by his friends, people like Al Hirt and Timothy Hutton and hers, people like Sonny Bono and Rush Limbaugh. "It started with a cocktail party," James said. "Then when it was time to get married we just opened the doors and people carried their drinks into where the ceremony was. After the wedding we had a parade—we had a brass band and everybody just kind of marched down Bourbon Street. People were throwing things and jazz music was playing." After the wedding, James said, "I was destined to be a wussy male. The three most important women in my life are Mary, Hillary Clinton, and Miss Nippy."

As the long knives came for Bill Clinton, James and Mary Matalin had two beautiful baby girls and were spending a lot of time out in the country playing what James called "air golf," shooting juice bottles with air rifles. They were happy. Mary talked about opening a mom-and-pop restaurant sometime in the future. "I'd call it I-55 for the interstate that runs through

Illinois. He'd cook. I'd be the bartender." James's vision of the future was less roseate: "When this era of our life is over and we're flat on our backs, we'll stand on a street corner with a sign that says — 'Will Bicker for Food.' "

They were already bickering about the long knives. Mary told James he was "obsessive-compulsive" about Kenneth W. Starr and that when he criticized him, James was "projecting." Mary said, "It is not political. Ken Starr is not political. He doesn't want to put Bill Clinton out of office. You see the world in such stark terms, James."

"Such stark terms" . . . yes indeed, James could see the stark, squalid ugliness of it . . . all of it, including what Mary's fellow Republicans were whispering behind their backs, besmirching the love they felt for each other. James thought of his brother up there in Woody Creek, watching the world like a fiery-eyed hawk on his big-screen TV. Hunter would see the stark foulness of this. Doc would know how to deal with it.

Mary's Republicans were saying that the only reason Mary Matalin loved James Carville was because he reminded her of Lee Atwater, her one, good, true, and dead love.

That Mary Matalin had been deeply devoted to Lee Atwater, her political mentor, who died in 1991 of a brain tumor at the age of forty, was true. She had a copy of a blues CD on her wall that Lee, who played a mean blues guitar, had made with Isaac Hayes. It was inscribed "Dear Mary, You have gotten me through many storms. I deeply love you." It was also true that Mary spoke of Lee's political savvy the way she spoke of James Carville's. "Lee was a genius. He had an understanding of human nature and cultural trends."

And there were obvious similarities between the two men. They both loved reruns of *The Andy Griffith Show*. They both loved their mountain cabins. Lee was from the South, too, from South Carolina, and had the same irrepressible, foot-tapping, twitchy energy as James. The same aggressive political attitude. "Republicans in the South could not win elections by talking about issues," Lee had said. "You had to make the case that the other guy, the other candidate, is a bad guy." Even in his rhetoric, Lee sounded like James. Running against Dukakis, Lee had said, "I'm going to strip the bark off the little bastard . . . I'm going to make Willie Horton his running mate," and he had devised a vicious ad that forever tied Dukakis in white voters' eyes to black crime.

Lee, too, was a master of the deadly leak. When black ministers came to him asking to support Ronald Reagan and asking for voter registration money, Lee told them the Reagan campaign was broke and suggested they go to John Connally, who was running against Reagan. Then he leaked to the Bush campaign, also running against Reagan, that "Connally was buying the black vote." Bush then attacked Connally and Connally fired back at Bush. And the two campaigns badly wounded each other—while Lee's Reagan campaign kept rolling along. It was the kind of shrewdness Mary had loved about Lee and the kind of shrewdness Mary loved about James, and it led her to conclude that "they would have loved each other. Lee would have loved James."

But the whisperers were whispering about something much more. Married and with children, Lee had had a reputation as a notorious womanizer and Mary had worked closely with him, so the whisperers were assuming that they had been lovers. And then Ed Rollins, the Republican campaign wizard who'd beaten James in New Jersey with Christine Todd Whitman over James Florio, had come right out and said it: "I always thought part of Mary's attraction to Carville had something to do with Lee. For the last year of his life, she ran the Republican National Committee in his absence, saw him every day, and directed much of his medical care. In many ways, she was *as much of a wife* as Sally at the end. I wasn't the only one of her friends to believe that Carville was Lee's surrogate in Mary's eyes." It was a revolting thing to say. James was nothing but Lee's surrogate? The reason she loved and slept with James was because she couldn't have a dead man?

The particular, cruel horror of it was that Lee had behaved bizarrely in his final year . . . but he had a tumor the size of a hen's egg growing in his brain. Lee *was* with another woman for much of his final year—Mary's friend Brooke Vosburgh—in the same house with his pregnant wife, Sally, and their kids, and they lay on Lee's bed and held hands. Lee was dying and losing his mind at the same time. Brooke was there with Sally's permission, both women trying to give comfort to a man who was in excruciating pain, who was having visions, who imagined himself with Brooke as Napoléon and Josephine, who found Jesus, who insisted on detailing all of his affairs to Sally in a plea for forgiveness, who became so paranoid that he had all his visitors frisked and his food tasted for fear of poison, who was suicidal near the end, begging his mother to kill him.

Lee "married" Brooke in a mock ceremony in which they used paper clips for rings. Lee tried massages and Tibetans and holistic healers. He tried hand-squeezed watermelon juice. And at the end, Lee concluded that he couldn't beat his nightmarish ailment. "Cancer is not a Democrat," Lee said. He died with Sally holding his hand.

Mary knew that what Ed Rollins was saying and what the others were whispering was meant to hurt James, to belittle him, to make him look like he was being cuckolded not only by a dead man but also by the dead king of modern political campaign managers, Atwater beating Carville even from the grave in a battle of the big swinging willards, with Mary as the prize. A showdown on the most macho and the most political levels. And Mary also knew that she was being belittled and denigrated, too, as a groupie whose love for Elvis had made her marry an Elvis impersonator. But what struck her the most about what Rollins was saying and the hall mice whispering was the obscene way in which Sally Atwater was being humiliated. Her husband was dead and Sally had to hear from his own Republican colleagues about yet one more possible betrayal.

James didn't say much in response to Ed Rollins or the whispers. He knew his chick loved him. He sat on the porch, squinting at the sun with his reptilian eyes. Mary Matalin knew her husband well. The long knives would be in for the fight of their lives.

He took it to Kenneth W. Starr and Newt Gingrich and Henry Hyde and Tom DeLay and Dick Armey and Bob Barr and Ed Rollins and all the other chickenshit, stuck-up, tight-ass, nose-high, pork-belly Republicans . . . like that other coonass took it to Ned Beatty in *Deliverance*. James was screaming "Sooey! Sooey!" at the top of his lungs and riding their pampered, powdered, mottled selves into their own excrement. It seemed as if he was waging an airwave filibuster, outshouting, outscowling, out-finger-pointing the editorialists and commentators calling for Bill Clinton's resignation or impeachment. His bearing suggested a possessed man who was witnessing a biblical obscenity and had been touched by the Holy Spirit to defoliate it off the face of the earth.

"Kenneth W. Starr," James snarled, "is obsessed with getting the president. This is a slimy and scuzzy investigation. This man is not out to get the truth, he's out to get Bill Clinton. . . . I am going to have a war against Ken Starr. You can strap it up! Here we go! Let 'er rip, boy! . . . This guy is serving a master other than the truth. . . . What he ought to do is just crawl under the same rock—tobacco-money rock—that he crawled out from under. Let him go into oblivion as one of the truly sad, tragic, despicable characters of the last twenty years of this century. And thank God this poor man is going to go back to representing cigarette companies, exploding gas tanks or whatever he did for a living before this. . . . I don't like Ken Starr. I don't like one damn thing about him. I don't like his politics, I don't like his sanctimony, I don't like his self-pity, I don't like the people he runs with. I don't like his suck-up, spit-down view of the world, how he kisses up to the powerful and abuses the life out of regular people. . . . I'm like a clown. If you watch the rodeo and the bull riding, and you get thrown from the bull, it's the clown's job to get between the bull and the cowboy. Starr's the bull and the president's the cowboy. . . . Ken Starr can go jump in a lake. He is a citizen of the United States, just like anybody else he can be subject to criticism. If he wants by some kind of fiat to declare himself above the Constitution, I'm not going to pay attention to it. He's a public figure, the people who work for him are public figures. . . . I'm not going to shut up, Mr. Starr, you can tell your hit men over there, I'm not going to shut up. If the Holy See and the United Nations ask me, I'm not going to shut up!"

Snarling . . . hissing . . . crouching . . . kneecapping . . . Mack-trucking . . . T-boning . . . lunging . . . sumo-wrestling . . . *Deliverancing* . . . on all the talk shows, morning, noon, and night, on the TV shows he called "the hot-air circuit," foaming at the mouth, gouging eyes, spilling blood, going for the throat, saying, "I'd rather be a constipated, mangy, flea-bitten dog that howls at the moon than be disloyal to Bill Clinton," threatening to put TV ads on the air against Starr, offering to raise money for campaign ads against Gingrich.

Starr was only one front of his bayou jihad. "Cueball Carville will be rolling into battle against Newt Gingrich," he announced, "because this entire thing has been under the orchestration, supervision, and direction of Newt Gingrich." He went for the jugular, "reminding everyone" that Gingrich had left his first wife and two teenage children, that his first wife had had to take him to court because he refused to provide adequate child support, that Gingrich's church had had to take up a collection to help his kids, that Gingrich had tried to reach a divorce settlement with his wife in her hospital room as she was battling cancer. He reminded people that Gingrich had been fined $300,000 by the House for ethics violations and that Bob Dole, Nixon's soul brother, had loaned him the money.

"Newt Gingrich is making every decision about this investigation,"

James said. "I've tried to work up some human feelings for him. I've really tried. And then I remembered him saying that I—and the people who believe as I do—caused convicted murderer Susan Smith to push her children into the lake when, in fact, she had been living with a Republican official who was a member of the Christian Coalition and who was molesting her. And if that weren't enough, Gingrich then said that this horrible case in Chicago where somebody ripped the unborn child out of a woman happened because of people like me and my friends and those I work for. . . . And then he talks about family responsibility—hell, his own church had to take up a collection for his kids! No Democrat ever blamed a Republican because someone drove her kids into a lake or ripped a fetus out of somebody. I mean, it was a Republican in Kentucky who had the First Lady hung in effigy at a rally. It was a Republican who said the president better have a bodyguard to come to North Carolina for his personal safety—Senator Jesse Helms. . . . The Republican party is dead. The Congressional Republican Party is dead. Those guys don't even know whether to wind their ears or scratch their watches. . . . They're a school bully yard. That's what those congressional Republicans are. They bully everybody. They bully anybody and then somebody comes up and they take one hit and they run. They're crying. And right now they're all under their mama's skirt. This is a school-lunch-cutting, government-closing, right-wing-worshipping, sex-obsessed, president-hating party."

Cueball Carville's crusade was hitting the bull's-eye. Kenneth W. Starr's approval ratings were tumbling. Republican pollsters issued warnings to their candidates about the upcoming November elections. It was as though James, this creepy-looking, nontelegenic freak were tapping into the American public's central nervous system and mainlining it full of outrage. Conservatives like Bill Bennett asked, "Where is the outrage?" And the answer was in front of their held-high noses. Right there. Directed at *them!*

Thanks to a great extent to Corporal Cueball. The long knives knew they were in trouble. Congressman Bob Barr talked about subpoenaing James to testify in front of the House Judiciary Committee. Sam Dash, ethical adviser to the Starr investigation, said James "seems bent on influencing potential witnesses and grand jurors in pending cases" and was "skating close to charges of obstruction of justice." James responded by saying he had "subpoena envy" and vowed, "I ain't gonna shut up! Even if the Vatican and the World Court ask me, I ain't gonna shut up!" Commentator Chris Matthews called what James was doing "road rage, not politics." Defrocked Clinton adviser Dick Morris said James was becoming "a demented fringe advocate, a laughingstock."

He didn't care what they said. He didn't shut up. James turned up the volume. "Henry Hyde," he said, "is a captive of the right wing and has decided to succumb to the will of Jerry Falwell." James issued new reminders: that Senator Phil Gramm had once invested in a porn movie, that right-wing billionaire Richard Mellon Scaife was going to fund Starr's professorial chair at Pepperdine University. Republican minority whip Tom DeLay, James said, was "a fool. This guy has led them down one disaster after another. He's been sniffing too much of his hair spray. He just breathed in too much hair spray." Representative Dan Burton, James said, was "a kook. Let's just call a guy what he is. He's a plain out and out kook. Wasn't me that shot a watermelon up in my back yard. It was Dan Burton."

A month after Corporal Cueball declared his war, only 34 percent of Americans said Starr was impartial. As James kept at it, Starr's approval rating sunk to 11 percent and the Republicans found themselves decimated in the November elections. James characteristically hailed his seeming victory. "The real Nixonian character in here—and people understand that—is Ken Starr. And by the way, Ken Starr is more unpopular now with the American people than Richard Nixon was when he left office."

Then they got him back. The story was out all over the Internet, flying through the E-mails. James Carville had brutally beaten up his wife, Mary Matalin, Rockville, Virginia, police lieutenant Bobby Masters was quoted as saying. The story first broke in the *Montgomery County Ledger.*

It was a hoax. The whole thing was a hoax. Character assassination designed to befoul what James Carville held most sacred in the world: his relationship with Mary. It never happened. There was no Rockville policeman named Bobby Masters. There was no *Montgomery County Ledger.* But the phony story was aired in twenty-five states by American Family Radio, which was owned by the American Family Association, which was headed by the Reverend Donald Wildmon, Christian antiporn advocate and good friend to the Reverend Jerry Falwell.

James decided it was time to go up to Woody Creek to see his bastard big brother. He needed some help here. The fate of the republic was at stake. He realized he hadn't won anything yet. These slime wouldn't quit unless they were liquefied. They were like the Terminator. A million-footed rabble of Bible-spouting robots.

Hunter was an old and wizened warrior who had been fighting them his entire life. Hunter knew what James was dealing with. That's why he had booby traps around his place. That's why he had so many guns. That's why he had so much ammunition in his house. Doc wasn't afraid of facing stark reality . . . nor of acting *starkly*.

They needed some apocalyptic firepower, the bastard and his crazy big brother knew. Something megaton to blast the slimy maggots and the shit-smeared rodents into the Kingdom Come for which the vermin incessantly begged the Lord. At this most fateful moment, the two bald warriors needed their own version of Nixon's "Plumbers," their own Bebe Rebozo who had the cash to buy the incendiary power they so badly needed.

But who had money big enough to buy a nuke? To buy an explosion hellacious enough to send the maggots and the rodents, in flecks and furry bits and pieces . . . heaven-bound?

Well, Hunter had a friend, Jim Mitchell of the infamous Mitchell Brothers, who had made millions . . . from porn.

Porn? These two babbling renegades were going to use porn money to save the republic? Porn money to clear the air of the sticky scent of oral sodomy, masturbation, and nonhygienic, tooth-decaying anilingus? Oh, such a perfectly sweet sixties revenge!

But wait, James had a friend, too, whom he'd met on a movie set. *His* friend had even more money than Jim Mitchell. *His* friend wasn't just a porn mogul, the Mike Todd or Joel Silver of porn. *His* friend was the assassinated Abe Lincoln of porn!

The maggots and the rodents were doomed. The Judgment Day which Pastor Pat Robertson kept urging upon them was finally here. Nuked! Exterminated! Sent to Kingdom Come! By the Abe Lincoln of porn.

[4]

Larry Flynt
Saves the Day

"I'm a dick person," Monica said to Linda Tripp. "I'm like hot to trot for the Big Creep."

Blacks were adamant, women were angry, but removal from office was still a possibility until Larry Flynt rolled his wheelchair alongside White House counsel Charles Ruff's in defense of Bill Clinton. Ruff was eloquent; Flynt was prurient. Ruff was inspiring; Flynt was dispiriting. Ruff was logical; Flynt was irrational. But in the end, it was Larry Flynt and not Charles Ruff who blackjacked and blackmailed Republicans into finally . . . finally giving it up.

The pornographer saved the president by threatening to reveal other acts of pornography committed by—this time Republican—politicians. Larry Flynt was a hero, a self-appointed, self-financed Kenneth W. Starr. It was Flynt's moment of epiphany: revenge upon the forces that had harassed him, jailed him, and then shot him. He saved the presidency by an act of indecency: extortion. They had forced him to put a pump into his willard and he had come back to cut their nuts off.

His weapon was an ad in the *Washington Post* that offered $1 million for information, photographs, and videotapes pertaining to the sexual indiscretions of Republican congressmen or senators. It was like hurling a lighted match into the tank of a gasoline truck. The blast was heard in every cubicle, office, cloakroom, and restaurant on the Beltway. Shrieks of outrage and alarm were heard on the Sunday-morning talk shows.

Salon magazine had already exposed Henry Hyde's extramarital affair. An announced *Vanity Fair* piece had revealed Dan Burton's illegitimate son. An Idaho newspaper had headlined the militia-defending Helen Chenoweth's six-year extramarital affair. The Bible thumpers were already taking a beating. And now here was Flynt, offering a fortune for dirt on people whose Christian Coalition supporters couldn't . . . wouldn't . . . tolerate much dirt. Flynt was turning the Christian Fundamentalists on their own swords. The pornographer would find the dirt, but it would be the fundamentalists who'd be unable to tolerate, let alone support, a man cheating on his wife or being at the center of a sexual threesome.

What frightened Republicans in Washington most was Flynt himself, the Caliban from the Ohio River Valley, a hillbilly shit-kicker who knew all about coldcocking someone with a roll of nickels or the butt end of a gun, a man who'd been fighting Republicans his whole sinful, miscreant life, a man angry, wealthy, and shrewd.

He was born in a hollow in Licksville, Kentucky, in Magoffin County, always one of the poorest in America. It was an area so rural that when one of its residents saw the first airplane, she said, "Oh, Lord, I knew you was comin', but I didn't know it was goin' to be so soon." When he was seven, little Larry Flynt said to his dad, "Betcha can't guess what I did. I just fucked Imogene!"—one of his first girlfriends. At nine, he had sex with a chicken, told by his friends that "its egg bag was as hot as a girl's pussy" and that "chickens wiggle around a lot more."

As a teenager, he was assaulted by a policeman who was a pedophile. At fifteen, he joined the army. His army tour complete at seventeen, he joined the navy. He ran whiskey and sold Bibles in his off-duty hours. Assigned to the carrier *Enterprise*, he was in the room when JFK was there on a visit. He wanted to shake the president's hand. So, to get his attention, in a metaphorical moment that would resonate through his entire life, Larry Flynt *stepped on JFK's toe.*

He started reading self-help books by Napoleon Hill, such as *Think and Grow Rich*. At a French whorehouse, he picked all twenty of the girls, had them strip naked and bend over to their ankles . . . and went down the line until his back went into spasms. He started taking amphetamines by the handful and drinking bourbon by the gallon. He married a young woman, and, discovering she was unfaithful to him, he fired a gun at her. He divorced her. He was sent to a state psychiatric hospital. He was given extensive electroshock therapy. He was eighteen years old.

He went into the bar business in Dayton, Ohio, and bought an old place called the Kiwi. He changed its name to Hillbilly Haven, put Hank Williams and Johnny Cash on the jukebox, and constructed a horseshoe pit in the backyard. It was the kind of place where at the end of the evening the floor was covered in beer and blood.

He prospered and bought other bars in the Dayton area. He almost killed a man when he brought the butt of his gun down between the man's eyes and the gun went off. He almost killed another man when he kicked him over and over again in the groin, the ribs, the stomach, and the face. He hit a man so hard once that the trigger guard of his gun bent and crushed his finger, taking a chunk of flesh out of it.

He set up a bar in Dayton called the Hustler Club, which featured topless go-go dancers. "I'm selling pussy by the glass and my customers don't care about the price of drinks," he said. He was making a lot of money and started other Hustler clubs around Ohio. He was doing so much speed, he'd go for four days without sleep. Sometimes he'd have sex with a different woman every four or five hours. "Have I fucked her yet?" he asked his brother once about a woman who looked familiar. His secretary kept count one week and told him he'd had sex with eighteen women. When Larry Flynt felt tired or stressed, he'd say, "I gotta go fuck somebody."

Bored with bars, he went into the magazine business. His idea was: "If you get models to spread their legs a little wider, you'll sell more magazines." He called his new magazine *Hustler*. "Anybody can be a playboy and have a penthouse, but it takes a man to be a hustler." He made some noise when he displayed a model in his new magazine with red-white-and-blue pubic hair. He made more noise with the magazine's first "pink shot." "Her vagina was open like a flowering rose, fragile and pink." He shook the whole country up in August 1975, when he published high-quality color photographs of Jackie Onassis nude. Even the governor of Ohio was caught buying a copy.

He fell in love with a young woman, Althea Leasure, a dancer at one of his clubs. Her father had killed her entire family. She grew up in orphanages, "where the nuns used to push my face into their crotch." At seventeen, Althea was already shooting heroin. Larry Flynt married her. Their arrangement was that he could have sex with any other woman but he couldn't kiss any other woman. Althea could have sex with any woman—she preferred women—but no other men. "We were happy," he said. "I slept with a lot of women. She slept with a lot of women." Althea loved him so much that she told him if he ever fell on hard times, she'd go out on the street and whore for him. Larry Flynt loved her so much that he made her the number-two person at *Hustler* magazine.

They moved to Columbus, the capitol of Ohio, and moved into a mansion once owned by a former governor. They put bulletproof glass on all the windows. In the basement, Larry had a three-foot replica of the chicken he'd had sex with as a child. In July 1976, in Cincinnati, he was charged with "pandering, obscenity, and organized crime"—all for publishing *Hustler*. "As far as I know," Flynt said of the prosecutor, "he couldn't tell a clitoris from a rutabaga." He called Ohio "the place where the dumb come to die." One friend, the novelist Harold Robbins, said that the prosecutor "reminds me of a marine drill sergeant, but he reminds me of the kind who, after kicking the shit out of some young recruit, would try to fuck him while making up."

The prosecutor *did* wear marine combat boots to court. He accused Flynt of "depicting Santa Claus in a lewd and shameful manner" in a cartoon that showed Santa with a monstrous erection. (The caption said, "Ho! Ho! Ho!") The prosecutor said *Hustler* was "the nightmare of a degenerate." Flynt was sentenced to twenty-five years in prison (later reversed by an appellate court). "Are we really living in a free country?" Larry Flynt asked as deputies hustled him off to jail.

Jimmy Carter's evangelist sister, Ruth Carter Stapleton, called Larry Flynt to talk to him about Jesus. She told him she even had fantasies about having sex with Jesus. He and Althea went to see her in their new "pussy pink" jet. They liked each other. On another flight in the pink jet—with Ruth but without Althea—Larry Flynt saw God. God was in a white robe and sandals and with him was the apostle Paul. A little guy with a beard, Lenny Bruce, was there with God, too. Larry saw somebody in a wheelchair and realized he was seeing himself in his vision. He freaked. Ruth stayed with him that night and held his hand, but Larry didn't strip her and tell her to bend over to her ankles. He told Althea about seeing God and Althea said, "The Lord may have entered your life, but twenty million dollars a year just walked out the door. Does this mean you'll be pushing dildos *and* crucifixes?"

In March 1978, Larry had to go to a small town in Georgia, Lawrenceville, where another obscenity indictment had been filed against *Hustler*. He was walking toward the courthouse with his lawyers when he heard gunshots. He felt like "a hot poker had been pushed" through his stomach. Then he was struck by a second bullet in the back. Eleven surgeries had to be performed to stop his bleeding. But he couldn't move his legs. A bullet had passed through the clump of nerves at the base of his spine.

For the rest of his life, he would be in the wheelchair he had seen in his vision. He was in excruciating pain. "No one could get an erection while suspended in a vat of boiling water." He went from one hospital to another, seeking relief for his pain. "I had been disemboweled and hung on a meat hook in my grandpa's smokehouse. I cried, screamed, and begged for relief."

He and Althea moved to Los Angeles and bought a house in Bel Air that had been owned by Errol Flynn, then Robert Stack, then Tony Curtis, then Sonny and Cher. Althea was running the magazine. Larry was eating Dilaudid, Valium, Percocet, Librium, Demerol, morphine, and drinking the morphine-cocaine compound for the terminally ill, the Brompton's cocktail. He overdosed regularly. He was rushed to the emergency room by ambulance six times. Twice, his heart stopped.

He was sued by Bob Guccione, publisher of *Penthouse*, and his girlfriend Kathy Keeton. Larry had run a cartoon of Guccione that suggested he was gay. He'd run another cartoon, this one of Keeton, suggesting she'd gotten syphilis from Guccione. Neither Guccione nor Keeton got the joke. Keeton's case wound up in front of the Supreme Court. Larry wanted to represent himself, but he wasn't allowed to by the Court. He sat in the audience and yelled, "You're nothing but eight assholes and a token cunt!" Chief Justice Warren Burger pointed to him and said, "Arrest that man!" They arrested him. Larry Flynt took his custom dress shirt off, and underneath it was a T-shirt that said FUCK THIS COURT! He had a limo outside with American flags all over the fenders.

At another court date, he wore an American flag as a diaper. He was, of course, always in his wheelchair and almost always dangerously loaded on drugs. He was arrested for desecrating the flag. At his hearing, he spat at the judge. The judge had him gagged. When Larry promised to behave, the bailiff took his gag off.

As soon as it was off, Larry told the judge, "Go fuck yourself!" The judge yelled, "I'm sentencing you to six months in a federal psychiatric prison! Get out of my courtroom!" Larry screamed, "Give me more, you chickenshit son of a bitch! Is that the best you can do?" The judge yelled, "Twelve months!" Larry screamed, "Give me more, motherfucker! Is that all you can give me, you chickenshit cocksucker!" The judge yelled, "Fifteen months!" Larry screamed, "Give me life without parole! You dumb motherfucker! Fuck you in your ass!"

Larry Flynt went to federal prison medical centers in Missouri and North Carolina. He threw his own feces into the face of a prison psychiatrist and screamed, "You motherfucker, you took everything away from me, but you can't take my heart!" He announced from his psychiatric prison that he was running for president and, describing Ronald Reagan, wrote, "Never has this planet ever had such a dumb, fascist, bigoted motherfucker as a world leader." Upon his release from government custody, he announced that all congressmen, senators, and Supreme Court justices would receive free copies of *Hustler*.

In November 1983, he published a satire of Campari's "First Time" advertising campaign. Behind the picture of the Reverend Jerry Falwell were a bottle of Campari and a glass of Campari on the rocks. The headline said JERRY FALWELL TALKS ABOUT HIS FIRST TIME. The text was a fake interview with Falwell.

"Falwell: My first time was in an outhouse outside Lynchburg, Virginia. Interviewer: Wasn't it a little cramped? Falwell: Not after I kicked the goat out. Interviewer: I see. You must tell me all about it. Falwell: I never *really* expected to make it with mom, but then after she showed all the other guys in town such a good time, I figured, 'What the hell!' Interviewer: But your mom? Isn't that a bit odd? Falwell: I don't think so. Looks don't mean that much to me in a woman. Interviewer: Go on. Falwell: Well, we were drunk off our God-fearing asses on Campari, ginger ale and soda—that's called a Fire and Brimstone—at the time. And mom looked better than a Baptist whore with a $100 donation. Interviewer: Campari in the crapper with mom . . . how interesting. Well, how was it? Falwell: The Campari was great, but mom passed out before I could come. Interviewer: Did you ever try it again? Falwell: Sure . . . lots of times. But not in the outhouse. Between mom and the shit, the flies were too much to bear. Interviewer: I meant the Campari. Falwell: Oh, yeah. I always get sloshed before I go out to the pulpit. You don't think I could lay down all that bullshit sober, do you?"

Falwell filed a $45 million libel suit and was represented in court, bizarrely, by *Penthouse*'s attorney, a man who had once referred to the reverend as "Foulwell." His case went all the way to the Supreme Court, and the justices voted, shockingly, eight to zero in favor of Larry Flynt. It should have been the greatest moment of his life, but it was almost an anticlimax. Althea died on June 27, 1987, of AIDS, contracted from either a heroin needle or a blood transfusion. She died in the bathroom next to Larry's bed. He had alerted the nurses that she was in there too long. He couldn't do anything to help her. His wheelchair wasn't next to his bed.

. . .

This was Larry Flynt, the man who announced now, in the year of Bill Clinton's impeachment, a $1 million reward for information about Republicans' sexual indiscretions. Conservative Republicans knew how Larry Flynt felt about conservative Republicans, sometimes even just plain Republicans. They remembered the *Hustler* cartoon showing Gerry Ford and Nelson Rockefeller and Henry Kissinger gang-banging the Statue of Liberty. They remembered the *Hustler* phone-sex ad for Jesse Helms—"Jesse Helms—Phone Sex—Blacks Preferred"—which included Senator Helms's office and home telephone numbers. They remembered the other cartoons of Jerry Falwell. One showed an old lady living in a dump, rats all around her, a can of dog food next to her, writing a letter: "Dear Jerry Falwell, I want to thank you for the inspiration and comfort your television broadcasts give me. I am enclosing the remainder of my Social Security money to help you keep up your fine work, as I know you need it." The other cartoon showed Satan sitting in a high-rise office, barking into a speaker phone, "Send Falwell in here. I want to see the look on the fucker's face." They knew that Larry Flynt knew—finally, after so many years—that the man who'd shot him was a white supremacist angered by an interracial photo spread.

Those in Congress knew how vulnerable they could be if someone was out there offering a million dollars for the sort of information Flynt was looking for. Congress really was, in Bob Dole's words, "Animal House." Rita Jenrette had even described having sex with her husband on the Capitol steps. There were hundreds of offices hidden away in the Capitol Building with crystal chandeliers and comfortable couches and mirrors, fireplaces, and decorated ceilings, rooms simply ideal for an intimate, hands-on chat with a young staffer.

And Speaker Newt Gingrich, God bless him, had restored an old, banned custom. Congressmen could sleep overnight once again in their offices, free to do whatever in-depth research on whichever subject was at hand. They were politicians, for Pete's sake, not saints. Who anywhere could withstand a million dollars' worth of this kind of scrutiny?

Not Newt, certainly, who was once caught bare-assed on top of his desk, conferring with an aide . . . who, it was even now being said, was too chummy with a young legislative aide, Callista Bisek, and allegedly with Arianna Huffington. Not Dick Armey, who was thrice accused of sexual harassment while he was an economics teacher in college. Not Tom DeLay, who'd bounced $5,300 worth of checks on the House bank.

And there was such a *history* of *human* behavior in Congress, too. Representative Dan Crane, caught having an affair with a Senate page . . . Representative Gerry Studds, caught trying to force pages into having sex with him . . . Representative Ken Calvert, a Christian Coalition favorite, caught half-naked in his car, getting a blow job from a heroin-junkie hooker . . . Representative Martin Hoke, caught on television saying, "She has *big* breasts!" about a television producer . . . Representative J. C. Watts, the Republicans' black poster child, exposed as the father of two illegitimate children.

Flynt, those who felt themselves vulnerable soon learned, wasn't fooling around. He was no Nixon-type operative, like the Night Creature's porcine bagman, the private eye Tony Ulasciewicz, who made so many raspy-voiced phone calls from public phone booths that he had to carry a bus conductor's coin belt on his belly. No phone booths for Larry Flynt! Larry King was his Ma Bell. "I have eight investigations going on," Flynt told King. "If they materialize, the Republican party is going to be in shambles."

He'd brought in a crack investigative reporter, Dan Moldea, who'd exposed Ronald Reagan's questionably close ties to Hollywood mogul Lew Wasserman and Teamster money, to run his million-dollar project. Also there to counsel Flynt was Rudy Maxa, a former *Washington Post* gossip columnist, who'd heard all the scuttlebutt through the years. There were rumors, too, which Flynt denied, that he was getting help trying to dig up Republican dirt from Terry Lenzner and Jack Palladino, private eyes who'd been employed by the Clinton campaign to do "opposition research."

Crazy man Flynt was being politically astute about all this, too. He said he was zeroing in especially on those Republicans who were calling for Bill Clinton's removal from office but had sexual skeletons in their own closets. Back off, Larry Flynt was saying. If you're dirty and you're calling for Bill Clinton's removal, I'll get you. It was extortion. What made it scary was that no one knew what Flynt had, what he could come up with, or what a million dollars would buy. It was like the best of thrillers, where the scares come from your imagination and not from what you see up on-screen.

The first development that struck people as odd was Newt Gingrich's resignation. Had it really been caused by the beating the Republicans took in the midterm elections? Or did Newt want to put himself out of the line of fire of any Flynt missiles? (His divorce months later and references to his affair with Callista Bisek would reignite speculation that it was Larry Flynt who'd toppled Newt Gingrich.)

The next development was a bombshell. There was no doubt this time. The incoming speaker, Bob Livingston, who liked to take Cajun knives into congressional meetings, resigned because he had been informed that Larry Flynt had information about him that he was going to publish. Livingston admitted to extramarital affairs, but he wouldn't directly respond to reports in Los Angeles that Flynt had videotapes of him in a threesome. Livingston's wife, Bonnie, called Flynt and begged him not to release the details of her husband's philandering. Flynt agreed. "The guy's resigned, you know?" he said. "What's the point?"

Bob Barr was next. The smug, self-righteous "prosecutor from hell," another Christian Coalition darling, denied that he had talked his ex-wife into aborting their child and had paid for it. But Larry Flynt had affidavits from Barr's ex-wife swearing to it. One of the staunchest abortion foes in America . . . caught urging the abortion of his own child.

As impeachment went from the House to the Senate, and as Flynt and his team kept digging, there was a noticeable shift on the part of some senators and other Republicans, who suddenly wanted to censure but not remove Bill Clinton. Commentators said the midterm elections had caused the shift, or the Gerald Ford–Jimmy Carter op-ed piece in the *New York Times*, but the more cynical wondered what effect Larry Flynt was having on the Senate trial.

Why would Pat Robertson suddenly do an about-face and come out for censure instead of removal? Why would Trent Lott suddenly work with Tom Daschle to limit the House prosecutors' efforts? Why would a senator like Richard Shelby of Alabama, who loathed Bill Clinton, suddenly start acting like the moderate he wasn't? Perhaps the real question was, What did Larry Flynt know and what would he do with it?

There was little need for anyone to point out how prone senators had always been to unsenatorial behavior. There was Senator John Tower, drunk, chasing his aides around his desk, his fly unzipped . . . Senator Joseph Montoya, who had a special secretary, whose only duty was to give him a blow job every afternoon . . . Senator Orrin Hatch, who'd had a former porn star named Missy Manners on his staff . . . Senator Chuck Robb, doing coke and having sex at the Pierre with twenty-one-year-old beauty queen Tai Collins (well, he *was* married to Linda Bird Johnson) . . . Senator Strom Thurmond, still known, at age ninety-six, around the Senate as "the Sperminator" . . . Senator Daniel Inouye, reprimanded by the Senate for unwanted sexual advances to aides. . . .

When it was all over and Bill Clinton stayed in office, nobody thanked Larry Flynt, the hillbilly kid from Licksville, Kentucky, for saving the presidency of the hillbilly kid from Hope, Arkansas. Groups like the National Organization for Women, who so desperately wanted Bill Clinton to stay in office, didn't say thank you to the man some feminists described as "every bit as dangerous as Hitler." The media patted members of the Senate on the back for their temperance and moderation.

Only one person acknowledged what Larry Flynt had done, and he did it with his action and not his words. John F. Kennedy, Jr., invited him as his guest to the very public National Correspondents Association dinner in Washington. The son of the woman whom Larry Flynt displayed nude in *Hustler* sat next to the man in the wheelchair, who'd built his empire on Jackie's naked flesh. There had to be an overwhelming moral imperative for JFK, Jr., to be sitting there next to America's immoral pornographer.

[5]

The Ace of Spades

"I have a crush on Vernon Jordan I think," Monica said.
"Oh, that's not at all surprising," Linda Tripp said. "He's very crushable."
"I'm going to tell the Big Creep," Monica said. "That would make him jealous."

Another centimeter and Vernon Jordan would have had to pull his own wheelchair alongside those of Larry Flynt and Charles Ruff to defend Bill Clinton. Like Larry Flynt, Vernon Jordan had taken a .30-06 bullet in his body, too, and for the same reason as Flynt: racial prejudice.

But that was a long time ago and it *had nothing to do* with what Kenneth W. Starr was doing to Vernon Jordan now, targeting him in his investigation, thinking in his Mad Hatter folly that Vernon Jordan would compromise or implicate the president of the United States. *Or did it?* Was Starr taking a shot at Vernon Jordan the same way the Klansman, that American Nazi party member, had taken a shot at him in Fort Wayne, Indiana, in 1980?

Starr didn't have a prayer. Even if he were right, even if Vernon Jordan and Bill Clinton had conspired to obstruct justice, to convince Monica to lie in the Paula Jones case, there was not a flicker of possibility that Vernon Jordan would cop to it. He was a man who had *taken a bullet* for what he believed in, and he and Bill Clinton believed in the same things. He was a man who'd walk down the darkest alley to help a good friend and *do* what had to be done. He was a man who could not only handle himself on the street and in the boardroom and in the locker room and at the dining table; he was a man who took charge, who, by the sheer power of his presence, *overcame.* "We're just buddies," he said about his friend Bill Clinton. "I eat in his kitchen, he eats in mine. If Hillary is in town, she comes to dinner. If he's in town, he comes to breakfast." And Bill Clinton said about his friend Vernon Jordan, "The last thing he'd ever do is betray a friendship. It's good to have a friend like that." Vernon Jordan said, "I always knew he was going to be president." And Bill Clinton said, "What attracted me to Vernon was that he was a very large person, larger than life."

That he was. Standing six foot four in his Brooks Brothers suits, Turnbull & Asser shirts, a Churchillian Davidoff cigar in his hand, Vernon Jordan was a charismatic black man whose oratorical flourishes were as powerful as Martin Luther King, Jr.'s. He could be a macho man in the company of other macho men and he could be dazzlingly, effortlessly seductive in the company of women. He could quote the Bible, slap a back, or tickle a funny bone. He could also fold his arms in front of him and fix his steely gaze on someone and say, "You don't know what the *fuck* you're talking about!" He could be smiling, carefree, *loose*, and then freeze the room with his scowl. He was a student of people and knew what made each one of them tick. He was a man never to be messed with and a man who never forgot. He was Sidney Poitier mixed with Richard Burton. He was who Denzel Washington wanted to be. He *was* what his white boardroom friends called him. Vernon Jordan was the Ace of Spades!

In 1997, sixty-two-year-old Vernon Jordan (or his second wife, Ann, a former assistant professor at the University of Chigago's School of Social Work) was on the board of directors at American Express, Xerox, JCPenney, Dow Jones, Sara Lee, Revlon, Bankers Trust, RJR Nabisco, Union Carbide, and Ryder. He was a director of the Ford Foundation and the Brookings Institution. He had received a fellowship to Harvard's Institute of Politics and an honorary degree from Brandeis. He was one of three executive partners in the most powerful political law firm in Washington, a firm whose clients included the People's Republic of China, the Chilean Exporter's Association, the government of Colombia, the Korean Foreign Trade Association, and varied Japanese multinationals.

He counted among his friends former president George Bush and former secretaries of state Cyrus Vance and James Baker. "Vernon knows more corporate leaders, more labor heads, more foreign heads of state than anyone I know," said William T. Coleman, Gerald Ford's transportation secretary. His Washington power breakfasts were the stuff of legend, as was the fact that Vernon Jordan chatted with the waiters and the waitresses as much as with his powerful guests. He and Ann were picked as one of America's

"Power Couples" by *Forbes* magazine. Most people in Washington, including Linda Tripp, felt he was the most powerful lawyer in town, making well over a million dollars a year. Yet he never walked into a courtroom or wrote a legal brief. He was a power broker, a problem solver, a fixer.

Rarely seen in the spotlight, the Ace of Spades was always observing . . . whispering . . . backstage. He didn't much like the glare of the spotlight, turning down Bill Clinton's offer to be the first black attorney general of the United States, turning down a seat on the Foreign Intelligence Committee, turning down being commissioner of the National Football League. When IBM needed a new CEO, they went to Vernon Jordan—to tell them whom to hire.

He was comfortable in the offstage tabernacles of the powerful and the wealthy, like the Century Club in New York or the Bohemian Grove in northern California, though he had a wicked sense of humor, which he displayed at these moneyed *white* places. The first time he ate at the long-segregated Century Club, he ordered watermelon. Asked to give the headliner Lakeside Talk at the Bohemian Grove, he titled his speech "The Coming Revolution": "I figured that would interest people or scare them enough to boost attendance. There was always the possibility that some people might think I would show up wearing bandoliers and carrying grenades. But I was with the Urban League, not the Black Panthers." He was the Ace of Spades, hobnobbing with the powerful and the privileged but letting them know that he knew that *white* boys were the ones he was dealing with.

With the possible exception of deputy White House counsel Bruce Lindsey, Vernon Jordan was Bill Clinton's best friend. As former White House counsel Lloyd Cutler put it, "Presidents need to have someone they can relax with. He is a good, loyal friend." William Coleman said, "He is as close to the president as anyone I know since Bobby Kennedy was so close to his brother."

Their friendship went all the way back to the seventies, when Vernon Jordan traveled around Arkansas as the head of the National Urban League and met Bill Clinton at a fund-raiser. After his election, Bill Clinton's first dinner in Washington was at Vernon Jordan's home. The Clintons and the Jordans had Christmas Eve dinner every year there, as well. The Ace of Spades and the president golfed together all the time, chatted twice a day. Vernon and Ann and Hillary and Bill even vacationed together. Vernon ran Bill's 1992 transition team and Ann was cochairman of Bill's 1996 inauguration.

It was the Ace of Spades to whom the president turned when he wanted to find out if Colin Powell was interested in being his secretary of state . . . when he needed a representative to attend the inauguration of Taiwan's first democratically elected president . . . when the way had to be smoothed for Les Aspen's resignation as secretary of defense . . . when Lloyd Cutler had to be approached to replace Bernie Nussbaum as White House counsel . . . when Web Hubbell, about to resign as associate attorney general to face criminal charges, needed a job. When Vince Foster committed suicide and Bill Clinton went down to his widow's house, it was Vernon Jordan who went with him and who then stayed with him in the White House until two o'clock in the morning.

Even White House staffers knew how much clout the Ace of Spades packed. When George Stephanopoulos wanted an office in the White House closer to the president's, directly within the Oval Office suite, he didn't ask Bill Clinton; he asked Vernon Jordan, and Vernon Jordan got the office for him. (Stephanopoulos called him "our wise man.") Perhaps the closeness between Vernon Jordan and Bill Clinton—the *brotherhood* between them—was most vividly portrayed in the photograph of the two of them that Vernon Jordan often showed friends. They were standing shoulder-to-shoulder, singing "Lift Every Voice and Sing," often called "the black national anthem," and Bill Clinton had inscribed it: "From the only WASP who knows the lyrics."

Vernon Jordan and Bill Clinton were also best friends on a male level. "What we talk about mostly is pussy" was Vernon Jordan's response to a reporter who asked him what he and the president talked about on the golf course. He was as sexual a man as Bill Clinton; long known as a "lady-killer," who was sometimes overheard at banquets mock-whispering about some young woman's finer points. He could be heard at those same dinners chortling over titillating gossip or letting his voice soar in the telling of a bawdy tale.

He didn't seem all that concerned about his reputation: "I like people. I've always liked people. I like all kinds of people and I'm not going to stop liking people. The interpretation of people's thoughts about that has absolutely nothing to do with my professional responsibilities." Arms folded and scowling, he had another response, too: "I know who I am. I am the custodian of my morality and ethics. I am, on that, answerable to myself." His wife didn't seem to mind his reputation, either: "I'm sure women find him attractive. *I* do."

Sometimes Vernon Jordan just laughed about his reputation and said, "Nothing wrong with a little locker room talk." His reputation extended to his interest in finding work for young people, especially young women. "Much is required of those to whom much is given," Vernon Jordan said about his job-placement efforts.

A young woman for whom he'd gotten a job said, "When you're a woman, an attractive woman, and Vernon does something for you, there is an expectation that there will be some extracurricular activities." Another young woman said, "He's flirtatious. That's just his style. I don't remember anybody hostile saying, 'Vernon hit on me.' I just can't think of a time people were angry about it. People roll their eyes and say, 'Oh, that's Vernon.' " Even Monica felt his sexual power. "Give him a hug for me," she told Jordan, talking about the president. "I don't hug men," Vernon Jordan told her.

For Washington insiders, there was one public moment that was all-revealing about the intimacy of the relationship between the president of the United States and the Ace of Spades. It happened at a state dinner in 1995. The president was sitting next to a hot young blonde, and sitting next to her was Vernon Jordan. The president observed the Ace of Spades flirting with her and said, "I saw her first, Vernon!" And Vernon Jordan and Bill Clinton laughed and laughed.

"Vernon knows a lot of stuff about the president and his personal life," former White House press secretary Dee Dee Myers said. "But he'll never trade on it. Vernon understands how power works better than anyone I know. He talks to the president about everything, I think, but it would diminish his power if he talked about it. He protects the president, his friend." Mary Frances Berry of the U.S. Commission on Civil Rights said, "Vernon is an old hand. He knows the issues. He knows what the political problems are. He knows where the bodies are buried."

This was the extraordinary man . . . Bill Clinton's brilliant, battle-scarred, distinguished, hard-nosed, sexual, loving black brother . . . whom Kenneth W. Starr was counting on to finger the president of the United States for obstruction of justice.

He was named for George Washington's Mount Vernon home . . . lucky that he wasn't named, like one of his brothers, for Warren Harding. He grew up in Atlanta's segregated projects—his father was a mail clerk for the army. His mother ran Mary Jordan's Catering Service for the wealthy whites of

Atlanta. He was his mother's son. "If you got some money," she told him, "you can do most anything you want. . . . Never forget your base, never forget where you came from. But even if you were born in the projects, always carry your smile, and that smile will carry you a long way." When Vernon Jordan came back from someplace, his mother would ask him, "What did you see? What did you hear? What did you learn?"

As a little boy, he stayed close to the projects. "You knew there was colored water and there was white water," he would say later. "You knew you sat upstairs in the theater and it was a way of life. You understood that. It never meant you accepted it." When he was ten, he saw the white world. Vernon Jordan went with his mother to the homes of the prominent wealthy, where she catered parties. He either bartended or helped her in the kitchen. He would sneak out of the kitchen sometimes to watch the wealthy white people. Watching a group of lawyers at Atlanta's white Lawyers' Club made a lifelong impression on him. "I liked the way they dressed. I liked their manners. I admired their bearing, the way they articulated the issues, if not the substance of their positions."

The schools he attended were as segregated as the bathrooms, the streetcars, and the lunch counters. Vernon Jordan studied hard, got excellent grades, and played basketball. He was accepted at DePauw University in Greencastle, Indiana. He was the only black in his class, one of five in the school. He appeared in the school play and even wrote a play about white racism. He continued playing basketball. He was vice president of the school's Democratic Club. He was a political science major, with a minor in history and speech. He won first prize for oratory in a state contest. He graduated with distinction. He wanted to go to law school but didn't have the money. He went to Chicago and became a bus driver, working sixteen hours a day, and got into Howard University.

Graduating with honors from Howard, he got job offers from many of the big East Coast white law firms. He turned them all down. He went back to Atlanta. He hurled his formidable intelligence and energy into being a part of the civil rights movement. He became a clerk in the law office of distinguished civil rights attorney Donald Hollowell. His personal hero was another Atlanta black civil rights attorney, A. T. Walden, who for years had argued doomed cases in front of white racist judges. "I can remember him standing erect and tall. To see him was to want to walk like him and talk like him."

In 1961, as a twenty-four-year-old law clerk, he accompanied Charlayne

Hunter, the first black admitted to the University of Georgia, to class. News footage showed a tall Hollywood-handsome young black man using his body as a shield and a wedge to get the frightened Hunter through a sea of crazed, spitting white faces screaming, "Die, nigger, die!"

At a moment in history when racial violence threatened to engulf America, Vernon Jordan was forming his own philosophy. He rejected the Panthers and Rap Browns and Stokely Carmichaels, who urged picking up the gun and cried, "Burn, baby, burn!" Vernon Jordan believed in political power as the road to equality, in voter registration, and in the economic boycott. He believed in the brain and not the firebomb. He believed in the idea of a black intellectual elite of social activists who would fight verbally in courtrooms and boardrooms to ease the burden of the less educated. He believed in the ballot box, not the soapbox. "You've got to have an intellectual, working black elite," he said, "and you can't get that standing on the corner."

He joined the NAACP and traveled all over the South, calling for economic boycotts of companies and industries that wouldn't hire blacks and coordinating voter registration drives. He became director of the voter education project of the Southern Regional Council. He worked relentlessly, driving himself, sleeping in church halls, *forcing* black people by sheer will to register to vote. By 1968, the South had nearly 2 million new black voters, the number of black elected officials had jumped tenfold, and Vernon Jordan was a nationally known civil rights leader.

Author Taylor Branch remembered him: "He had an aura of being luminous and glamorous as he was supervising people registering voters five years after it had gone out of fashion." The Reverend Ralph Abernathy called him "one of the ablest and articulate voices in the civil and human rights movement." Vernon Jordan was so well respected within the movement, even by black nationalists, that he became a high-level mediator within the movement itself.

When he was about to run for Congress in 1970, he was asked to become head of the United Negro College Fund. He gave up his own political ambitions to further the cause of black education—which he felt was perhaps the worst of black people's problems. A year later, when Whitney Young, executive director of the National Urban League, drowned, he was asked to replace Young. He accepted.

Vernon Jordan believed that the struggle was shifting from the South to the ghettos of American cities and believed the Urban League could do something to help. He believed that for white corporate America, the Urban League was a much easier alternative than dealing with the more incendiary cries for black power. Vernon Jordan hammered the white corporations for job training and early-education programs. He saw the Urban League as a bridge between white executives and the urban poor.

As Drew S. Days, former director of Civil Rights in the Justice Department, said, "He was able to make an important link between the Civil Rights Movement and the corporate world. He was hard-nosed in showing corporate leaders why it was often in their interests to provide support." A corporate leader who worked with him at the time said, "Vernon cannot be manipulated. He's a tough customer. You can never get Vernon to do something because you want him to do it. He knows how to say no."

Vernon Jordan soon had a $100 million budget to work with, supplied by corporate America and the federal government. "If I do a good job here," he said, "black people are not the only beneficiary, so is the country. The country has a vested interest in black people doing well." When he was not in boardrooms, hammering corporate execs, he was making speeches across America, urging Americans to do something about the nightmare of existence in the inner city.

One of those speeches took place on May 29, 1980, at the Marriott Inn in Fort Wayne, Indiana, where the Fort Wayne chapter of the Urban League was having its dinner. In his speech, he condemned "the blind enthusiasm of the country's move to the right, especially the move toward a balanced budget at the expense of social programs." At the dinner afterward, he met thirty-six-year-old Martha C. Coleman, a member of the Urban League's Fort Wayne board of directors, a secretary at International Harvester, a white divorcée who had been married to a black man. After the dinner, Vernon Jordan went to Coleman's house, where, according to her, they had coffee and played the stereo.

At two o'clock that morning, she drove him back to his room at the Marriott. On the way there, stopped at a red light two miles from the hotel, a car full of white teenagers pulled up next to them. They started screaming obscenities and racial epithets at the interracial couple and drove off. Coleman drove him to the hotel, and when Vernon Jordan got out of the car, a .30-06 bullet (the kind used to hunt bear and deer) struck him in the lower back, just left of the spinal cord.

"As soon as the projectile entered, there was an explosive effect like nothing I've ever seen before," an emergency room doctor said. "It was purely a miracle that it missed the spinal column. Had it exploded a millionth of a second later, there would be absolutely no chance for survival." The gunshot ripped a fist-size hole in Vernon Jordan's back. He underwent five surgeries.

Fort Wayne police, seeing that he had been with a white woman and knowing she had been married to a black man, called it "a domestic-type thing." They made much of the fact that he had spent hours alone with Coleman at her house "with the stereo playing." John E. Jacob, executive vice president of the Urban League, held a press conference, saying the organization had "grown increasingly disturbed over the diversion of public attention away from the horrible nature of the crime and onto matters of speculation, innuendo, and gossip."

Characteristically, in one of his first public statements after the shooting, Vernon Jordan said, "It is significant to note that, since over the years many blacks died on a highway because no hospital would take them because they were black, here in 1980 I would get shot in a little town like Fort Wayne and be rushed to a hospital where the internist in the operating room was black, the anesthesiologist was black, and the surgeon was black. Now what that suggests is that there has been some progress."

The man who'd waited for two hours on a grassy knoll to shoot Vernon Jordan was a thirty-year-old drifter from Mobile, Alabama, who'd renamed himself Joseph Paul Franklin—in tribute to Benjamin Franklin and Paul Joseph Goebbels, Hitler's propaganda minister. He was a sometime member of the American Nazi party and the Ku Klux Klan. He had the grim reaper and the American eagle tattooed on his forearms.

He had already sent a threatening note to President Carter and had visited Chicago, hunting for Jesse Jackson. He would say many years later that he "just happened to be" in Fort Wayne when he heard that Vernon Jordan would be speaking there. His intent was to start a race war in America, and he was so angry that Fort Wayne police were calling Jordan's shooting a "domestic-type thing" that he quickly drove to Cincinnati and gunned down two black teenagers.

Born James Clayton Vaughn, he was unable to see with his right eye at birth. Both his parents were alcoholics. He rarely went to school. "I made very low grades. The only time I got an A was in conduct. I was one of those really quiet kids." At eleven, staying with his uncle in Georgia, he was already carrying a loaded rifle as he roamed the woods. "I was just pretending like I was shooting, but I wasn't really shooting it." At twelve, he shot a pistol for the first time. At sixteen, his brother gave him a 16-gauge shotgun, took him into the woods, and taught him how to hunt.

For the rest of his life, he "always had a gun." He watched hundreds of television Westerns and would make believe that he was a cowboy. He never liked the sheriff; it was the outlaw he felt himself to be. He liked to dress up as a cowboy, but he always dressed in black—black cowboy hat, black boots, black jeans. In his midteens, he started reading Nazi literature. "Once you consciously go over the stuff over and over again, it just goes down in your conscience and you begin to think that blacks and Jews aren't even people at all."

By the time he left Mobile, at seventeen, he had developed a deep hatred for blacks, especially those who were dating whites. He got married twice. Both marriages lasted a year. Both wives said he'd beaten them.

On September 21, 1976, he turned up in a Washington suburb. He saw a black man and a white woman walking down the street and sprayed them with chemical Mace. He jumped bail and never stood trial.

Early in 1977, he set a bomb that destroyed the Beth Shalom Synagogue in Chattanooga, Tennessee. He was also connected a month later to the bombing of a Washington home belonging to an Israeli lobbyist.

He started robbing banks like the outlaws in his Westerns to support himself. Before he was caught, he'd robbed sixteen of them.

Later in 1977, he was driving his 1972 Capri through Madison, Wisconsin. He was stuck in traffic. The car ahead of him was driven by a black man. A white woman was sitting next to the man. They got through the traffic, but the same car was still ahead of him, driving slowly. He kept honking at them to speed up. The man pulled over to the side and came to Joseph Paul Franklin's car. Franklin had just robbed a bank. He had a stolen gun with him. "That was done on the spot of the moment. I hadn't planned it. I just whipped the pistol out and shot him right there." He shot the woman, too, and drove off. "It just happened to be two people I totally hated. Once whites begin having sex with blacks, they aren't even human."

Still in 1977, he shot and killed a Jewish man outside a synagogue in Missouri.

In February 1978, he shot and killed an interracial couple strolling through an Atlanta neighborhood.

In July 1978, he shot a black man in Chattanooga as the man was speaking to his white girlfriend outside a pizza parlor.

"It was my mission. I just felt like I was engaged in war with the world. My mission was to get rid of as many evildoers as I could. If I did not, then I would be punished. I felt that God instructed me to kill people."

In 1979, he shot a black cabdriver who was speaking to a white woman in Atlanta's Piedmont Park.

On May 29, 1980, hearing that Vernon Jordan was in Fort Wayne, he parked his car on the side of Interstate 69, raised the hood as though he was having car trouble, and walked up the hill to the grassy knoll facing the Marriott Inn.

In June 1980, he shot two black teenagers in Cincinnati, Ohio. In July 1980, he killed two black hitchhikers in West Virginia. In August 1980, he killed two black men and two white women jogging together in Salt Lake City, Utah.

On October 28, 1980, he was finally caught in Lakeland, Florida, after he'd sold his plasma to a blood bank for five dollars. His wanted poster had been sent to all blood centers. President Carter, whom he'd threatened earlier by mail, was due in Lakeland on a campaign stop hours after his arrest. Police officers said they "could not rule out the possibility" that Franklin's presence in Lakeland at the same time was "more than coincidence."

All told, he would be charged with twenty murders.

In 1997, he was on death row in Missouri, still awaiting execution. Law-enforcement officials from across the country were coming to interview him, trying to tie him in to other killings. He seemed to enjoy the attention. "Blacks still aren't my favorite people," he said. Prosecutors called him an "animal," but he smiled and said, "I'm Jesse James or Billy the Kid. I look at myself as an outlaw of the Wild West. They didn't go around killing innocent women. I would never do that, either."

Sometimes Joseph Paul Franklin seemed to be holding court. He told Atlanta detectives who wanted to visit him that he'd only talk to them if they brought a "pretty woman" for him to gaze at during the interview. They brought a female deputy and Franklin stared at her breasts and leered and licked his lips for two hours.

When Kenneth W. Starr's Mad Hatter folly finally came to fruition . . . when the preacher's son got the Ace of Spades up in front of his Republican congressional snipers, what happened was that Vernon Jordan *did to them* what sniper Joseph Paul Franklin had tried to do to him: He blew them away. He blew them to smithereens. He did not miss the spinal cord.

Q: Was your assistance to Ms. Lewinsky, which you have described, in any way dependent upon her doing anything whatsoever in the Paula Jones case?

A: No.

Q: And that is exactly the point, that you looked at getting Ms. Lewinsky a job as an assignment rather than just something that you were going to be a reference for.

A: I don't know whether I looked upon it as an assignment. Getting jobs for people is not unusual for me, so I don't view it as an assignment. I just view it as something that is part of what I do.

Q: During the course of the meeting with Ms. Lewinsky, what did you learn about her?

A: Enthusiastic, quite taken with herself and her experience. Bubbly, effervescent, bouncy, confident. Actually, I sort of had the same impression that you House managers had of her when you met with her. You came out and said she was impressive, and so we came out about the same place.

Q: And did she relate to you the fact that she liked being an intern because it put her close to the president?

A: I have never seen a White House intern who did not like being a White House intern, and so her enthusiasm for being a White House intern was about like the enthusiasm of White House interns—they liked it.

Q: Did she make reference to someone in the White House being uncomfortable when she was an intern, and she thought that people did not want her there?

A: She felt unwanted—there is no question about that. As to who did not want her there and why they did not want her there, that was not my business.

· · ·

Q: And sometime after your meeting on December 11 with Ms. Lewinsky, did you have another conversation with the president?

A: You *do* understand that a conversation between me and the president was not an unusual circumstance.

Q: I understand that.

A: All right.

Q: Let me be more specific. Did he [Clinton] indicate that he knew about the fact that she had lost her job at the White House, and she wanted to get a job in New York?

A: He was obviously aware that she had lost her job in the White House, because she was working at the Pentagon. He was also aware that she wanted to work in New York, in the private sector, and understood that that is why she was having conversations with me. There is no doubt about that.

Q: And he thanked you for helping her.

A: There is no question about that, either.

Q: And on either of these conversations that I've referenced . . . did the president tell you that Ms. Monica Lewinsky was on the witness list in the Jones case?

A: He did not.

Q: And did you consider this information to be important in your efforts to be helpful to Ms. Lewinsky?

A: I never thought about it.

Bang! A single bullet fired from a grassy knoll! Vernon Jordan had won a Purple Heart in what he considered his war for social progress. He had been decorated with the medal of honor by black people, many white people, by presidents, by corporations. And Kenneth W. Starr and his white-bread congressmen thought they were going to beat up on him?

In October 1998, Joseph Paul Franklin told an Ohio judge, "You are just a representative of the satanic system and you'll be judged by Jesus Christ."

"I won't have twenty notches on my gun when I am," the judge responded.

Joseph Paul Franklin had by then admitted one more shooting: the March 1978 wounding of *Hustler* publisher Larry Flynt in Lawrenceville, Georgia. He had seen a pornographic interracial photo spread in *Hustler*, Franklin said, and he "just happened to be" in Lawrenceville when Flynt's trial began. *In the right place at the right time . . .* It wasn't the porn that had bothered him; it was the interracial couple.

Within the context of Bill Clinton's impeachment, it was a heart-stopping coincidence. Bill Clinton was saved from removal from office to a great extent through the efforts of two men—the Ace of Spades, who stuck by him, and the pornographer, who scared the bejesus out of all of Washington. *And the same man had shot both of them!* What if he had been a better shot? What would have happened to Bill Clinton then? What if Jesse Jackson had been in Chicago when Franklin went looking for him?

What if Franklin hadn't been busted by the time President Carter got to Lakeland?

Joseph Paul Franklin represented everything my generation loathed and had tried to change in American society: racism, anti-Semitism, the cowboy myth, the love of guns, the sexism, the wife battering. He was a twisted, demonic foot soldier who didn't like blacks and interracial couples any more than did the Night Creature, the Ratwoman, the Bag Lady of Sleaze, or Führer Man.

Hillary spoke of a "vast right-wing conspiracy," and many of us were sure she had used the phrase opportunistically, pragmatically, mendaciously to save her husband and their presidency. But were we really supposed to believe that the man who named himself for Goebbels "just happened to be" in Fort Wayne, Indiana, and Lawrenceville, Georgia, when Vernon Jordan and Larry Flynt were there? This wasn't some factoid Oliver Stone had conjured to con us into buying a ticket. Or a piece of gonzo Hunter Thompson had emitted from his fevered brain. *This was real.*

And if it was all part of a great, unseen, and continuing shadow war for the heart and soul of America, what commentators euphemistically referred to as "the culture war," then where would it end? JFK went down and so did Bobby and so did Martin and so did Medgar and so did Vernon Jordan and Larry Flynt. And Bill Clinton almost went down just as surely, but in a different way, saved by men who had already taken bullets. From one grassy knoll to another . . . where would the next grassy knoll be?

(6)

Al Gorf
Loves Tipper Galore

The day the *Starr Report* was released was one of the saddest and happiest days of my life.

I knew that the president I'd served and admired would be left with a legacy most accurately characterized by the kind of rock and roll lyrics that had so outraged Tipper. And I knew that, finally and forever, I could rid myself of the awful paranoia that in 1993 Bill had victimized Tipper in ways analogous to the manner in which he had abused Monica Lewinsky.

I knew that if anything had happened between them, Ken Starr and his zealous army of investigators would have discovered it. He could have destroyed both Bill *and* me with one report about a vice president cuckolded by his commander in chief. He would have destroyed a love story even greater than the one Erich Segal wrote about us.

The Rock of Gibraltar of my life has been my love for my wife of nearly thirty-three years, the mother of my four children, the woman I first called Tipper Galore after we saw a James Bond movie together when we were in college.

My mother didn't like her at first. "She has no credentials," Mother said, wanting me to date "sophisticated" women from around Boston. But then she didn't like Bill, either. "Bill Clinton is not a nice person; don't associate too closely with him," she said. "He grew up in a very *provincial* atmosphere."

I love my dear old mother, but she's a professional snob and she's often—well, I'll put this in the kind of alpha male terms my new media adviser, Naomi Wolf, wants me to use.

Mother is often full of shit.

. . .

Mother was "Mrs. Senator Ma'am" and my dad was "Mr. Senator Sir" to the help as I was growing up on the eighth floor of the Fairfax Hotel in Washington, D.C. My father was Albert Gore, the distinguished liberal populist senator from Tennessee, and my mother, Pauline, was his smartest campaign adviser.

Dad, who'd once played the fiddle with the Carter Family on the radio, now decked himself out in English tweeds and divinity school blue suits. Mother, who'd been a waitress when they met, was now the president of the Congressional Wives Forum and the president of the Women's Speakers Bureau of the Democratic National Committee.

They were gone much of the time and I was mostly alone in the apartment with my black nanny, Ocie Bell, who'd put the food out on the table and make it look "pretty" for me. When they were in town, we went for sunset strolls, parading up and down in front of the embassies on Embassy Row, or I was up on the Roof Garden of the Fairfax with them, drinking milk while they had their highballs.

My dad called me "honey" and took me with him to committee meetings at the Senate. He let me float my toy submarine in the Senate pool. He introduced me to Vice President Nixon and the vice president rocked me on his knee. He took me to Saturday-afternoon dance lessons and showed me how to do the waltz. He accompanied me to violin lessons, too, but Mother made him stop. "Future world leaders do not play the violin," Mother said.

Sometimes, when I was bored and they were out of town, I sneaked up to the Roof Garden and dropped water-balloon bombs on the limousines waiting at the curb. I met President Kennedy—first at a party at our apartment and then on the phone. My dad let me listen in as the president called some people "sons of bitches." My dad even sneaked me into President Kennedy's private office when he was out of town. I sat in his rocking chair.

My parents enrolled me when I was in the fourth grade at St. Albans, a private school near our apartment, where a great many Kennedys and Roosevelts had gone. St. Albans, to use a Naomi Wolf word, sucked. The other kids called me "Al Gorf."

I was a good kid, though, just like I'd been a good little boy. I had a teacher who said to me many years later, "You were so mature and advanced, I had almost to look at you to see if you were a child or a man." I was a bored child.

The only good news was that the Jockey Club, the city's fanciest restaurant, had opened on the first floor of the Fairfax Hotel and I could sashay into the kitchen any time and eat whatever I wanted. Dad started sending me in the summers to the small town in Tennessee named Carthage, where he was from and where we had a farm. I had to do farm work every day with some of Dad's acquaintances. Clean the hog parlors for a summer, then back to the Jockey Club and St. Albans.

It was that same routine for a lot of years—St. Albans, my parents gone, and the farm in the summer, my parents rarely there. I didn't have any close friends.

I played football and basketball and I listened to the radio all the time: Jackie Wilson, Sam Cooke, Chuck Berry. A black doorman at the hotel liked me and sometimes he took me into the alley behind the Jockey Club and we tossed a football back and forth.

In school, Al Gorf learned how to balance a broomstick on his nose for a half hour. And in Carthage, Al Gorf saw a girl sitting in a car listening to Ray Charles and went up to her.

I was thirteen and she was sixteen—*Donna* Armistead—the Ritchie Valens song was out about then and I was in love with it—and I asked Donna to go out with me. We went to a drive-in with some of her friends, and the next day I asked her to go steady. She agreed.

And they called it puppy love, but I had a girlfriend now when I went back to St. Albans. I wrote her twice a day and I called her every Saturday night at 7:30. In my junior year at St. Albans, Mother and Dad were gone so much that I moved into the dorm. I slept as long as I could each morning before chapel, using a clip-on tie and cutting the back out of my shirts so I could just put them over me like a T-shirt under my jacket. Or I'd wake up at three in the morning sometimes and get dressed for the next day and go back to bed.

In Carthage, Donna and I would kiss a lot and make out and pet, but we'd never go all the way. We were the Ken and Barbie of the Tennessee hills. Once, when Donna and I were in the basement of my parents' house in Carthage, Mother was in town and she came running downstairs. We were on the couch, rubbing hard against each other, and Mother broke us up and told me to take a cold shower. I did. Another time, Donna and I were parked in a lover's lane and headlights were suddenly behind us. I jumped out of the car so fast, I was wearing her shoes. My dad was standing there. He said, "What do you think you're doing? Don't you think it's time we were getting on home?" We got on home.

In my senior year at St. Albans, I was on the varsity football and basketball teams. We sucked. We won one and lost seven at football; we won two and lost fourteen at basketball. When the school yearbook came out, it said, under my picture, "People who have no weaknesses are terrible."

I went to a couple of the school debutante dances, moving Al Gorf around to Johnny Mathis, but I still wrote Donna twice a day. I went down to see the Beatles at Washington Stadium with three classmates. They all loved John; Paul was my favorite. I celebrated graduation by driving around town in my father's Chrysler Imperial, alone, and tossing cherry bombs out the window. One of them bounced back into my lap and almost ended Al Gorf's sex life, which had hardly begun.

I was probably closer to Powell, the doorman at the hotel, than to any of my classmates. Powell and I had Jackie Wilson in common and I knew so much about music that we never ran out of something to talk about. I knew that Lefty Frizzell was in jail in Roswell, New Mexico, the night the flying saucers landed . . . that Jerry Lee Lewis almost killed Paul Anka on an Australian tour . . . that Ray Charles was a bigger stud than Elvis . . . that Brenda Lee was a thirteen-year-old midget.

I asked Powell if he'd take me down to the Howard Theater, a fabled R&B house, to see James Brown, and he did. James Brown knocked me out and I swear I almost had an orgasm watching that business he did with his cape at the end of the show.

I met her at my graduation dance. She was with somebody else. I saw her across the room; a vision of wispy blondness, long hair, angelic face, mirror-bright blue eyes. Marianne Faithfull with a dazzling cinematic smile. Oh, pretty woman!

We talked a little bit. Her name was Tipper Aitcheson. Her mother had nick-named her after a thirties big-band hit called "Tipi Tipi Tin." I couldn't take my eyes off of her. A case, Tipper said later, of pure animal magnetism.

I called her the next day and asked her to another graduation dance that same night. We danced and danced. Everything and everyone else melted away. It was the first time Johnny Mathis ever sounded really good to me.

She liked me. I couldn't believe that I was with the most beautiful girl I'd ever seen and that she liked Al Gorf. She said she thought I was funny and fun. She was sixteen, a junior at St. Agnes, an Episcopal girls school in Arlington, Virginia.

Tipper was crazy about the Stones, especially Mick. She played drums in a girl garage band called the Wildcats. She adored the naughtiness of "I can't get no girly action" in "Satisfaction." She drove an ice blue Mustang. She had dated one of my classmates, one of the fast and cool guys, and had given him a 45 of "Get Off of My Cloud," writing "Rolling Stones Forever!" on the record in French. She had also dated another classmate, another fast and cool guy, and had inscribed his yearbook, "Have all the fun you want, but someday I'm going to marry you!"

She lived in her grandparents' house in Arlington, where she'd grown up. Her parents had divorced when she was an infant. Her father had beaten her mother, who'd twice been hospitalized for depression. She'd been teased by the other kids in school for "not having a father."

She had an off-color, sometimes bawdy sense of humor. Definitely not Paul McCartney. I took her out all the time, but they were definitely not Stones-type dates. I'd put my suit and tie on and we'd go to fancy restaurants and then to the theater. We had chateaubriand a lot, even downstairs, at the Jockey Club, where I introduced her to my friend Powell, the doorman.

I was hopelessly, desperately, madly, gloriously in love with her. It wasn't just love, either. I realized quickly that she was my friend, the best friend I'd ever had. I called Donna in Carthage and told her the truth. Donna burned all the love letters I'd sent her.

I felt awful. All those years with Donna, and I'd never once asked her up to Washington. She was a part of my summer experience, along with cleaning the hog parlors. A farm girl down in the hills for a senator's son to use until he met his debutante. Is that what Donna was? Is that what I had done? I hoped not. I truly, remorsefully hoped not.

I kept Tipper's picture on my desk my first year at Harvard. She was in her senior year at St. Agnes. I was tossin' and turnin', turnin' and tossin', tossin' and turnin' all night. I was in pain without her. I went back to see her whenever I could.

I bought a motorcycle, and there was no better feeling in the world than Tipper snuggled into me, her arms wrapped around me, and that roaring between my legs. I drove it back and forth to Harvard.

I got myself elected freshman council president. Our big issues were clean rooms, the Princeton mixer, and the quality of the turkey salad and the meat loaf. I won a couple of beer-chugging contests, able to down a sixteen-ouncer in three seconds. I went for lonely midnight rides on my motorcycle around Memorial Drive. I even sort of participated in the annual spring riot, hundreds of guys blocking Memorial Drive by pretending, on their hands and knees, that they were looking for their contact lenses. I made the freshman basketball team, but I sat on the bench most of the time.

Gentle on my mind was Tipper. I took her down to meet my parents. Mother was cold, but Dad liked her. He told me she had "lovely, beautiful, sparkling eyes." He said she was "pleasant" and "shapely," about as far as my dad would go in that area. He was even more impressed with her when she came down to breakfast the next morning. "She had every eyelash in place! She was dressed for an evening ball!"

I asked Tipper what she thought of my dad and she said, "Do you remember Oedipus?" God, that made me laugh!

Tipper came up to Boston on Spring Weekend, with her grandmother tagging along as chaperone. We went to see the Temptations. Please come to Boston, I begged her, and she said yes, she'd come to Garland Junior College, a short ride from Harvard on the subway.

The world changed the beginning of my sophomore year. Beer chugging was out. Smoking dope was in. And Tipper was there. I lived in Dunster House and passed out on a lot of couches. Or Tipper was in my room. It was as though I were living inside her, stoned or straight.

We read Wallace Stevens to each other. We went to see Doc Watson together. We liked to touch. To hold hands, to have an arm around each other. She said to Al Gorf, "You've got the greatest legs!" She made us some very special cookies.

We talked about living beyond the sea. She was going to paint and I was going to write. We talked about going to Tennessee and living in the hills, in a commune, growing vegetables. Sometimes we'd hang out on the lawn, both of us wearing bib overalls, laughing at my new Texas friend, Tommy Lee Jones, as he paced along a path by the Charles. He wore blue velvet—jacket and pants—held a rose, and recited lines from Shakespeare in a stoned, down-home twang.

Laughing as Tommy suddenly said, out of the blue, deep into his black turtleneck existentialist phase, "I just realized I'm gonna die." I grew my hair long (my dad was angry) and flipped out over *Star Trek* and *2001: A Space Odyssey.*

Tipper and I hated the war in Vietnam. We got into the protests, but I had to be careful. I didn't want to do anything to hurt my dad, whose increasing liberalism was getting a lot of Tennessee voters more and more angry.

He asked me to go to the Democratic National Convention in 1968 with him and, even though I hated to be away from Tipper, I went. I was on the convention floor, helping him write a speech, while the whole world was watching what was happening outside. On election night, Tipper and I prayed for Hubert Humphrey. Instead, the man my dad called "the Vilest Man" became president.

Yesterday all my troubles seemed so far away. Now I had to deal with the draft. I thought the war was immoral. I was head over heels in love. And I was the son of a senator from a rural state who'd be up for reelection in two years.

My dad told me to make my own decision and that whatever it was, he'd support it. If nothing else worked, Tipper wanted to go to Canada. But Mother laid it down: If I didn't go into the service, I'd destroy my dad's political career.

I enlisted. Tipper and I cried and held each other. It wasn't fair, but I felt I didn't have any choice. I could not destroy my father's life. I even volunteered for Vietnam. I knew how good that would look for my dad—to have a son in combat during a campaign.

I was assigned to Fort Rucker. "Mother Rucker," we called it. I looked at myself in the mirror and didn't recognize the grunt in the buzz cut I was looking at. I called Tipper, in her senior year now, every day. I hung out with soldiers who hated the war as much as I did.

On weekends, some of the guys and I would rent a motel room and get stoned, listening to Cream and Hendrix and Zeppelin. I saw and loved *Easy Rider, M*A*S*H*, and *The Strawberry Statement*. I read and loved *Dune, The Beastly Beatitudes of Balthazar B* and *One Flew Over the Cuckoo's Nest*. Meanwhile, I'd won "Supernumerary of the Guard" three times for having the sharpest-looking uniform and the shiniest boots.

I almost got into trouble once—picked up by state troopers in a field near a freeway, looking for the perfect four-leaf clover to give to a buddy headed for Nam. I explained to the state troopers what I was doing and why, and, thank God, they let me go.

Our wedding was at the National Cathedral, right next door to St. Albans. The love of my life wore a train of white lace and carried a bouquet of orchids and white carnations. I wore army dress blues. The organist played the Beatles. She loved me! Yeah yeah yeah!

We moved to Rucker, lived in a trailer full of cockroaches, and drove a VW camper. We stayed in bed much of the time. I felt alive again. She was there, holding my hand, touching me, making me laugh. I thanked God each night and day for His blessing.

Dad was in trouble. The Vilest Man had targeted him. Because of his friendship with the Kennedys, he was being attacked as "the third senator from

Massachusetts." Haldeman, Nixon's chief of staff, wrote a memo telling an aide that "Gore's cocktail-party liberalism offers a chance to rebut his folksy image" and told the aide to dig up a list of dinner parties Mother and Dad had attended, including the menus—"the Frenchier the better."

Dad's Nixon-picked Republican opponent said, "Our college campuses are infested with drug peddlers, our courts are disrupted, buildings bombed, schools threatened. Our law officers are threatened, beaten, and murdered. Pornography pollutes our mailboxes. Criminal syndicates infiltrate legitimate businesses. Rapists, robbers, and burglars make our streets and homes unsafe." Dad and liberals like him, of course, in this vilest view of the world, were to blame.

I tried to help Dad as much as I could. We did a TV ad together, with me in uniform, where Dad said, "Son, always love your country." Dad even got his fiddle out again after all these years and played "Turkey in the Straw," but it didn't do much good. His ads showed him riding a horse or playing checkers with the old-timers on the courthouse lawn. The Nixon people portrayed him as a man out of touch with his constituents, a wealthy social snob in a Tyrolean hat and a red vest, a man who fought for the little guy but couldn't stand his presence, the southern regional chairman of the eastern liberal establishment.

Ironically, even my attempt to help him by volunteering for Vietnam proved useless. I'd go to Vietnam, I was told, on the first transport *after* the election.

"A damnation!" my dad called it, when he lost on election night. "The causes for which we fought are not dead," he said. "The truth shall rise again."

I cried, for Dad and for myself. I had enlisted in a war I hated in order to help him. And now he had lost anyway. And after he had lost, I was going to Vietnam, risking my life for nothing, leaving behind and alone the woman who was my life.

Rat fuck. I had rat-fucked myself.

How's that for a Naomi Wolf word?

I was in-country for six months. I was a military journalist. I talked about Tipper so much that a buddy, Mike O'Hara, felt like he knew her.

I smoked a lot of dope. I bummed a lot of cigarettes. I listened to a lot of music. I bodysurfed, pulled O'Hara out of a riptide, and saved his life. The guys called me "Brother Buck," not Al Gorf, and told me I "had my shit in the bag."

I heard that Tipper was depressed and crying all the time. I was depressed and crying when no one could hear me.

I took my turn regularly on the perimeter in those little firebases out in the boonies. Someone would move; we'd fire first and ask questions later.

I saw men and women cut in half by Huey gunships.

I never had to come face-to-face with someone whom I had either to kill or be killed by.

I promised God that if I survived, I would atone for my sins, and purify myself.

I blasted Dylan and dreamed about Tipper.

Our company had a pet snake, a mammoth python we called "Moonbeam." It ate the pack rats, which were everywhere around us, but it liked chickens the best.

We'd go into the villages and buy fat chickens and then we'd offer the chickens to Moonbeam, who'd swallow them in one gulp.

I watched that python devouring, its eyes lidded, cruel, and impassive. Stoned one night, watching it feed, I thought, The snake is Vietnam, swallowing America.

Tipper Gore! Tipper Galore! I'm here! I'm back! I made it! I survived! God did I miss you! God do I love you! Oh my God, I love you so much, so much, so much, so much.

Tipi Tipi Tin, Tipi Tipi Tan, Tipi Tan Tipi Tan—all day, all night, Tipi Tan Tipi Tan, all day all night in the sand . . .

I was angry and bitter. She soothed me. I had dreams of carnage and bloodshed. She healed me. I went to divinity school and atoned. She helped me. I purified myself. She held me. I became a newspaper reporter at a place that had already hired Bobby Kennedy's son, Arthur Schlesinger's son, and Hank Aaron's daughter. Tipper took pictures.

We made a baby. Then we made another baby.

I wasn't a very good newspaper reporter. We had to do something with our lives. What should we do? Live on a commune and grow vegetables? Live by the sea and paint and write?

We had babies now. We were parents now.

What should I do, Tipper Gore, Tipper Galore, Tipi Tipi Tin, Tipi Tipi Tan?

Should I run for Congress?

Yes.

Yes?

Yes!

She kissed me.

I made my announcement, and just before I did, I threw up.

. . .

We moved back to Washington when I was elected and lived in the same house in Arlington where she grew up. The girls went to the same public elementary school she had gone to. The school crossing guard was the same one who had helped her cross the street.

Mother tried to buy "proper Washington clothes" for Tipper, until I stopped it. My wife was more beautiful, curvier, than I'd ever seen her. She built a darkroom in the house and freelanced some of her photographs. She worked in volunteer shelters for the homeless. She wore jeans and was mostly barefoot at home.

I was a congressman. I wore a blue suit, a red tie, and scuffed shoes every day. I kept a computer to one side in my office and a case of Tab on the other. I came up with my first nationally quoted good line: "The tax system is a national joke that hurts when you laugh." I studied every issue myself that I was interested in. I didn't want staffers making decisions for me. I investigated unsafe infant formula. I found a conspiracy to overprice contact lenses. I held hearings to toughen warnings on cigarette packs. I held hearings on organ donations. I learned that if you want to get your colleagues' attention in Congress, the best way is to let them see you on TV or in the paper.

I played basketball at the House gym. Al Gorf was the master of trick shots. Al Gorf could carom the ball off the rear gym wall and get it into the basket. Al Gorf could lie on his back at half court and throw it over his head for a score.

The beautiful Mrs. Tipper Gore and I attended formal state dinners, where she nibbled my ear.

We had three girls. We wanted a boy. We read a book. We put it into practice.

Tipi Tipi Tin, Tipi Tipi Tan . . . but she wasn't . . . tan. She was snow-white back there. No tight underwear for me, lots of coffee, deep, deep penetration, and no missionary position.

Deep, deep penetration, over and over again, at her thermometer's beck and call, in those dazzling mounds of miraculous snow.

We got our boy.

She was angry. The baby-sitter had brought home a Prince CD and the last song on it, "Darling Nikki," said, "I .net her in a hotel lobby masturbating with a magazine."

There were videos on MTV that the girls were talking about. Van Halen's "Hot for Teacher"—in which a teacher stripped—and "Mötley Crüe's "Looks Can Kill"—with women kept in cages by men wearing leather.

Tipper set up the group called Parents' Music Resource Center with other congressional wives. She went public. There was my beautiful wife on the CBS evening news talking about "Bondage and oral sex at gunpoint." There she was at home, telling me that Prince sprayed his audience with water to simulate a woman's body fluid, that Wendy Williams pretended to masturbate onstage with a jackhammer.

The music industry lashed back at her. Frank Zappa, who'd been one of our favorites at Harvard, called her a Nazi. Wendy Williams told her that she was just afraid our own daughters would masturbate.

I was proud of the strength of her conviction, but I wondered, Are we getting old? What about the Stones' "Starfucker" and the Kingsmen's "Louie Louie" and all those other daring rock songs we'd laughed about in school? Tipper was the one who'd loved rock and roll raunchiness, while I was the McCartney fan. She seemed to almost obsess about Prince and how he'd appear onstage naked in a purple bathtub. But wasn't that just rock and roll showbiz, not all that far removed from James Brown's cape?

She laughed when she heard Ice-T's response to her . . . but I couldn't.

"Think I give a fuck about some silly bitch named Gore? Yo, PMRC, here we go, raw. Yo, Tip, what's the matter? You ain't gettin no dick? Your bitchin' about rock and roll, that's censorship, dumb bitch."

I couldn't even bear to tell her about the tape that had been sent to every member of Congress, the tape that all the staffers were listening to and cackling about:

> *She got pouty lips*
> *She got juicy tits*
> *She got hungry hips*
> *She got funky pits*
>
> *Ride, Tipper, Ride*
> *Your lips so wide*
> *Ride, Tipper, Ride*
> *You're burnin up inside*
>
> *She got big blue eyes*
> *She got a hefty size*

She got milky thighs
She got cherry pies

Ride, Tipper, Ride
Don't pay Al no mind
Ride, Tipper, Ride
Baby go hog-wild

Ride, Tipper, Ride
Wiggle that behind
Ride, Tipper, Ride
Move it side to side

We both laughed when she finally got support from a rock superstar who said she was right. Paul McCartney!

She hung in, though, and never backed off. A few years later, when I was running for president, she said, "We're just trying to get his name recognition up to mine."

I ran for president and got my butt kicked—Mother sent me a note that said, "Smile. Relax. Attack"—and our boy got hit by a car and we nursed him back to health.

I wrote a best-selling book and got tagged as "the Ozone Man," and Tipper and I and the kids went out on a houseboat, where I grew a beard, and we decided I wasn't going to run for president again.

Tipper got up on a stage and played drums with the Grateful Dead. And at a National Correspondents Association dinner, with photographers all around, she stuck her tongue deep into my mouth.

When Bill Clinton asked me to be his vice-presidential running mate, she didn't want me to do it. We had decided on that houseboat to focus on us and the kids. But I remembered what my dad had said at the moment he lost: "The truth shall rise again!" So Tipper said, "Okay, here we go. Let's save the world."

I liked Bill Clinton. I thought he wanted to do good things for America and I knew I could help him. He was an instinctive politician and I was a cerebral one. He went with his gut and I went with my head. He was John Lennon and I . . . would always be Paul McCartney.

I knew how different we were. We were jogging in Little Rock before the convention and he said, "Ooh, lookit that ass!" as we jogged by some high school girls. He liked to tease, too. When Perot dropped out, he called me and said, "I'm pickin' a new VP. You were my choice in a three-man race, but now we're down to two and I'm goin' with Bob Kerrey."

Tipper and I did a bus tour all over the Midwest with Bill and Hillary, and that's when I saw, for the first time, how much Tipper liked him. He made such a huge deal out of the fact that he and Tipper shared the same birthday. He was touching her all the time—casual little touches on the arm or the elbow, holding her blue eyes with his, telling her how much of an "asset" she was going to be to the campaign.

She told him about her mother's hospitalization for depression, and right away he told her he was going to make her the head of a White House mental health program. We were supposed to leave two days into the tour, but Tipper was having so much fun, she said, meeting the crowds, she said, that she wanted to stay another two days.

Watching Bill with her, watching Bill with other women on the campaign, I felt that what somebody had said in the paper was right: Tipper and I were about to become national chaperones while the country was going off on a blind date with its first rock and roll president.

I hoped I was right about Tipper being a chaperone right along with me—because some of the papers had already picked up on her "friendship" with Bill. She and Bill, one magazine said, shared "a certain fun-loving spirit," and the same publication said that, personalitywise, Hillary and I were more alike. And maybe there was some truth in that, too. On that bus tour once, I told Hillary she looked "cute" up on the stump, and she laughed right in my face.

I wondered on that tour, too, whether Bill was still smoking some dope. He was so cobwebbed in the morning, he could hardly talk. He started hitting his stride around noon. "Allergies," Bill told me.

We were Butch and Sundance, the press said, but I remembered the movie and I thought, What about Katharine Ross? Wasn't she with both guys, both Newman and Redford, one after the other?

Was Tipper Katherine Ross?

I couldn't remember the darn ending: Which one did she wind up with?

·   ·   ·

Tipper, I saw, as we dove full bore into the campaign, was more energized than I'd seen her in a long time, sticking her tongue into my ear on the plane, shooting water guns at the media, more energized intimately with me, too, than she'd been in a while.

I wondered about that, too. Was that me? Or was it Bill's presence? The effect he seemed to have on almost every woman, the effect Al Gorf had never had and never would. Tipper even called me on *Larry King Live,* disguising her voice, and came on to me.

Nervous about her, I got a little energized myself. On the campaign plane, I'd yell, "I f-e-e-e-l good!" like James Brown, and I'd use a food tray as a snowboard and surf down the aisle during takeoffs.

Sure enough, when we won the White House, Bill named Tipper the head of the Mental Health Task Force, gave her an office in the EOB, right next to the White House, as well as a small staff. So she went to the White House each day, and I knew she saw him sometimes . . . to discuss mental health?

She was acting like a much younger Tipper, I thought, or was it that I was getting old and she wasn't? She jumped on the back of a White House staffer's motorcycle one day and they went tearing around town, with Tipper lifting her arms high sometimes, like she used to do with me. And a friend of mine told me he'd run into her at Reagan National Airport—"completely grubbed out"—in jeans, no makeup, sitting at the bar in a baseball cap and sipping a beer. She dove into Lake Michigan with all her clothes on. She started Rollerblading.

I heard that Bill liked me, too. "What does Al think?" I heard he'd ask when I wasn't there at a meeting. And James Carville, I heard, felt that I had "unbelievable message discipline."

I tried to be as supportive of Bill personally as possible. When we played miniature golf, I threw the game. When we jogged together, I slowed down, and Bill said afterward once, "I want to thank Al for not running me into the ground." I sat down at my own computer and did a last-second rewrite of a speech he was making.

I could make him laugh. He was ranting and raving about how the congressional Democrats never had anything good to say about him, and I said, "I'll speak to them!" And Bill laughed so hard, he had a sneezing fit.

He was supportive, too. After a tough press conference where the media roasted me, he came out of the Oval Office, put his arm around me, and said, "Fuck 'em! You did great!"

He always had that twinkle, though, just a slice of rock and roll: He came into a meeting once and stood by the door, his face frozen, arms stiffly at his side. "Hi," he said, "I'm Al." I laughed.

And as I was heading out on a fund-raiser, he said, "Hey, Al, don't forget to shake hands at the rope lines!"

I was the vice president of the United States—"I did a better job on him than on my husband," Mother unfortunately told the press—in an office eighteen feet from the president's, wondering if the love of my life was in there with Bill.

I knew that Bill had told someone, "I really like Al; he's real smart. But Al's always seeing something when there's nothing." And I thought to myself, He's talking about policy and politics, isn't he? And not Tipper, right?

I thought back, too, to the whole business with Prince, that near obsession Tipper had had with him, to all the talk about whips and kink. Was that, too, an indication of some kind of unrealized yearning on Tipper's part? I knew Bill had those yearnings, too. I had heard the Gennifer Flowers tapes, the same ones where he said, "Al Bore is the boringest man I've ever met."

Tipper Gore, Tipper Galore, Tipi Tipi Tin, Tipi Tipi Tan, I've always loved you the best that I can.

I was so paranoid, I bought an astrology book to see what Tipper and Bill had in common. It said:

Brilliant and capable, you can do anything you set your mind to. Be careful who you let into your life. When it comes to relationships, people expect you to have few faults. Surprise—you are not perfect, and you know it. However, this may be difficult for others to accept.

Accept? Tipper and Bill? Never!

I looked up my own date, March 31. It said:

You distrust everything people tell you. Try to dwell less on things that go wrong in your love life. An unconventional marriage may alleviate this.

An unconventional marriage? Tipper and Bill? Or Tipper and Bill and me? Or Tipper and Bill and Hillary and me?

Never!

.   .   .

And then, when the *Starr Report* came out, I realized and was convinced that it was all in my head. That I had put it there. Because I loved her so much and because I was getting older and because Bill, on that silly alpha male level, is a better man than I am, Charlie Brown.

On the day he was impeached, I sat in his office with him and watched him cry. I cried with him. I held his hand.

Tipper said about the House managers: "It's going to be an interesting day when the American people truly get intimate with the minds of those people. I'm on the edge of my seat."

So Naomi Wolf, who is a brilliant and beautiful young woman, is trying to make me into an alpha male. It can't be easy for her, if you believe what they say about me.

I'm the man who lives behind a Plexiglas shield, tone-deaf to his own flat notes, humorless, stiff, wooden, a father reading to his toddlers when he speaks. I've got a Boy Scout manner, look like a soap opera doctor, and wear pants that are too short. I clap like a marionette and the sleeves of my dark blue suit are lined with flagpoles.

I'm a mannequin; when I turn, my whole upper body turns with me. I'm as graceful as someone skating on a wooden floor. My arms dangle lifelessly from my shoulders and I seem to have no joints above the waist. I'm a self-important goody-goody who looks as if he were born in a coat and tie.

I'm Cyborg Gore, the Computer Geek in Chief, Robo Veep, and Kaw-Liga the Wooden Indian. I'm the fat boy in the school yard you just love to torment. *Al Gorf!*

But that's okay.

Tipper Gore loves me.

Tipper Galore loves Al Gorf!

Somebody asked her what books I keep on the nightstand, and Tipper Gore said, "Are you kidding? He's living with me. You think he's going to read a book at night?" I call her when I leave the office because I know she wants time to comb her hair and put her lipstick on. When I get home and she's jamming in the backyard with the kids, playing the drums, I grab my harmonica and join in because she has told me that I have a "sweet and pretty" voice. We have a dress-up Halloween party; last year, Tipper and I were mummies.

We still go to the movies, sit in the balcony with our baseball caps, and hold hands. She gave me a bumper sticker yesterday that said NIXON IN 2000. HE'S STILL NOT AS STIFF AS GORE.

.   .   .

When Paul McCartney's wife, Linda, died, I held Tipper Gore as tightly as I could all night.

Naomi Wolf used to be an adviser to Bill before she became alpha male adviser to me. She's married to a White House speechwriter.

There was a book called *Face Time* out about a year ago. It's about the wife of a White House speechwriter, and she has an affair with the president of the United States.

Do you remember how when *Primary Colors* came out, everybody said it was fact and not fiction? I wonder—what if *Face Time* isn't fiction, either? Do you think Naomi and Bill . . .

Oh, heck, don't even think about it.

There I go again, Mr. President!

I'm just being . . . me.

When I was a little boy wandering around inside the Fairfax Hotel, there was an old man who had an apartment there. He was very tall and he had a cane, and whenever I saw him by the elevator, he'd make a terrible face at me and then laugh as I ran away. His name was Senator Prescott Bush. And come November, I'm going to kick the living shit out of his smirking grandson.

Is that alpha male enough for you?

(7)

Hitler's Whore

Monica was obsessing. Trying desperately to take her mind off of It. Off *herself*. She was sewing again, making bags and scarves for her family and friends. But she found herself blanking, zoning out, agape at the set, which showed her to herself, twenty-four hours a day, in the most unflattering light.

She couldn't escape from the image of herself going down on him. She felt violated, raped, as though anyone who saw her saw her only on her knees. She felt she was a whore, "Hitler's whore," she told her girlfriends. So she obsessed. She trembled. She cried. She sobbed. She was hysterical.

Andy Bleiler was the final betrayal. Her first real boyfriend, her first true love, the man who'd taken her virginity, and he was live on all the networks, standing in front of his house in Portland with his wife, *holding a press conference*! And calling her a liar and a whore. Andy and Kate and a lawyer, trashing her, stripping her naked and showing her to the world in the merciless glare of TV lights, saying she "had a pattern of twisting facts, especially to enhance her version of her own self-image," saying, "She spoke of sex a lot; she's fairly obsessed with that," telling the world about her abortion even, making it seem as though she'd purposely gone to the White House to seduce the president. Kate called her "a *Fatal Attraction* type" and said that *she'd* said, "I'm going to the White House to get my presidential knee pads." They made her sound like a pathetic mess, revealing that she'd called them as much as five times a day from Washington. She watched Andy, and all she could do was cry and take the pills her shrink had given her. *Whore! Fat whore!* Now even Andy was saying it.

Every day was a nightmare. Trying and being unable to sew. Taking her pills. Eating more and more. Getting fatter. Unable to go out. Unable even to step outside on the balcony of her apartment because there were cameras on the street aimed up there. Trapped with the TV and the Internet, switching channels and surfing, watching the fat whore through *their* eyes, watching and reading each new account. Yesterday it was Andy and today it was her very first so-called boyfriend, Adam Dave, whom she had only kissed, saying that they'd had sex and that she liked to be handcuffed to the bed. *Fat, kinky whore!*

She switched the channels and saw a film clip of Bayani Nelvis, her friend the White House steward, on his way to the grand jury. Seeing him hurt almost as much as seeing Andy Bleiler and Adam Dave. Nel was wearing one of her ties. One of the ties she had given the Creep, which said to her that the Creep had thought so little of her gift that he'd given it to his steward. *But of course! Why would any man keep a present from a fat whore?*

She'd even gotten a letter yesterday, which she'd sent on to her lawyer, from a woman in New York who said that Starr was after her, too; who admitted she'd had affairs with lots of famous married men but not with the Creep. The woman didn't know what to do. *A whore turning to another whore for advice!* She switched channels again and watched Dr. Joyce Brothers. "Can you imagine," Dr. Brothers said, "a young man bringing Monica Lewinsky home to his parents and saying 'I'm going to marry Monica Lewinsky'?"

When they weren't talking about her, they were talking about her mother. Her poor violated mother. It reminded her of that old movie she'd seen with Sophia Loren where mother and daughter are raped, gang-banged, right next to each other. Raped first by Starr, then by the media. Her mother had almost collapsed in the grand jury room. A wheelchair and a nurse had to be called for her. Her attorney took her to the bathroom, where she fell to the floor, hysterical. When she came home that night, her mother curled up in the fetal position on the kitchen floor, sobbing. Her shrink had to come to the apartment in the middle of the night.

The White House had called it Starr's "Throw Mama in Front of the Train" strategy. Her father had said, "To pit a mother against a daughter, to coerce her to talk, to me it's reminiscent of the McCarthy era, of the Inquisition, and even, you know, you could stretch it to the Hitler era." Her mother had said, "What a better way to force someone to do what they don't want than to threaten those they love? My own family saw that technique used very effectively by Joseph Stalin, which is why they left Russia."

All this imagery piling up—McCarthy, the Inquisition, Hitler, Stalin—but the media didn't want to hear any of it. They were implying that her mother had *encouraged* her in her pursuit of the president. They were implying that her mother had pursued Peter Strauss for his money the same way that Monica had pursued the president. They were almost saying that her mother had staged her collapse in front of the grand jury in an orchestrated PR effort to make Starr look like Savonarola. They didn't care that her mother now was as hysterical as she was, taking *her* pills, seeing *her* shrink. *Who cared about a whore? A fat whore? A fat, kinky whore? Hitler's whore?*

She switched channels, and there was Linda Tripp. *Her!* She wished her *kids* would die! She wished her stupid dog *Cleo* would die! She had called her hairdresser the other day and Ishmael had said Linda was going to *him* now! Linda had taken her life, her dignity, her privacy from her. Now she was taking her hairdresser, too!

And every time she saw her on the tube, she was wearing something that Monica had given her—that old coat, the fake Chanel bag she'd brought back from Korea. Like Linda was taunting her through the media—See, you got me all this cheap shit, Monica; now it's payback time! You're Hitler's whore because you didn't get me a *real* Chanel bag!

She felt so alone. Sure, her mother was there for her, but her mother was a train wreck, too. Could a train wreck help rebuild a train wreck? What could they do—share their pills and exchange prescriptions? Have conference calls with *both* shrinks? Reassure each other with old stories about how the Spellings unintentionally forgot to invite her to Tory's birthday party when she was a little girl? Compare intimate notes about the affair her mother didn't have with Pavarotti and the affair she had with the president?

She had no one to go to who was strong enough to give her a helping hand. Her lawyer? Ginsburg? She had to laugh. Even feeling suicidal . . . she had to laugh. What was she doing with this putz? How had her dear father albatrossed her with this flaming, unmitigated schmuck? This medical-malpractice lawyer who was on the tube every time she switched the channel. Such a rube!

He thought he was so slick. She told him to stop doing all these shows, and he said, "If you don't feed the bear, it'll eat you because it's hungry. If you feed the bear too much, it'll crap all over you. But if you feed the bear just enough, he'll leave you alone." Oh, sure, just enough. That's why the media was leaving her alone, right? Where the fuck did he get off? She read what he'd said to *Time* magazine. He'd called her mother "aggressive" and said Monica was "a caged dog with her 24-year-old libido." Her own lawyer. "Caged dog," meaning bitch in heat. *Whore!*

He told the press that he'd kissed her inner thighs when she was six days old and said, "Look at those little *pulkes.*" Inner thighs? Her own lawyer giving the public an image of her inner thighs? Her *pulkes?* He had to say *that* when the world already saw her as a whore? He had to give them her *inner thighs?*

Ginsburg gave her the creeps. Asking her all the time for more intimate details of what had happened in the hallway. Sitting at dinner at her house with her family and saying it was *his understanding* that the president liked only women with dark pubic hair. At the dining room table! She was the whore of the Western world and she obviously had dark pubic hair, and Ginsburg . . . at the dinner table! . . . Her step-mother had to leave the room. Writing that essay for *California Lawyer* that was going to say, "Now, Mr. Starr, thanks to you, we will know if another's lips aside from the First Lady's have kissed the president's penis." *Aside from the First Lady's?* Uncool, inappropriate, and gross!

How about the time she was doing a photo shoot in Malibu and Ginsburg showed up, took one look at the blue chiffon dress they had her wearing, and said, "The president is going to cream his pants when he sees this." A nice classy photo shoot with Herb Ritts on a sunny private Malibu beach and her own lawyer has to ruin it for her. *Cream his pants* like he'd creamed them before. Or cream the blue dress maybe. Her own lawyer! Who was supposed to protect her from the gang bang.

But who was getting a hard-on instead, maybe, watching, wanting more intimate details, thinking about her inner thighs, her *pulkes,* her dark pubic hair, her lips, creaming his pants, in line at the gang bang. . . .

She thought about all the other women who had been, for a while, America's whores, the world's whores, famous for no other reason except that they had somehow been caught with or without their panties down, kneeling down or lying down, with famous men. They were all over the channels and the Internet now . . . thanks to her.

They thought they had finally resumed anonymous lives, and now they were being yanked back naked onstage for the world to remember once again for their whoring. Just when they thought their ravaging fifteen minutes of gang bang were over, their now-aging bodies were dragged out to be scrutinized, mocked, poked, and violated again . . . *thanks to her.*

They were bit players now in a drama in which she was starring. They had starred briefly themselves, but in much smaller and dingier venues. Going down on a congressman was not going down on the president of the United States. Being Wayne Hayes's whore was not being Hitler's whore.

She wondered, watching these women on *Hard Copy* or *Montel Williams* or *Geraldo* if this was what was going to happen to her, too. Back on the tube for a few bucks ten or twenty years later, reminiscing about the blow jobs the same way old ballplayers talked about getting the hit in the bottom of the ninth that won the World Series. Signing autographs in red ink with a happy face and a smeared pair of rubber lips. Smiling until your facial muscles hurt, in order to prove that the long-ago gang bang didn't hurt anymore.

She knew that the women she was watching or reading about now, the women who were being violated again—thanks to her—didn't have much to smile about. Was Meredith Roberts, Bob Dole's old mistress, smiling as she lived alone with her cats, saying, "Life is very hard. I wish it would just end"? How about Elizabeth Ray, that fat old congressman's mistress, who lived alone with her dog? Or Fawn Hall, who hid Iran-Contra papers in her panties for Oliver North—out in L.A., battling heroin addiction and crack, saying, "Ollie treated me like a piece of Kleenex"? Or Vanessa Pernach—bitten by Marv Albert—who said, "I have an *A* stamped on my forehead. *A* for Albert. No one's going to want to date me now." Or Jessica Hahn, saying jokingly to Gennifer, "If you fix me up with Bill Clinton, I'll fix you up with Jim Bakker." And Gennifer's response: "No offense, but I wouldn't fuck him on a bad day." *Celebrity whores. Superstar whores. And she was the* biggest *whore.*

It could have been worse. Really. Really? Yeah, *really.* She thought about Megan Marshack, who was twenty-one when she met the vice president of the United States, Nelson Rockefeller, who was married and almost seventy. Monica thought she could almost sort of *recognize* Megan, a Valley Girl from L.A. who grew up in a house at the foot of the Hollywood sign. Megan was big-boned, attractive, tall, smart, ambitious. A history and journalism major. Megan went down to San Clemente as a college journalist, got on the Nixon press bus, met the hotshot Washington journalists. Megan had an affair with one of them. He helped her get a job in Washington as a radio reporter for the Associated Press. Megan went to interview Vice President Rockefeller. She knew how much Rocky liked Oreo cookies. So she bought a box, took all the cookies out, wrapped each cookie separately, and gave him the cookies.

Rocky liked the cookies, liked Megan. Rocky hired Megan to work for him for sixty thousand dollars. He put her in an office right next to his with a private entrance. Rocky took her to New York as an art adviser, loaned her $45,000, bought her a big raccoon coat, a nice Gucci bag.

Then, one night when they were together at a hideaway town house, Rocky had a heart attack and died inside her. Megan Marshack was *the femme fatale of all time.* Well, thank God the Creep didn't do that to me, Monica thought. The killer blow job. The blow job to end all blow jobs. The orgasmic assassination of William Jefferson Clinton. Willard rigid in rigor mortis. Hillary's Ultimate Humiliation.

She felt an overwhelming sadness as she heard and heard again about these women. She felt, too, that she didn't even belong among them, let alone be the star of their sad dinner-theater circuit. God, poor pathetic Elizabeth Ray, who got her start as a beauty queen from North Carolina by popping the pageant judges. Elizabeth's dream was to be Marilyn Monroe. The fat old congressman paid her to be his mistress and put her on his staff. "I can't type, I can't file, I can't even answer the phone," Elizabeth Ray said. The fat old congressman married another staffer. Elizabeth Ray wasn't invited to the wedding. Humped and dumped.

She got angry and stormed into the congressman's office. The congressman had the Capitol Police escort her out. She went to the *Washington Post* and spilled the beans. "I always pick 'em," she said. "My problem is that I always choose the bad guys. For one or two days they treat you right, but then . . ." She moved to New York and hooked up with a gambler, then a stage producer. Humped and dumped. Humped and dumped again.

"Playboys, gamblers, and politicians," Elizabeth Ray said. "I always go for them. I'm spoiled. I'm used to staying in top hotel suites, having limos pick me up and flying to Atlantic City and having a Rolls-Royce pick me up. But I really pay for it." She wrote a book about the fat old congressman, called *The Washington Fringe Benefit*. She took acting lessons from Lee Strasberg and Stella Adler. She appeared for one week as a singer in a bar in McKeesport, Pennsylvania. She got a role in a Chicago dinner-theater production and a job covering the Democratic National Convention for a men's magazine. She posed naked for the magazine, too. She saw her shrink often. "The day that there's no hope, he said he'd tell me." Elizabeth Ray had a nude portrait of herself stretched out on a white sheet holding a rose, like Marilyn. And she lived alone with her dog.

Then there was Fanne Fox. A stripper called "the Argentinean Firecracker." With another fat old congressman. Pulled over by the park police in Washington with the congressman and two others. Everybody drunk. Fanne, panicked, jumped out of the congressman's car and dived into the Tidal Basin. A camera crew scanning police radios was there when she got out. She said she was in love with her fat old congressman. He ran for cover, his career over. "I learned not to drink with foreigners," he said. Humped and dumped.

She tried stripping under a new name—"the Tidal Basin Bombshell." She wrote a book called *The Stripper and the Congressman*. She did "promotional work" for a men's magazine and posed in the nude for it. She tried to kill herself. She spent time in a psychiatric ward. She made a sex movie called *Posse from Heaven,* which was a double entendre the producers thought would be a gold mine. "What happened happened," she said. "So that can not be repaired completely. But some things can be mended enough to allow you to live comfortably and not be completely ashamed of yourself."

Was this going to be Monica's future? Acting lessons? A week at a bar in McKeesport? A book? Posing nude? A sex movie? Seeking hope from a shrink? Suicide attempts? Time in a psychiatric ward? Humped and dumped and humped and dumped over and over again in individual mocking replays of the gang bang that initially violated and ravaged her? Endless sorrow? Not being *completely ashamed?* Tragedy? And talk shows?

Endless self-exposing talk shows? She remembered something Gennifer had said: "I was doing a talk show over the phone at home. I had to go to the bathroom so bad I couldn't wait. But the show was only half-finished and I could hardly excuse myself right in the middle of it to go use the potty. Desperate for relief, I looked around the kitchen and got the brilliant idea to use a bowl. So as I continued to answer questions about Bill Clinton and me, I proceeded to tinkle into the bowl. Luckily it wasn't stainless steel, and so it didn't make any noise." *Tinkling into a bowl while doing a talk show?*

Only Donna Rice gave her hope. Donna Rice was a party girl when she met Gary Hart, who met her through Don Henley of the Eagles. Donna had even had a blind date with Prince Albert of Monaco. And then Donna Rice did those tacky blue jeans commercials, before Marla Maples, where she said, "I have no excuses. I only wear them."

But Donna Rice didn't write a book. Donna Rice didn't pose nude. She didn't take acting lessons. She didn't do any cheap movies. She didn't even do the talk shows. Donna Rice got married. She found God. She was the head of an organization called Enough Is Enough, which battled pornography on the Internet. No Atlantic City, no limos, no humped and dumped. A life. Donna Rice had a life and was doing something she believed in.

It's so unfair, Monica thought, as she switched her channels. *Wait! Oh my God! Oh my God!* There she was! On the Fox News channel! The *other* Monica, Nixon's Monica, Crowley. *Holy shit!* The host was introducing her as "Monica Lewinsky," and the other Monica was saying, "Talk about a Freudian slip!"

It's so unfair, she thought. Here she was, cooped up in her prison of an apartment, and here Nixon's Monica was, trashing her and trashing the Creep and saying, "Nixon would have counseled Clinton to avoid stonewalling and make good on his promise to provide more information rather than less, sooner rather than later."

Nixon! Nixon's Monica was saying that *Nixon,* the total liar, would have told the Creep, the almost-total liar, to stop lying? How could they believe her? Or when she said that Nixon "was like a grandfather to me." Yeah, right. When she'd already told the world that she got "moral support" to write her books from that guy Roger Stone, the freak who advertised with his wife in the swingers' magazines. *"Moral support" and Grandpa Dick, yeah right!* It was *s-o-o-o* unfair.

She switched the channels and felt herself beginning to obsess again—Oh God! Oh God! Oh God!—about all these whores, these other whores . . . speaking to her, getting inside her. *No!* That was it right there. That's where she made her mistake. They were not whores any more than *she* was a whore or Monica Crowley was a whore. It didn't matter what people thought! It didn't matter if that's what the media insinuated! They were women who had either fallen in love with or been used by cynical, deceitful men. Just like her. She had fallen in love with *and* she had been used by a cynical, deceitful man. They were women who had made a mistake just like she had made a mistake. They were human just like she was. They were her sisters.

She felt better now. She felt so much better, she turned off the set and called downstairs to the Watergate Bakery and ordered up another chocolate mousse cake. She remembered the happy endings that some of her sisters, some of her fellow gang-bang victims, experienced.

Vanessa Williams, of Miss America fame, was singing with Pavarotti. . . . Jessica Hahn, of Jim Bakker fame, had her nose, teeth, and breasts redone. . . . Gennifer Flowers was lecturing in colleges. . . . Connie Hamzy, the groupie from Little Rock, was running for Congress and campaigning in a thong bikini. . . . Tai Collins, of Senator Chuck Robb fame, was writing *Baywatch* episodes in L.A. . . . Koo Stark, of Prince Andrew fame, hosted a London TV show. . . . Rita Jenrette, who made love on the Capitol steps, lived in a million-dollar penthouse and sold commercial real estate. . . . Fawn Hall was beating her addiction to heroin and crack. . . . And Fanne Fox, at the age of forty-five, was happily married and had given birth. There *was* life after the gang bang! As Rita Jenrette said, "Succeeding is the best revenge." As Judy Exner of JFK fame said, "I was twenty-five years old and in love. Was I supposed to have better sense than the president of the United States?"

Monica was *s-o-o-o* happy she wasn't a whore, *s-o-o-o* happy she wasn't Hitler's whore, a nice Jewish girl like her. She was *s-o-o-o* happy that she'd discovered her sisters. Her doorbell rang. Her chocolate mousse was here. As she sliced into her cake, she saw her future: Everything would be just fine.

Monica would dump her schmucky lawyer and make a deal with Starr. The baseball hat she wore would become a fashion item. People would applaud her as she went into a restaurant. A Gallup poll would find her among the most admired women in the world, tied with Queen Elizabeth.

She would pose in *Vanity Fair* with the stars and stripes. The Creep would say nice things about her. Andy Bleiler would dump his wife, regret what he'd said in his press conference, and try to come crawling back. She'd lose a lot of weight and maybe she'd let him. And if, after Hillary dumped the Creep, sometime down the line, and if she was still skinny, and if the Creep was in town one night . . .

[8]

The Ugliest Story
Ever Told

"I think he even horrifies himself in his rational moments,"
Linda Tripp said to Monica. "Like 'Holy shit, what am I doing? If
they think that one's bad, what would they ever do to me with this
one?'"

After the midterm November election of 1998, when Republicans had
their political future handed to them on a feminine ebony platter, it
looked like the impeachment of Bill Clinton by the House of Representatives was as likely as Hillary doing a porn movie.

Yet it was a porn movie in the form of a hard-core FBI interview that was
responsible for Bill Clinton's impeachment by the House of Representatives six weeks later. Without this raw FBI file, seen by more than forty
Republican congressmen in the high-security evidence room of the Gerald
R. Ford Building, moderate Republicans would have voted against impeachment. At the end, Bill Clinton was impeached not for what he was charged
with: perjury and obstruction of justice. He was impeached for an alleged
rape.

The FBI interview of Juanita Broaddrick, known as Jane Doe #5 in the
Starr Report, had been sent to the House Judiciary Committee as a supplement by Kenneth W. Starr. It was never made public. The FBI had been
sent to interview Broaddrick because Starr was looking for evidence of
obstruction of justice. Starr found none, but he sent the interview itself to
the Judiciary Committee, which placed it in the guarded room. Not one
Democrat went to read it. But, at majority whip Tom DeLay's encouragement, forty Republicans, most of them wavering moderates, did. They

described themselves to their colleagues as "horrified" and "nauseous" after they read it.

Few of them asked what the FBI interview was doing there. If Kenneth W. Starr found no evidence of obstruction of justice pertaining to Jane Doe #5, then why was the interview with her even sent to the House? How was it relevant?

It was the hot, rancid potato that Kenneth W. Starr tossed to Tom DeLay, who tossed it to the congressmen who seemed like they might vote against impeachment. It was a Hail Mary pass that scored a Republican touchdown and got Bill Clinton impeached before Larry Flynt saved him from removal.

The story the congressmen read was ugly: In 1978, Juanita Broaddrick, attractive and well built, was thirty-five years old. She'd graduated from a nursing school and now owned a nursing home of her own in Arkansas. Bill Clinton, running for governor, then the attorney general, visited her nursing home during his campaign. Broaddrick was married to her first husband. Clinton asked her to drop by and see him at his campaign headquarters in Little Rock. She told him she was due there at a nursing seminar the following week. When she got to Little Rock, she called Clinton's office and was told to call him at his apartment. She did, and they agreed to meet for coffee in her hotel's coffee shop. When he got there, Clinton called her from the lobby and said it was too noisy. There were too many reporters there. He asked if he could go up and have coffee in her room. He went upstairs.

He'd been in the room less than five minutes when he moved close to her as they looked out the hotel window at the Arkansas River. He put his arms around her. She tried to resist him. He forced her onto the bed, holding her down. He bit her upper lip and kept her lip in his teeth as he ripped her panty hose open. He raped her. She was crying. She felt paralyzed.

Finished, he got off the bed and put his pants back on. She was in shock, sobbing. He went to the door. He put his sunglasses on. He turned back and looked at her. "You better put some ice on that," he said, and was gone.

A friend found her on the bed an hour later. She was in shock. Her lips had swollen to double their size. Her mouth was badly bruised. Her panty hose were torn open at her crotch. "I can't believe what happened," she kept sobbing to her friend.

. . .

After Bill Clinton's impeachment by the House, Tom DeLay tried it again with the Senate. "You never know how those senators are going to vote if they go down to the evidence room," he said. By then the Internet was full of gossip about Juanita Broaddrick and the story she told.

Bill Clinton was not the first president of the United States to be accused of rape. Selena Walters, a young, hot-looking Hollywood starlet, was sitting in a Hollywood nightclub with her date one night in the early fifties. A strikingly good-looking man hit on her. She knew who he was. "I'd like to call you," he told her. "How can I get in touch with you?" She gave him her address. Her date took her home and she went to bed.

At three o'clock in the morning, she heard someone beating on her door. It was the good-looking man she'd met at the club. She opened the door.

"He pushed his way inside and said he just had to see me. He forced me on the couch and said, 'Let's just get to know each other.' Then it was the battle of the couch. It was the most pitched battle I've ever had. I was fighting him. I didn't want him to make love to me. He's a very big man and he just had his way."

Ronald Reagan was asked about Selena Walters's account in 1991 as he was on his way into church. He didn't deny it. What he said was, "I don't think a church would be the proper place to use the word I would have to use in discussing that."

It was a story that had been around Arkansas since 1980. Juanita Broaddrick told close friends what had happened and she told her second husband. She and her husband ran into Bill Clinton one day and her husband grabbed him by the hand and said, "Stay away from my wife and stay away from Brownwood Manor [her nursing home]." In 1980, a man running for governor against Clinton went to see her and asked her to go public with her story. She refused. She didn't want trouble, and she'd heard too many nasty stories on the grapevine about what had supposedly happened to those who had somehow crossed Bill Clinton. She was scared.

In 1984, she got a congratulatory note from him when her nursing home was judged the best in the state. "I admire you very much," he had handwritten on the bottom. In 1991, she was called out of a meeting on state nursing standards. Bill Clinton waited for her in a stairwell. He said he was a "changed man," took her hands, apologized, and asked if he could do anything to make it up to her. She told him to go to hell and walked away.

Shortly afterward, she read in the newspaper that he was going to run for president. In 1992, a former business associate publicly told the story he had heard from her privately and urged her to come forward. She refused. When the Paula Jones attorneys approached her about the story they had heard, she made out an affidavit saying it was all untrue. Her attorney prepared the affidavit with the help of White House counsel Bruce Lindsey.

But when Kenneth W. Starr's FBI men came around, her twenty-eight-year-old son, a lawyer, told her, " 'This is another whole level.' She knew it was one thing to lie in a civil trial so she could get away from all this, but another to lie to federal agents and federal prosecutors and possibly a grand jury."

Now, as Bill Clinton's Senate trial approached, a tabloid wrote a story about her and said that she and her husband had both been paid off to keep quiet. She and her husband were hardworking, honorable people who lived on a hilly forty acres filled with horses and cows. Juanita Broaddrick was fifty-six years old and looked like the sort of mother or grandmother everyone wanted. She loathed Bill Clinton and loathed what the tabloids had written about her and her husband. She thought, for the first time, about going public.

And what effect would it have on the Senate trial, Tom DeLay and his Clinton-hating fellow Republicans wondered, if Juanita Broaddrick's story became public? What effect would charges of rape have even on Democratic, pro-Clinton senators with strong female constituencies? The American people, as the midterm elections showed, had gotten over the blow jobs and the cigar . . . but could they get over a rape? Could they look the other way? Or would Juanita Broaddrick be the final straw . . . after Jones, after Willey, after Lewinsky . . . that would remove Bill Clinton from office? If only somehow this story could get out there.

Juanita Broaddrick's phone was ringing off the hook with interview requests. A Fox News crew chased her down the highway as she sped away. *Time* magazine sent reporters, who claimed they were there to cover a tennis benefit. ABC wanted to fly her to New York to talk to Barbara Walters.

She had read about Kathleen Willey and liked her on television. She found Willey's story to be believable. She called Willey in Virginia and asked her for advice: "It just helped me to be able to talk to her, someone who had been through an interview that was so uncomfortable. She told me that, yes, she would do it again." Willey told her to "be calm and tell the truth." Willey even offered to fly to Arkansas to help her.

Juanita Broaddrick decided she was ready to go public. She agreed to speak to Lisa Myers of NBC News. Myers was there the next day, January 20, right in the middle of Bill Clinton's Senate trial. Broaddrick was videotaped from midmorning until evening. She told Lisa Myers *everything*.

She was told NBC would run the interview on January 29 on *Dateline*, during the Senate trial. It didn't run on the twenty-ninth. The Senate vote on impeachment was quickly approaching. It was scheduled to take place on February 12.

News of the Myers interview with Broaddrick was all over the Internet. Drudge not only had Lisa Myers's details; he hammered away at NBC for not airing the story as the Senate clock ran down. He said NBC News president Andy Lack "stood by as the White House manipulated NBC owner General Electric." He quoted an unnamed NBC source as saying "Andy Lack should resign. Resign now. We have to save our face."

He wrote, "It's not clear if White House Press Secretary Joe Lockhart has been in touch with NBC news." No one knew what that meant. Either Lockhart was or wasn't in touch with NBC News. If Drudge didn't know that Lockhart had been in touch, he had no business throwing it onto the Internet as a possibility.

An NBC spokesman said the Broaddrick interview was still "a work in progress." The network said it had to cross-check dates and speak to others to make it, as Lack said, "a rock-solid report."

Broaddrick said she felt "so betrayed" by NBC for not running the story. "I honestly don't know why they haven't run it," Broaddrick said. "But one has to wonder, considering that I gave the interview as the Senate trial was going on."

The Reverend Jerry Falwell asked his followers to "inundate" the producer of NBC's nightly news for not running the story, and NBC was bombarded with phone calls and E-mail. Republican trial manager, Representative Chris Cannon of Utah, told MSNBC: "Everybody knows in Washington that your colleague Lisa Myers has Jane Doe #5 on videotape and you haven't broken the story." Rupert Murdoch's Fox News anchor Brit Hume wore a button on the air that said FREE LISA MYERS! The *Washington Post* reported that Myers and Washington Bureau chief Tim Russert were "frustrated by their inability to get the story on the air. They and other advocates believe that each time they come up with further corroboration, NBC management raises the evidentiary bar a little higher."

An NBC source said that one of the reasons the network was hesitating was that the father of the chief corroborative witness, the woman who'd found Broaddrick after Clinton allegedly raped her, was murdered and Clinton had pardoned the murderer. The rape had taken place in 1978 and the pardon in 1980. The witness hadn't said anything corroborating Broaddrick until *after* 1980, the year her father's murderer was pardoned.

Sure, many countered, but Broaddrick didn't say anything publicly until *after* 1980, either—so how could the witness's corroboration be suspect?

As hard as Drudge tried, hammering away at NBC, this one didn't work like Lewinsky had. With Lewinsky, he broke the story and the media felt forced to follow him. But this was an old story and the same ploy was ineffective: The major news media did not feel compelled to write about Broaddrick just because Drudge had stolen Lisa Myers's details. They were waiting for NBC.

They were still waiting on February 12 when the Senate voted not to remove Bill Clinton from office. NBC was still researching the story and a lot of people were saying the story would never run. The impeachment crisis was over. America was finally free of its blow job and cigar noose. Would Americans now want to contemplate ripped panty hose and a bitten lip?

Dorothy Rabinowitz was known among her friends in the media as "a right-wing ideologue." Her employer, the editorial page of the *Wall Street Journal*, as opposed to its news section, was known as a right-wing sheet that, according to Vince Foster's note, had driven him to suicide.

The editorial page had treated seriously not only allegations that Bill Clinton was a big-time coke dealer involved with the Colombian cartel but that he had been involved with the murder of dozens of people. The editorial page was a journalistic haunted house—while the rest of the paper was well balanced. For the editorial page, every day was Halloween.

Now, with the Senate trial over, Dorothy Rabinowitz went to see Juanita

Broaddrick at her small-town Arkansas home . . . in a limousine. And Juanita Broaddrick told her *everything*. And the *Wall Street Journal* published a very long news story about her allegations, not in the news pages, where it belonged, but on its right-wing editorial page. And, now that it was out and everybody was talking about it and this was, after all, the *Wall Street Journal*, the *Washington Post* and the *New York Times* published their own stories.

It was the Drudge ploy all over again, as executed by Rabinowitz. And now that the *Post* and the *Times* had provided the details of Juanita Broaddrick's story, NBC aired Lisa Myers's interview . . . now that the Senate trial was over and Bill Clinton hadn't been removed from office.

Broaddrick was as believable as anyone I'd ever seen on television. She told the details and more. She described Bill Clinton at the moment of the rape as "a vicious, awful person." She said, "My hatred for him is overwhelming." She said she came forward because "I just couldn't hold it in any longer." She said she didn't want her granddaughter to ask, "Why didn't you tell what this man did to you?" She said she wasn't interested in a book deal or a lawsuit, but that "all of these stories were floating around . . . and I was tired of everybody putting their own spin on it." She said, "I do not have an agenda. I want to put all of these stories to rest."

She said, "I just told him — 'No.' You know, 'Please don't do that.' Then he tries to kiss me again. And the second time he tries to kiss me, he starts biting on my lip. He starts to bite on my top lip and I tried to pull away from him. And then he forces me down on the bed, and I just was very frightened. And I tried to get away from him. I told him 'No!' because I don't want this to happen, but he wouldn't listen to me."

Asked about Broaddrick's allegation, President Clinton said, "Well, my counsel has made a statement about the issue . . . and I have nothing to add to it." The president's counsel, David Kendall, called the charge "absolutely false."

Those who defended Bill Clinton pointed out that:

1. There was no physical evidence.
2. No one else was present.
3. She didn't remember the date or the month that it allegedly happened.

4. She never screamed.
5. She went to a Clinton campaign fund-raiser three weeks after she was allegedly raped.
6. The year after she was allegedly raped, she accepted a Clinton appointment to a nonpaying post on a state advisory board.
7. She denied the rape under oath in an affidavit for Paula Jones's lawyers.
8. She conferred with Kathleen Willey, who had been embarrassed by the White House release of her letters to Bill Clinton, before her interview with Lisa Myers.

As former White House counsel Lanny Davis said, "It is not corroboration because her girlfriend said she had a swollen lip. That doesn't make the charge of rape a fact. . . . How do we know that she didn't lie to all her friends? We know that, voluntarily, without anyone influencing her, she swore out an affidavit that she now says she lied about."

And yet, a poll taken a week after her interview with Lisa Myers showed that 84 percent of Americans believed Juanita Broaddrick . . . believed that the president of the United States was a rapist.

It didn't matter. We were a tired people, tired of pornographic imagery on the evening news, tired of feeling we were mired in filth. This was the worst . . . and we didn't want to hear it.

It was like the reaction to the *Starr Report* when it was released. The details themselves came to Bill Clinton's defense. Our heads had been forced into the mud for over a year and we wanted to free ourselves. To countenance that *this* was the president of the United States, *our* man in the White House, this person who put his shades on and said, "You'd better put some ice on that," was too much to ask of us.

Bill Bennett had it right: "Judging from most of the media and most of the public reaction, the silence on Capitol Hill, most people are just too tired to inquire into the question as to whether the President of the United States committed rape." The managing editor of the *New York Times*, Bill Keller, said, "Legally it doesn't seem to go anywhere. Congress isn't going to impeach him again. And, frankly, we've all got a bit of scandal fatigue."

As the *Washington Post* wrote, "Had NBC aired the interview during the Senate impeachment trial and the furor over Monica S. Lewinsky, it might have had a significant impact on the national climate." NBC had acted either ethically, nailing down the details of a complex and incendiary story, or had, cynically and corruptly, made a decision for its own reasons to protect the president of the United States.

In either case, NBC News president Andy Lack or his superiors or General Electric had saved Bill Clinton from removal from office . . . as surely as Vernon Jordan and Larry Flynt had.

The day after the Lisa Myers interview with Broaddrick aired, Bill Clinton was in Tucson, Arizona, giving a speech about saving Social Security and Medicare. He spent more than fifteen minutes in an auditorium greeting well-wishers as Bachman-Turner Overdrive blasted "Taking Care of Business" from the speakers. He received kisses and hugs from several women at the front of the crowd. A small group of protesters stood outside the auditorium with placards that said I BELIEVE JUANITA, PAULA, AND KATHLEEN . . . MR. CLINTON, DID JUANITA BROADDRICK CONSENT? . . . JAIL TO THE CHIEF! . . . GET OUT OF OUR HOUSE! . . . STAY AWAY FROM OUR DAUGHTERS! . . . RAPIST!

On Matt Drudge's TV show, after the Broaddrick interview on NBC aired, Drudge said, "There's all this talk behind the scenes in the media that a second woman has made sexual claims against Bill Clinton. I don't know if it's true, but it's out there." Dick Morris said, "People don't rape once." Lucianne Goldberg said, "The new allegation is assault, not rape. It occurred after he became president and comes from someone who cannot be faulted. I expect her to come forward in the next month." No one came forward.

In his new book, published shortly after Broaddrick's interview, Michael Isikoff quoted Elizabeth Ward Gracen, a former Miss America, as telling a friend she had "rough sex" with Bill Clinton when he was governor of Arkansas. Isikoff wrote, "Clinton got so carried away that he *bit her lip.*"

He was still in office, but the party was over. You could hear the fat lady singing for him across the land. People didn't want to look at him anymore.

Playing with your willard, accepting homage to your willard, was one thing . . . *this* was another. Yeah, rock and roll, gotta put the shades on, dude, before you walk out the door . . . when she's bruised, sobbing, paralyzed on the bed.

Revulsion. That was the word. There he was on TV, smiling, taking care of business, but it didn't work anymore. Juanita Broaddrick had shown us more than we ever wanted to see. He had come into our homes, where we welcomed him. He was cool. We thought he was one of us. The first rock and roll president of the United States. The first black president of the United States. The first playboy president of the United States. We had welcomed him into our homes . . . and he had befouled our walls. Maybe some of us thought we'd smelled something, but Juanita Broaddrick took us there and pointed to it: *He had befouled our walls!* We couldn't wait to get the smell off. The election campaign of 2000 began the instant we shut the set off when Juanita Broaddrick's interview ended on NBC.

The *Washington Post* reported that before Broaddrick went public, she "talked and exchanged E-mail with scandal impresario Lucianne Goldberg."

Oh no, I thought, not again. *In the right place at the right time . . .* Please God, not again! She had told Tripp to tape Monica. She had made sure Drudge leaked the Lewinsky story so the rest of the media would follow. Now Drudge had leaked the first Broaddrick details to the world. Drudge had revealed NBC's reluctance to run the interview. The *Wall Street Journal* had followed Drudge. And all this time, Lucianne Goldberg had been talking to Broaddrick?

Sweet Jesus, I thought, was it possible that a cackling, chain-smoking, croak-voiced sixty-something Bag Lady of Sleaze diagrammed all, or at least most, of these plays? And was it possible that, through Juanita Broaddrick, Lucianne Goldberg had accomplished what she had set out to do—the assassination of the president of the United States?

Lord, I thought. Bill Clinton . . . as slick as he was, as sick as he was, as smart as he was, as dumb as he was . . . never had a chance. Richard Nixon, the Night Creature who'd created Lucianne Goldberg, had exacted his infernal, Machiavellian revenge.

(9)

John Wayne McCain
Chickens Out

I let you down, pal. No, not by making that speech about the Ayatollahs Robertson and Falwell. No, not by saying the Crown Prince twists the truth like Bill Clinton. And no, not by showing up at the big California debate on the monkey screen instead of in person.

But by being the good soldier that I am and have always been.

I listened to Bob Dole, my friend, my fellow war hero, my fellow Republican. Bob Dole did to me what those gooks couldn't do in Hanoi. He talked me into quitting. He talked me into giving up.

Hey, you want straight talk, my friend? I could've been the president of the United States. But I chickened out.

Me! The Punk, McNasty, John Wayne McCain, the White Tornado, Luke Skywalker, heir to Barry Goldwater's Senate seat, friend to Ronald Reagan. I didn't have the balls.

How's that for straight talk? Are you any less heartbroken yet?

Okay, so I said to my fellow Republicans, come on, guys, let's stop sipping the Kool Aid with Jim Jones. Let's appeal to the real Americans and not the anti-abortion fanatics and the southern Grand Dragons and the gay-bashing, Jew-hating, nigger-lynching holy-holies.

And my fellow Republicans said to me: John, we've respected you until this moment for being a tough guy with those Commie cocksuckers in Hanoi, but now we see that the middle finger you jabbed at them was an act, a part of your programming as the Manchurian Candidate. John, goddamn it, you're a Commie cocksucker, too, even though you became one against your will.

Then they tarred and feathered me, screwed me, and lynched me while they glugged down their Jim Jones Kool Aid.

.   .   .

And that's when Bob Dole convinced me not to belly up to the table and put it up there to see whose was the biggest. Jesse Ventura was begging me to do it. Two polls showed me only a few points down behind Gore and the Crown Prince.

And that's when I revealed to myself and the average Americans who'd given me all that money that I was more of a Republican than an American. That was the moment, my dear friends, after they'd screwed me, that I screwed you.

That's when I went back to the empty chambers of the Senate and left you—those of you who had voted for the first time, those of you who had believed in me, those of you who had given me the dollars you couldn't afford to give—in the same old hopeless, futile lurch you've been in all these years and with all those other candidates.

I was a politician after all, you now saw. For a moment there, I'd made you forget that. For a moment there, I'd forgotten it myself.

The reason I ran for president was to give America back to you, to take it away from the toothless call girls who sit next to me in the Senate and are paid to take care of the special interests and the lobbyists. The reason I ran was to turn the world right side up again from the America where Bill Clinton is introduced before a speech as a "tough, battle-tested, principled" president and praised for his "undaunted courage and bravery." The reason I ran was because in the 1996 election, voter turnout among eighteen- to twenty-five-year-olds was the lowest in history.

The reason I ran was to give the American people access, total access, to the man who led them. No more Robopols, rope lines, and lying, full-a-shit spin doctors who wanted to "control the story of the day" and "stay on message." No more politicians who spoke like programmed Furbies. I also wanted to take the MOTEL SIX sign off the Lincoln bedroom and be a president, not a bellhop.

I'm a romantic and an adventurer. When I was a kid, my heroes were Hemingway characters like Robert Jordan, who died for a cause he believed in.

I felt there had to be a reason why I wasn't dead. God had to have something in mind that I had to do. I don't mean just the five and a half years in Hanoi, the broken arms, ribs, shoulder, teeth, and knee, the dysentery, the puking, the torture.

There was a plane crash in Corpus Christi, too, when I was in training, when my engine conked out and I fell into the bay. And another plane crash in Philadelphia, when my engine blew and I fell onto a beach. And the power lines that almost brought me down in Spain. And the carrier *Forrestal,* when I was about to take off and got hit by one of my own guys' rockets, creating a firestorm that killed a lot of men. And then, above Hanoi in my Skyhawk, getting hit by that SAM missile that blew my wing off and sent me ejecting into a lake.

But I survived. Miracles. All of them. Why does God spare a man on all those occasions? So he can drink and be merry, for tomorrow he may die? I didn't think so.

But like I said, I grew up reading Hemingway, *before* he killed himself.

I thought about running for president as Bill Clinton was going through impeachment, and when I wrote it down on a piece of paper, it made no sense:

1. Much of my own party hated me.
2. My party was already blowing the trumpets, heralding the coronation of the Crown Prince.
3. I had had as many zipper problems as Bill Clinton.
4. I had dumped my crippled wife of fifteen years and traded her in for a sexy young babe loaded with big bucks.
5. My own mouth was my biggest enemy. I had said and I knew I would continue to say some dumb-ass, tasteless things.

I thought about my list for weeks and figured I didn't have a prayer of becoming the president of the United States.

So I said, I'm running.

I decided that I am the way I am, that I can't help it. I'm a flawed human being. I'm going to let the American people see my flaws and let them decide.

My grandfather Slew smoked and drank and crashed five planes. He finished 79th out of 116 in his class at Annapolis. He became a full admiral. My father, "Good Goddamn" McCain (as in "I don't give a good goddamn") drank more than my grandfather, which was a helluva lot. He finished 423rd of 441 in his class at Annapolis. He became a full admiral.

I didn't drink as much as they did at Annapolis, but I was always a member of the Century Club, an exclusive society of those students who had earned a hundred demerits. I was an arrogant, undisciplined, insolent midshipman who felt it necessary to prove his mettle by challenging authority. In short, I acted like a jerk. I outdid Slew and Good Goddamn. I finished fifth from the bottom of my class.

I had myself photographed in James Dean poses. I went over the wall to visit greasy-floor strip clubs. When some older women wouldn't let me pick them up, I yelled, "Shove it up your ass!" at them and got arrested. When a commander asked if I knew who he was, I said, "Frankly, Commander, I don't give a rat's ass!"

I am like my grandfather Slew, who was always ready to fight. When the Japanese surrendered, my grandfather told a friend, "This surrender has come as a kind of shock to me. I feel lost. I don't know what to do. I know how to fight, but now I don't know how to relax. I am in an awful letdown period. I feel bad." A week later, he had a heart attack and died.

And I am like my father, Good Goddamn, who always liked beautiful women. My mother is a beautiful woman and she has an unmarried identical-twin sister. Both my mother and her sister were always around Good Goddamn McCain. "How do you tell 'em apart?" somebody asked him. "That's their problem," my dad said.

My friend Gary Hart says I've got a little boy inside me trying to get out. He's probably right. On the other hand, gee, *Gary Hart?* Talk about having a little boy inside you!

I hired Mike Murphy as my strategic consultant and chief media adviser, probably because he likes convicted felon Chuck Berry as much as I do. A couple of years ago, *Cosmopolitan* picked Mike as one of America's most eligible bachelors. I was very impressed with that, too.

He's thirty-seven years old, has long blond hair, a stubble, wears thick glasses, black leather jackets, Hawaiian shirts and sneakers. He calls himself a "rock and roll Republican" and is known as the "Mr. Groovy of politics."

He's the guy who did the ad that stuck Pat Buchanan's Mercedes up his ass. He's also the guy who put the lumberjack shirt on Lamar Alexander. (Great shirt, wrong guy.) He's also the guy who ran this high-road ad against Senator Chuck Robb in Virginia: "Why can't Chuck Robb tell the truth? About the cocaine parties where Robb said he never saw drugs? Or about the beauty queen in the hotel room in New York? Robb says it was only a massage."

Mike Murphy had been doing this for twenty years when I hired him. He had run campaigns out of his dorm room at Georgetown. He had won eighteen races for the statehouse or the Senate. Mike said to me, "Make the charge and let the other guy spend a million dollars to explain it. . . . We must be confrontational and define ourselves through our enemies." He bragged that in one campaign, he focused on the rape of a nine-year-old girl to prove that his opponent was soft on crime.

I liked him immediately. I called him a lot of names during the campaign. "Murphistopheles" and "the Swami" and "oo8, Bond's idiot brother."

But all I said to the press after I hired him was, "Mike Murphy is the worst low-life scum I've ever been associated with in my entire life. In some ways, he's worse than my Vietnamese interrogators."

Mike was pleased with that. I think he liked me immediately, too.

Murphistopheles and I went over my personal soft spots. Talking to Murphy about soft spots is like confessing everything to a defrocked whiskey priest who went to the joint for rape and robbery. *Why did the Republican establishment, especially so many senators, hate me? Besides the fact I tried to take their soft money bribes away?*

Well, I told Murphy, sometimes I literally growled and shook my fist at them. I got into a scuffle with Sperm Thurmond once on the Senate floor after he physically tried to stop me from speaking on a bill. I cussed another Republican colleague out on the Senate elevator, and I said, "Only a chickenshit would create a chart like that!" to another colleague on the floor. I said to that suck-ass Mitch McConnell, during a debate, "You said it was okay for us to vote for the tobacco bill because the tobacco companies would run ads in our favor." And I broke with Ronald Reagan over putting troops in Lebanon. Then I tried to stop some of the old girls' favorite pork-barrel self-diddlings: An aircraft carrier the navy didn't want, which was to be built in Trent Lott's hometown; $1.1 million for a manure disposal project; $750,000 for a study of grasshoppers.

But that wasn't even the real reason why they hated me, I told Murphy. They hated me because I don't think leadership means compromises, coalitions, and deals. They hated me because I'm a loner and like being one. They hated me because once I take a position on something, I won't change that position as a favor to the venerable round-heel sitting next to me. They hated me because I was uncooperative and a general pain in the ass—which was the same damn reason my North Vietnamese captors hated me.

Murphistopheles smiled.

What about dumping my first wife? Murphy asked.

I am a flawed human being, I told Murphy. Carol was faithful and true to me while I was in prison. She didn't deserve my treatment of her.

Look, I said, she was a beautiful woman when I married her—tall, a model. I was in bliss. She had two kids. I adopted them. We had another child. Then I went to Nam. I talked about her in prison all the time. I called her "Long Tall Sally."

I came back. I was crippled up. She had been in a car wreck. She was four inches shorter from surgeries than when I had last seen her. She was in a wheelchair. She'd put a lot of weight on.

We tried. It didn't work anymore. We were a golden couple when we'd met. We weren't that anymore. It hurt to remember how we'd been.

I started cheating on her, and then I met Cindy. Tall, model-like, beautiful. I fell in love with her. She was my *new* Long Tall Sally. A year after we met, I filed for divorce. Carol was in shock, but she understood. She said I was forty and wanted to be twenty-five again.

It looked bad, I know, not only because Cindy was so much younger and beautiful but also because she was the heir to a Budweiser distributorship. Some people said I was like Bob Dole—dumping the woman who'd helped him to walk again. I don't know. All I can say is that I tried to do the honorable thing with Carol—alimony, child support, giving her both houses.

Over time, we healed it. Carol tells the press, "I'm crazy about John McCain. I love him to pieces." Like Bob Dole's ex-wife, she supports my campaigns. I was the best man at our eldest son's wedding. Our youngest son works at the beer distributorship.

The breakup was a human tragedy. It was my fault. All of it. I didn't marry Cindy to use her for my political gain, I married her because I love her. And I have to tell you, the fact she doesn't look like Sabina Forbes helps.

Murphistopheles laughed.

A zipper problem, really? Murphy grinned. An old coot like you?

Not anymore, I said to him, but I wasn't always an old coot. Even at Annapolis, we had a group of guys, the Bad Bunch. It was the James Dean thing I told you about. Being on liberty with me, one of the guys said, was like being in a train wreck.

Women liked me. I had a friend, Dittrick; he used to tag along, hoping for sloppy seconds. The guys used to say—no shit—I'd walk into a room and you could hear the panties drop.

I went to Rio on a destroyer and met this little blond honey who was a fashion model. *Oh man!* The guys put her picture in the Academy magazine—the caption was "So nice to come home to." I remember being on a terrace with her and a bottle of champagne and a bucket of ice. *Oh Christ,* believe me, she wasn't dressed for dinner.

Then there was a girl who was a stripper—Marie, "the Flame." She used to clean her fingernails with a switchblade. And in Meridian, Mississippi, we had toga parties and bands from Memphis and guys were flying in to party all the way from the West Coast. All those Mississippi girls. *Sweet Jesus!*

I was tired a lot. I was exhausted a lot. I thought I'd die. I don't understand why I *didn't* die. I probably came closer to dying than on the plane crashes or on the *Forrestal.* I had to wade through fire to stay alive on the *Forrestal*'s deck, but that deck wasn't as hot as those Mississippi girls I'd plowed through.

Murphistopheles said, "That's enough. I can't bear anymore."

Tell me about Vietnam, Murphy said.

It's Christmas Eve, pal, I said to him. The slant-eyed cocksuckers are playing Christmas carols. Dinah Shore. Dinah Shore all the time. Jesus Christ, do you have any idea how much I hate Dinah Shore?

One of the gooks tells us there's going to be a Christmas service. I'd been in solitary for nine months. I was the scarecrow the crows were done with.

Okay, they hobble me into this room full of more flowers than a Mafia funeral home. We're seated on benches—about fifty of us POWs. We've got to sit apart so we can't talk. Some gook priest is up there at an altar. Then I see all these photographers. Flashbulbs. Movie cameras. The cocksuckers are setting us up, I think, for some propaganda film. They're just using Dinah Shore to suck us into their plot.

I get up and grin and start waving at the other guys. "Hey, howya doin', man? How's it hangin'?" One of the cocksuckers says, "No talking! No talking!" and tries to get me back on my bench.

I say, "Fuck that!" and turn to the guy nearest me and say, "Hey, pal, my name's John McCain. What's yours?" He's a scarecrow, too, but the crows aren't done with him yet.

A gook we called "the Soft Soap Fairy" says, "McCain, no talking!"

I go, "Fuck you!" real loud. I go, "This is fucking bullshit! This is terrible! This isn't Christmas! This is a propaganda show!"

I turn back to the guy I've just met. I go, "I refused to go home. I was tortured for it. They broke my rib and rebroke my arm."

The Soft Soap Fairy yells, "No talking! No talking!"

Another guard, the one we called "the Prick" runs over and screams, "No talk! No talk! No talk!"

I go, "F-u-u-u-u-ck you, you slant-eyed cocksucking motherfucking son of a bitch!"

I go hobbling around the room to the cameras, giving them the finger, going, "Fuck you! Fuck you! Fuck you!"—a scarecrow gone berserk.

Murphistopheles said, "You make it sound like fun." He was smiling.

I smiled at him, too. I said, "It wasn't *all* fun."

What are some of the stupid things you've said? Murphy asked.

I told him my Chelsea Clinton joke. "Why is Chelsea so ugly? Because Janet Reno is her father and Hillary is her mother." I had called Leo DiCaprio an androgynous wimp and Ross Perot nuttier than a fruitcake. I had called an old-age home named Leisure World "Seizure World." People with Alzheimer's, I said, "couldn't hide Easter eggs anymore." I had referred to Congress as the "Fort Knox of hypocrisy" and the Senate as a place where "most of the members don't have a life."

Murphistopheles said, "Well, at least it's all true."

How do you think we should use the POW stuff? Murphy asked.

We should low-key it, I told him, like I've always done. When I was first running for Congress in Arizona and my opponent accused me of being a carpetbagger, I said, "As a matter of fact, the place I've lived longest in my life was Hanoi." When I was criticized for leaving Carol, my pea-brained brother Joe McKmart told the press, "Here's a guy who wouldn't accept a Get Out of Jail pass from the North Vietnamese for five and a half years—so the guy is certainly not going to bail out of a marriage unless there just isn't anything there." When I was accused of using my influence to help businessman Charles Keating, I said, "Even the Vietnamese didn't question my ethics."

Low-key! Besides, I said to Murphy, by the time we go into New Hampshire, my book, which is mostly about what the gooks did to me, will be out and A&E will be airing the documentary called *John McCain, Hero or God?*

Murphistopheles cackled.

It ain't easy to campaign against a crippled POW wrapped in Old Glory, I said to Murphy. That, at least, is what one of my first congressional opponents said.

Murphy started noodling lines he thought the media would pick up. McCain survived prison camp; Bush survived summer camp. McCain survived getting his arms, ribs, shoulders, and knees broken; Bush survived trading Sammy Sosa. McCain got a silver star; Bush got daddy's car. McCain got over dysentery; Bush got over the tooth fairy. McCain's a hero; Bush is a zero. McCain's a man; Bush ran.

"We need a low-key visual reminder," Murphy said, "like Dole clutching his pen in his right hand all the time."

Murphistopheles thought about it and smiled a sociopathic smile.

"We let the press see Cindy spraying your hair," he said. "It reminds everybody you can't lift your arms above your shoulders."

That, I thought, was hellishly Murphistophelian.

With a pocketful of good luck charms, including an old penny and an American Indian medicine bag, I started campaigning in New Hampshire. I didn't feel like Luke Skywalker, I felt like the Elephant Man. We didn't have any crowds; we didn't have any money; we hardly had any volunteers. In the beginning, it was mostly Long Tall Sally and Murphy and me.

"My friends," I said at one town hall meeting after another, "I will say things you agree with and some things you don't agree with. But I promise you this. I will always tell you the truth, no matter what. You have my solemn promise. You may disagree with me often, but I will never embarrass you. We need to reform government. We need to reform politics. We need to reform the military, the education system. We need to reform the tax code, which would lead to greater freedom for all Americans. Anyone who is satisfied with the status quo should vote for somebody else. But anyone who believes that America is greater than the sum of its special interests should stand with me."

The folks gawking at me like a circus freak didn't like the truth sometimes, but I told it anyway.

"Who won the war in Vietnam?" somebody asked at a town hall meeting.

"We lost," I said.

"So you think a gay person could be a good president of the United States?"

"Absolutely," I said.

A caller on a radio talk show said to me, "You are misinformed."

"No!" I barked. "*You* are misinformed!"

Anyone anywhere could ask me anything. No rope lines. No security. No team of advisers. No entourage. No airs. No pomp and circumstance. They didn't know how to handle it. They couldn't fathom I'd stay at the town hall meeting until every question was answered. They didn't know how to react to the way I handled the meetings, either.

When a question was long and garbled, I said, "Come on, get to the point. Spit it out!"

When it was time to introduce local politicos, I said, "We have several Spanish-American War veterans here today."

When I saw someone in the crowd who looked wacko or was dressed oddly, I invited them up on the stage and gave them the microphone.

Murphy, I noticed, was doing his rock and roll best on TV interviews, which often included Bush aides, to back me up.

"May I finish?" a Bush aide asked.

"No, you may not!" Murphy said.

"Don't spin me," Murphy told a Bush aide. "I'm in the racket."

"You *are* the racket, man," the Bush aide said.

My favorite was Murphy with Tim Russert and a Bush aide on *Meet the Press*.

"How do you beat Al Gore in the November election?" Russert asked.

"Well, it'll be tough," the Bush aide said.

"Nominate John McCain," Murphy said.

He introduced me to a crowd by saying, "John McCain is the skunk at the garden party in Washington."

And I responded by pointing to him and saying, "That's what happens when you hire people from the prison release program."

We had begun. I was running for the highest office in the land. I was telling people the truth as I saw it. This is what my life had been spared for: gawking strangers. I hadn't had so much fun since I was firing rockets, dropping bombs, and shooting off guns.

I was nuts. That, at least, was what some of my colleagues in the Senate were whispering to the press off the record, while the word they chose for attribution was *temper.*

What got me wasn't what they were saying. I *am* probably a little nuts, but not as nuts as Slew and Good Goddamn McCain were; or as nuts as my screw-loose brother Joe McKmart, a former newspaper reporter, who once wrote a fake story about Mickey Mouse divorcing Minnie Mouse; or as nuts as my mom, who's eighty-seven years old and just bought a new car to drive to places like Outer Mongolia and Uzbekistan.

What got me was that they were saying I had *been driven crazy* by my five and a half years in captivity. So. I had been in prison for five and a half years for the love of my country, and now they were saying that the love of my country disqualified me for the presidency. Poor John had *suffered too much.* So he couldn't be president. The reason poor John did all those town meetings, they said, was because, after all that time in caged solitary, poor John had a compulsive need to talk.

"Where do they get all this shit?" I said to Murphy one day, and he laughed and said, "Careful—temper!" That hippopotamus who's the governor up in Michigan and wants to be the Crown Prince's footstool so badly, Engler, farted that I was a "hot-tempered psycho." *Saturday Night Live* did a skit saying I couldn't eat without a blindfold. I wasn't allowed to be angry, a reporter explained to me, but being tense or irritated was okay.

Irritated? Tense? Hell, I was so pissed off, I felt like going down to the Senate chamber and body-slamming and head-butting those chickenshit assholes.

Murphy and I started making fun of the whole thing.

"Well, you gotta be a little nuts to want to be president," I said.

We allowed CBS to film our prep for the first debate, and Murphy stood there in a nauseatingly hideous Hawaiian shirt and said, "Senator, you killed a guy on the way here to the debate. You're a screaming, hotheaded maniac. You're exploding every minute. Do you have the temperament to be president of the United States?"

"Well," I said. "You know, that really makes me mad."

The other reason they thought I was crazy was the bus. We thought about calling it the Bullshit Express but settled on the Straight Talk Express instead.

We rode the bus up and down New Hampshire every day and we let the reporters (Murphy called them "the scrums") ride with me *all the time.*

It had never been done in American politics before—full access all the time and nothing off the record. Since the media, to most Republicans, is the enemy, I was eating with the enemy, pissing with the enemy, snoring with the enemy almost twenty-four hours a day. So I *had* to be nuts!

Full access all the time . . . at a time when Clinton had never even answered one question about Juanita Broaddrick, when Lockhart tried to call only on his pals in the White House press room, when everybody still remembered Ronald Reagan cupping his ear and pretending not to hear questions about Iran-Contra. Most scrums were so cynical about politicians that, in the beginning of my campaign, they seemed almost insulted by "full access all the time." I was being manipulative, they told me, by not manipulating them. Since most scrums were used to politicians lying, a politician who told the truth had to be lying by telling it.

They didn't know whether to shit or go blind when they boarded the Straight Talk Express and realized they could ask me anything about anything and it was all on the record. I remember one day when a scrum got on for the first time. "Senator," he said, "can I ask you a couple of questions?"

"We answer all questions on this bus," I told him. "And sometimes we lie. Mike Murphy is one of the greatest liars anywhere."

The scrum blinked his eyes. I looked at Murphy and said, "Aren't you, Mike?"

Murphy grinned and nodded and I turned back to the scrum and said, "Murphy has spent his life trying to destroy political careers."

Murphy said, "I'll have yours destroyed by election day."

The scrum was gaping at us, his jaw hanging.

Murphy said to him, "The problem with the media is, you're obsessed with process, with how many left-handed, independent soccer moms are going to vote."

"In other words," I told the scrum, "you're assholes."

Like the gawking voters, the scrums were astounded by the truths I told them.

"Why are you running for president, Senator?"

"Because it's mandatory for any senator not under indictment or in detox to lust for the presidency."

"How do you feel about the media, Senator?"

"It's the first opportunity that I've had to meet with card-carrying members of the Communist party."

"What has your favorite day of the campaign been?"

"My favorite day of the campaign was that day we went over to New York and I saw all you guys pushing one another out of the way and slipping on the ice."

"What was your life like as a naval aviator?"

"I drove a Corvette, dated a lot, spent all my free hours at bars and beach parties, and generally misused my good health and youth."

I liked John F. Kennedy, Jr., a lot, and the final editorial he wrote for *George* magazine compared my candidacy to Luke Skywalker fighting the Death Star. So we started screwing around on the bus with light sabers and playing John Williams's *Star Wars* theme on the loudspeaker.

One day, I clutched my chest melodramatically and told the scrums, "It's the Death Star! They're firing from all directions! Luke may not make it."

We said our unofficial campaign slogan was "Burn it down!" in honor of Stokely Carmichael and black power, or "Eradicate evil!" in honor of George Lucas and Ronald Reagan.

Murphy told the scrums there was a line he wanted me to use in a debate with the Crown Prince. "When there's a world hot spot, there's no second chance."

I told them I had come up with a line the Crown Prince could use in his campaign. "When the scouting reports come in to the Texas Rangers, there is only one lonely man in a dark office."

"This campaign," Murphy said, "is the amazing Wallendas!"

"Quick," I said to him, "hand me a chair!"

"I'll get your unicycle for you," Murphy said.

After a while, the scrums realized that this was a movable circus and they started to enjoy themselves. Connie Stevens was on the bus with us one day, and I said to them, "I first met Connie at a USO dinner." They all wrote it down. Then I said, "But I was with her vicariously several times." They all wrote it down. Then I yelled, "I hate Eddie Fisher!" and they all stopped writing.

In a more serious vein, I told them that if I was ever elected president, I'd hold weekly press conferences like JFK and would also meet with ten members of Congress each week for a televised question and answer session.

"Couldn't that be embarrassing?" one of the scrums asked, like he'd just found a revelation in the Torah.

"Absolutely," I said.

Something wild was going on out there. I could feel it in the crowds, which were bigger and more gaga at each stop. I saw something in the way they wanted to touch me that put chills down my back. I saw something in their eyes when they looked at me that humbled me. "No more Clinton-Gore! No more Clinton-Gore!" they yelled when they saw me, yelling it like we'd yelled "Beat Army!" at the Naval Academy, their faces blazing, their voices hoarse.

There were people with signs saying VEGETARIANS FOR MCCAIN! HIPPIES FOR MCCAIN! CARNIVORES FOR MCCAIN! There were signs that said CINDY IS A BABE! One day, I saw a mob of people come tramping through a muddy construction site just to get a look at me. My book was a big best-seller by now, and they came to the town hall meetings and rallies, holding it close to their hearts. A mother told us she had been at a Bush rally and had left because her three-year-old kept asking to see me.

I kept telling them the same thing: "I won't lie to you! I won't embarrass you! We have to reform this government!"

I said, "I'm going to beat Al Gore like a drum!" and the crowds went crazy.

I said, "This is the beginning of the end of the truth-twisting politics of Bill Clinton and Al Gore," and they screamed, "No more Clinton-Gore! No more Clinton-Gore! No more Clinton-Gore!"

Our rallies ended in pandemonium. *Star Wars* blasting. Confetti guns showering the air. The deejay we'd hired with the five earrings, who'd just come off tour with the Foo Fighters and Nine Inch Nails, spinning Fat Boy Slim. A tape of Dick Vitale yelling, "Let's do it, baby! Let's do it!"

We took a day away from New Hampshire and spent it in New York, and I saw the same electric zip in the crowds there, like they'd eaten the wrong Arizona mushrooms. The Crown Prince and his rubber-mouthed governor pal, Pataki, another footstool volunteer, were trying to keep me off the ballot. Murphy suggested we hold a press conference across the street from the Russian embassy. "In Russia, there will be more than one name on the ballot," I said. "In New York, unless something happens, there will be only one name on the ballot— George W. Bush!" The crowds kept screaming, "No more Clinton-Gore! No more Clinton-Gore!"

We weren't prepared for what happened on election night in New Hampshire. Nineteen points! The Crown Prince was humiliated. He didn't even want to call me. He tried to have an aide call one of my aides, and only when my aide told him to stuff it did the Crown Prince make his obligatory call. Nineteen points! The biggest primary turnout in New Hampshire's history! The biggest new voter turnout in New Hampshire's history! The biggest young voter turnout in New Hampshire's history!

Oh, what a great ride! We got the covers of all three Communist news magazines. Red Army commandant Mike Wallace said he was considering taking a leave from *60 Minutes* to become my press secretary. Commissar Jay Leno was faxing us jokes to use on the stump. We raised $5 million on the Internet in the next week. They were talking about "the McCain Mutiny." There were people out there who called themselves "McCainiacs." An aide to Al Gore said, "McCain's not just a man. He's become an idea. The idea that he's not just politics as usual. It's powerful stuff." The latest poll showed me dead even with the Crown Prince in South Carolina, our next primary stop, where I'd been twenty-seven points behind last week.

The Crown Prince looked like he'd peed himself in public. His highness fled back to Austin amid stories that he traveled with his own fluffy pillow.

"I think you're going to be nominated," Murphy said to me, "and then you're going to be president."

And then Murphistopheles, who had no business saying this, added, "You poor devil."

We knew South Carolina was a major part of the Crown Prince's attempt to rig the game—the redneck and fundamentalist fire wall erected to keep him safe from any damage those crazy Yankees might have done. It was the primary purposely scheduled immediately after New Hampshire for that reason, an attempt to get the Bible-thumping populace to whitewash whatever graffiti may have been sprayed on the Crown Prince's royal carriage.

But we thought we could beat Bush at his own game. There were more veterans in South Carolina than in any other state, and when we arrived, at three in the morning, we were greeted by a crowd of cheering kids. Our bus was pulled over by an inbred Highway Patrolman, who stopped us because he wanted to meet me. Still, it was a state where T-shirts were being sold with Lincoln's picture and the words SIC SEMPER TYRANNIS—"thus ever to tyrants"—which that other androgynous wimp actor had shouted before he shot Lincoln.

When the Crown Prince made his first appearance in the state at Bob Jones University, the musk of his New Hampshire pee still in his pores, we knew how scared he was. Bob Jones didn't permit interracial dating, didn't permit gay alumni to visit, considered Catholicism a satanic cult and the Pope the Antichrist. Bob Jones was the symbol of the old-time, racist, lynching South, the Eagle's Nest of the cross and pitchfork Nazis. George and Laura Bush were introduced there as "sweet spirits who love the Lord." By appearing there, the Crown Prince came out of the Compassionate Conservative closet and was sending a frantic SOS to the South Carolina Reich to save him because he was one of them.

When I first saw the Crown Prince in South Carolina, I thought he was trying to impersonate me. He had a big sign behind him that said he was now the Reformer. He, who had spent much of his life within the shadow of the White House, was now the Outsider. He had a bus now. He was doing his best to string entire paragraphs together. He moved his private security detail out of camera range. He suddenly attended town hall meetings and what he called "media avails." He had stolen whatever had worked for us, even our chant. His people walked through crowds yelling, "No more Clinton-Gore! No more Clinton-Gore!"

And now they had their own confetti guns, their red-white-and-blue Nixon balloons stashed somewhere in an Austin castle.

I was pissed. "This stuff isn't going to work," I said to Murphy, "it's transparent."

"You've got to remember," Murphy said, "Republicans are the Stupid party."

When Dan Quayle became the first prominent Republican to fly into the state to endorse the Crown Prince, I saw how right Murphy was. With David Letterman and others saying George W. Bush was "the next Dan Quayle," they brought Quayle in to endorse him? What *was* this? A ritualistic passing on of dunce hats? Final proof of the genetic enervation of the aristocracy? A piece of wicked political sabotage Murphistopheles had pulled off?

Then the Crown Prince stood there smirking next to that clown who attacked me for "forgetting about veterans once he returned from Hanoi." This was slashing at the place in my heart where I live and breathe! Nothing is more sacred to me than veterans' benefits and rights.

We couldn't let it go. It hurt too much. Bush had stood there simpering while that crotch rot told his sordid lie. "We will run a tough campaign," Murphy said. "Like McCain said, we're ready to punch back. We're not Bill Bradley."

Murphy wrote an ad saying the Crown Prince "twists the truth like Bill Clinton." The Crown Prince ran around in circles, shrieking. It was like I'd pissed into the fountain of holy water at St. Peter's. Comparing George W. Bush to Bill Clinton? It was a burn-at-the-stake offense! After beheading and dismemberment! The crosses and the pitchforks in the farm fields of the South Carolina Reich were raised to the sky!

Oberführer Pat Robertson attacked my campaign chairman, Warren Rudman, as a "vicious bigot" in taped phone calls all over the state. This was like Bill Clinton calling George Washington a liar. Chris Matthews of *Hardball* saw it for what it was: "They went after Warren Rudman because he is Jewish. They were playing that card." Of course they were. The card was part of the Bob Jones hand. Get the crosses and the pitchforks out to support the Crown Prince against the niggers, the Catlicks, the kikes, the faggots, the dykes, and John McCain.

Trying to say that he didn't know about the Robertson tape was another transparent Crown Prince lie. Sitting right at George W. Bush's table as a paid campaign consultant, part of his official team, was Babyface Ralph Reed, the former head of the Christian Coalition, which was founded by Robertson. Storm trooper Reed was Oberführer Robertson's pet ferret.

I went on a talk show in South Carolina one day and a caller asked me, "Did you ever commit adultery with prostitutes in Subic Bay?"

. . .

That was nothing, though, compared to what I discovered was going on . . . in E-mails, faxes, leaflets, talk shows, and telephone "push polls" organized by the crosses and the pitchforks as the Crown Prince smirked, turned away, and held his nose. This is what they were saying about me and my family:

I wasn't tortured during the war. I had sex with another POW and several of my captors. I had ratted out other POWs in Hanoi. Cindy was a drug addict, unfit for the White House. Cindy had to have a hysterectomy because I'd given her a venereal disease. Cindy's dad had ties to a murder. Cindy had a deformed uterus and that's why I was cheating on her. I was having an affair with Connie Stevens. I helped arrange the murder of a man who was going to expose us. I had black illegitimate children. My adopted Bangladeshi daughter, Bridget, was one of them, her mother a black prostitute.

They were trying to dirty me so badly that those who believed I was something new and clean in the dirty world of politics wouldn't come out to vote. They were trying to kill the magic. They were trying to disillusion those who, for the first time in a long time, believed in someone. They didn't want new voters; they wanted only their corrupt friends and allies to vote. They wanted to depress America and make her more cynical. They didn't want excitement; they wanted boredom. They wanted to kill hope. They didn't want anything to change. They were the cancerous sphincter muscles of the status quo, their reek undisguised by the perfume of holy water.

When a woman at a rally told me about how her fourteen-year-old son broke down in tears after getting a push-poll call telling him I was a liar and a cheat, I told Murphy we weren't running any more negative ads.

"They're killing us," Murphy said. "We've got to run them. People say they don't like negative ads, but negative information is an important part of their decision making. It works."

"I don't care," I said. "I don't want to wake up after a victory and feel dirty. I'm not going to take the low road to the White House."

I thought about the Crown Prince and remembered him boyishly hugging me at the first debate in New Hampshire. It was all this "I love ya, man! You're my buddy! I'm proud of ya!" Then I'm suddenly this awful guy and the only thing that has changed is that I beat him like a drum in New Hampshire.

Our campaign was never the same after South Carolina. Chris Matthews was on the mark again. He called what George W. Bush did a "scorched-earth campaign . . . close to the allied bombing of Dresden."

I'd put it a little differently. It was Adolf Hitler's rampaging goons celebrating Kristallnacht.

We won Michigan, killing off Engler's footstool dreams forever, and the Crown Prince never even called to congratulate me, but I didn't give a shit about that by then. I was still angry. No, I was *horrified* by what I'd seen in South Carolina. South Carolina took me back to Hanoi: rats scuttling in the cell, open, seeping sores, a turd floating in a well.

I'd started talking about it in Michigan already, about "the Christian Right, the Extreme Right," about "the bunch of idiots who run Bob Jones University." I said, "My friends, my party has lost its way. I think a lot of Americans feel that the Republican party doesn't represent them anymore and that we have too narrow a focus. I believe we have to make sure that everyone is on the playing field, that there is an equal opportunity for everybody, that we will not favor one group over another, particularly as a result of financial contributions."

And then I flew my Skyhawk into Virginia Beach, Virginia, Pat Robertson's home, and I targeted Robertson and his smarmy Axis ally, Jerry Falwell, personally: "We are the party of Ronald Reagan, not Pat Robertson," I said. "The political tactics of division and slander are not our values. They are corrupting influences on religion and politics. . . . Neither party should be defined by pandering to the outer reaches of American politics and the agents of intolerance, whether they be Al Sharpton or Louis Farrakhan on the Left or Jerry Falwell or Pat Robertson on the Right."

The next day, on the bus, I called Robertson and Falwell "agents of intolerance" and an "evil influence" over the Republican party. "To stand up and take on the forces of evil," I said, "that's my job. You're supposed to tolerate evil in your party in the name of party unity? That's not what the party is all about."

Murphy told the scrums, "The speech was right. The speech is why he's running."

"It's a home run," Murphy said to me.

But I knew my wing had been shot off. I knew my Skyhawk was crashing and I was going down with her. There was no ejection mechanism in a presidential campaign. "John McCain is dead politically," said Lyn Nofziger, who I always thought was Ronald Reagan's smartest political adviser. I had done pretty much what John Anderson, another Republican, had done in 1980, when he opened fire on the National Rifle Association.

.   .   .

Maybe I just should have called them nutbags and phonies.

Pat Robertson keeps predicting the end of the world as casually and as often as weathermen in Arizona predict thunderstorms.

Jerry Falwell thinks Tinky Winky is gay because he's purple and carries a purse and has a triangle on his head.

Pat Robertson rails against premarital sex but adjusted his wedding date to hide the fact the child was conceived out of wedlock.

Jerry Falwell said he asked Jimmy Carter, "Sir, why do you have known practicing homosexuals on your senior staff in the White House?" He also said The Antichrist will be "a Jewish man who is alive today." (Warren Rudman probably.)

Pat Robertson was taped at a Businessmen's Fellowship event, saying, "Satan begone . . . a hernia has been healed. If you're wearing a truss, you can take it off. It's gone! Several people are being healed of hemorrhoids and varicose veins!"

Jerry Falwell, discussing welfare recipients, said, "That crowd ought to be left to starve until they decide that a job is a good deal."

Pat Robertson called himself an expert in tax law on his résumé although he had failed the bar exam in New York State and never practiced.

Jerry Falwell sold a videotape on his TV show that accused Bill Clinton of being a murderer.

Pat Robertson said, "A Supreme Court ruling is not the law," and that Congress should "ignore a Supreme Court ruling if it so chooses."

Jerry Falwell demanded a federal task force to consider quarantine or imprisonment for gay people who have sex after they've been diagnosed with AIDS.

On second thought, I'm proud of myself. *Evil* was exactly the right word.

A lot of the rest of it is a blur. They put on more lying ads in New York and California, and the Crown Prince appeared everywhere with Catholic priests sticking out from under his robes. Governor Pataki's rubber face rigidified into a permanent ass kiss.

Murphy showed me some "soft negative" ads he wanted to run in response to their new slanders, and I said no.

I scurried like a red-eyed, white-haired specter up and down the country, saying, "Tell Governor Bush and his cronies to stop destroying the American political system!" and "Governor Bush and his buddies are stealing this election!" and "No young American will ever vote again!"

I did the California debate on the video screen because I was afraid that if I was in the same room with the Crown Prince I'd either kill him or be dragged away in a strait-jacket, or both. I remember getting ready for that debate in a studio in St. Louis and suddenly drawing a blank and Murphy leaning down and saying to me, "It's okay. It's okay." And I remember saying to him, "Murphy, he may be a dishonest candidate running a vicious campaign, but in the end, nobody gives a shit."

The day before Super Tuesday, my Murphistopheles and I had a chilled vodka together and he told me he thought that, as a result of what we'd done, his career with the Republican party was over.

Murphy said, "John, we made you the most popular politician in America, but they won't nominate you."

I said, "Murphy, they'd rather lose the election than nominate me."

I ended it on a bright and crisp day at my house in Sedona after Super Tuesday. Long Tall Sally stood there holding my hand. It ended not with "Hail to the Chief" but with the instrumental version of the theme song from *Rocky,* not with my hero Teddy Roosevelt but with Sylvester Stallone.

I said Long Tall Sally and I were going to Bora Bora. I said I expected to support the Republican nominee.

Murphistopheles cried and I choked up.

I'll tell you what I think of the nominee I will support for president, the Crown Prince, George W. Bush.

David Letterman is right when he says he is "the next Dan Quayle" and that his slogan should be "a dumb guy with connections."

But the real Crown Prince revealed himself to David Letterman weeks after the man had had quintuple bypass surgery.

Dave asked, "What does it mean that you're a uniter, not a divider?"

And George W. Bush said, "That means when it comes time to sew up your chest, we use stitches instead of opening it up, is what that means."

What it really means is that he's not just dumb. He's dumb *and* mean.

When I was a POW, we'd tell each other the stories and scenes of movies we'd seen. My favorite was *One-Eyed Jacks.* My favorite scene was Marlon Brando calling Slim Pickens a "scum-sucking pig."

The Crown Prince, the Republican nominee I will support for president, is a scum-sucking pig.

.　.　.

Long Tall Sally and I went to Bora Bora. We sat in the sun. We listened to my spiritual adviser, Chuck Berry. It wasn't easy to go cold turkey. I tried to make believe and I kept using the phone to talk to my staff for temporary fixes to help me with my withdrawal.

Jesse Ventura kept calling me, telling me about polls that showed me only three or four points behind in a three-way race.

Bob Dole kept calling me. I love Bob Dole. He's one of my oldest friends. I traveled with him on the campaign trail in 1996 to try to keep him smiling. (It wasn't easy.) He'd almost picked me as his vice president.

Party unity, Bob Dole said to me. He kept beating me with it. *Party unity, John, party unity, party unity! This party has been good to you, John. You're a lifelong Republican, John. Your mother is a Republican. Your mother attended every day of the Alger Hiss / Whittaker Chambers hearings and she rooted for Chambers. You love your mother, John! You're not a Hiss man, John!* Bob Dole beat me like a drum.

In the end, I told Jesse I couldn't do it. I *am* a lifelong Republican. I *do* love my mother. I'm *not* a Hiss man. Jesse and I made a date to meet in a shark cage sometime somewhere. I don't know, maybe navy SEALs *do* have more balls than navy fliers. He wears his feather boa more often than I wear mine.

I went back to the Senate, and Trent Lott called me "one of our brothers," although he also said, "We're not going to hold a parade or anything for him." I did an interview with Dan Rather and he said, "The leaders of your own party, left to their own devices, would cut your heart out and throw your liver to the dogs."

I read some articles that had piled up in the office during the campaign. Frank Gamboa, my roommate at Annapolis, said, "He'd push the limits at Annapolis, he'd push the edge, but John never went *over* the edge." My numbnuts brother Joe McKmart said, "John was always a guy who pushed the boundary, but he always knew what the boundary was." And David Broder of the *Washington Post* wrote, "John McCain is the chairman of the Senate Commerce Committee by sufferance of the Senate Republican Conference and that is a very important incentive for him to stay and be a loyal Republican."

"I failed myself. I failed my fellow Americans. I failed my family, and I failed my country."

Those were the words I used to describe how I felt about signing a confession after Vietcong torture.

·   ·   ·

Chris Matthews said to me, "You were a rock star, but it's more important than music. It's the country you had in your hands."

Goddamn it, Murphistopheles, I told you I was a flawed human being. Goddamn it, Murphy. *Goddamn it!* We had fun, didn't we?

[10]

The Man with the Golden Willard

"He must, like, belong to the CD of the month club or something," Monica said to Linda Tripp. "Well, I looked at his CDs. It's really weird. Like he has these CDs that are really weird. Like sax for lovers and stuff. Uch!"

Warren Beatty for president? Oh my! *Warren Beatty?* In this cigar-choked, willard-gagging climate? The Man with the Golden Willard? *In the White House?* Even for Hollywood, a town noted more for mind-numbing plot twists than logic, it was mind-numbing news. God how I loved Hollywood! Even after a quarter century of contributing mind-numbing plot twists of my own, I still didn't understand it.

Warren for president made about as much sense to me as the marriage between Barbra and James Brolin. Barbra is about as fervently Jewish as Golda Meir, and here she had married a redneck cowboy who had called me one Sunday afternoon in the late eighties and yelled at me about the attorneys I was using in a negotiation to buy his house. "You and your goddamn Jewboy attorneys!" Barbra's future husband had said. *Ohhkay.* Now Warren Beatty was going to be president. His biggest previous political accomplishment had been getting Paul Simon and Art Garfunkel to reunite for a McGovern fund-raiser.

When I heard that his candidacy had been first floated by Arianna Huffington—"We need someone who can pull the nation around the fire and draw us together"—I figured that it was a treacherous plot hatched by the opportunistically right-wing Sorceress, a secret plan to embarrass liberals further. Let the liberals huzzah around Warren, let the public fall in love, and then expose the man's satyriasis, his praying mantis need for woman flesh, his narcissism, his megalomania.

Forget blow jobs and masturbation as fireside dinner table talk; now we'd be discussing priapism and male nymphomania, although, in a line that made the whole town roar, the *Los Angeles Times* referred to Warren as a "political virgin."

I wondered how the poor battered feminists would react to the Man with the Golden Willard . . . who had bedded at least three generations of movie stars; whose conquests included Leslie Caron, Julie Christie, Madonna, Natalie Wood, Joan Collins, Diane Keaton, Isabelle Adjani, Mary Tyler Moore, Michelle Phillips, Britt Eklund, Joni Mitchell, Liv Ullmann, Carly Simon, Diane Ladd, Rona Barrett, Jessica Savitch, Jane Fonda, Vivien Leigh, and Annette Bening; whose favorite introductory line to women had for so long been, "What's new, pussycat?"; whose own sister, Shirley MacLaine, said, "I'd like to do a love scene with him just to see what all the yelling is about."

There were obvious and special Clintonian parallels. "Three, four, five times a day, every day, was not unusual for Warren," former fiancée Joan Collins said. "*And he was able to accept phone calls at the same time.*" A friend said, "Warren wants the entire world to go to bed with him." Rona Barrett, an old friend, said, "I love Warren, but I think he's a whore."

Warren admitted, "Sometimes I wake up about four a.m. and I'm scared for a minute because I wonder where the hell I am," and allowed that "if I tried to keep up with what is said about me sexually, I would be speaking to you from a jar at the University of Chicago Medical Center." Woody Allen said, perhaps euphemistically, that if reincarnated, "I'd like to be Warren's fingertips."

In other ways, Warren was strikingly un-Clintonian. One of Hollywood's most esteemed liberals, Warren was not, personally as opposed to ideologically, a great egalitarian. One movie crew disliked him so much that they locked him into the jail cell in which he'd been shooting a scene. (Warren said, "All right, so I'm not buddy-buddy with the crews. I don't get paid to be friends with them and they don't get paid to be friends with me. Making pals of grips and electricians is not an actor's most important job on the set.") Told by Jack Warner to go to the White House to meet JFK if he wanted to play him in *PT 109*, Warren said, "If the President wants me to play him, tell him to come here and soak up some of *my* atmosphere." And when a reporter asked about a batch of unpaid bills on the floor of the car Warren was driving, Warren said, "I can't be bothered with things like this. I keep telling those people to send their bills to my business managers if they want to get paid."

Hollywood, though, always looking for a new kick, was in high dither. Robert Evans's magnificent candle-glowing whorehouse was a smoke-filled room where not box-office grosses but platform planks were being discussed. This was Warren's second home, a place he'd spent so many nights in stimulating company, plotting moves to fulfill nubile voters' needs and desires, staying forever young, plugged into the current social fabric. Warren even had his own seat in Bob's screening room—right next to Jack's—Warren maybe taking oh so cool peripheral glances in the darkness at the masses of faceless but well-rounded voters who had to sit on the floor.

Bob himself was so excited. Warren's candidacy or noncandidacy or potential candidacy or near candidacy . . . was an absolute tonic to the effect of his strokes, and he could almost see himself as President Beatty's Kissinger or Dave Powers or Bobby Baker or Vernon Jordan. This was so much more fun than writing his letters to stamp out Alzheimer's or humming around the house wearing the George Bush White House baseball cap that Marlin Fitzwater had given him. More fun even than the parties back in the grand old days before he was broke. President Beatty would guarantee "the kid would stay in the picture forever," drowning out the whispers about the cocaine conviction and that body found out in the desert.

Pat Cadell was back in business, too, rejuvenated like Evans, but looking a little gray around the edges, looking, indeed, almost unrecognizably different from the way he did in the Jimmah and Governor Moonbeam days, looking like he'd been withered by defeat and time, that old liberal spark dimmed by trying to write TV shows around commercial breaks. And it was whispered that Gary Hart hovered in the background, too, Svengali to his former Svengali, just as he'd once been Svengali to McGovern, one of the greatest electoral bust-outs in American history . . . Gary Hart, whose act of cowardice in withdrawing from the 1988 race sealed his fate forever as yet another gutless political wonder.

What a curious crew, I thought, Warren and the Sorceress and Evans and Cadell and Hart. It was a scam, I felt. It had to be. Warren was such a navel-contemplative control freak, such a self-involved snob that he would never expose himself (sorry) to the hoi polloi. Not to the general mass of the hoi polloi, as opposed to individual, well-structured ones. Not politically, as opposed to sexually.

In many ways, he was the very opposite of Bill Clinton as a political and psychosexual animal. Bill Clinton went into a room and seduced en masse. The triumph of his en masse seduction turned him on and he had to relieve himself with some faceless voter. But Warren held himself aloof and superior en masse. He seduced individually and relieved himself individually.

Bill Clinton liked pressing the flesh and laying on hands. Warren needed his own grand space. He didn't like to be touched in well-lighted rooms. The flesh he liked to press was horizontal, not vertical. Bottom line: Bill Clinton was a politician who could act; Warren was an actor acting the role of politician.

Bill Clinton, for example, knew that a politician had to be a whore for the cameras. Cameras could invade him from a thousand different angles at any moment. He'd been invaded so often, he couldn't feel it anymore. Warren tried to give cameras only his right profile. He tried to control the lighting, the distance, and the shutter speed. To Bill Clinton, a camera meant any schmuck at any campaign appearance. To Warren, a camera meant Vilmos Zsigmond or Helmut Newton. Not to mention that in his last couple of movies, it looked as if Warren had given instructions to be photographed through gauze.

It was the narcissism of the actor as opposed to the politician. Actors had to approve the cover art on magazines. Politicians had to grin and bear it. Actors made their living with their faces. Politicians made their living with their faces, too, but there were, at least in most cases, other dimensions in the package. In a town filled with narcissistic actors, Warren Beatty, I knew firsthand, won the prize in the Cracker Jack box.

He lived for more than a decade in the penthouse suite of the old Beverly Wilshire Hotel, and days after he moved out, I found myself there, staring at his mirrors, staring at myself. I had come from Marin County to spend a day on a set and the studio had taken out the penthouse suite for me. But I had finished my business early and was in a studio-supplied limo on the way back to the airport when I was struck by intense nausea and stomach cramps. I sought relief in a couple of gas station rest rooms, but both the nausea and the cramps were worse, and I remembered the accommodations the studio had reserved for me at the Wilshire.

I instructed my driver to take me there, checked in, and was led to what had been Warren Beatty's penthouse suite. There were mirrors everywhere—*everywhere*—on the walls, the ceiling. The suite was one big mirror. You could see yourself from every angle. I saw myself. I was sweating, pale, with a greenish hue. I raced for the bathroom. There were mirrors all over the bathroom, too. I left the bathroom door open and saw myself sitting there, not just in the bathroom mirrors but in the living room mirrors, as well. I saw myself looking godawful from six different angles. I saw myself wiping myself and throwing up from six different angles.

I thought, What sort of man wants to look at himself *all the time*, twenty-four hours a day, every day? Doing *everything* that human beings do. Was this routine benign Hollywood narcissism or self-devouring, all-encompassing neurosis? Did Warren Beatty enjoy watching himself defe-cate? Because he'd put himself in a living space where he was *forced* to watch himself defecate. Was this the ultimate Hollywood hubris, to watch yourself on the can? Or was it self-punishment for his life of opulent excess? Was *this* how he kept in touch with ordinary Americans? Was this the daily self-abnegation that fueled his bleeding liberal heart?

An hour later, I checked out of the Wilshire and went back to the airport. My various evacuations had cost the studio $2,800. I wondered how it would appear on the production budget.

Considering him now as our possible new president, I remembered, too, the experience (some in Hollywood called it a "near-death experience") that I'd had with him on one of my movies—*Jade*, produced by Evans. It was an experience many in Hollywood had had with Warren, who was also an Academy Award–winning producer and director.

The word on Warren in Hollywood was that he had unmade more movies he'd been involved in than he'd made. He considered himself not an actor, not a star, but an auteur. Or, to use the Sorceress's word, a "story-teller." Warren would commit to do a movie and then he'd work with the writer to rewrite the script. Then he'd work with the director to redo the schedule. Then he'd work with the cinematographer to redo the shots. Then he'd work with the costume designer to redo the costumes. Then he'd work with the hair person and redo the hair. Then, when everything had been redone to his satisfaction, he'd pull out of the movie. He'd claim he'd lost confidence in the script, which he'd forced to be rewritten to his design. He'd claim he'd lost confidence in the director, who was suffering a nervous breakdown.

The studios had let him get away with it for a long time, even though he hadn't had a hit movie in many years, because he was Warren Beatty. He was, even though he had to be shot through gauze, a legendary star. After all this money—the rewriting, rescheduling, rehairing, and so on—had been spent for nothing, the studio, exhausted, would tire of the project itself— "It's got the clap," as they say in Hollywood—and the movie would never be made.

Knowing all this, when Evans suggested Warren as the lead for *Jade*, I suffered a near relapse of the symptoms I'd relieved myself of in Warren's penthouse suite many years before. I truly felt a near-death experience, saved only at the last minute. Yes, Warren liked the script. Of course, he had a lot of ideas for it. He'd have to sit down with me at length and go over it. And he wanted $8 million. I was saved only because the director was Billy Friedkin, married to studio head Sherry Lansing, who loved her husband and didn't want to undo his movie with Warren Beatty. Warren was replaced by David Caruso, who had many fewer ideas, who wouldn't stick his nose into Billy's schedule, and who wanted only $2 million.

It all made me wonder how this "storyteller" who'd never written a script by himself, this auteur who'd always gotten his way for many years in Hollywood, would fare in the White House. Would he want to redesign the lasers in the Tomahawk missiles? Would he veto every bill unless he could sit down and rewrite it with Trent Lott and Dennis Hastert? Would he take two years and seventeen speech writers to deliver *last* year's State of the Union address? Would the White House photographers be hired from *Vogue?* Would Bob Evans be in charge of hiring White House interns? Would the Oval Office, the hallway, the bathroom, and the private study all have mirrors on the ceilings and walls? Would "What's new, pussycat?" replace "E Pluribus Unum" on our currency? Would he show better judgment than the time he'd turned down playing JFK in *PT 109?* (I imagined what that would have done for his candidacy: Warren running *as* Jack.) Would *Reds* posters be sold at his inauguration? Would Madonna be named attorney general? Would Annette Bening, who had the hair for it, become the new Hillary? Would stills of Annette in *The Grifters* be on the cover of *Time?* Would the Sorceress be his press spokesperson? Would she cast her spells on him? Would the golden willard stay true to Annette?

What also troubled me was that while he was a "storyteller" and an auteur, Warren was still, underneath all of it, an actor. And in my experience, actors were only as good as the lines somebody wrote for them. I didn't think Warren was a dummy—that wasn't the problem—although my experience had taught me that many actors quite happily and successfully were.

The problem as I saw it was that good actors really got into a part . . . and sometimes got stuck there even if they were supposed to be someone else in the next movie. Actors in film stayed in the part for at least two months, actors onstage often much longer. But a president had to play a different part every hour of every day. Threaten terrorists at noon, praise cops at two, chat up the House Republicans at four, welcome Tony Blair at six.

What if Warren got stuck? He was, after all, a Method actor, which meant a lot of intense preparation. What if he couldn't switch parts fast enough . . . after having supervised seventeen drafts of all the different speeches? What if his actor's training itself bollixed him all up? If he was still at his tell-off-the-terrorists mode with Tony Blair? If he was in his praise-the-cops mode with the House Republicans?

Fearing that I'd really hit on something, I thought about *Bullworth*. It was Warren's last movie before word of his candidacy, and Warren had played a politician who told the truth. It was classic Method actor syndrome, I thought. That's what all this was about! Warren had fallen in love with the part! Warren had been brilliant in the part! *And he still wanted to play the part!*

What could he do? He couldn't reshoot the movie over and over again, could he? The studios wouldn't let him get away with that—maybe once, but not anymore. It was like Stallone playing Rocky over and over again for so many years, but Warren wasn't Stallone; Warren had a social conscience, true lefty beliefs he had formed in penthouses and limousines all over the world.

Warren could play Bullworth for the rest of his life and get away with it . . . if he did it on a public stage and not a soundstage. It was like watching himself on all those mirrors. He could watch himself playing Bullworth, improvising the already-written and already-shot script on TV, on the prime-time network news!

The improvising, I realized, would be rehearsed, mannered, and styl-ized—right there in the script, as most actors' improvisations are, but it would be fun. He would be playing Bullworth, and Bullworth was fun. Bull-worth liked to say the *F* word, and Warren had advised Bill Clinton to fire up his stump speech in 1992 by shouting *fuck* a few times. I could see it now: The first president caught on camera saying the *F* word. This wouldn't be like Bob Kerrey telling his homophobic joke on-camera or George Bush talking on-camera about kicking Ferraro's ass. It was good Hollywood advice, really, used in movies since the seventies to punch up dialogue that was putting everybody to sleep, the white equivalent of blaxploitation's *motherfucker*.

My fellow Americans, I don't know what the fuck's wrong with the economy, but I'm working on it. . . . Fucking Saddam . . . Fucking Milošević . . . Fucking Arafat . . . Fucking schvartzes—but no, that was Evans's word; Bullworth and Warren, hip Hollywood liberals, would never use *schvartzes*.

As the buzz about Warren ricocheted crazily around Hollywood, the non-candidate, possible candidate, potential candidate, near candidate made a speech at the Beverly Hilton that was possibly the biggest Hollywood event until the cocktail party for the Dalai Lama. Warren was accepting the Eleanor Roosevelt Award from the ADA for "a lifetime of creative and political integrity." (*Dick Tracy? Ishtar?*)

It was in the ballroom of the Beverly Hilton, and Warren arrived in his shades, with Annette on his arm. The shades weren't dorky like Clinton's, Annette was prettier than Hillary, and Warren even pressed the flesh. Well . . . he shook hands. Not pumping hands like Feinstein or Boxer or the old-style macho pols, but touching them a little fey, Euro-trashy, almost New Age.

He began by saying, "I had in mind a different kind of lighting—could we get the candles going again?" He made a dull speech—a few shouted *F* words would have helped—saying Al Gore and Bill Bradley weren't really liberals. The speech played like a movie written by seventeen screenwriters, visually interesting but nada at the core. Warren wasn't playing Bullworth and he was as boring as Al Gore separated from Clinton. Half of Evans's whorehouse was there, applauding, even though Warren was upstaged by Dustin Hoffman, who, in his last movie, *Wag the Dog*, had patterned himself after Evans.

Dusty introduced Warren this way: "Warren Beatty wouldn't make the mistakes of other presidents. Unlike Richard Nixon, he would have burnt the tapes. Unlike George Bush, he would have come up with something better than being 'out of the loop.' Unlike Bill Clinton, he would have never trusted a twenty-two-year-old girl to be discreet." Those who knew Warren said that Dusty had to be making dumb jokes: Warren wouldn't have burned the tapes; he would have made ten thousand phone calls to two thousand women asking their advice . . . and as far as trusting a twenty-two-year-old girl was concerned, almost all of the temptresses at Evans's house were in their early twenties.

Dusty also said that as a nine-year-old boy, Warren called Eleanor Roosevelt to praise her and began the conversation by saying, "Eleanor, what are you wearing right now?" Then Penny Marshall introduced Warren by saying that she'd had thirteen thousand telephone conversations with him over the years and he'd begun every one by saying, "Penny, what are you wearing right now?" Then Gary Shandling introduced Warren by translating the presidency into Hollywood terms: "If you get elected, make sure you get your name above the title of the country."

Hollywood insiders admired Warren's gargantuan chutzpah. He was in his sixties. He hadn't had a hit movie in ages. His last movie had flopped. His next movie, about a man having a midlife crisis, had been rescheduled (surprise!) and was rumored to be not very good. He wasn't getting paid what he had once been. Adam Sandler was making more money than he was. And now he had put himself back on prime-time television, getting nightly exposure on the news . . . just as the video of *Bullworth* was about to be released.

Warren had figured out a way to get a *Wag the Dog* kind of box-office bump for *Bullworth*'s video and for his next movie. Bill Clinton had bumped up *Wag the Dog*. Now, by implying that maybe he wanted Bill Clinton's job, Warren was delivering his own bump. For *his* movie.

It was a con job that soon had other practitioners. Activist attorney Gloria Allred started a boomlet for actress Cybill Shepherd's presidential candidacy. Cybill immediately became Clintonesque.

A magazine headline read CYBILL — "I'M HOT TO TROT." And Cybill was quoted as saying, "I'm horny most of the time. There are few activities in life as pleasant as sex. And now that I'm suddenly single, I definitely feel very horny. I was always horny—I don't know how to say it other than that." She made a list of "America's Sexiest Men," which she called her "hit list of specimens," the first time within anyone's memory that a putative presidential candidate released a hit list instead of a position paper. Her specimen / positions included Clint Eastwood, Kevin Costner, and Ted Turner.

Surprisingly, few people in Hollywood were surprised about Cybill's candidacy. They knew she didn't have a movie, didn't have a television show, and was making car commercials. Floating a presidential candidacy was a classy stepping-stone, people felt, back to prime time.

Maybe noting all the free air Warren and Cybill were getting, Arnold

Schwarzenegger dropped hints that he "could" be a candidate in California's next gubernatorial election. "I think about running for office many times," Arnold said. "The possibility is there, because I feel it inside. I feel there are a lot of people in politics that are standing still and not doing enough. And there's a vacuum. Therefore I can move in."

While the Big Guy sounded like he was being honest—"I inhaled. Exhaled. Everything"—he did have a new movie coming out (the last couple had bombed) and some studio heads were worried about his bankability at a time when other action stars like Stallone, Seagal, and Van Damme were already roadkill. A little high-minded, socially committed ink or air never hurt.

As the Warren, Cybill, and Arnold noncandidacies were dissected and parsed on the evening news, the world's master parser, Bill Clinton, came to a Hollywood fund-raiser at the home of director Rob Reiner.

Ronald Reagan, writer-director Mel Brooks told Bill Clinton, was the greatest actor in the history of Hollywood and had turned in his best performance at the White House. "If you didn't know any better," Brooks said, "you'd think Reagan was the president. He even fooled Gorbachev."

"If President Reagan could be an actor and become president," Bill Clinton said, "maybe I could become an actor. I've got a good pension. I can work for cheap."

But it would never happen. Warren Beatty was no Bill Clinton, and Bill Clinton was no Warren Beatty. They did, though, have something in common. As the balmy Evans kept saying, over and over again, humming his life's mantra to anyone who'd listen: "Pussy hair, my boy, is stronger than universal cable."

(11)

George W. Bush Defines Himself

Listen, I gotta tell you somethin'. This is the God's honest truth here. If you think my dad is a wimp, that's . . . *good*. Cuz I'm a *compaysionate* conservative and George Herbert Walker's wimpiness . . . works for our message. He's such a nice guy, my dad, isn't he? Hell yes, he really is.

Okay, you want the truth? I'll tell you the truth, but don't tell nobody, cuz this stuff's not ready for prime time. Not this stuff. We've spent a lot of damn money obfuscatin' this. Here goes: I'm not like my dad at all! I'm not a nice guy! I'll kick your fuckin' ass, boy, if you fuck with me! I'll bust your kneecap! I'll gouge your eye! I'll bust your nuts! I'll make you cry! (*Did you see the big tough war hero, John McCain, the day after I busted his chops on Super Tuesday?*) I'm a "political terrorist," hoss, as that high-ass honey Mary Matalin said.

Ain't nothin' "Poppy" about me! Cuz I'm my mama's boy, Bar's son, and my asshole little brother, Jeb, he calls her "the enforcer."

You wanna hear a good one? The best damn one I heard in a long time? Thanks to Bill Clinton's pecker, I'm gonna set myself in the Oval Office. Thanks to Bill Clinton's pecker, the pigeons are gonna come home to roast. No more abortion. No more affirmative action. No gay marriage. No gay rights. No hate crimes. Prayer in the schools? Hell yes! More jails, tents, barracks to keep the thugs and the scum off the streets? Hell yes! The death penalty for fourteen-year-olds? Hell yes!

Hell yes, thanks to Bill Clinton's pecker, I'm gonna shove it up William Sloane Coffin's coffined dead ass, finally, after all these years. Chaplain Coffin, sir, you pompous Yankee dickhead, listen up! You never shoulda said to me that my dad—my own dad!—lost to a better man when he lost for the Senate. *I'm gonna destroy everything you believed in!*

And you, Bill Clinton, and you, Hillary, you uppity skank, you never shoulda kept my mom and dad waitin' for a half hour at the inauguration. *I'm gonna dismantle all your programs!*

And you, Al Gore, you Buddhist-kissin' bag of wind, you never shoulda made Donna Brazile your campaign manager against *me*—the same schemin' voodoo Ebonics witch who told the press in '88 that George Herbert Walker was hosin' his secretary. *I'm gonna be your controllin' legal authority!*

Hell yes, the pigeons are *all* gonna come home to roast, every one of 'em!

You don't get it, do you? Not even the big-britch media superstars, not even Mr. Rather, who tried to coldcock George Herbert Walker on prime time. None of you get it! I am my mama's boy, and that means there's gonna be blood and hair on the walls!

Remember Mom sayin' she wanted to hang Saddam Hussein? Remember Ferraro and *bitch* rhymes with *rich?* I'm a shit-kicker, partner, not the preppy from Andover. I grew up on George Jones and Johnny Rodriguez, not Fleetwood Mac hippie music. I wear cowboy boots with the state of Texas star on 'em, not tasseled loafers.

Hey, I'm the guy who went up to Al Hunt of the *Wall Street Journal* and his wife and his little kid and called him a "fuckin' son of a bitch." With his *little kid* there! I'm the one who says, "No comment, asshole!" to reporters I don't like! I'm the guy who went into John Sununu's office and told him his ass was grass and made him boo-hoo blubber! I'm the one who okayed the Dukakis in the Tank and the Willie Horton ads!

And when all the big chips were on the table and it was time to show and tell, when the media was snotful and ready to sneeze about George Herbert Walker and Jennifer Fitzgerald, I'm the guy—my mama's boy!—who went in to see my father and said, "You gotta tell me the truth, Dad, you been gettin' some of Jennifer's tail?"

You know how tough my mom is? So tough that when my little four-year-old sister died of leukemia, Bar went out and played golf the next day. Well, son, I'm just as tough! I ain't afraid of nobody or nothin'! I love my dad, but he got my dander up once, and I said to him, "Hey, you wanna go right here? One-on-one? *Mano a mano?*" Hell, I've always been like that. Mom had a miscarriage; I'm the one who drove her to the hospital, said to her afterward, "Mom, ain't you gettin' too old to still be havin' babies?"

The media put this preppy sweater on me, but that ain't bad. Shit-kickin' don't buy a lotta votes in the North and the Midwest. *Compaysionate* conservative don't mean callin' a guy a "fuckin' son of a bitch" with his little kid there or imitatin' to a reporter that murderin' chickenshit Tucker beggin' for her life. So maybe the preppy sweater, worn to rags and riches by George Herbert Walker, is gonna come in handy in the general election.

But it ain't me, babe. *This* is me! Bob Bullock, Texas lieutenant governor, sticks it to me with a bill in the legislature. There's a roomful of people there. I grab the son of a bitch by his lapel. I say, "If you're gonna fuck me, you gotta kiss me first!" I pull his ugly face right up to mine. He's got his mouth open, not knowin' what the fuck. I stick my old tongue in there. Yeah! *That's* me, hoss!

They say I grew up rich, the silver wine opener up my butt and all that, but that don't mean I noticed it stickin' out of there. I was in Midland fuckin' Texas, not in Palm Beach or Newport or Martha's Vineyard. I crawled under the high school stadium and got forty feet up on the crossbars, climbed the light poles all around the stadium, got sent to the principal's office for throwin' a football out the window and puttin' makeup on like Elvis. I didn't give a shit about school; I wanted to be Willie Mays and play outfield for the Giants. I worked hard at hittin' the curveball, not hittin' the books. I collected baseball cards, not straight *A*'s. What I liked most about my dad, who mostly wasn't there, was that he could catch a baseball—no shit—with the glove behind his back.

I was out all day ridin' my bike with the other kids—Texas kids, shit-kicker kids—learnin' to cuss, suckin' on young beers. I got a little older and we'd drive over to Odessa. They had whores there and dirty and oily honky-tonks. You raised hell in Odessa was what they said; you raised a family in Midland. I sure as shit didn't have no silver wine opener stickin' out of me when I was doin' all that. Ain't no little honey's lips got split by no wine opener.

I noticed somethin' pretty young, though. I was a guy. I knew how to be a guy. Truth is, a lotta boys and men don't know how to be guys. I sure did right away. And guys liked me. I knew how to grin and tell a dirty joke. I knew how to pat somebody on the back or on the ass. I knew how to look somebody in the eye and hold their eyes on mine or wink or squeeze a bicep while I was talkin' to 'em. I knew how to cuss up a storm, turn the air blue with a stream of bad words, turn filth into locker room poetry. I knew how to rock on the heels of my boots and bob my head around. I loved Midland fuckin' Texas.

Then they sent me up to Andover. Up in New England. It was colder than Tricia Nixon's you know what. East Coast spoiled brats, phonies who hardly knew who Willie Mays was, let alone his lifetime battin' average against left-handed pitchin'. I tried out for everything, but all I got was cheerleader. Yeah, I know, you don't have to tell me. But don't try to *define* me with that. That don't mean shit about shit. It don't make me Richard Nixon, either, just because he was a water boy or a cheerleader or whatever the diddly shit he was.

By the time I got to Yale, it was hittin' the fan. The antiwar stuff. Hippies. A heaviness hangin' over everything. That whole downer scene. Everybody gettin' drunk on their own guilt—we were here havin' toga parties—they were havin' recon parties in the rice paddies. Big deal! You know what? Listen, this is the God's honest truth. It's not that I was for the damn war or against the damn war. I just didn't give a damn!

I still went to see as many ball games as I could and I discovered the pure-joy bliss of drinkin' Jack Daniel's with iced Budweiser behind it. Sometimes I mixed up a garbage canful of screwdrivers. Sure, I tried a little loco weed, who didn't? Even Tricia Nixon did. Bill Clinton may have been off protestin' against the war in England or Prague or Moscow or Hanoi (my dad's CIA friends say he was in Hanoi), but I was in New Haven, gettin' busted for stealin' a wreath off a store's door with my fraternity brothers or gettin' almost busted at Princeton for tryin' to pull the goalposts down.

I wasn't wallowin' in how awful everything in America was, because I didn't see anything that was awful. I loved my fraternity brothers and I loved hearin' the pledges squeal when we put ΔKE on their asses with a red-hot coat hanger. And I loved hearin' some bead-wearin', peace-lovin', social-conscience little nitwit squeal when I made her feel good.

Mom and Dad were livin' in River Oaks, outside Houston, by then, and on vacations or in the summer, I was hangin' out with Lacey Neuhaus (who'd almost marry Teddy Kennedy one day)—*I guess Teddy and me got at least one thing in common.* And with Tina, who was a sizzlin'-hot handful and the actress Gene Tierney's daughter. (Gene Tierney was one of JFK's millions, so I guess I sorta indirectly *got somethin in common with JFK, too.*) Then I met Cathy, who was smart, sexy, and blond and who belonged to the country club. We got engaged, but then we broke up and *not*—hell no!—because her stepfather was Jewish, either.

You would've thought back then, readin' the papers and lookin' at the TV that this country was comin' apart, but I didn't get it. I didn't see that. What I saw was the media sensationalizin' everything.

There were a whole lotta young people like me who didn't grow their hair long and clack around with beads and smell like the inside of a fortune teller's. Truth is, there were more of us than there were of them. The fact that it was easier to get laid than ever before wasn't our fault. And to turn it down? At that age? (Bill Bennett, back then, used to date Janis Joplin! I'm not shittin' you, cowboy. Bill "Book of Virtues" Bennett and drunk-as-a-skunk, fuck-the-doorknobs Janis! True story!)

Hell, I wasn't *changed* by any of it. Alterin' my conscience like a lot of 'em. I still listened mostly to George Jones and Johnny Rodriguez. I still liked beer better than loco weed or . . . anything else. I still cussed up a storm. (Mom wouldn't play golf with me, I cussed so much.) I still went to as many ball games as I could. I swam. I jogged. I played ball. I still couldn't hit the damn curveball. I was still smokin' and chewin' tobacco.

The only part of Yale I really liked, besides the Dekes, was Skull and Bones, which was a different kind of fraternity. To get initiated, I had to lie down bare-assed in a coffin half full of mud. Then they locked the lid. (*Fuck John McCain and his war hero stories! That never happened to him!*) But what was fun was this braggin' we did. We had to brag the details of our sexual scores to the other braggers of Skull and Bones and they had to brag theirs. We knew everything about what everybody had done to whoever. So one day, you'd hear about this little old girl and the tricks she knew, and the next day, you'd call her and maybe experience 'em for yourself. It was like we were givin' tips on outboard power motors or sides of beef.

After Yale—Yale went completely to shit right after I left, thanks to Bill Clinton and his skank and the Black Panthers and the kind of college president who let protesters piss into the wastebasket in his office—I had a problem. I didn't wanna go to Vietnam, not because I had Clinton's fancy-ass, high-falutin theological differences with the war—but because I didn't wanna get my young ass shot off.

Then I heard about this Texas Air National Guard outfit and I went to see the guy and I told him who I was and he said fine. I wanted to be a fighter pilot anyway, after hearin' all my life about Dad gettin' to be a hero as one. And it's not like there wasn't a need for fighter pilots to defend our borders.

What if Castro's air force tried to take Galveston out? This was back in the good old Cold War days, don't forget. The guy with the shoe, remember? The bald Russian? The fat one? He beat on the table with his shoe and said he'd bury us!

I liked the Texas Air National Guard. Lt. Lloyd Bentsen III was the senator's kid and Capt. John Connally III was the secretary of the treasury's kid, and I met half the Dallas Cowboys team, who'd all signed up. I spent fifty-three weeks of flight trainin' school in Georgia, at Moody Air Force Base, in the shit-flake town of Valdosta. I learned how to fly a jet and got high on the sound of the burners. I drank a lotta beer and a whole lot more whiskey, and the women in Valdosta . . . aw, man! They just about trucked 'em in there from all over the piney woods, little halter tops, hot sweat, and iced beer, and I scratched my itch . . . from all the mosquitoes, oh yeah!

It was out of hand—no shit—I'm the first to admit, part of my feckless and irresponsive youth. Georgia peaches, yessir, Georgia peaches, Georgia peaches! The Officers' Club—wasn't nothin' but a shack, a stump house, a tin roof, a hot tin roof, up there on the roof on a summer night, a girl in a halter top on a tin roof on a summer night, pussycat on a hot tin roof . . . aw, shit, aw, man . . . jukebox blarin' George Jones, "White Lightnin'," real hot, so fuckin' hot, tubsful of iced Bud, sweat drippin' off me, took my shirt off, still sweatin', sweatin' like a pig, took my pants off, singin' "White Lightnin'! White Lightnin'! White Lightnin'!" got up on the bar, bare-assed . . . *No! Hell no! Forget it! Didn't happen! Never happened! Wouldn'ta done that! No fuckin' way! Naked? On the bartop? Hell no! Hell no! Naked? With all those guys in there? . . . Why? . . . I'm not . . . Hell no!*

One day at the base, I got a call from Dad. The air force was sendin' a plane for me. President Nixon had a big idea. He thought Tricia and I'd be perfect for each other. I had seen pictures of Tricia Nixon, not bad, nice tits, but still . . . whoa! *Nixon's daughter?* Dad said Nixon did this kind of thing sometimes. He'd arranged Julie's marriage to David Eisenhower. A joinin' of the clans. A joinin' at the hip. The Nixons innerbleed with the Eisenhowers.

Well, we were a clan, too. The Nixons breed with the Bushes. Sort of like, I guess, intermarriage between Knights of the Round Table families. Nixon had been good to Dad, campaignin' for him, knightin' him our UN delegate. The plane was on its way to take me to dinner with Tricia Nixon in Washington.

"Be nice to her," Dad said.

Nice? How nice? What did that mean? How nice did I have to be? The guys at the Officers' Club shit a brick. *Tricia Nixon?* I was bein' flown to Tricia Nixon like some boy bimbo bein' served up on a silver platter at Barney Frank's house.

We had dinner. It was a nice dinner. That's all I'm gonna say. Tricia has her . . . qualities. Definitely not as stiff as her father. Nixon was even nicer to Dad afterward. Campaigned hard for him in Dad's Senate race. Knighted him the chairman of the Republican National Committee. Told Gerry Ford to crown Dad head of the CIA. I did what I had to do. I was nice to her. Tricia liked me. *I love my dad.*

Yeah, but it was out of hand! That whole time was out of hand! My reckless and irresponsible youth! After flight school, I rented an apartment in Houston. A one-bedroom at the Chateaux Dijon. All singles. Four hundred units. Eight swimmin' pools. Secretaries. Ambitious secretaries. Secretaries on their own for the first time in their lives.

Away from mommy and daddy for the first time in their lives. All-day volleyball in the pool. All-night relays inside.

It was all so out of hand that when George Herbert Walker came to town, campaignin' for the Senate, and asked me to go with him, I did, but I took my shirt off, walkin' behind him, bare-chested. I was beautiful, trim, tanned. I don't know what the fuck I was thinkin'. Half-naked with my dad. Showin' myself off. (Jeb, my asshole little brother, lost it in those years. Hair homeless-long, smokin' weed like Winstons.)

I had to figure out what I was gonna do with my life. I got into the Harvard Business School, back up north in alien territory. Barry Goldwater was right. He said that entire part of the country except Kennebunkport should be chain-sawed and set out to sea. There were protests every other day. For Cesar Chavez, against the CIA. Dick Gregory spoke and said young white people were "America's new niggers." The same heaviness that I'd felt at Yale, the same guilt-stewin' rhetoric, the same claustrophobia. I just couldn't give a shit.

I went down to Fenway and saw the Red Sox. I wore my old Texas Air National Guard jacket to class. Let 'em get a load of that while they were handin' out their antiwar leaflets. *Uh-huh, that's right, a genuwine bomber jacket, darlin', with genuwine stains on it!* I chewed tobacco and took a spitoon into class with me, spittin' loud so they could hear the plop-plop as they planned their civil disobedience against Gallo wine. What did I care about Gallo wine? I don't drink cheap wine.

I went down to a place called Hillbilly Ranch, outside Boston, with, you betcha, my jacket on. George Jones was in town. When it came time for my yearbook picture at Harvard, I wore a polo shirt and a pair of khakis torn at the knee. Everybody else wore a suit and tie. Yeah, uh-huh, I knew they would. That's why I made sure my polo shirt was rumpled.

I didn't know what the hell I was gonna do. Harvard Business School usually means an East Coast corporation, but I couldn't do that. Honest to God, I felt physically refrained in that part of the world. The hangin' heaviness. The spacious claustrophobia. The stewin' guilts. Everybody a victim of some kind or other.

I drove out to Arizona to try to breathe, and on the way there I stopped in Midland and saw some of the friends I'd grown up with. And the answer came to me while I was talkin' to 'em. *This* is where I was happiest. Under the big hot oily sky, havin' a beer and sippin' whiskey inside the air-conditioned country club with real people. Talkin' about Nolan Ryan and the Astros and the Rangers. People here knew how many career home runs Willie Mays had hit. People here weren't full of psychobabble horse manure. They weren't proud, unhappy, chest-beatin' victims.

They were Americans, shit-kickers, oil and grease cowboys just tryin' to live life on their own gumption, not tyin' themselves up like a rodeo calf with guilts everybody around 'em is beatin' into 'em. I wasn't claustrophobic in Midland; I didn't feel physically constrained. I could breathe. I was free. I could rock back and forth on the heels of my boots.

I rented a back-alley guest cottage that was an outhouse dump. After a week there, it felt like home. Dirty laundry everyplace. Empty pizza boxes under the bed. Beer cans with gray fuzz growin' out of 'em. The bed frame was broke. I lassoed it together with some chili-stained ties. My Olds Cutlass needed a paint job. I spray-painted it. One of my friends got me a sweater at a thrift shop. I wore it all the time.

I was makin' connections in the oil business, down at the Petroleum Club, down at the country club, hangin' around the big-money guys in their ostrich Lucchese boots, doin' what I'd always been able to do with guys . . . the eye contact, the butt slap, the dirty jokes, the shit-kickin' jive that I had in my bones but not in my blood.

Sometimes, when I saw Dad, I thought I saw him lookin' funny at me. Dad was a Texan, but he could never shit-kick—remember that whole pork-rind-eatin' publicity later on? Dad even threw his horseshoes funny, like he didn't want any mud or dirt sloppin' up on him. I thought I saw Dad eyeballin' me enviously, thinkin', How does he do it? How does he shit-kick so well? It was workin' fine for me in Midland. Yeah, I had been to Harvard, but the dump I lived in was on Harvard Street in Midland.

The drinkin' helped, too. The old moneybags in Midland loved to drink, and I did, too. I don't mean sippin' scotch like my little asshole brother Jeb does; I mean shooters of whiskey and tequila and lots of iced Bud. I drank a lot with 'em and I talked a lot about poontang with 'em and they loved me. I told 'em all the poontang stories I'd heard at Skull and Bones and some of my own stories, and these old boys thought they were in heaven.

Smokin', drinkin', talkin' pussy, eatin' ribs. All that wasn't there yet was money. But I knew we'd get there, too, when I jogged by one of the biggest money guys and pulled his runnin' shorts down to his ankles and the old boy almost shit himself, he laughed so hard.

Hot damn, I was havin' fun. Back home. Back among people I loved. In the real America. The real red-blooded, red meat, real feelings, no psychomanure America. I knew I was drinkin' too much, screwin' around too much, but I wasn't hurtin' nobody except maybe myself. I didn't have any responsibilities to nobody else.

Juicin' up at the Nineteenth Hole, the country club bar, stuffin' my face with Tex-Mex at La Bodega, playin' George Jones on the honky-tonk juke boxes of

Odessa. One night Willie Nelson came into Odessa and I was in town, tonkin', with a couple buddies, and we decided to see Willie. Lord knows, we'd had too much whiskey, but that still don't explain to me how we wound up onstage, right behind Willie, singin' backup.

A good part of my time, I gotta admit, I spent playin' poker, just like I'd spent a good part of my time at Yale and Harvard playin' it, too. But it was different playin' it in Midland now. It wasn't a game here; it was like the final part of the equation in bein' a good ole boy shit-kickin' success story. You smoke, you drink, you laugh, you cuss, you wear pointy-toe boots, you tell dirty jokes, you wink, you eat red meat, you talk pussy, you get pussy . . . and you win at poker.

I set up a little drillin' company with the old guys' help, and things were lookin' good. I was gatherin' momentum and impotence. But I was drinkin' too much. A friend of mine was callin' the bars and the liquor stores and tellin' 'em to sell me nothin' but wine or beer. And then my best buddy got leukemia and I was shitfaced for a whole week, wakin' up parched, pukin' in the shower, makin' a Bloody Mary as soon as I got out.

I knew my biggest talent was lookin' folks in the eye and smilin' and touchin' 'em on the arm and gettin' what I wanted from 'em. Men gave me bucks for my company. Women liked bein' in my company. There was a lesson in that, and you gotta be sharp enough in life to read the lipstick handwritin' on the motel room mirror. If men and women fell in love with me, there was a life to be had inside that. I'm not bisexual, so that left politics.

Out of the stump house and up on the stump! My dad had done it and so had my grandpop, but I thought I was better than them at gettin' people to give me their money or their selves. My grandpop had such a thick broomstick up his butt, he couldn't be elected to the Kennebunkport PTA today. And my dad had to work real hard and never did succeed—the pork rinds again—at bein' more down-home than earnest.

All I had to do sometimes was a little badass boot rockin' and back porch butt pattin' and sugary-eye gazin' and explicit winkin' and pointin' a sassy finger . . . and the money and the pussy fell into my lap.

I announced that I was runnin' for Congress, and a month later I met Laura, my wife and my love, and now the mother of my children. Aw, hell, we'd "met" before, when we were in the seventh grade, but I wasn't really lookin' at anybody back then except Willie Mays. This time, we met at a backyard barbecue.

She was shy and on the quiet side. She'd been a grade-school teacher in

Houston and was a librarian now in Austin. She was a reader—she'd spent her whole life with her pretty nose in or around smelly old books. It surprised the hell out of me that she'd lived in the same bordello apartment house, the Chateaux Dijon, in Houston while I was there. But then Laura wasn't the type to play all-day volleyball and all-night relays.

I made her laugh. She was a great listener, and I talked a lot. Plus, she was smart and beautiful, the perfect girl for me. As Mom said, I got hit by a white lightnin' bolt. Laura wasn't any gigglin', mechanical-bull West Texas hosebag. She was a serious, reality-time woman. I was in love. Asshole Jeb, when Laura met everybody, right away Jeb said, "Brother, did you pop the question, or are we just wastin' our time?" She called me "Bushie," and I called her "Bushy," different spellin', for different reasons. We still call each other that.

There was a prime-time political consideration, too, that had never occurred to me. I had announced the run for Congress and I knew they were gonna try to define me as this drunken, wild, and crazy pussy hound. Well, they couldn't define me like that anymore. I was married now. To a librarian. To a schoolteacher. Laura, though I'd never thought about it, defined me now. I had found myself not just a smart and beautiful wife. I had found myself a voter-friendly and mandate-potential *definition*.

No mandate, though. The voters weren't that friendly. I got licked by a Democrat who defined me as a drunken and wild and crazy pussy hound, Bushy or no Bushy. Damn I was pissed off! I was happy, too, with my new wife and everything, but I was pissed off! I guess I started hittin' the Jack Daniel's pretty hard again.

Bushy was all right about it—I can't complain. She cooked what I liked—meat loaf, tacos—and she didn't say anythin', but she'd leave books around the house about the dangers of boozin'. Alcoholism. I'd read 'em and keep boozin'.

Our little girls were born. I was doin' fine with business, settin' up a new company, workin' the phone, hustlin' old family friends—the FOBs—the friends of the Bushes, which includes a helluva lot more people than the other FOBs—the friends of that SOB.

But somethin' was off. I didn't know what. Maybe it was that after all these years as a nomad, now I was a husband and a father.

I liked bein' a husband and a father—that's not what I'm sayin'. But I liked drinkin' and raisin' hell and howlin' at the moon with George Jones, too, though there wasn't any "strange," if you know what I mean, in the mix. It was all Bushy. Makin' meat loaf. Her nose in a smelly old book. So I don't know . . . you know . . . but somethin' was off.

That's when Jesus saved me. Not Jesus, really, but Jesus in spirit. Billy Graham. I'd known Billy for a long time, thanks to my dad, and one day we were walkin' around together at the summer house in Kennebunkport and Billy told me about his own boy, Franklin, who'd come to Jesus finally after drinkin' every hour and comin' into everybody else.

And Billy asked me, "Son, are you right with God?"

I told him that Bushy and the girls and I went to Midland Methodist every Sunday and that I even taught Sunday school sometimes.

Billy put his hand on my shoulder and said, "You didn't answer my question, son. Do you have the peace and understanding with God that can come only through our Lord Jesus Christ?"

There was somethin' about the way Billy looked at me that was like takin' one of the hot hangers we used on the pledges in the Deke house at Yale and puttin' it into my heart. I told him I felt somethin' off in my life and about the Jack Daniel's and the iced Budweisers.

Billy said, "To be without God in this life is to be terribly lonely. If there is one thing I want you to take back to Texas, it's this. God loves you, George, and God is interested in you. To recommit your life to Jesus Christ, you have to give up that one last demon before you can become a new man. Give it to Him; George, He'll take the burden and set you free."

I thought about it when we got back to Texas. To *recommit my life to Jesus Christ? God loved me? The last demon? A new man?* It sounded good, but I wanted more Jack Daniel's. I wanted my iced Bud. I wanted another Winston or a big fat cigar. I chose Jack Daniel's over Jesus Christ. An iced Bud over God.

On my fortieth birthday, Bushy and I went to the Broadmoor Hotel in Colorado Springs with some friends. We had a six-course dinner, sixty-dollar bottles of wine, brandy, some Jack Daniel's back in the room, a few cold Buds. I don't remember a whole lot after Bushy and I got back to the room, except that she left and slept in one of the other rooms.

I didn't treat her that night like you should treat the mother of your children. May God forgive me—it was a George Jones moment. I got up the next mornin' with vomit over me. I looked in the mirror and I started to cry. I begged Bushy to forgive me. Drinkin' was over. Smokin' was over. George Jones was over. Sex was over, like it had been for a while (except for Bushy).

I'd come to Jesus.

I was a man now, finally, like Billy's son, Franklin, except Franklin was twenty-two when it happened, and I was forty. I would make love no longer to the demons Jesus Christ had freed me of. I would make love to America. I would put all that wasted energy now into lovin' up America, into makin' this an America worthy of God's name.

I'd made love to Budweiser and then to bimbos and then to Bushy, and now I would make love to America. Come to Jesus, literally! I felt like I had discovered a callin' that I had seen vague glimmers of at Yale and Harvard.

I would make love to America and by my hard and deeply felt exertions and insertions, I would transform her. I'd turn her out. Inside out. No more heaviness. No more victims. No more guilt. No more self-indulgence. I would make her forget, through my soft words and hard-thrustin' actions, the pervert tricks she had been trained to perform in the sixties. Abortion. Gays in the military. Gay marriage. Women at work and not, like Bushy, at home with their kids.

I would teach my beautiful America the virtues of self-reliance, responsibility, consequence for your actions. And abstinence. No more street-corner trickin' for the America I loved! No more special-interest whips and chains! No more empowerment-group blow jobs! No more advocate-group daisy chains! Missionary position all the way!

I had to pump myself up first, before I could seduce, make love to, and transform America . . . like Rocky before he fought Muhammad Ali in the movie. The trainin' sequence, remember? Before you step into the ring with all the bright media minicams on you. *Baseball!* It was ideal. As American as apple pie, the catsup inside what would be the hamburger bun of my candidacy . . . to serve America . . . to be a public servant . . . to get her off the street corner.

Baseball! I bought into the Texas Rangers. I became the general partner of the Texas Rangers. I didn't sit in the owner's box; I sat in a regular seat behind first base, with Roger Staubach, the Captain of America's Team, right next to me sometimes. I pissed in the same urinal the fans did. I signed baseball cards with my picture on 'em. I jogged in the afternoon in the outfield. I hung out with Nolan Ryan on the pitcher's mound before games. I met Willie Mays and told him all his stats. I built a brand-spankin'-new stadium and sold the team for a $16 million personal profit.

How's that for a Rocky trainin' sequence, huh? I'd come to Jesus and I had become a high priest at the same time of America's own religion, baseball, where battin' averages and ERAs—the important ones, not the women's kind—were mumbled like prayers among the faithful.

I joined my dad's campaign as an adviser in 1988. That's when I met Pat Robertson. He knew all about me from Billy. Word spreads fast among sinners saved. Oh, we weren't friends right away. He was runnin' against Dad, so we had to bring him down a notch or two, leakin' that stuff to the press about what his close friend Jimmy Swaggart had asked that hooker to do to him.

But we respected each other. Pat Robertson and Jerry Falwell can get the vote out. Their friends and neighbors and admirers will show up in flatbeds and pickups and buses, wearin' little crosses and wavin' little American flags. They vote for Jesus. The votin' booth is their church on election day. By the time 1992 came around, Pat and Jerry Falwell and Jim Robison and I were friends.

They knew how true-blue I'd been born again. They knew that my dad talked the talk but that I walked the walk. No more drinkin'. No more smokin'. No more George Jones. No more sex (except for Bushy). They were in the same boat. Nothin' left except meat loaf, tacos, America, and Jesus. They were in the room with me when I testified to my Lord Jesus Christ, my Savior.

Dad made a big mistake. He thought the way to win was to appeal to the center and *fake it to the Religious Right*. Bullshit. Pat and Jerry and the others recognize bullshit when they see it. They're experts. A lot of little white churches are out there in smelly farm fields. The way to win is to lock up the Religious Right— make them *know* how much you believe in what they believe in—and then *fake it to the center.*

Tell everybody you're a *compaysionate* conservative, a uniter, not a divider—talk about goo-goo soccer-mom issues like education, health care, and breast cancer—and make sure Pat Robertson tells the faithful that what you believe in . . . to his own *personal* witness . . . is the death penalty, outlawin' abortion, lettin' the gays die off from AIDS, and Jesus Christ our Savior.

I'm gonna be the president of the United States. I'm better at lookin' in your eyes and suckin' up your votes and pain than Bill Clinton. I got a sexier wink cuz my eyes been inside more dark places than he's dreamed of. And I'm not pussy-whipped, either. Bushy does what I tell her to do. She don't wanna experience no more George Jones moments, now does she? Hey, you don't ever see scratches on *my* face.

Remember when Bill Clinton was gonna be impeached and Pat Robertson suddenly said just censor the bozo (my dad's word), don't remove him? Why do you think he did that? I'll tell you why. He knew I was gonna be the next president of the United States and it would help me if Bill Clinton stayed around and everybody could swallow in our humiliation and his misery.

I hope asshole Jeb, that dumb shit—not only did he *marry* the first *Mexican* girl he ever slept with, she was the first *girl* he ever slept with—doesn't give the game away. Bannin' affirmative action in his state, gettin' the endorsement of groups that hate gays. Callin' for the abolition of the education department, flat out opposin' gay rights and abortion gives a little sneak preview in Florida of what George W. Bush's America is gonna look like. In Florida, the highways are full up with prisoners on chain gangs. Asshole Jeb, my little brother, spendin' his nights watchin' reruns of *American Gladiators* . . . lettin' the cat out of the bag, sayin, "The age of relativity is over! There *is* absolute truth! You *are* responsible for your actions!"

Jeb smoked too much bad loco weed, I think. Talkin' heavy stuff like "Politics is a contact sport." Callin' himself in college "a cynical little turd." What kinda upbeat, vote-catchin', middle-of-the-road *compaysionate* message is that? Where's the funny face or the rainbow at the end of "cynical little turd"?

I'm willin' to do anything to be the president of the United States. Not for me. I could give a shit. For America. For Jesus Christ. For your kids. For my kids.

Anything! We gotta get rid of John McCain? Yeah, well, they turned him into a robot Commie while he was makin' himself into a big hero, didn't they? Or, hey, doesn't he have some illicit kids? Black kids, maybe? I don't say that, Pat doesn't say that, Jerry doesn't say that. Some voice on the phone whispers it at midnight. Mudslingin'? Hell no! Just a little enlightenment in the shadows of the under-pass on the information highway. Steve Forbes? Hey, wasn't his dad a homosex-ual who had little Arab boys goin' down on him? *Al Gore?* Don't make me laugh. I've *got* Al Gore. He's dead meat. It's all over. We're gonna show the world his bald spot. Dad wasn't head of the CIA for nothin'. They don't call Mom the Silver Fox for nothin', either.

We're takin' this country back. Thanks to Bill Clinton's pecker. Thanks to peo-ple thinkin' about Bill Clinton's pecker. Thinkin' pecker thoughts right down to the minute they go into the votin' booth. And I'm gonna take the high, bold road all the way . . . *compaysion*, inclusion, empowerment, entitlement. . . . I'm gonna postpone execution dates and kiss babies and hug mongol-faced kids. . . . I'm gonna charm the skinny waitresses and flabby soccer moms into giving me what I want. . . . I'm gonna stash the cowboy boots and wear tasseled loafers. . . . I'm a leader, not a misleader! I'm an insider, not an imbiber! I'm an imbiber, not a di-vider! I'm a reformer, not an informer! I'm a deformer with results! Hell, I'll even sit down with the log-sized Log Cabin Republicans, and with whatever other fairies who wanna meet. How's that for *compaysion?*

Sometime in my second term, with an all-Republican Senate and House, I'll do two things. I'm gonna hang Saddam Hussein by his nuts for Mom and I'm gonna reward Ken Starr to the Supreme Court for Dad. He shoulda done it when he had the chance—both with Saddam and with Ken—but he wimped out. Well, hell, ain't nobody perfect. I love my dad.

Read my lips! We've won! And that rhymes with *fun!*

Read my lips? No, sir, that's not the way *I'd* say it. I'd say:

Move your hips! I'm comin'!

[12]

Billy Comes Out to Play

"You'll die," Monica said. "You will die. You're gonna smack me. What do you think I said to him? What's the worst I could say?"

"God only knows," Linda Tripp said.

"I said, 'I love you, Butt-head.'"

"What did he say?"

"Nothing," Monica said. "He just kind of hung up."

As time passed, the distractions piled up (and so did the bodies) . . . endless Kosovo and then Columbine and then JFK, Jr., and then the guy in Atlanta who went to war with two brokerage houses.

During that period of time, with eighteen endless months left in his term, Bill Clinton came out to L.A. often to hang out and play a little golf. On one trip, he came, officially, to attend the Women's Soccer Championship between the United States and China at the Rose Bowl. He came alone; Hillary was doing summer stock in rural New York in the new show called *A Time to Listen!* Bill Clinton had a few days to kick it and chill with his Hollywood buddies.

A week or so before the game, Mark Canton, the former head of production at Sony, now a producer at Warner Bros., where his career began, contacted his friend Rudy Durand. Mark was still in the middle of a messy divorce from his wife, Wendy Finerman, who had won the Academy Award for producing *Forrest Gump*. He was a man with a remarkable string of hit movies, whom *Newsweek* magazine had once called "moronic." Mark Canton asked his friend Rudy Durand if he'd like to join him in his box at the Rose Bowl for the Women's Soccer Championship.

Rudy Durand was offended by the invitation. First, because Mark didn't call himself, but assigned the call to his assistant. Second, because if Rudy wanted to join Mark and his new girlfriend, Amy—Mark's marriage blew when wife Wendy walked into Mark's studio office and found him on top of his desk with Amy—in Mark's box at the Rose Bowl, it would cost Rudy a thousand dollars a ticket.

Rudy Durand, who was sixty-four years old, to Mark's fifty-one, was not a man to trifle with that way, to issue an invitation through an assistant at the cost of a grand. He was a man with a fascinating history, even for Hollywood, a place where people invent and reinvent themselves every few years. According to Rudy, his curriculum vitae included stops in Washington (as an advance man for JFK), in Palm Springs (as Frank's running buddy), and in Vegas (Frank had introduced him to some of the boys).

Then he came to Hollywood and wrote and directed an odd little movie called *Tilt*, which had lots of pinball machines and Brooke Shields. When Warner Bros. took the movie away from him and recut it, Rudy sued the studio for interfering with his artistic vision. The suit stretched endlessly (as antistudio suits will), for nearly a decade . . . a time during which all Rudy Durand, blacklisted now, did was pursue his case. Not through lawyers, by himself! Some people said he had become the best nonlawyer lawyer in town. He argued the case in front of a federal appeals court himself, made the Warner attorney literally vomit during his presentation, and won . . . $7 million, tax-free.

No, Rudy Durand was not a man to trifle with, as one of the town's top agents learned one day when he made a joke that Rudy Durand took personally. Rudy went up to him and said, "What did you say? What the fuck did you say? Either stop making jokes or get a new comedy writer. You hear me, you cocksucking motherfucker? You want a fucking war with me? You piece of shit?" And all the agent, a powerful man in Hollywood, could say was, "I know who you are. I didn't mean anything. I'm sorry."

A lot of people in town knew who Rudy Durand was, like Kelly Preston, now married to John Travolta, who met Rudy when she was a waitress at Gladstone's on the PCH, and let Rudy take some revealing (and un-Scientological) pictures that she still wanted back. Rudy Durand met Bill Clinton on a golf course and the two of them liked each other. That's why, when Rudy Durand called Mark Canton back about the women's soccer game at the Rose Bowl, Rudy Durand said, "Naw, I can't go with you. I'm going to the game with the president."

And Mark Canton, who had never met the president of the United States, said, "*You are?*"

. . .

It was a whopping, bald-faced lie. Fuck Mark Canton, Rudy Durand thought, this self-inflated dwarf who couldn't even play a decent round of golf, this Peter Sellers character who seemed most interested in the celebrity photos adorning his office walls. Fuck him! If Mark Canton wanted to play these stupid games with him, Rudy Durand thought—the assistant's call, the grand—he'd nuke his skinny little ass with the president of the United States.

On the morning of the day before the game, Bill Clinton called Rudy Durand. He was in L.A. at his friend Ron Berkle's house (Ron owned Ralph's supermarkets) and Bill Clinton wanted to know if Rudy felt like playing golf with him. Rudy said he'd love to but that he was booked; he was playing with Pete Sampras that day. Pete had just won Wimbledon.

"Can I use your name to get into the Riviera?" Bill Clinton asked Rudy. He hated the Bel Air Country Club, where the houses were almost on top of the course, where there was little privacy, where a telephoto lens could easily capture a wet, chewed-up cigar in the mouth of a wet and sweating president.

"Sure," Rudy said.

"Well come on over," the president said, "if you get a chance."

When Rudy went out on the golf course with the strikingly good-looking Sampras that day, he saw all the Secret Service agents in the distance, and as he started heading that way on his cart . . . he saw Mark Canton, too, playing with his own group of friends not far away. Rudy drove over to Mark and his friends, with Sampras alongside him, and Mark could barely contain his overbubbling excitement: "Rudy, Rudy, the president's here!" Rudy told Mark that he could see that, that even Ray Charles could see that, and he introduced Mark to Sampras.

"I'm Mark Canton," Mark Canton said to Pete Sampras. "I've produced . . . " And he listed a series of movies, many of which he *hadn't* produced . . . but some of which had been made under his aegis at Sony.

"I'll see ya later," Rudy said to Mark, and started driving down the fairway to where the president was teeing off. As he drove, he heard the Secret Service squawk boxes going "Six-five! Six-five!" (Rudy's own code number) and he knew Mark Canton was hearing it, too, and gasping openmouthed. *Rudy had his own code number!* As he approached the president, Rudy slowed down; he didn't want to disturb him. Rudy Durand believed that the three finest feelings in life were "a great climax, hitting a golf ball," and what Rudy described as "the pyramid": great food going down the pipe and into the digestive tract.

So he waited until the president hit his golf ball, and then he and Pete Sampras went over. The president, Rudy saw, was with Sly Stallone, once the box-office heavyweight and now, like Bill Clinton, caught in the headlights of a kinky sex scandal. Some Hollywood hookers had written a book alleging that Sly had built a glass contraption above his bed. They had to relieve themselves on the glass, they said, while Sly watched, stretched out on the bed below, and did the Bill Clinton thing with his right hand.

The president turned to Rudy and hugged him. Sly asked the president if he knew that Rudy was the best producer in Hollywood. Rudy introduced Sampras to both of them and the president praised Sampras for representing his country with such class and distinction at Wimbledon.

Rudy suggested that they all meet when they were half-finished with their games . . . at the Halfway Clubhouse between the tenth and thirteenth holes. The president and Sly, seemingly getting along well together, certainly with enough to talk about, agreed.

"Can you do me a favor?" Rudy asked the president of the United States.

"Sure," Bill Clinton said, drawing him a little aside for privacy, "what is it?"

"When we're at the Halfway House, can you say, 'Hey, Rudy, are you still coming to the game with me tomorrow?' "

"Sure," Bill Clinton said. "Do you *want* to come to the game tomorrow?"

"Hell no," Rudy Durand said, and both of them, good friends, laughed.

"What's it about?" Bill Clinton asked.

"I'll tell you later."

The president asked about a few mutual friends like Jack Nicholson — who had just been reaccused by a thirty-two-year-old hooker of beating her so badly in 1996 that she'd suffered brain damage — and they went off in different directions on the golf course.

When Rudy and Sampras were nearly halfway finished, Mark Canton came by on his cart and Rudy told him they were going to meet Bill Clinton and Sly at the Halfway Clubhouse.

"Can I come with you?" Mark asked.

Rudy said he supposed so.

"I'll ride in the cart with you!" Mark said.

"I'm riding with Pete," Rudy said. "Follow us over."

Mark Canton said, "Rudy, please! I've gotta get a picture with him for my wall. You gotta promise me, Rudy, please. I heard the White House photographer's with him wherever he goes. Can he take a picture of us?"

"I don't see why not," Rudy Durand said.

When they got to the Halfway House, Bill Clinton and Sly were already there. Mark said hi to Sly and Sly asked the president if he knew that Mark Canton was the best producer in town.

Mark Canton shook Bill Clinton's hand and said, "Mr. President, I'm Mark Canton. I'm a producer . . ." And he listed the same credits he'd listed to Pete Sampras, in the same order.

The White House photographer came by and Bill Clinton put one arm around Sly and one arm around Rudy . . . and Mark Canton leaned into the picture as far as he could.

Bill Clinton started heading away with Sly, and then the president of the United States turned back and said loudly, "Rudy, are you still coming to the game with me tomorrow?"

And Rudy said, "Hell no, I wouldn't want to be seen with you."

And Mark Canton looked the way he must have looked the night that Wendy walked in on him with Amy. Unbelievable! Un-fucking-real! Not only was the president checking to see if Rudy would still be his guest . . . but Rudy was so close to him that he could tease him like that.

Mark Canton went over to the White House photographer to make sure he got the picture, and Bill Clinton, who was watching Mark Canton now and laughing with Rudy, said to Rudy, "You want me to put a little mustard on it?" Rudy laughed and Bill Clinton said, loudly enough to make sure Mark heard it, "I'll send the helicopter for you, Rudy, if you're busy. Come on!"

Mark Canton shook his head as Rudy and Pete Sampras drove away, and he didn't hear Pete say to Rudy, "Who was that asshole?" And Rudy answered, "That's Mark Canton, producer."

The next morning, Rudy's phone rang and an official from the Chinese embassy asked if Rudy would like two tickets to the official People's Republic of China box at the Rose Bowl championship soccer game. Rudy had just done several deals with Macao and Chinese financiers and he accepted the two tickets. He called his friend Jack Nicholson and told him about the two tickets in the Chinese box, and Jack Nicholson, who was supposed to attend in Mark Canton's box, said, "I'll come with *you.*"

Moments later, Rudy Durand's phone rang again; it was Mark Canton. "Jack's going with *you?*" Mark asked.

"That's what he said," Rudy said.

"But he was supposed to come with me."

"Where's your box?" Rudy Durand asked.

"On the ten-yard line."

"Shit," Rudy said, "That's almost in the end zone."

"It's not in the end zone," Mark Canton said; "it's on the ten-yard line."

There was a pause, and Mark Canton said, "Where's *your* box?"

"You mean the official box of the People's Republic of China?" Rudy asked.

"Yeah."

"It's on the fifty," Rudy Durand said. "Right next to Bill Clinton's. Right in the middle of the field!"

Mark Canton asked Rudy Durand if he and his party could follow Rudy's and Jack's limo to the Rose Bowl. Mark had heard the Secret Service squawk boxes going "Six-five! Six-five!" and knew that security at a public circus like this one could wind up being embarrassing if you didn't have your own code number.

That's what happened. Rudy and Jack in the lead, and then Mark's party's limos; among the passengers, Dennis Hopper and his wife and two kids, pissed off that it had cost them four thousand dollars to see this game. Dennis, the ultimate sixties icon, the Easy Rider himself, who'd gone on after that monstro/boffo hit of a movie to write and direct something called *The Last Movie* (which was so bad, it almost was Dennis's last). Dennis, once a human Dumpster of LSD, longtime former resident of that holy place, Taos, now hanging out with Mark Canton.

It was going to be like a sixties reunion: Dennis and Jack, also an *Easy Rider* graduate, and Bill Clinton, the former Street Fightin' Man who didn't inhale.

When they got to the security gate at the Rose Bowl, they were all whisked through—"Six-five! Six-five!" said the squawk boxes again, magic words—and when they got off the elevator and started heading for their boxes, the president of the United States heard the "six-five" announcements, too, and stuck his head out of his box and yelled, "*Hey, Rudy!*"

He invited Rudy and Jack into his box and introduced Rudy to his personal guests, Gray Davis, the governor of California, and L.A.'s mayor, Richard Riordan.

"I want you to meet the best producer in Hollywood" was the way Bill Clinton introduced Rudy Durand to the others. And boy, did Rudy get a kick out of that!

Then Jack and the president schmoozed off in a corner for a while, grinning, enjoying each other, two horndogs who liked each other's scent. Jack Nicholson had even come to Bill Clinton's public aid during the darkest impeachment days, appearing at a rally at the Federal Building in Westwood with Barbra, who wore a ditsy little hat some people said she'd worn in *The Way We Were*.

Jack Nicholson liked Bill Clinton a lot, a whole lot, better than he even liked Fidel Castro, almost as much as he liked Robert Evans, who kept Jack supplied with endless boxes of windup dolls, misty, vacant-eyed midwestern farm girls who'd come to Hollywood to be stars and who were now on the hairy, varicose first leg of that trip.

When Jack Nicholson and the president were finished schmoozing, they gave each other a hug, and then the president gave Rudy Durand a hug, and the Marine Corps guard in the box saluted Jack (as marines everywhere did after *A Few Good Men*).

Jack and Rudy went over and sat in the Chinese box, smack square on the fifty-yard line. The good old USA won the game. A great time was had by all.

Bill Clinton went back to Washington, but he would return soon. Rudy and Jack played some golf the next day. Mark Canton got his picture for his wall. He was so happy about the picture, he gave Rudy Durand a deal to produce two movies, the kind of deal Rudy hadn't had in Hollywood for a long time.

It was all thanks, Rudy Durand knew, to Bill Clinton. Hollywood . . . and Rudy Durand . . . and Sly Stallone . . . and Mark Canton just loved Bill Clinton!

(13)

Hillary Bares All

He'll end up like Nelson Rockefeller, his heart exploding as he grunts and groans on top of some young slut who's flattered him into being his aide. It's funny . . . I campaigned for Rockefeller in 1968, you know. The Democratic National Convention was about to become a symbol of a changing world, and where was I? At the Republican one, campaigning for Rockefeller. Make of that what you will, those of you who, like Barbara Olson, consider me the last Communist, who accuse me of having worked for a Communist in Berkeley, who say that Saul Alinsky was my Karl Marx. (Dick Morris was enamored of Saul, too, and he works for Trent Lott and Rupert Murdoch now.)

Did you read the Barbara Olson book? Did you know that her husband, Ted, is one of Ken Starr's best friends? Did you know that her publisher, Al Regnery, who's published so many books trashing Bill and me, has the same exact interests as Bill? Police who were called to his house found Al's porn stash, including a book with colored photos of "oral sex and the placing of objects into the vagina." I've done my research, as you see. I've *always* done my opposition research.

But getting back to Bill: I once deluded myself into thinking that maybe in our dotage he would settle down. That atherosclerosis (from cheeseburgers) and flaccidity (from overuse) would sober his priapic drunkenness. I say "deluded myself" because, thanks to the marvels of modern medical science, that is no longer a possibility. No one ever considers the heartbreak that Viagra means to a woman like me.

You know, it was never very good with us, even in the beginning, when there *was* a was. Oh, he said it was good for him, but I somehow never believed him, even before I had the evidence, before I went through his pockets looking for phone numbers as soon as he was asleep. I tried to please him. I shaved my legs and armpits, even though I felt the act was a betrayal of my beliefs. God knows, all of you know how many times I tried changing my hair. Not that he was ever Adonis himself, with his pale gut sticking out of his T-shirt, his thighs like the flabby Crisco fat of a man who was twenty years older. But I tried. And kept trying. And kept trying. Until the pain and humiliation congealed into an angry black clump in my heart. It wasn't enough that he was cheating—he was rubbing it into my face.

I wondered for a while if that was a part of his thrill. He wanted to take Gennifer into that bathroom at the statehouse as I stood only a few feet away. He knew I saw them together outside that bathroom door. He brought that whore to the airport to kiss him good-bye. He knew I knew who she was. And on the morning we left for Washington after the election, at 5:15, he had to see that slut down in the basement, knowing that I was upstairs, knowing that I knew, knew even that she was wearing a raincoat with nothing underneath it. Was it any wonder, do you think, that I turned away from him when he moved to kiss me for the cameras at the inauguration? I'm not his prop. I am no one's prop. The fucker can't do me that way. Unless I want to be done.

I knew everything. I know about all of them. I've *always* known everything. God, do you have any idea of the pain knowing everything has entailed? I *had* to know to be able to protect him. To be able to protect *us*. We wanted to go to the White House. We've always wanted to get to the White House. The sluts and the whores, the bimbos and the groupies had to be silenced, neutralized. The stakes were too high. They had to be made to understand that if they spoke about what he had done with them, their own frailties and weaknesses would be exposed. They had to be reminded—by the troopers, by Terry, by Palladino—of their own *humanity*. They had to get a vulnerability wake-up call. Opposition research, really, that's all it was. If you tell someone what you did with him, the world will find out that you fucked half the high school football team on the fifty-yard line—even if you didn't. That sort of thing. An antidote to self-righteousness, an inoculation against a gag reflex to take fifty thousand dollars from the *National Enquirer*.

I trust Terry Lenzner. I worked with him on the Watergate stuff. He knows who the good and bad guys are. He knows that reality-checking a whore is a venial and noble sin in the pursuit of keeping the bad guys out of the White House. But consider the position it put me into relative to my own heart. I *had* to know all the filth to know whom to silence. But it was filth that poisoned me against him with each piece of information. In the process of saving him, I was destroying him inside myself. But even if it meant his destruction within me, I *had* to destroy him in order to save him. It became the nightmare equation that had been worked out by the Pentagon in Vietnam, the equation that I had railed against and loathed so much: You have to destroy the village in order to save it. I was napalming my own heart and soul. I laughed when they called me Joan of Arc in the media. If they only knew. I was burning my own most intimate feelings at a stake of my own creation.

Why, you ask? Why would anyone do that to themselves? Is anything worth that price? *Power?* Power by itself, you mean? Power as a concept, as the ability to make people do things? No. Fuck that. Fuck power as a concept. I've never been interested in power that way. But power to accomplish goals that would make America a better place to live? That would make this country a more compassionate, more sensitive, more human place? Yes, I plead guilty to a quest for that kind of power—in the name of children, women, black people, gay people, the elderly, the disabled, the ill. In the name of the millions of repressed, unempowered, disenfranchised—yes! A thousand times yes! *That* is worth the humiliation and pain and inner destruction I've sentenced myself to. A reality check to a nation to remind it of its own humanity . . . the way Terry and Palladino and the troopers had to remind the whores and sluts and bimbos of theirs.

Is there anything wrong with wanting to make this a better America? My pain is *mine.* I've decided to take it upon myself. I'm not causing *you* pain. My aim is to better *your* life. But if I've taken that upon myself, then why do you quibble with the means I've chosen—the means I've *had* to choose? To get into a position where I can better *your* life, do *I* lie?

Of course I lie. Could Bill have been elected and reelected if I had said, Yes, he turned the statehouse and the White House into a whorehouse? . . . Yes, I've seen him so stoned, he was incoherent? . . . Yes, he was Brer Rabbit, dodging the draft? . . . Yes, his greatest talent is to seduce, whether it's a voter or a bimbo?

Could I have told the truth and said, *I* care about making this a better America; *he* cares about glory and victory and whores and doesn't give a shit what position he takes in order to get all of those things? Could I have said, some of the good things that this administration has achieved have been achieved because he is *afraid* of me? Afraid to disagree with me? Afraid I'll hit him? Afraid I'll leave him and destroy whatever vestige of his presidency and his posterity is left?

Yes, I've learned to lie and I lie well. I've learned to con the media and the voters with the sort of uplifting, bathetic, soporific ideas that I know will soften my image as Saul Alinsky's ill-begotten daughter. *It Takes a Village* and children's rights and health care and Social Security and Medicare—how can you not love me for waving those good-hearted flags?

Yes, I lie about him, and when the going gets rough and his approval ratings are down, I lend myself in those moments—if I so choose—as his prop. I let him tell that story of how the maids barged in on us in the residence as we were in bed, letting him imply that we were sleeping together and having sex. Or the time, during his darkest hours, when I allowed a photograph to be "surreptitiously" taken showing the two of us embracing in our bathing suits. I even let the world see my big butt just to try to keep Bill Clinton in office.

What hurts me most isn't what he does with his whores anymore; it's what he says to them. He told Gennifer about how he dreamed he could take a walk with her on a sunny day down a leaf-strewn street. He told the intern he had nothing in his life except his work. He called me Hilla the Hun and the Warden. Even if he betrayed me sexually, he didn't have to betray me that way. There's nothing in his life except his work? My God, even if I don't exist, even if he views me as his jailer, what about Chelsea? First he does his filth with a slut almost his daughter's age and then he just about tells his slut that his daughter doesn't exist in his life?

He has no right to be angry at me, but his actions show he is in a rage. I saved him countless times in Arkansas, I saved him on *60 Minutes* in New Hampshire, and I saved him from being removed from office. Had I left during impeachment, the whole country would have been applauding and he would have had to check himself into some place like Menninger. I've come to the conclusion over the years that he has one use for a woman. And I've come to the conclusion that I'm not a woman to him.

He has somehow desexed me in his own head, although I sometimes wonder if he ever really looked at me that way. He made me into his adviser/sister, his pol/buddy. Maybe I was wrong not to try to be more feminine in our Arkansas years, but maybe I was right not to shave or even shower that much—because I sensed that he wasn't attracted to me intimately . . . and in revenge, I wanted him to feel revulsion. Maybe it horrified me that I was married to a drooling sexual pig and that's why I was the way I was. Here he was . . . the enlightened, sensitive, empathetic New Man, the hero of the PTAs and the soccer moms, a candidate and a president who would empower women. And here I was . . . profoundly lonely, abandoned by him intimately, the woman he desexed, getting him out of trouble with women he'd used as living hand towels.

He rarely touched me that way, and even when he did, I questioned the dynamic, the underlying stimulus. One of the rare times I'm talking about took place in Arkansas. Vince and a young woman who was an associate and Bill and I went out to dinner and we all had too much to drink. We were walking outside afterward and Bill and the young woman started fooling around, kissing. And Vince started kissing me and holding me.

I could see Bill and her and he could see Vince and me. Our driver, a trooper, was nearby, watching all of us. Bill and I got back in the limo and he pulled the divider up and we had sex right in the backseat. He fucked me like he hadn't fucked me in a long time. And all the time he was inside me, I thought, You prick! You phony bastard! You're not fucking me; you're fucking that young blonde! You're not inside me; you're inside her! You're not squeezing my tits; you're squeezing hers! But I'm the one who hurt afterward . . . not her.

Vince's death was the final evidence to me that I had been right about all the humiliation I'd shouldered and the lies I had told. Because those motherfuckers at the *Wall Street Journal* killed Vince Foster as surely as if they had pulled the trigger. Those motherfucking, racist, Neanderthal, troglodyte, right-wing creeps who wrote their foul rag of an editorial page. When they wrote that scurrilous and false editorial about him, Vince took himself out of a politics he considered too dirty to be a part of. They assassinated his character, and it was like Vince said—"Fuck you! You want my character? I'll give you my body! I will force you to see what you've done!" My lovely Vincenzo Fosterini, always there for me in any way I wanted. And now they'd taken him, the forces of darkness I had fought against for so long, the forces that had to be kept at bay, in the gothic wilderness, out of the White House—if the America I believed in with every ounce of my body was to survive.

When it was the same editorial page of the same *Wall Street Journal* that broke the story of Juanita Broaddrick's alleged rape, I wasn't surprised. It was almost morbidly funny; they were calling me the last Communist and it was the ultimate symbol of capitalism, the *Wall Street Journal,* that had wounded me the most, not just once but twice.

I don't know what to tell you about Juanita Broaddrick. It's very difficult, almost impossible, for me to talk about her. I knew back in Arkansas already what people were whispering, and he, as always, denied it. I think I kept myself from really confronting it until I saw the videotape of her on television. I threw up afterward. I felt like taking a shower, but I knew it wouldn't do any good. I knew in my core that she was telling the truth. I sat alone in a room and thought about having had the same thing inside me that he had forced into her. And I had wanted it inside me and even remonstrated with him when he hadn't put it there. And now it had been exposed to me on national television in a grotesque, ugly manifestation . . . an instrument of torture. Yet it was also the instrument that had fathered Chelsea.

I wondered how that could be. A piece of flesh that could cause both excruciating misery and the greatest joy, suffering and celebration. I knew I didn't want it inside me anymore. No, that's not right: I knew I would never allow it inside me anymore. It was a thought that I knew was moot and profoundly sad, too, because I knew he didn't *want* to put it inside me anyway. This would relieve him of the painful obligation he felt once or twice a year. The pain I felt from what he had done to Juanita Broaddrick . . . the pain that would now cause the most intimate loathing I'd felt for any man . . . would probably be doing him a favor. He wouldn't have to go through his yearly charade with me anymore.

Sometimes I wonder what happened to the boy at Yale whom I fell in love with. At other times, I wonder whether I simply misperceived him—maybe he was always that way and I just didn't see it. I thought he had an inner life, a mental life that would deepen and root itself through the years. I didn't know that even the words *deepen* and *root itself* would turn into a cheap, dirty joke for me, a cruelly exact double entendre. I don't know how I didn't see that the boy I met at Yale would turn into a man interested not in his mind but in his dick, who would spend free hours not with the classics but with phone sex, whose idea of enjoying nature was jumping into the bushes with some slut.

I remember the day he gave me *Leaves of Grass* and how we'd read stanzas to each other for weeks. And I remember the day I learned that he'd given *Leaves of Grass* to the intern, too. And in the years between giving me my cherished leather-bound volume and giving the intern hers, something inside my husband crashed and burned. *I think.* Or it was just a ploy on both occasions, a little something to make me . . . and her . . . feel good about him. Maybe when he gave me that book and when he gave it to her . . . he was doing nothing but responding to an internal poll taken by his ego: I'll give them some poems; they'll like that.

I don't have a whole lot of people to talk to now that Vince is gone. My mother is too old and Chelsea too young to talk about most of these things. I'm hurling myself into the Senate race. Who knows? I may sit down in an intimate moment in my private study with a young intern one day and tell him or her that I have nothing in my life but work. I've been working out a lot and I finally feel good about my hair. It surely is about time, isn't it? It's fun being called "regal" and "glamorous" by the media and I liked being called "the First Lady of Miramax."

Hah! Hollywood was always supposed to have been *his* turf. In between the Senate race and his trips and mine, we certainly don't see each other much, and we talk infrequently. What am I supposed to say to him—Hey, asshole, you been reading *Leaves of Grass* lately? I know what he's doing because I know everything. He's playing with himself—what did you think?

I talk to Eleanor a lot in my own way. She convinced me to run in her home state. All I'm doing is continuing the same struggle she began. God knows, I feel we have so many things in common, although I envy her the closeness of her relationship with Lorena. I don't really have a Lorena in my life now, but maybe I will. Eleanor and I talk a lot about Bill and Franklin. It's funny how the intern even referred to herself as Lucy Mercer in that note she sent Bill. And most people don't know that Bill has always felt a real closeness to FDR, too, thanks mainly to his friendship with Jim McDougal, who idolized FDR and was always telling FDR stories. And, of course, there is yet another connection: Bill, bless his heart, told Gennifer I was a lesbian, and Eleanor really was one for much of her life. A lesbian with a philandering husband who used her to breed a gaggle of kids and then had nothing to do with her intimately. There you go, Bill Clinton's role models, JFK and FDR. I'm surprised Bill didn't come equipped with two dicks.

Eleanor was telling me a story up in the solarium the other day that really made her laugh. She confronted Franklin about Lucy, and Franklin promised to break it off. Then she discovered that they were meeting secretly. FDR had the Secret Service drive him across town in his limo each day. And Lucy would be waiting for him on some prearranged street corner. She'd jump in and do what he liked and then the Secret Service would drop her off on another street corner, where she'd wait for the bus and go home. I didn't laugh much, though. I remembered Bill's jogs around the statehouse in Little Rock and around the mall near the White House here.

I just thought of something. This *does* make me laugh. When Bill and I got married, the minister's name was . . . the Reverend Nixon. I'm not kidding. With a thousand ministers to choose from, we picked Nixon to bless our marriage. Isn't that funny? We took our vows before God and Nixon.

[14]

Willard Comes Clean

Billy doesn't love Hilla the Hun. He never has. He loves *me*. He's always loved me, from the time we were both little. When his parents were fighting and he ran into another room crying and all upset, *I* was the one who sat with him. He touched me and played with me. Only *I* could give him peace. Only *I* could self-soothe him and modulate his anxiety. Only *I* could make him feel good about himself. As we grew and he suddenly got fat, only *I* could convince him to lose his belly. He *wanted* to look down and see me and play with me. But he couldn't see me because of his belly. Then he lost it, and I could look at him and he could look at me. We still play the same way now that *we've* grown so *big!* Before that *60 Minutes* interview, before his grand jury appearance, before a State of the Union speech, Billy plays with *me* and *I* give him the same inner peace I gave him when we were little.

I was his friend when he had no others. He knows that, even today. He's so proud of me sometimes, he overdoes it. Kathleen Willey, Dolly Kyle, Monica—he put their hands right on me. He said, "Kiss it!" minutes after he'd met Paula Jones. It's good for my self-esteem, you know, not that I've ever had a lot of problems with my self-esteem sagging. Even when we were little together, Billy and I had a lot of fun with girls. Tinkerbelle. Snow White. Natasha in *Bullwinkle*. His cousin's Barbie doll. Suzy the dolphin. All those slave girls in *The Ten Commandments*.

Billy's worked me hard my whole life, but I'm not tired. I've never been inoperative. I've always had a lot of get-up-and-go. He's never had to eat shark-fin soup or oysters or mandrake root or rhino horn. I've always taken care of his health. My activity has kept his prostate healthy, and the exercise I provide him helps diminish the toxic effect of all the saturated fats he regularly poisons himself with.

But still, the attention he pays me is nice. Nurturing. Enabling. Empowering. Reassuring. He reassures me in other ways, too. Did you ever notice how Billy keeps his hands in his pockets a lot? I'm his good-luck charm. His lucky penny. His rosary. His grasp of reality. He even hums me songs under his breath some- times—"I Can't Stop Loving You" and "You're My Soul and Inspiration" and "Please Please Me" and "Mama Told Me Not to Come." Billy Joel's "Captain Jack" is our favorite song. He treats me with sensitivity. He never tries to hem me in and lets me have my own space to breathe. No condoms. No tight bikini shorts—it's mostly boxers. Billy can seduce a whole crowd, but he knows from experience that he'll need me when we go home. When Hilla goes into the other room. When it's just Billy and the K-Y jelly and me.

Billy and I have enjoyed life. A lot of my peers, I know, are exposed only to darkness. To toilets, urinals, bedsheets, underwear, or vaginas. I've seen a lot of the lighted world. I've seen the Oval Office, the private study, the photos of Billy on the walls of Nancy Hernreich's office. I've seen the crashing surf at Malibu from a lot of different angles. I've seen almost all of the rooms of the governor's mansion in Little Rock, especially the basement. I've become a student of hotel decor and, thanks to vacations and out-of-town fund-raisers, Louis XIV night- stands in Beverly Hills, Bloomfield Hills, and the Hamptons. I've seen almost as much sunshine as Billy, especially around the Ozarks. I'm an overachiever who's been externalized with an air of grandiosity.

I've enjoyed the perks of his success. But I was there, too, in the bad times. In adolescence, when I feared he and his friend Five Finger Mary were going to rip me out by the root. In Arkansas and Oxford, when I was sure I would die of overwork and overexposure. Billy and I were indiscriminate in those halcyon days. We closed our eyes and thought of pig farms. We put a flag over her head and did it for Betsy Ross. I kept thinking of what his mother had said when we were boys: "That little girl over there is so ugly, we have to tie a pork chop around her neck so the boys will play with her."

The Oxford years were our "We Shall Overcome" years. I kept saying, "Not a chance. Never." We spent much of our time in our individual ways there protest- ing the war. McNamara was wrong about "progressively escalating pressure" defeating the Vietcong, but Billy used me to apply the principle to our mutual satisfaction. America's entanglement in Vietnam led to a lot of our entangle- ments at Oxford. "Peace Now!" Billy kept nobly yelling, and those dumb, dis- armed English girls misspelled or misheard the word. I radiated in those days as though I were wearing Day-Glo paint.

I was there in the other bad times, too. In the White House, when all Billy wanted to do was to let an age-inappropriate Monica lick me. She wanted to lick me with this goovno on her tongue to give me chills. I couldn't ever convince

Billy to let me empower myself inside Monica, to give her my unconditional, rubberless love. But he did finally allow me to act out an inappropriate, intrusive flow. That led to Monica's feelings of codependence on me.

And that, unfortunately, led to the worst times of all, when Billy and I hit the front page and the evening news together. The whole world was talking not just about him but also about me. It should have been a time of triumph for me, finally publicly given my due. My ultimate empowerment! But it was the worst time because suddenly Billy was almost afraid to touch me. It was like when we were kids and he went through a stage of reading the Bible. Onan, he informed me, was put to death for spilling his seed on the ground. But he soon realized I was much more fun than chapter and verse.

He was afraid again now, even when we were alone, even when I grew into his pocket. I knew he was overreacting to all the preachers and the soccer moms, but he was treating me as if I weren't even there anymore, attached to him. I was afraid that he was afraid that Hilla was checking his sheets or his underwear for signs of my life, like his grandma had checked us when we were half-grown. Thank God for Carly Simon! The worst of times ended for me in the middle of our international crisis, when we hugged Carly Simon at the Martha's Vineyard airport. Billy rediscovered me hours after that hug.

I know, too, that I've been exceedingly fortunate with what Billy has chosen to do for a living. He's a people person who seduces other people for their votes. If I get something out of it, too, well, he still gets the vote, doesn't he? He decided he wanted to be president, thankfully, instead of, say, a football star. He doesn't go out there every weekend and let me get beaten up. Cup or no cup, it still hurts. He prefers to watch others get theirs beaten up on TV. I don't mind seeing that. Billy and I agree. A bed is much better than a football field. I score. He groans. She yips. *We* win. And go off together into our Disney World.

I've been exposed to a lot of precious people. I like the word *precious* very much. It's what Gennifer called her internalized *me*, her buried little honey pot, her hidden feelings. Truth to tell, Pookie was the most precious I've met. Pookie wanted to eat me alive. Billy would buy lingerie with her and I'd start to feel instinctively grandiose.

We've always been suckers for clothes. Thongs. String bikinis. Monokinis. Hot pants. Leotards. Body stockings. Wet T-shirts. Armholes. Chunky zippers. Dog collars. He'd have Pookie move around in bed wearing her white nightie with the garter belt. All the time she did that, he was holding on to me like I were a snake on meth. Then he turned me intrusively loose inside her precious and I felt obsessively, compulsively grandiose.

The things that happened between her precious and me constituted a monumental impropriety. Don't just take my word for it; look at what happened to Pookie after me and Billy. Pookie went on to have a total body experience with a *world-champion rodeo rider,* Larry Mahan, who sure knew a great ride when he saw one. That was *after* she left riding partner Evel Knievel, who was used to jet-engine Harley hogs under his loins. Then she married a man named Finis Shellnut—I'm not kidding, really—whose willard she calls "Big Tex."

But Pookie hurt my feelings when she went public. She talked about Billy's "overheated eye contact" and how she liked Billy's lips, especially "the way that bottom lip kind of turned to the side as he spoke." *Spoke?* With Pookie, Billy, and me, it wasn't about "speaking." It wasn't about lips. It wasn't about Pookie and Billy. It was about *me.*

It was about the overheated one-eye contact *I* was having with her precious. To hear her tell it, it was about the lace teddy she was wearing and the scented candles in the room. It wasn't about that. It was about *me, me, me* and Pookie's precious. I loved Pookie's precious! I couldn't get enough of Pookie's precious! Pookie's precious was paradise! Now, alas, paradise lost.

Billy frightened me with Hilla for a while, but I quickly learned he meant to have the Hun for himself, not me. Even when he was engaged to her, we were cheating with someone else's precious and we were cheating on that someone else's precious with a third precious, living a precious life. . . . I didn't mind that he kept Hilla mostly away from me. I knew in my capillaries that Hilla didn't like me. She was full of hostility toward me. I had zero interest in doing inner therapy with her. I thought she viewed me as some kind of necessary and traumatic self-punishment.

I just didn't feel I belonged in there. It was a dry and cold place. I sensed she always had another hidden agenda, and I wasn't interested in probing her underlying issues. I kept worrying she'd hurt me somehow. But Billy seemed to sense this, too, and didn't call on me more than two or three times a year. Maybe, to be frank, the problem is that Hilla's precious has a self-worth as big as mine. Maybe Hilla's precious wants exactly the same attention that Billy has gotten me so used to during the years. Maybe Hilla's precious wants to be me with people kneeling at *her* feet.

Then there was Monica. I think, had it all turned out differently, I could've had a lot of fun with her. Beverly Hills girl, you know. Orange ice wigs. Silk scarves. Handcuffs. Mirrors. Poppers. Altoids. Dirty jokes. All of that. Pookie in training maybe. Get rid of the baby fat, the helmet, and I had visions of sugar-plums, ice, and hot candle wax dancing in my head. She was a young woman with great interpersonal, inappropriate potential. I liked Monica, standing there stark naked in boots. I liked her fleshpot lips. And Billy, no surprise, liked her hooters.

Billy and his thing for balloon-bread ba-ba-zoom hooters! When we were kids, peaches, tomatoes, cantaloupes, and eggplant turned us on. Going to the grocery store meant a change of underwear. A melon patch was an orgy. In those days, of course, he'd notice something, *anything,* and I'd try to jump out of his pants. A big juicy tomato. A rare steak. The smell of fresh catfish. The curves on a Cadillac car. The carburetor in a Cadillac car. Courtesans on their way to church in Hot Springs. The minister's daughter in Hot Springs. The minister's wife in Hot Springs. The smell of rain in Hot Springs. *Anything.* Anything at all, and Billy and I would be off to play. Good days. Fun times. Lots of laughs. Lots of showers. Lots of underwear.

Not like now, when they're trashing me everywhere and for the first time in my life I'm worried about sags in my self-esteem. They say I'm too small and point out that Marla Maples calls the Donald's "Trump Tower." Well, I'm not too small. I'm not a seven-footer carried around by Shinto priests or one of those Ja-maican purple creepers or Long Dong Silver. But from what Truman Capote said, I'm probably bigger than Jack's or Bobby's . . . not as big as LBJ's, who called his "Jumbo." They whisper slanderously about pimples and warts and God knows what pus-filled whatnots. They make me sound like some sort of Frankenpenis hunched to the side or humpbacked.

I have to hear about my supposed afflictions on talk radio. Can you imagine being *me* and hearing about myself on talk radio? (I've never wanted fame—to be displayed at the Smithsonian like John Dillinger's; to be kept in a bottle and sold like Napoléon's.) They accuse me of wearing a Winnie the Pooh tattoo like Michael Jackson or being imbedded with a pump like that big action-movie star. Dirty-minded lies. The politics of personal destruction taken to a new high or low (depending on my mood).

Please! I'm healthy and all-American! I've always been user-friendly, equal-opportunity, global, and all-inclusive. I'm from Arkansas, for Jiminy's sake! I know Billy sometimes acts like I'm from Missouri, the Show Me State. But I'm not. I don't have any pimples or warts. I don't wear any Disney tattoos. I don't have any pumps. Billy doesn't have to moan "Squeeze me! Squeeze me!" to get me to stand up on my own two . . . I've been traumatized by all this. Maybe Billy needs to find me a warm and friendly (and moist) support group to help me.

He's hurt me, too. No, not *that* way—I'm used to his touch; I've grown accustomed to his pace. But with his words and with that one single, unforgettable intrusive action. Why did he have to talk about me as a worn-out old organ, able only to pee twenty times a day? (Even that wouldn't be my fault; it's not fun being hostage to your prostate.) Why did he have to humiliate me by putting that cigar where I so badly wanted to go? Why did he allow his cigar and not me to be total with Monica's totality?

I was unzipped, externalized, watching when he did that. Why didn't he keep me zipped, instead of making me so undignifiedly drool at the sight of the cigar inside the object of my turgid emotions? Why did he force me to watch him put the cigar there, as he later forced Monica to watch as he projected me over that rudely inappropriate sperm bank of a sink? What an awful, hurtful thing to do to your dearest and oldest friend, who's *never* let you down, who's risen to every occasion, even in those challenging Oxford years, when I was sleep-deprived but grandly functioning *all the time.*

Even so, I felt sorry for Billy when our old and dear friendship was so heartlessly exposed. They called him a "masturbator," as though it was something bad, instead of the basis of our love for each other. "Masturbator" didn't bother me. I felt it was a tribute to the hold I had on him and the hold he had on me. But then they started calling him a "musterbator," too—a chronic masturbator and a chronic *musterbator:* the psychological term for a man who has to succeed at everything or loses all sense of self-esteem. Then they tried to make it sound like this musterbation, not me, was the cause of all the fun we've had together. Like Billy had a mental deficiency of some kind. Like it was a damaged part of his brain and not me telling him to find us another precious he could tease me on into.

I felt slighted again, but I thought, Be fair. Consider Billy. How would you like to be viewed by the whole world as a masturbating musterbator or a musterbating masturbator? The shrinks kept piling it on, talking about Billy's need for abstinence (no way!), rehab (we'd still have each other), and a multiplicity of twelve-step programs. Editorialists even wrote about twelve-step programs he'd be perfect for, programs from "the top down and the bottom up." (I like tops down and bottoms up.) Even the liberals were talking about twelve-step programs, even people as inappropriate as Gary Hart and Bob Packwood.

I've tried to cheer Billy up any way that I can. I've given him advice: Get a grip, Billy! . . . You can't keep a good man down, Billy! . . . The dog will have his day, Billy! . . . Win one for the Zipper! . . . Masturbation now! Masturbation tomorrow! Masturbation forever! . . . Give me liberty or give me death! . . . Speak softly and carry *me!* . . . I am not crooked! . . . *Ich bin ein* Derringer! . . . None dare call it pleasin'! . . . Squeeze the Charmin! . . . In your heart, you know I'm right! . . . Just say yes!

I've even rapped to him to cheer him up and remind him that we're made for each other:

> *You make a speech, I pluck a peach*
> *You tell a lie, I poke your fly*
> *You campaign, I leave the stain*
> *You sleep with Hilla, I need a pilla*
> *Gennifer Flowers, I'm hard for hours*
> *You want fame, I want a dame*
> *You want glory, I want whorey*
> *You like to think, I like kink*
> *You like politics, I like licks*
> *You like power, I like to deflower*
> *You're a coward, I'm empowered*
> *You're a Lefty, I'm hefty*
> *You're a boomer, I boom her*
> *You're alone, I'm a bone*
> *You're a hick, I'm a prick*
> *Your hunger makes me plunder*
> *Your smile makes me grow a mile*
> *Your hand is the Promised Land*
>
> *You take a flight to a foreign land*
> *For twelve long hours I'm in your hand*
> *And when our trip is finally done*
> *I've left my mark on* Air Force One
> *For better or worse, it's me and you*
> *So stop feeling so low-down blue*
> *We're gonna be together on our dying day*
> *Forever and ever in your hand I'll stay*
> *You think you've got me in your hand*
> *But I'm the one who's in command.*

"I am in control here!" said Gen. Al Haig, known as Alexander the Small, when *his* Billy, Ronald Reagan, was wounded by the politics of personal destruction. *And I am!*

I am his search engine, his Minuteman long-range guided missile, his Sears Tower, his ruby slippers, his Hope diamond, his eternal flame, his Rose-bud . . . his Lord.

I am his banana peel, his smoking gun, his Mannlicher Carcano rifle, his Kathy Smith speedball, his John Dean, his Bruno Magli shoes, his Dodi Fayed, his Mark Chapman . . . his doom.

Thank you to:

Ed Victor
Sonny Mehta
Michael Viner
Peter Gethers
Paul Bogaards
Tina Brown

A NOTE ON THE TYPE

The text of this book was set in Electra, a typeface designed by
W. A. Dwiggins (1880–1956). This face cannot be classified as
either modern or old style. It is not based on any historical model,
nor does it echo any particular period or style. It avoids the extreme
contrasts between thick and thin elements that mark most modern
faces, and it attempts to give a feeling of fluidity, power, and speed.

The alternate text was set in Meta Plus, a sans serif face originally commissioned for the German Post Office (Bundespost) in
1984. Although the project was eventually canceled by the Bundespost in favor of staying with Helvetica, Erik Spiekermann com-
pleted the design as a digital font in 1989, and it was published in
1991 by FontShop International as part of their FontFont type library.

Composed by North Market Street Graphics,
Lancaster, Pennsylvania
Printed and bound by Berryville Graphics,
Berryville, Virginia
Designed by Virginia Tan